What's New Study Guide

Microsoft Project 2010

Dale A. Howard
Gary L. Chefetz

What's New Study Guide

Microsoft Project 2010

Publisher: Chefetz LLC dba MSProjectExperts
Authors: Dale A. Howard and Gary L. Chefetz
Cover Design: Emily Baker
Copy Editor: Tim Clark
Cover Photo: Peter Hurley

ISBN: 978-1-934240-16-8

Library of Congress Control Number: 2010925077

Published and distributed by Chefetz LLC dba MSProjectExperts, 90 John Street, Suite 404, New York, NY 10038. (646) 736-1688 http://www.msprojectexperts.com

Contents

Introduction ... vii

Download the Sample Files ... vii

Module 01: What's New – Microsoft Project 2010 User Interface ... 1

Introducing Microsoft Project 2010 ... 3

Understanding the Ribbon ... 4

Using the Task Ribbon ... 4

Using the Resource Ribbon ... 6

Using the Project Ribbon ... 7

Using the View Ribbon ... 7

Using the Format Ribbon ... 8

Collapsing the Ribbon ... 10

Using the Backstage (File Tab) ... 11

Using Navigation Features ... 24

Using Shortcut Menus ... 24

Using Built-In Keyboard Shortcuts ... 26

Zooming the Timescale Bar ... 26

Using the Zoom Slider ... 28

Customizing the User Interface ... 29

Customizing the Ribbon ... 29

Customizing the Quick Access Toolbar ... 35

Importing/Exporting a Custom Ribbon ... 41

Module 02: What's New – Views, Tables, Filters, and Groups ... 45

Reviewing the Microsoft Project Data Model ... 47

Understanding New Views ... 47

Applying a View ... 49

Understanding Changes to the Default Tables ... 50

Applying a Table ... 51

Understanding New Filters ... 52

Applying a Standard Filter ... 52

Applying a Highlight Filter ... 53

Understanding New Groups ... 55

Applying a Group ... 56

Module 03: What's New – Project Planning ... 61

Creating a New Project from a Template ... 63

Creating a New Project from a SharePoint Task List ... 63

Creating a New Project Using an Office.com Template 66
Defining a New Project 68
Setting Project Options 69
Setting the Task Mode Option 69
Setting Options in the Project Options Dialog 70
Setting General Options 71
Setting Display Options 72
Setting Schedule Options 74
Setting Proofing Options 79
Setting Save Options 81
Setting Language Options 82
Setting Advanced Options 83
Setting Add-Ins Options 86
Setting Trust Center Options 87
Saving a Project as an Alternate File Type 92
Saving a Project File as a PDF or XPS Document 94
Understanding Reduced Functionality with Older Project File Formats 96
Opening a Project Created in an Older Version of Microsoft Project 98
Saving a Project to SharePoint 100
Sharing a Project via E-Mail 105
Module 04: What's New – Task Planning 107
Auto-Wrapping Task Names 109
Inserting Summary Tasks 109
Inserting a Summary Task for Selected Tasks 110
Inserting a Milestone Task 111
Using Manually Scheduled Tasks 112
Linking Manually Scheduled Tasks 114
Understanding Schedule Warnings and Suggestions 117
Using the Respect Links Feature 118
Using the Task Inspector 118
Creating a Manually Scheduled Summary Task 120
Understanding Task Scheduling Changes 122
Module 05: What's New – Resource and Assignment Planning 123
Inserting New Resources in the Resource Sheet View 125
Assigning Resources to Tasks 126
Using the Task Entry View 126
Using the Assign Resources Dialog 127
Using the Team Planner View 131

Leveling an Overallocated Resource in the Team Planner View ... 133
Dragging Tasks in the Team Planner View ... 135
Changing Schedule Information in the Team Planner View ... 137
Customizing the Team Planner View ... 140
Printing the Team Planner View ... 144
Detecting and Resolving Resource Overallocations ... 146
Module 06: What's New – Project Execution ... 151
Rescheduling an Unstarted Project ... 153
Rescheduling a Task ... 156
Setting Tasks to Inactive ... 159
Understanding the Peak Field ... 163
Synchronizing with a SharePoint Tasks List ... 169
Adding Fields to the Task Synchronization Process ... 175
Reporting Progress Using a SharePoint Tasks List ... 181
Module 07: What's New – Reporting ... 187
Using Enhanced Copy and Paste ... 189
Understanding New Fields ... 193
Using the Active Field ... 194
Using the Task Mode Field ... 194
Using the Scheduled Fields ... 195
Using the Warning Field ... 196
Using the Baseline Estimated Fields ... 197
Formatting the Gantt Chart ... 202
Using the Format Tools ... 202
Using the Columns Tools ... 205
Using the Bar Styles Tools ... 207
Using the Gantt Chart Style Tools ... 212
Using the Show/Hide Tools ... 212
Using the Drawing Tools ... 214
Formatting Other Views ... 217
Using the Timeline with the Gantt Chart View ... 218
Adding a Task to the Timeline ... 220
Formatting the Timeline View ... 221
Adding Tasks Using the Contextual Format Ribbon ... 225
Exporting the Timeline View ... 229
Creating a New View ... 231
Creating a New Table ... 232
Creating a New Filter ... 234

Creating a New Group 234
Creating the New View 237
Using the Add New Column Feature 242
Creating a New View by Customizing an Existing View 248
Resetting a Default View after Customization 250
Using Visual Reports Improvements 252
Using New Features in the Compare Project Versions Tool 256
Index 261

Introduction

Thank you for choosing *What's New Study Guide Microsoft Project 2010.* We designed this book as a quick learning guide to get you up to speed with the new features in Microsoft Project 2010. The content of this book derives from the *Ultimate Study Guide Microsoft Project 2010: Foundations,* (ISBN: 978-1-934240-13-7). Consider obtaining *The Ultimate Study Guide Foundations* for a complete learning experience and reference manual, which includes the new features in Project 2010 presented in context with Project Management Institute (PMI) best practices and project management cycle.

Microsoft Project 2010 introduces exciting new features representing profound changes to the software functionality, including the ability to manually schedule tasks, a feature added to ease the transition for people who use Excel to manage their projects. From the new ribbon-based user interface and backstage, to the incredibly handy new Timeline view, Microsoft Project 2010 is packed with new features and changes that you can use to enrich your scheduling experience.,

The 2010 edition introduces a new planning support feature, the Team Planner view, that provides you with the ability to apply tasks to resources as an alternative to the traditional model of applying resources to tasks. You should also explore Project's new collaborative capability that allows you to publish your tasks to team members through standard SharePoint task lists. The new Inactive Tasks feature allows you to exclude tasks from your project without losing your baseline or the original representation of the task in the Gantt chart.

Numerous smaller and more subtle enhancements round out the changes in Project 2010, making this version the most dramatically changed in more than a decade. This book covers all of these changes in depth. Be sure to download the practice files and work your way through the hands-on lessons. You will be up to speed in no time. Enjoy!

Download the Sample Files

Before working on any of the Hands On Exercises in this book, you must download and unzip the sample files required for each exercise. You can download these sample files from the following URL:

http://www.msprojectexperts.com/whatsnew2010

Module 01

What's New – Microsoft Project 2010 User Interface

Learning Objectives

After completing this module, you will be able to:

- Understand the features of the Ribbon
- Use the File tab to access the Backstage
- Use a shortcut menu to access the Mini Toolbar
- Use KeyTips keyboard shortcuts
- Zoom the Timescale using various methods
- Customize the Ribbon
- Customize the Quick Access Toolbar

Inside Module 01

Introducing Microsoft Project 2010 .... **3**

Understanding the Ribbon **4**

Using the Task Ribbon 4

Using the Resource Ribbon 6

Using the Project Ribbon 7

Using the View Ribbon 7

Using the Format Ribbon 8

Collapsing the Ribbon 10

Using the Backstage (File Tab) **11**

Using Navigation Features **24**

Using Shortcut Menus 24

Using Built-In Keyboard Shortcuts 26

Zooming the Timescale Bar 26

Using the Zoom Slider 28

Customizing the User Interface **29**

Customizing the Ribbon....29
Customizing the Quick Access Toolbar....35
Importing/Exporting a Custom Ribbon....41

Introducing Microsoft Project 2010

To the experienced user, the most striking new feature of Microsoft Project 2010 is the user interface, which conforms to the other applications in Microsoft Office 2010, such as Word, Excel, or PowerPoint. Previous users of Microsoft Office 2007 should find this user interface familiar. Figure 1 - 1 displays the Microsoft Project 2010 user interface after starting the application.

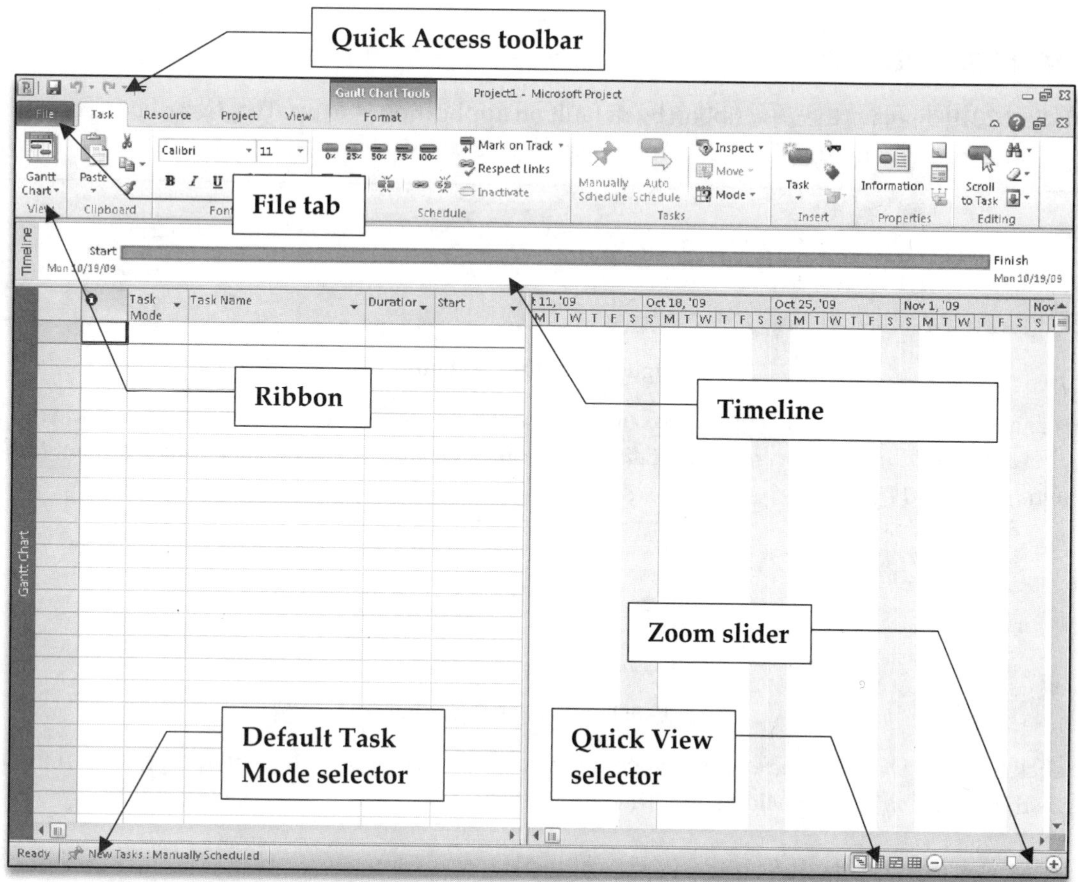

Figure 1 - 1: Features of the Microsoft Project 2010 User Interface

You use these new features as follows:

- Use the *ribbon* to access commands found on menus in previous versions of Microsoft Project.
- Use the *File* tab to access all file-related commands, such as Open, Save, Print, etc.
- Use the *Quick Access* toolbar to display frequently used commands such as Open, Undo, Save, etc.
- Use the *Timeline* to view the current progress of the project in any task view, such as the Gantt Chart view or the Tracking Gantt view.
- Use the *Zoom* slider to quickly zoom to pre-set levels of zoom in the Gantt Chart.
- Use the *Quick View* selector to apply four of the most commonly used views.
- Use the *Default Task Mode* selector to determine the default Task Mode for new tasks project.

I discuss each of these new features in this module and succeeding modules, along with many more new features.

Understanding the Ribbon

The most noticeable new feature in Microsoft Project 2010 is the *ribbon*, which replaces the familiar system of menus found in all previous versions of Microsoft Project. These familiar menus included File, Edit, View, Insert, Format, etc. Replacing these menus are a series of ribbon tabs that display the *Task* ribbon, the *Resource* ribbon, the *Project* ribbon, the *View* ribbon, and the *Format* ribbon for the current View.

Using the Task Ribbon

Microsoft Project 2010 displays the *Task* ribbon by default on application startup. The *Task* ribbon contains all of the buttons and commands you need for task planning. Figure 1 - 2 shows the *Task* ribbon.

Figure 1 - 2: Task ribbon

The system organizes the buttons and commands on the *Task* ribbon into eight sections, which include the *View, Clipboard, Font, Schedule, Tasks, Insert, Properties,* and *Editing* sections. The *Font* section also includes the *Font Dialog Launcher* icon, shown in Figure 1 - 3.

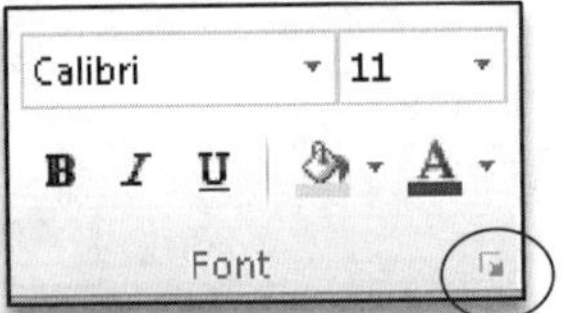

Figure 1 - 3: Font Dialog Launcher icon

When you click the *Font Dialog Launcher* icon, Microsoft Project 2010 displays the *Font* dialog shown in Figure 1 - 4. This dialog is the same *Font* dialog Microsoft Office Project 2007 uses.

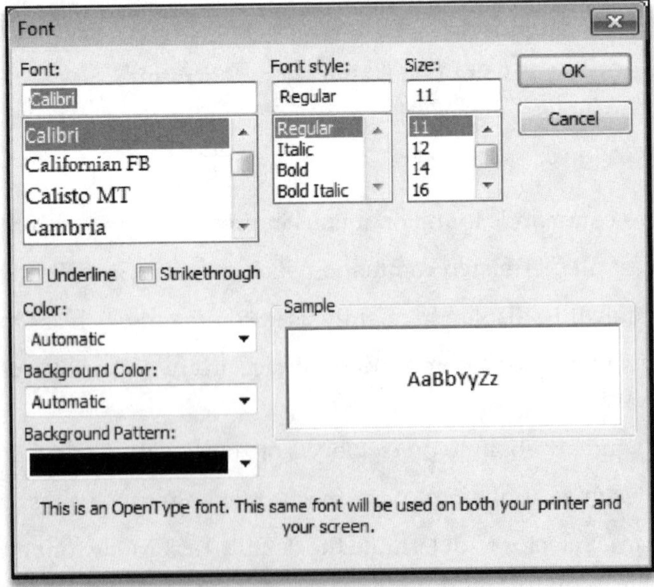

Figure 1 - 4: Font dialog

Table 1 - 1 and Table 1 - 2 document the corresponding Microsoft Office Project 2007 locations for the buttons and commands you see on the *Task* ribbon.

Microsoft Project 2010 Feature	Microsoft Office Project 2007 Location
View section	*View* menu View ➢ More Views
Clipboard section	*Cut, Copy, Paste,* and *Format Painter* buttons on the *Standard* toolbar
Font section	*Font* and *Font Size* pick list buttons, *Bold, Italic,* and *Underline* buttons on the *Formatting* toolbar Format ➢ Font
Schedule section	View ➢ Toolbars ➢ Tracking (for the progress buttons shown on the top row of the *Schedule* section) *Outdent* and *Indent* buttons on the *Formatting* toolbar *Split Task, Link Tasks,* and *Unlink Tasks* buttons on the *Standard* toolbar
Tasks section	No corresponding feature in 2007
Insert section	Insert ➢ Task

Table 1 - 1: Corresponding Features for the Task ribbon

Microsoft Project 2010 Feature	Microsoft Office Project 2007 Location
Properties section	Project ➢ Task Information *Task Information* button on the *Standard* toolbar Project ➢ Task Notes *Task Notes* button on the *Standard* toolbar
Editing section	*Scroll to Task* button on the *Standard* toolbar Edit ➢ Find and Edit ➢ Replace Edit ➢ Clear Edit ➢ Fill

Table 1 - 2: Corresponding Features for the Task ribbon (continued)

If you do not see a corresponding location in Microsoft Office Project 2007 for a button or command on a Microsoft Project 2010 ribbon section in the table, then that button or command is a new feature in Microsoft Project 2010.

Using the Resource Ribbon

Click the *Resource* tab to display the *Resource* ribbon shown in Figure 1 - 5. Use the *Resource* ribbon with any resource view (such as the *Resource Sheet* view) to manage the resources in your project. The exception to this statement is the *Assign Resources* button, which you can use with any Task view (such as the *Gantt Chart* view) to assign resources to tasks.

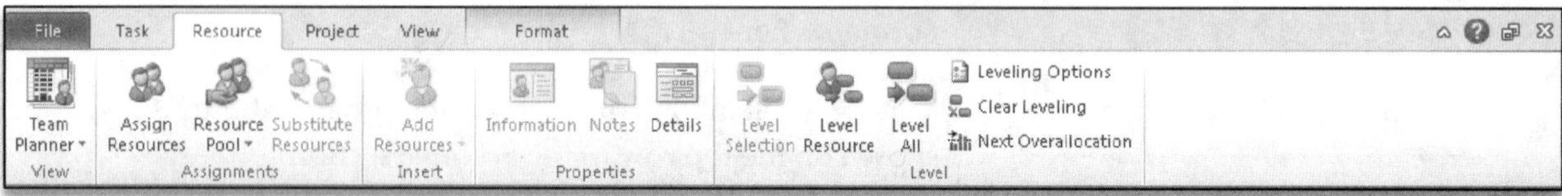

Figure 1 - 5: Resource ribbon

Table 1 - 3 documents the corresponding Microsoft Office Project 2007 locations for the buttons and commands found on the *Resource* ribbon.

Project 2010 Feature	Microsoft Office Project 2007 Location
View section	*View* menu View ➢ More Views
Assignments section	*Assign Resources* button on the *Standard* toolbar Tools ➢ Resource Sharing Tools ➢ Substitute Resources (available only when used with Project Server 2010)
Insert section	Insert ➢ New Resource Insert ➢ New Resource From…
Properties section	Project ➢ Resource Information *Resource Information* button on the *Standard* toolbar Project ➢ Resource Notes Resource *Notes* button on the *Standard* toolbar
Level section	Tools ➢ Level Resources

Table 1 - 3: Corresponding Features for the Resource ribbon

Using the Project Ribbon

Click the *Project* tab to display the *Project* ribbon shown in Figure 1 - 6. Use the *Project* ribbon to specify high-level information about your project or to generate reports for your project.

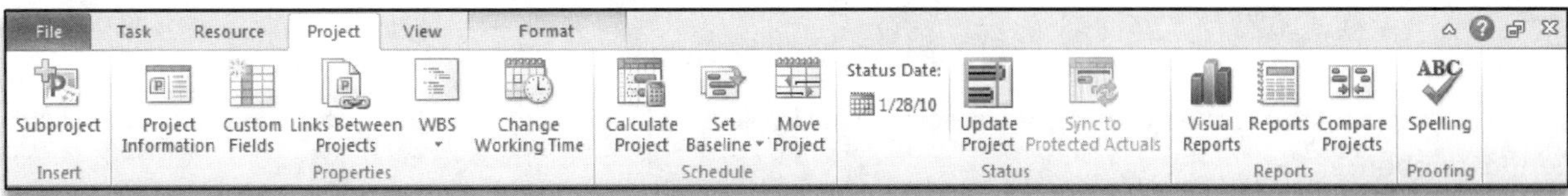

Figure 1 - 6: Project ribbon

Table 1 - 4 documents the corresponding Microsoft Office Project 2007 locations for the buttons and commands found on the *Project* ribbon.

Project 2010 Feature	Microsoft Office Project 2007 Location
Insert section	Insert ➢ Project
Properties section	Project ➢ Project Information Tools ➢ Customize ➢ Fields Tools ➢ Links Between Projects Project ➢ WBS Tools ➢ Change Working Time
Schedule section	Tools ➢ Options ➢ Calculation and then click the *Calculate Now* button Tools ➢ Tracking ➢ Set Baseline View ➢ Toolbars ➢ Analysis and then click the *Adjust Dates* button
Status section	Project ➢ Project Information and enter a date in the *Status Date* field Tools ➢ Tracking ➢ Update Project
Reports section	Report ➢ Visual Reports Report ➢ Reports View ➢ Toolbars ➢ Compare Project Versions
Proofing section	*Spelling* button on the *Standard* toolbar

Table 1 - 4: Corresponding Features for the Project ribbon

Using the View Ribbon

Click the *View* tab to display the *View* ribbon shown in Figure 1 - 7. Use the *View* ribbon to apply different views in your project, and to apply features of views, including tables, filters, and groups.

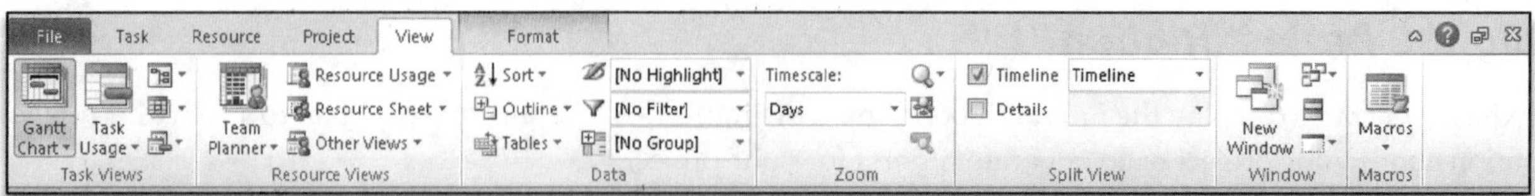

Figure 1 - 7: View ribbon

Table 1 - 5 documents the corresponding Microsoft Office Project 2007 locations for the buttons and commands found on the *View* ribbon.

Project 2010 Feature	Microsoft Office Project 2007 Location
Task Views section	View ➢ More Views
Resource Views section	View ➢ More Views
Data section	Project ➢ Sort Project ➢ Outline (or click the *Show* button on the *Formatting* toolbar) View ➢ Table 1 - ➢ More Tables Project ➢ Filtered For ➢ More Filters and click the *Highlight* button *Filter* pick list on the *Formatting* toolbar Project ➢ Group By ➢ More Groups (or click the *Group By* pick list on the *Standard* toolbar)
Zoom section	View ➢ Zoom *Zoom In* and *Zoom Out* buttons on the *Standard* toolbar
Split View section	Window ➢ Split View ➢ More Views ➢ Task Entry
Window section	Window ➢ New Window Window ➢ Select any open project Window ➢ Arrange All Window ➢ Hide
Macros section	Tools ➢ Macro

Table 1 - 5: Corresponding Features for the View ribbon

Using the Format Ribbon

You can use the *Format* ribbon only with the current view applied in the active project. Before you click the *Format* tab, select a view to format (such as the *Gantt Chart* view), and then click the *Format* tab. Microsoft Project 2010 displays the *Format* ribbon for the current view, and allows you to customize that view. Figure 1 - 8 shows the *Format* ribbon for the *Gantt Chart* view. Notice in Figure 1 - 8 that the software indicates that I am editing the *Gantt Chart* view by showing the *Gantt Chart Tools* header above the *Format* tab.

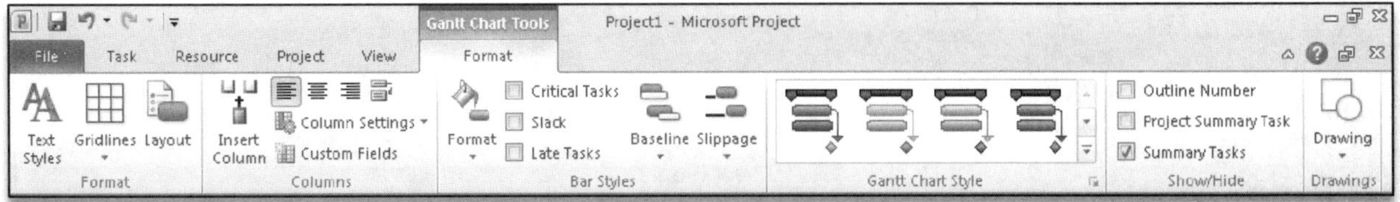

Figure 1 - 8: Format ribbon for the Gantt Chart view

Table 1 - 6 documents the corresponding Microsoft Office Project 2007 locations for the buttons and commands found on the *Format* ribbon.

Microsoft Project 2010 Feature	Microsoft Office Project 2007 Location
Format section	Format ➢ Text Styles Format ➢ Gridlines Format ➢ Layout
Columns section	Insert ➢ Column Tools ➢ Customize ➢ Fields
Bar Styles section	Format ➢ Bar Format ➢ Bar Styles *Gantt Chart Wizard* button on the *Formatting* toolbar
Gantt Chart Style section	Format ➢ Bar Styles
Show/Hide section	Tools ➢ Options ➢ View
Drawings section	View ➢ Toolbars ➢ Drawing

Table 1 - 6: Corresponding Features for the Format ribbon, Gantt Chart Tools

Remember that the *Format* ribbon shows the appropriate formatting options for your current view. This means that the buttons and commands on the *Format* ribbon vary widely depending on the formatting options available for the current View. For instance, Figure 1 - 9 shows the *Format* ribbon for the *Task Usage* view.

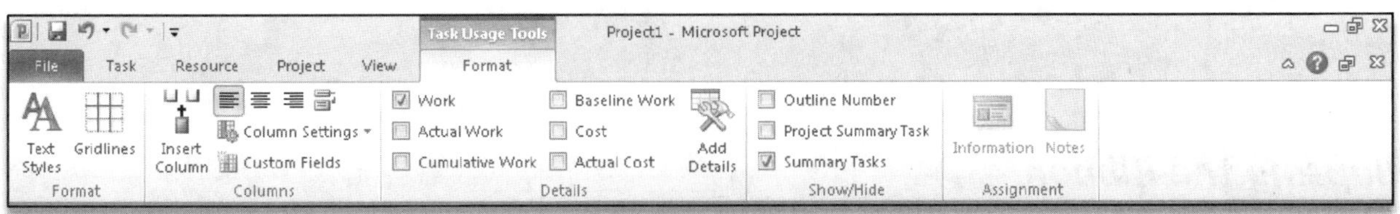

Figure 1 - 9: Format ribbon for the Task Usage view

Figure 1 - 10 shows the *Format* ribbon for the *Resource Sheet* view. Notice that the *Format* ribbon shows very few options with which to format the *Resource Sheet* view.

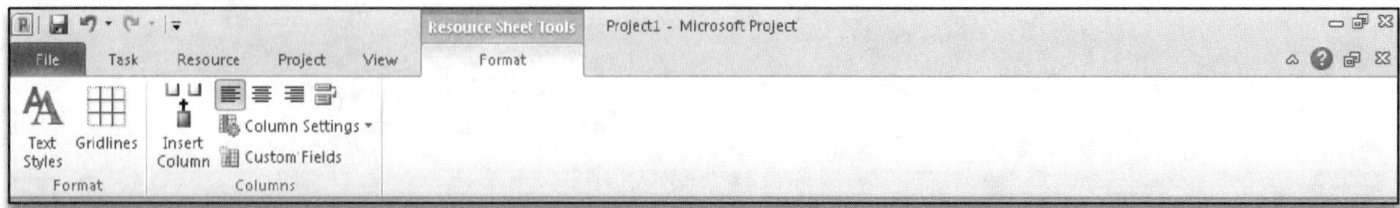

Figure 1 - 10: Format ribbon for the Resource Sheet view

Figure 1 - 11 shows the *Format* ribbon for the *Team Planner* view. The *Team Planner* view is a powerful new view included in Microsoft Project 2010. Notice that the *Format* ribbon for this view includes a number of buttons and commands not available when formatting other views.

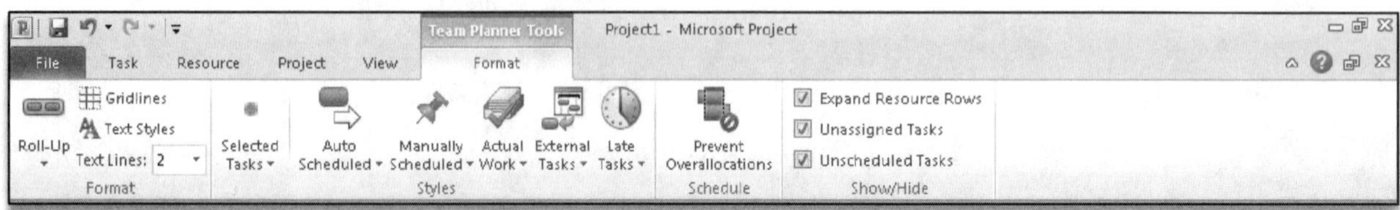

Figure 1 - 11: Format ribbon for the Team Planner view

Figure 1 - 12 shows the *Format* ribbon for the *Calendar* view. Notice that the *Format* ribbon shows very few options for formatting the *Calendar* view

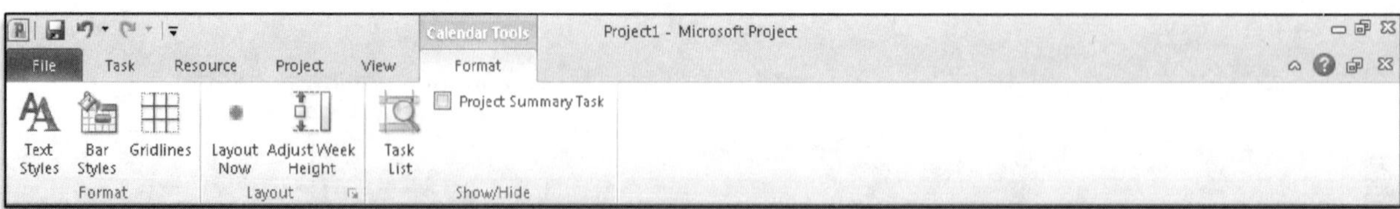

Figure 1 - 12: Format ribbon for the Calendar view

I do not document the buttons and commands available on the *Format* ribbon for every view. Keep in mind that every view offers a unique set of options for formatting. All task views, such as the *Gantt Chart* view and the *Task Sheet* view, include a common set of task formatting options. Likewise, all resource views, such as the *Resource Sheet* view and the *Resource Graph* view, offer a common set of resource formatting options.

Collapsing the Ribbon

Microsoft Project 2010 allows you to expand and collapse the *ribbon* by double-clicking any ribbon tab. For example, Figure 1 - 13 shows Microsoft Project 2010 with an open project after I collapsed the *ribbon*. Because of this, the application allows me to see more tasks in the active project.

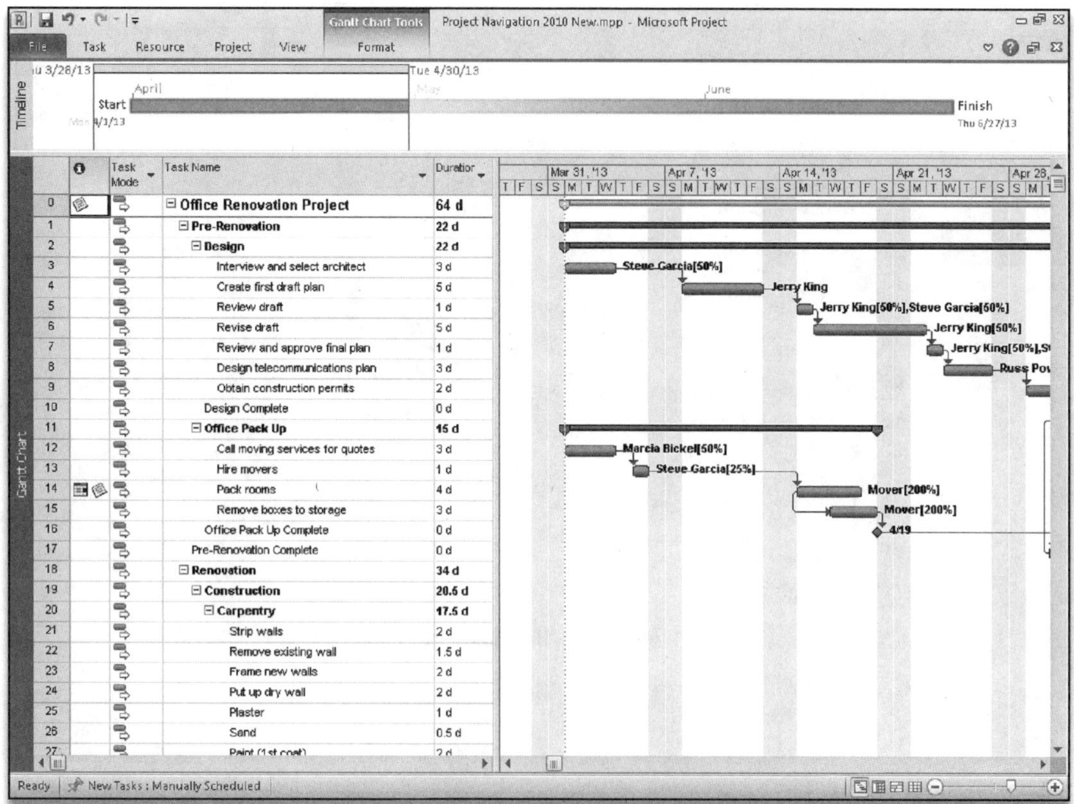

Figure 1 - 13: Microsoft Project 2010 with the ribbon collapsed

> You can also collapse the ribbon by right-clicking on any ribbon tab and selecting the *Minimize the Ribbon* item on the shortcut menu.

Using the Backstage (File Tab)

As I noted earlier in this module, you click the *File* tab to access the most commonly used file commands, such as Open, Save and Print. When you click the *File* tab, Microsoft Project 2010 displays the *Backstage* shown in Figure 1 - 14.

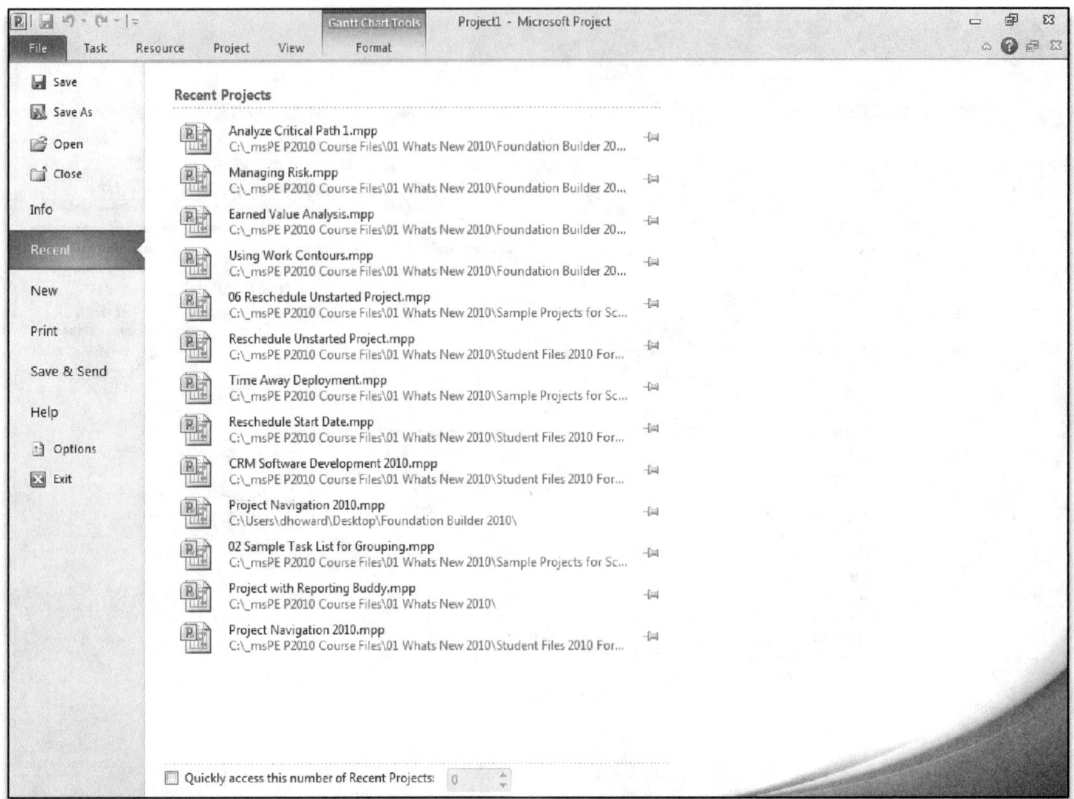

Figure 1 - 14: Microsoft Project 2010 Backstage

Notice in Figure 1 - 14 that the *Backstage* defaults to the *Recent* tab, and shows the list of files you opened recently. The left-hand menu on the *Backstage* contains six tabs, as well as commands that handle files above the five tabs and a number of miscellaneous commands below the tabs. In the *Backstage*, you can perform any of the following actions:

- Save a project file.
- Save a project file using a different file type.
- Open a project file.
- Close a project file.
- Specify information about a project file, such as the properties for the project.
- Open a recently used project file and specify the number of recently used files.
- Create a new project file.
- Print a project file.
- Share a project file with others.
- Access Microsoft Project 2010 help topics.
- Specify options settings for the active project and for the application.
- Exit Microsoft Project 2010.

You may see an *Add-ins* command item below the *Options* command in the *Backstage* menu if your system has an add-in that Microsoft Project 2010 recognizes, such as a bluetooth device.

To save the active project file, click the *Save* command from the *Backstage* menu. Microsoft Project 2010 saves the active project and then exits the *Backstage*.

To save the active project as an alternate file type, click the *Save As* command in the *Backstage* menu. The system exits the *Backstage* and displays the *Save As* dialog shown in Figure 1 - 15. This dialog allows you to save your project using an alternate file type, such as a Microsoft Excel workbook or a PDF file, or to save the project to an ODBC-compliant relational database. Select your alternate file type and location, change the name of the file if desired, and then click the *Save* button. The system exits the *Save As* dialog and returns to your active project.

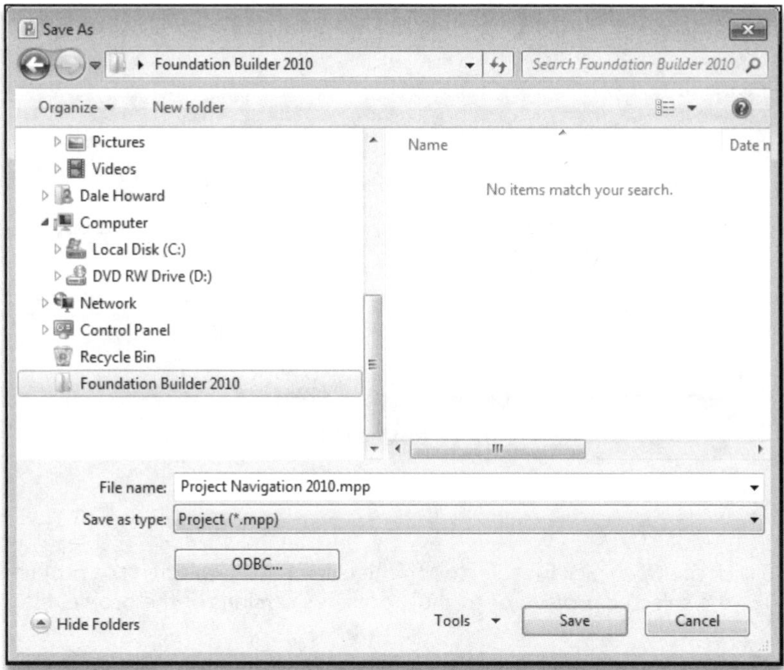

Figure 1 - 15: Save As dialog

To open any existing project, click the *File* tab to open the *Backstage* and select the *Open* command. Microsoft Project 2010 closes the *Backstage* and displays the *Open* dialog shown in Figure 1 - 16. The *Open* dialog offers you a number of ways to locate an existing project, including the following:

- Click one of the folders shown in the *Breadcrumb* bar at the top of the dialog.
- Click the *Previous Locations* pick list button at the right end of the *Breadcrumb* bar.
- Enter a search term in the *Search* field in the upper right corner of the dialog.
- Select a link in the *Favorite Links* list on the left side of the dialog.

- Click the *Folders* button at the bottom of the *Favorite Links* list and select the drive and folder.
- Click the *ODBC* button to navigate to an ODBC-compliant relational database.
- Click the *Save as type* pick list in the lower right corner of the dialog, and choose an alternate file type, such as an Excel Workbook file.

Select the project file you want to open and then click the *Open* button. The system closes the dialog and opens the selected project in Read/Write mode.

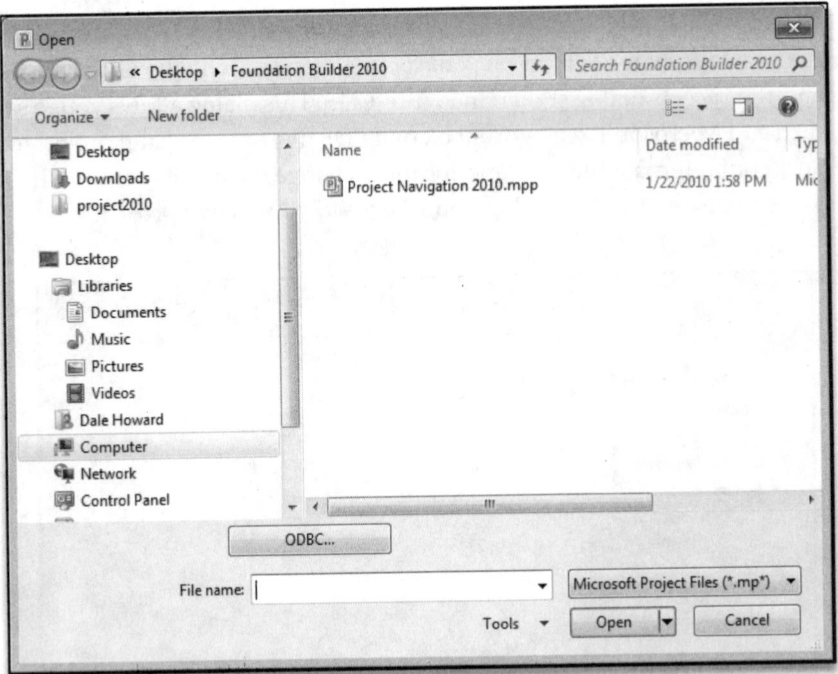

Figure 1 - 16: Open dialog

You can also click the *Open* pick list selector on the *Open* button to open the project file read-only, to open a copy of the selected project, or to show previous versions of the project file.

To close the active project file, click the *Close* command in the *Backstage* menu. The system exits the *Backstage* and returns you to your Microsoft Project 2010 application window.

To specify information about the active project, click the *Info* tab in the *Backstage*. Microsoft Project 2010 displays the *Information* page for the selected project, as shown in Figure 1 - 17. Notice the following about the *Information* page:

- The system displays the name and file path for the active project at the top of the page.
- The system displays statistics for the active project on the right side of the page.
- The system allows you to create and manage Project Server 2010 login accounts (available in only the Professional version of Microsoft Project 2010).
- The system allows you to access the *Organizer* dialog.

- The system allows you to specify Project Information about the active project.

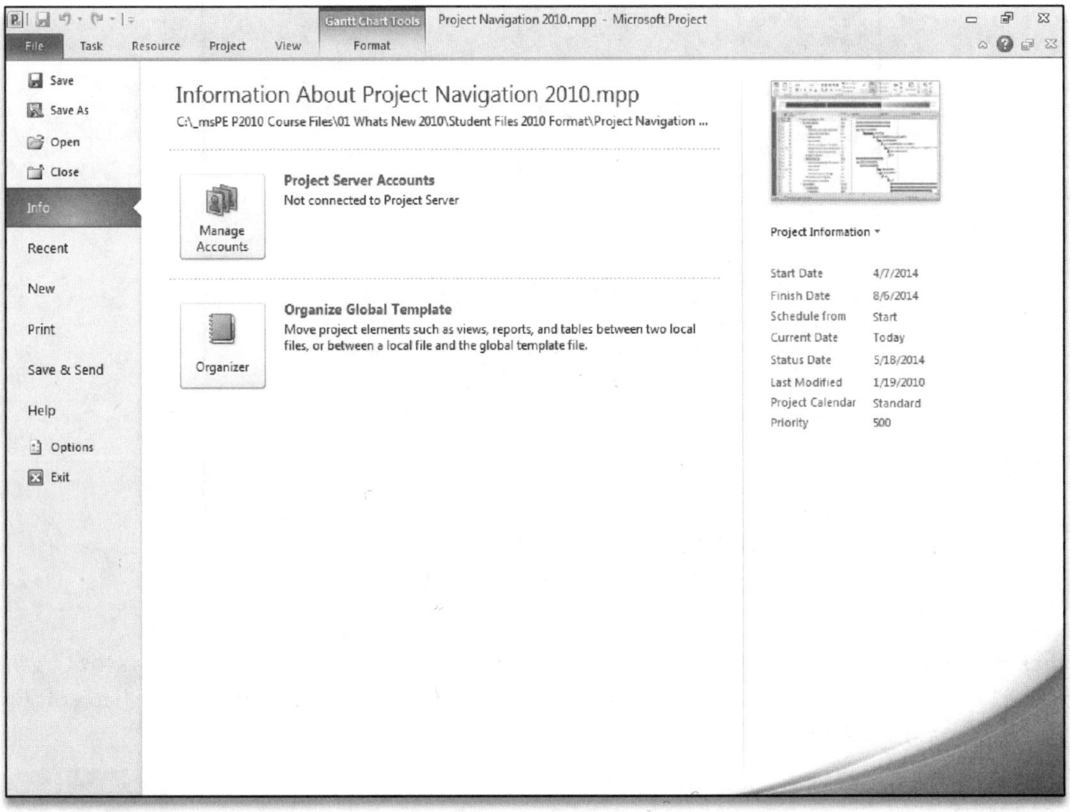

Figure 1 - 17: Information page for the selected project

When you click the *Manage Accounts* button in the *Project Server Accounts* section on the *Information* page of the *Backstage,* the system displays the *Project Server Accounts* dialog shown in Figure 1 - 18. This feature is available only in the **Professional** version of Microsoft Project 2010, and you use this feature to specify login information for your organization's Project Server 2010 instances.

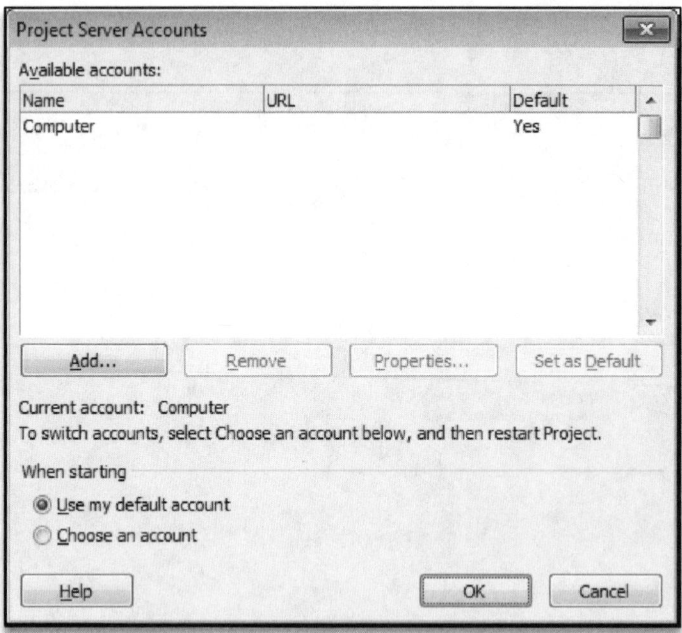

Figure 1 - 18: Project Server Accounts dialog

When you click the *Organizer* button on the *Information* page of the *Backstage,* the system displays the *Organizer* dialog shown in Figure 1 - 19. You use the *Organizer* dialog to manage default and custom objects in Microsoft Project 2010, such as Views, Reports, Tables, Filters, Groups, etc.

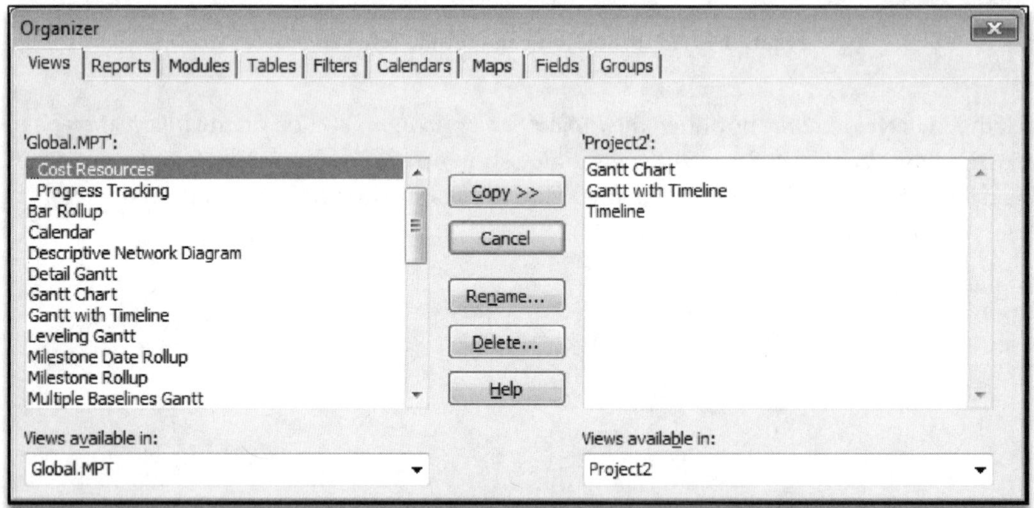

Figure 1 - 19: Organizer dialog

When you click the *Project Information* pick list in the upper right corner of the *Information* page in the *Backstage,* the system displays the pick list shown in Figure 1 - 20. Select the *Advanced Properties* item on the list to display the *Properties* dialog, where you can enter custom properties for the selected project. Select the *Project Statistics* item on the list to display the *Project Statistics* dialog.

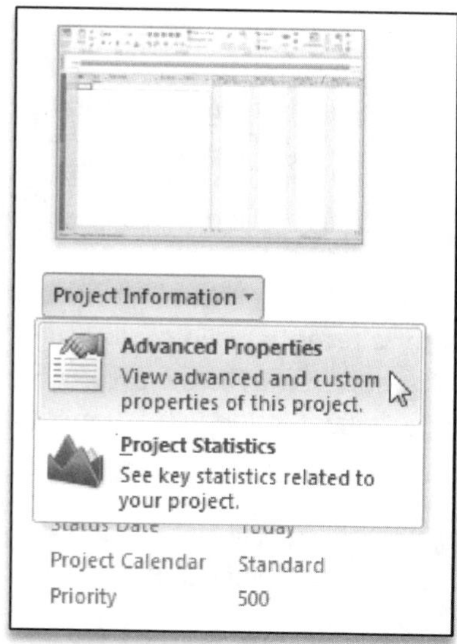

Figure 1 - 20: Project Information pick list in the Backstage

To open a recently opened project file, click the *Recent* tab in the *Backstage*. The system displays the recently used projects in the *Recent Projects* page shown previously in Figure 1 - 14. To add a specific number of recently used project files to the list shown on the left side of the *Backstage* page, select the *Quickly access this number of recent Projects* option at the bottom of the screen and then specify a number for this field. The system adds these projects to the menu on the left side of the page, as shown in Figure 1 - 21. Notice in the figure that I chose to display eight projects in the menu.

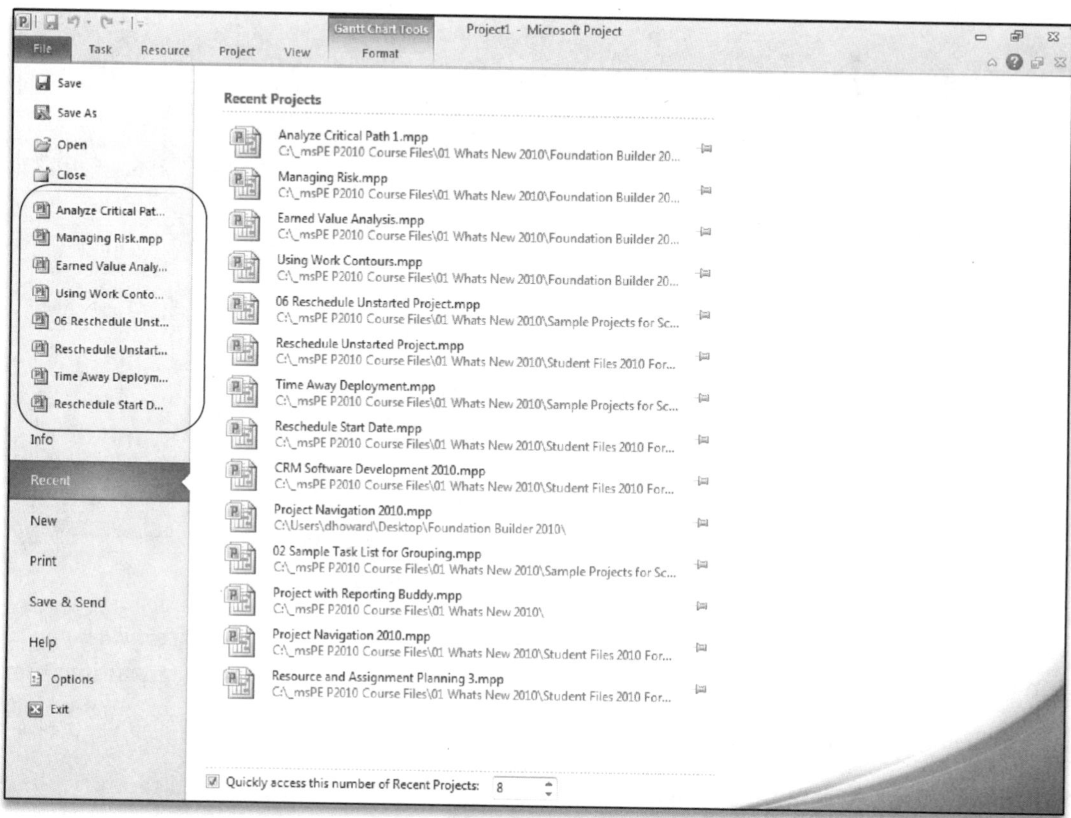

Figure 1 - 21: Recent files shown on the left side of the Backstage page

Microsoft Project 2010 limits you to no more than **17 files** in the *Quickly access this number of Recent Projects* field.

For any project file shown on the recently used file list, you can "pin" the file so that the system always displays this file at the top of the *Recent Projects* list. To "pin" a recently used project file, click the "pushpin" icon to the right of the project file name in the *Recent Project* list. The system moves the project file to the top of the Recent Projects list and displays an "unpin" icon, as shown in Figure 1 - 22. Notice that I "pinned" four recently used project files.

If you right-click on any of the projects shown in the *Recent Projects* list, the system displays a shortcut menu that allows you to perform additional actions such as removing a project from the display list or clearing the list of all unpinned projects.

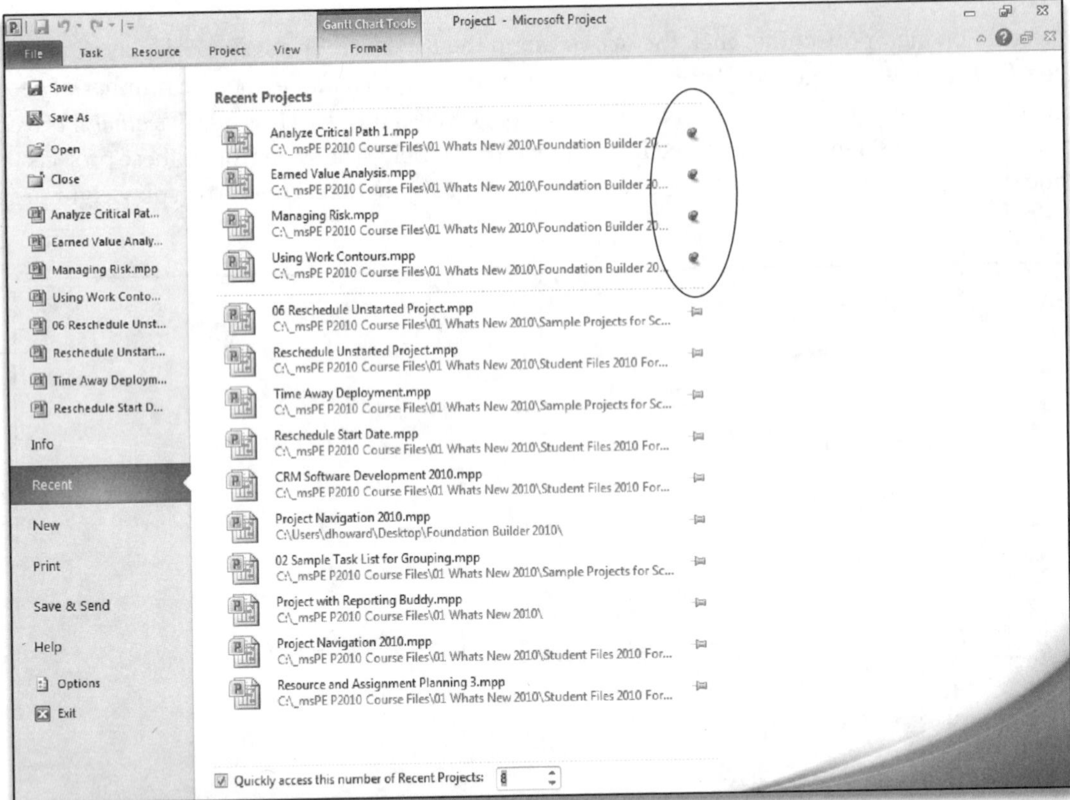

Figure 1 - 22: Pinned projects at the top of the Recent Projects list

To create a new project, click the *New* tab in the *Backstage*. The system displays the *Available Templates* page in the *Backstage* shown in Figure 1 - 23. Notice that you can create a new project in a variety of ways, including the following:

- Click the *Blank project* button to create a new blank project.
- Click the *Recent templates* button to create a new project from a template you used recently.

- Click the *My templates* button to create a new project from a custom project template you created.
- Click the *New from existing project* button to create a new project from an existing project.
- Click the *New from Excel workbook* button to import a new Microsoft Project 2010 file from an existing Microsoft Excel file.
- Click the *New from SharePoint task list* button to create a new project from a Task list in an existing SharePoint 2010 site (available only in the Professional version of Microsoft Project 2010).
- Click one of the icons in the *Office.com Templates* section to display available templates in Office.com.
- Type one or more key words in the *Search Office.com for templates* field and click the Start Searching arrow button to search Office.com for customized project templates.

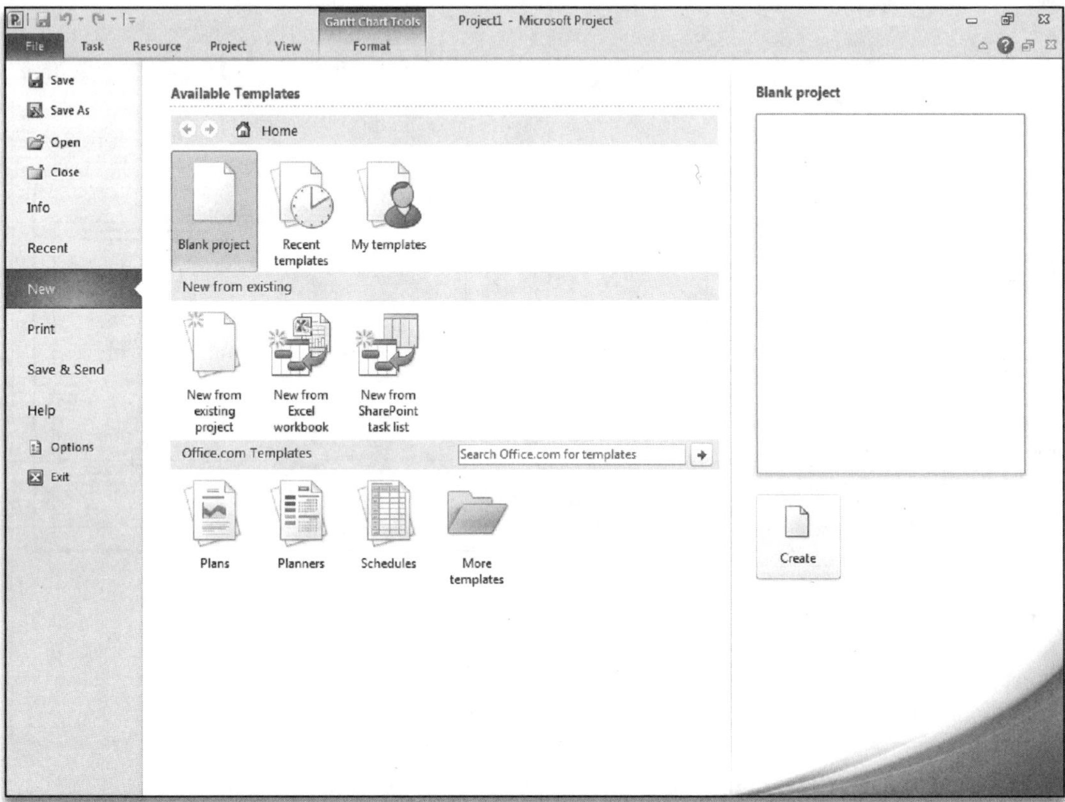

Figure 1 - 23: Available Templates page in the Backstage

To print the active project, click the *Print* tab in the *Backstage*. The system displays the *Print* page shown in Figure 1 - 24. On the *Print* page, you can control any of the following printing options:

- Specify the number of copies to print in the *Copies* field.
- Select an available printer in the *Printer* pick list.
- Set printer options by clicking the *Printer Properties* link.
- Specify the date range for printing project information by clicking the *Settings* pick list and choosing a predefined date range.

- Manually enter a date range in the *Dates* and *to* fields.
- Specify the number of pages to print by selecting values in the *Pages* and *to* fields.
- Specify the orientation of the printout on the *Print Orientation* pick list.
- Specify the paper size on the *Paper Size* pick list.
- Display the *Page Setup* dialog by clicking the *Page Setup* link.
- View the Print Preview of the project in the right side of the page.
- Navigate in the Print Preview using the buttons in the lower right corner of the page.

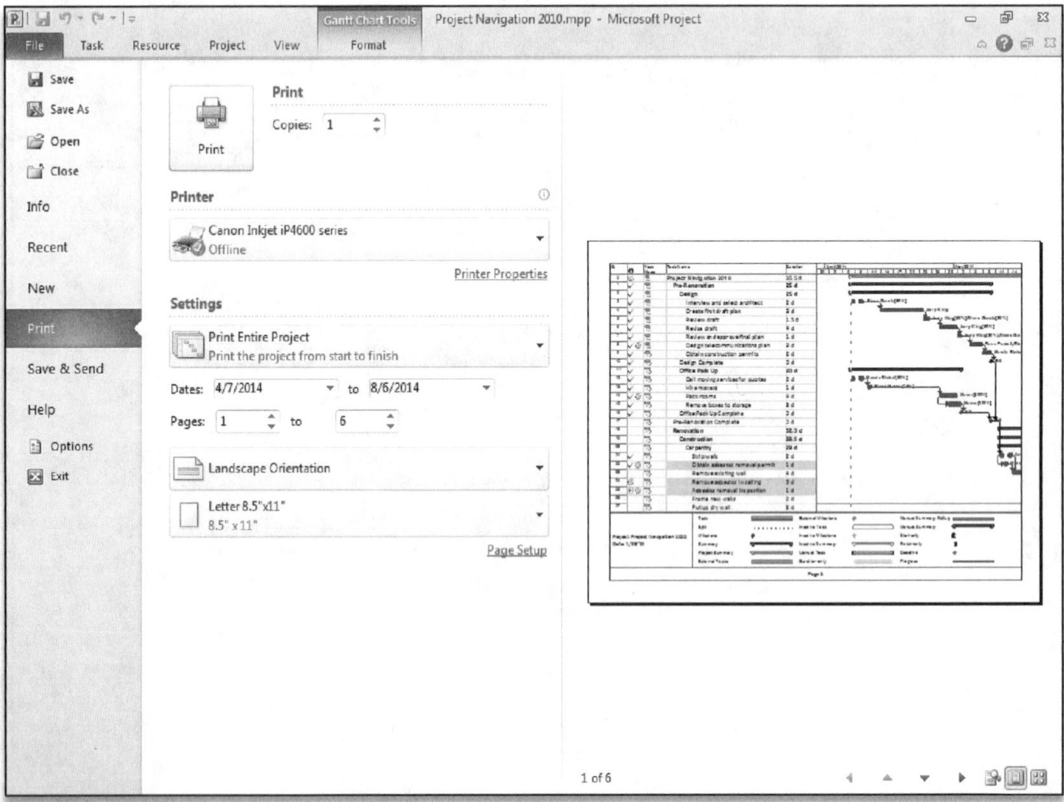

Figure 1 - 24: Print page in the Backstage

To share a project with others, click the *Save & Send* tab in the *Backstage*. The system displays the *Save & Send* page in the *Backstage*, as shown in Figure 1 - 25. Notice on the *Save & Send* page that Microsoft Project 2010 allows you to share your project file in a number of ways, including each of the following:

- Send the project file as an e-mail attachment.
- Synchronize the tasks in the project file with a Tasks list in a SharePoint 2010 site (available only in the Professional version of Microsoft Project 2010).
- Save the project file in a SharePoint 2010 site (available only in the Professional version of Microsoft Project 2010).
- Share the project with others using the Microsoft Project Online service.

- Save the project file to an alternate file type.
- Save the project file as a PDF document or an XPS document.

XPS documents are electronic paper documents saved according to XML Paper Specification standard. Hardware, software, and people can all read XPS documents.

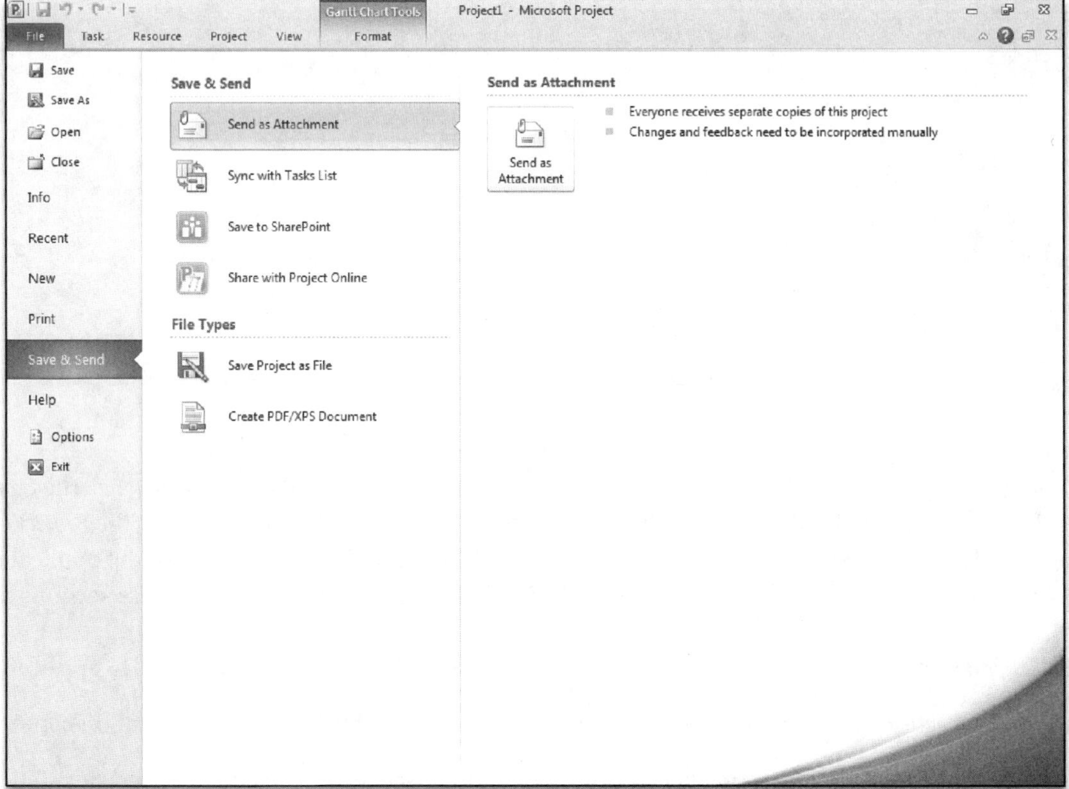

Figure 1 - 25: Save & Send page in the Backstage

Click the *Help* tab to display the *Help* page in the *Backstage,* as shown in Figure 1 - 26. Notice that the *Help* page contains four sections of options, including the following:

- The *Support* section contains icons that offer you Help articles and allow you to contact Microsoft.
- The *Tools for Working with Office* section contains icons that allow you to display the *Options* dialog and to help you to get the latest software updates for the software.
- The *Product Activated* section shows you the activation status of your software.
- The *About Microsoft Project* section shows you the version of Microsoft Project 2010 you are using.

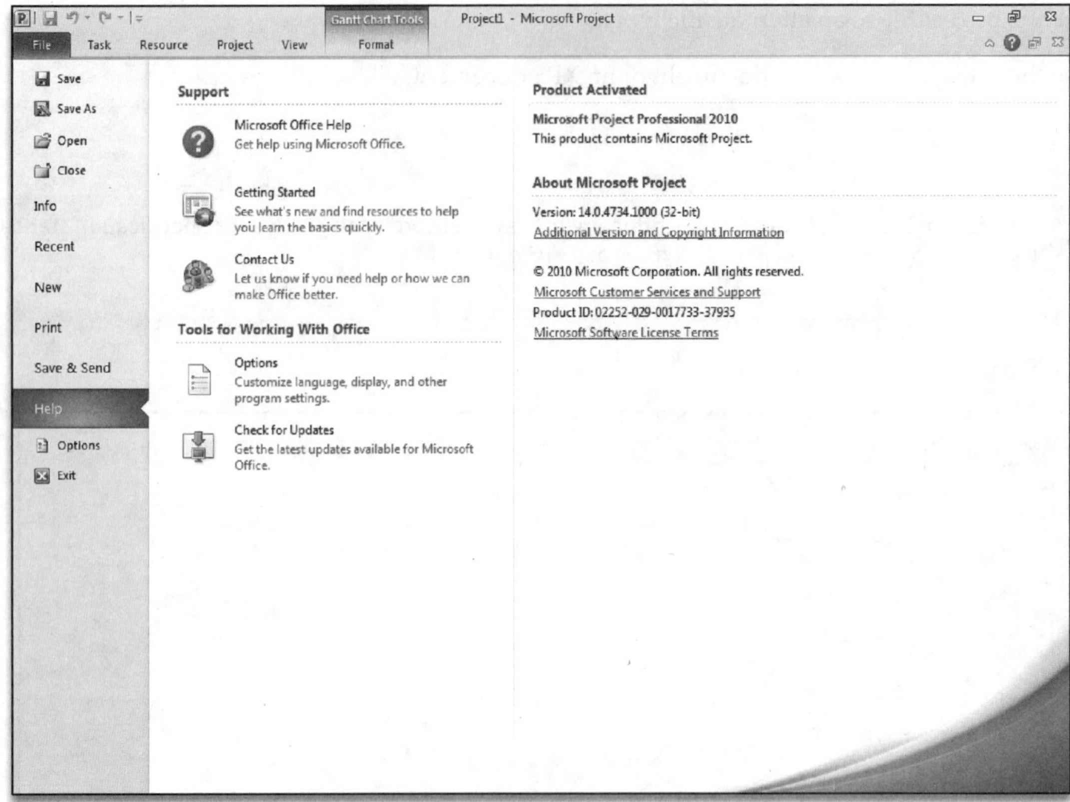

Figure 1 - 26: Help page in the Backstage

To specify option settings for the active project and for the Microsoft Project 2010 application, click the *Options* command in the *Backstage*. The system displays the *Project Options* dialog shown in Figure 1 - 27. In the *Project Options* dialog, you can specify settings for the active project as well as for the Microsoft Project 2010 desktop application. Notice that the *Project Options* dialog offers eleven sections in which to specify options settings. These sections include:

- The *General* section allows you to specify general settings for the Microsoft Project 2010 application.
- The *Display* section allows you to specify how Microsoft Project 2010 displays application content.
- The *Schedule* section allows you to specify options related to scheduling, calendars, and calculations for the active project.
- The *Proofing* section allows you to specify how the Microsoft Project 2010 application proofs and formats text in your project files.
- The *Save* section allows you to specify how and where the Microsoft Project 2010 application saves your project files.
- The *Language* section allows you to specify the language used in your Microsoft Project 2010 application.
- The *Advanced* section allows you to specify advanced options for the active project and for the Microsoft Project 2010 application.
- The *Customize Ribbon* section allows you to customize the ribbon by adding or removing tabs and buttons on the ribbon.

- The *Quick Access Toolbar* section allows you to customize the *Quick Access Toolbar* by adding or removing buttons.
- The *Add-Ins* section allows you to add and remove COM Add-Ins for Microsoft Office.
- The *Trust Center* section allows you to specify your level of security for macros written in the VBA programming language.

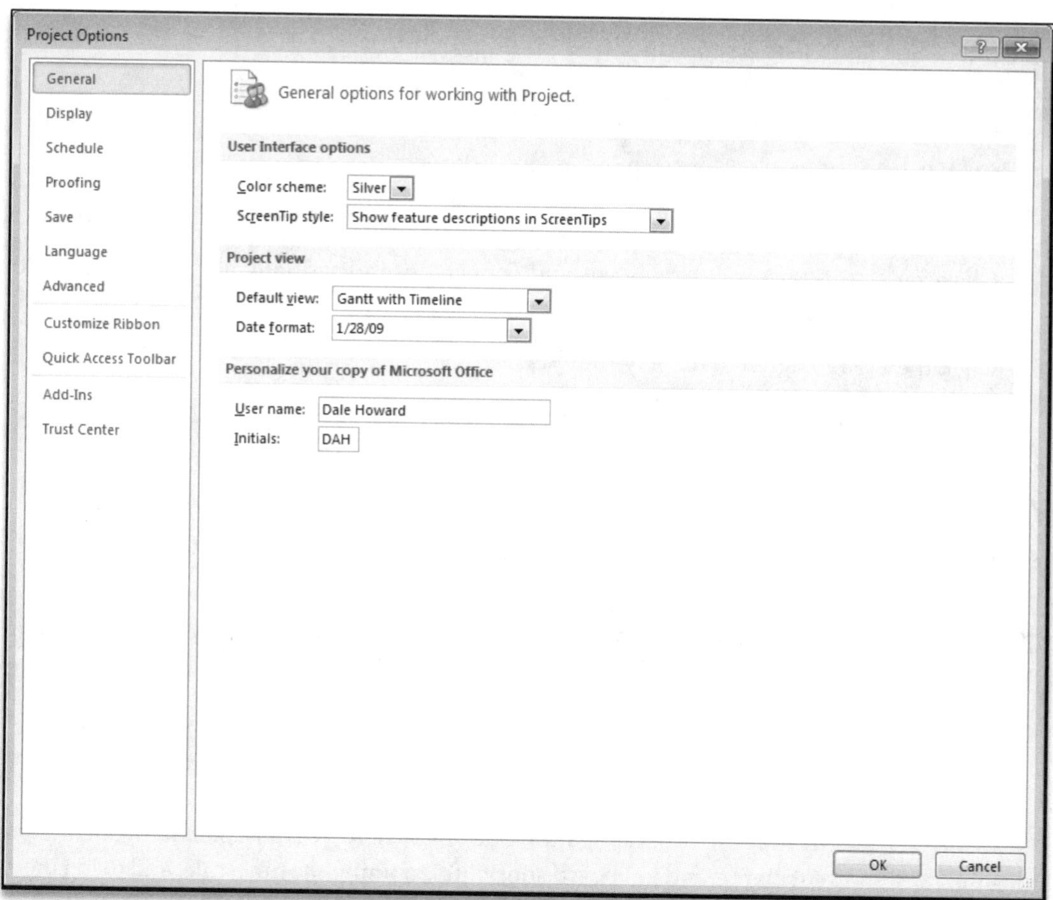

Figure 1 - 27: Project Options dialog

I present an in depth discussion of many of these *Backstage* features in succeeding modules in this book. To close the *Backstage* without taking any other actions, click the *File* tab again or click any other tab on the ribbon.

Hands On Exercise

Exercise 1-1

Explore the ribbon and the Backstage in Microsoft Project 2010.

1. Launch Microsoft Project 2010, if necessary.
2. Click the *File* tab and then click the *Open* command in the *Backstage* menu.
3. Navigate to your student folder and then open the **Project Navigation 2010.mpp** sample file.
4. Click the *Task, Resource, Project, View,* and *Format* tabs individually and study the buttons available on each ribbon.
5. Click the *File* tab again to display the *Backstage.*
6. In the *Information* page of the *Backstage,* click the *Project Information* pick list (upper right corner of the page) and choose the *Advanced Properties* item on the list.
7. Enter your name in the *Owner* field and then click the *OK* button.
8. Click *Recent, New, Print, Save & Send,* and *Help* tabs in the Backstage and study the options available on each page.
9. Click the *Save* button to save the **Project Navigation 2010.mpp** sample file and exit the *Backstage.*

Using Navigation Features

Microsoft Project 2010 offers four new types of navigation options to help you navigate in the active project. These options include improved shortcut menus and keyboard shortcuts, zooming the timescale, and using the *Zoom Slider*. I discuss each of the navigation features individually.

Using Shortcut Menus

If you are a previous user of Microsoft Office Project 2007, you are probably already familiar with the shortcut menu that the software displays when you right-click any object such as a task or a Gantt bar. Microsoft expanded the shortcut menu in Microsoft Project 2010 to include a longer menu of options and an additional shortcut menu section called the *Mini Toolbar*. When you right-click on any object, the system displays the *Mini Toolbar* and the shortcut menu simultaneously. For example, Figure 1 - 28 shows the Mini Toolbar and the shortcut menu when I right-click a task.

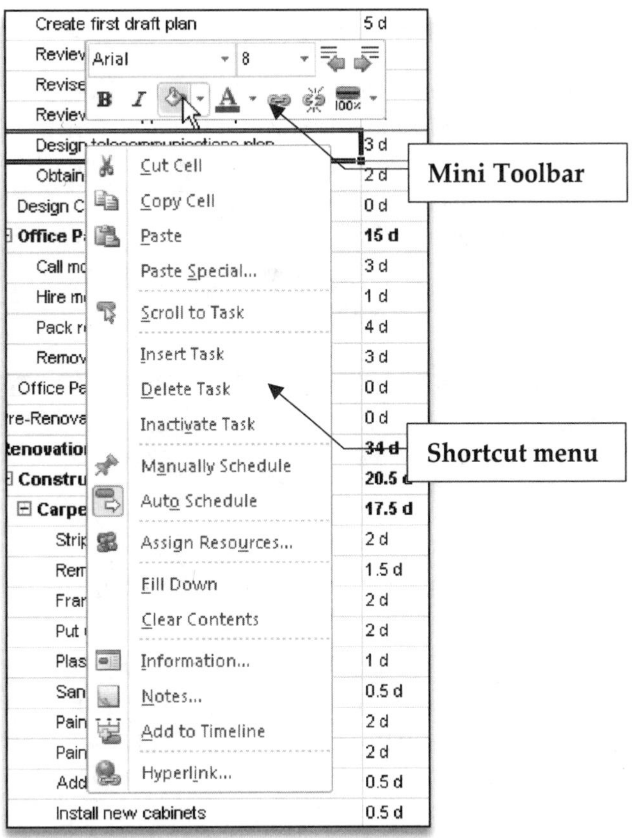

Figure 1 - 28: Mini Toolbar and shortcut menu for tasks

Notice in Figure 1 - 28 that the *Mini Toolbar* has buttons for the following actions: Font, Font Size, Indent, Outdent, Bold text, Italic text, Cell Background Color, Font Color, Link Tasks, Unlink Tasks, and Percent Complete. If you right-click on any graphical object in the Gantt Chart, such as a Gantt bar, the system displays the shortcut menu and *Mini Toolbar* shown in Figure 1 - 29.

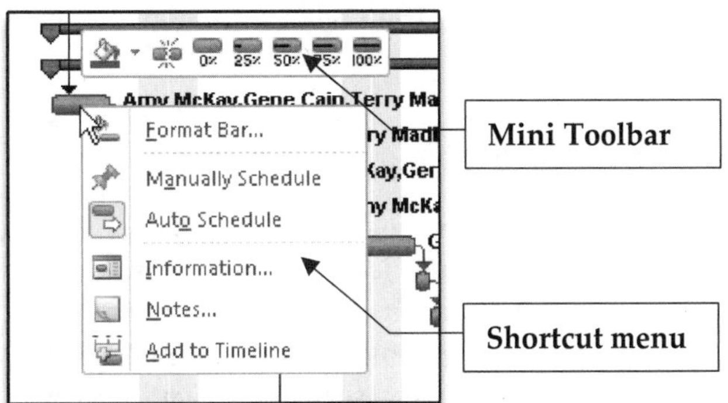

Figure 1 - 29: Mini Toolbar and shortcut menu for a Gantt bar

Notice in Figure 1 - 29 that the *Mini Toolbar* has buttons for the following actions: Bar Color, Split Task, 0% Complete, 25% Complete, 50% Complete, 75% Complete, and 100% Complete. Likewise, if you right-click on a resource, such as in the Resource Sheet view, the *Mini Toolbar* and shortcut menu offer a set of features exclusively for working with resource information.

Using Built-In Keyboard Shortcuts

For users who prefer using the keyboard to the mouse, Microsoft Project 2010 offers two types of keyboard shortcuts. The first type includes the same set of keyboard shortcuts found in previous Microsoft Office Project versions. You can continue to use keyboard shortcuts such as **Ctrl + S** to save a file and **Ctrl + C** to copy information to the Windows Clipboard. The second type is keyboard shortcuts called **KeyTips** for use with the tabs on the ribbon and for the buttons on each ribbon as well as the *Quick Access* Toolbar. To activate these keyboard shortcuts, press the **Alt** key on your computer keyboard. The system displays the KeyTips for each tab on the ribbon and for each button on the *Quick Access Toolbar*, as shown in Figure 1 - 30.

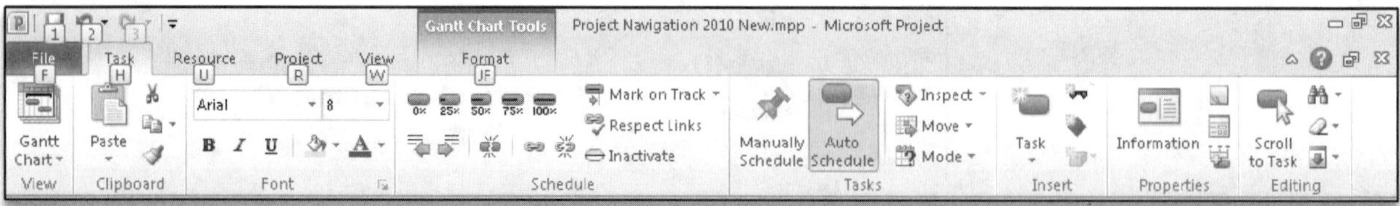

Figure 1 - 30: Ribbon with KeyTips for tabs

Notice in Figure 1 - 30 that **F** is the KeyTip for the *File* tab, **U** is the KeyTip for the *Resource* tab on the ribbon, and **2** is the KeyTip for the *Undo* button on the *Quick Access Toolbar*. With KeyTips activated, press the keyboard shortcut key for the KeyTip you want to use. When you press the shortcut key for a ribbon tab, the system displays the KeyTips for each button on the selected ribbon. For example, Figure 1 - 31 shows the KeyTips for the *Task* ribbon. Therefore, to activate the *Paste* button I must click the **V** key on my computer keyboard.

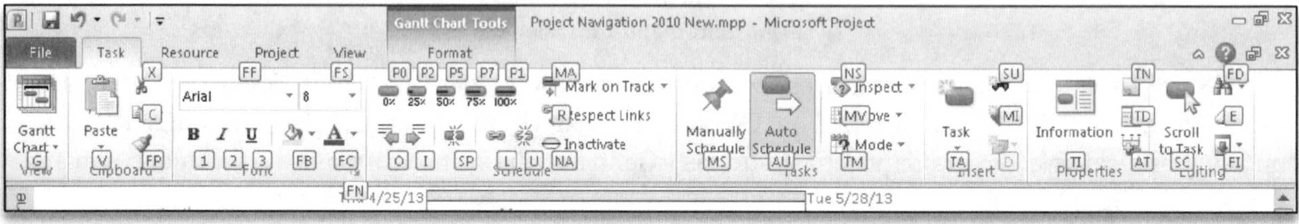

Figure 1 - 31: Ribbon with KeyTips for buttons

Zooming the Timescale Bar

Microsoft Project 2007provided you with two quick ways to zoom the Timescale using the *Zoom In* button and the *Zoom Out* button on the *Standard* toolbar, or clicking View ➤ Zoom to display the *Zoom* dialog. Microsoft Project 2010 now offers a single *Zoom* pick list button in the *Zoom* section of the *View* ribbon, which allows you to zoom in and zoom out, and offers two new zooming options: the *Zoom Entire Project* button and the *Zoom Selected Tasks* button. To zoom the Timescale, first apply any task view, such as the *Gantt Chart* view. When you click the *Zoom Entire Project* button, the system zooms the Timescale to display the entire time span of the project in the Gantt Chart, as shown in Figure 1 - 32.

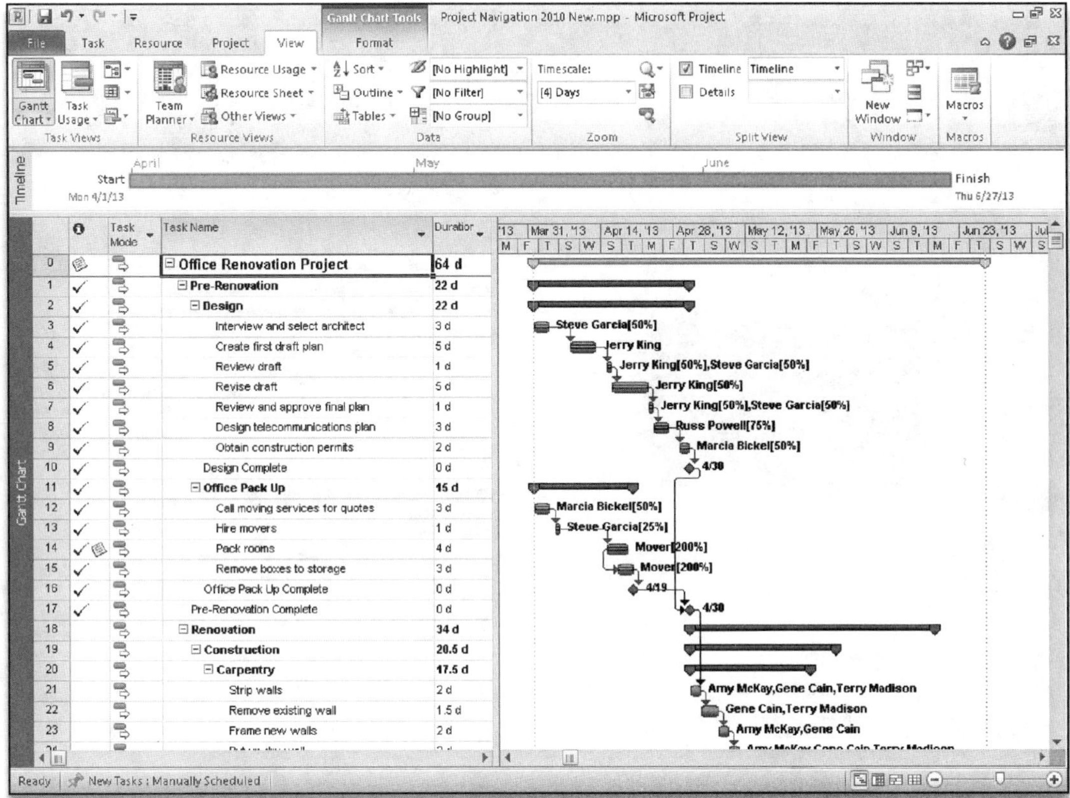

Figure 1 - 32: Gantt Chart view with Timescale zoomed to Entire Project

In the project shown in the figure above, the current level of zoom for the project is "2-Week Time Periods Over 4-Day Time Periods." To determine the current level of Zoom in a project, double-click anywhere in the Timescale. In the Timescale dialog, examine the zoom information on the *Middle Tier* tab and the *Bottom Tier* tab to determine the current level of Zoom applied to the project.

If you select a block of tasks and then click the *Zoom Selected Tasks* button, the system zooms the Timescale for the time span of the selected tasks. In Figure 1 - 33, I zoomed the Timescale to the time span for the tasks I selected in the Design deliverable section of the project.

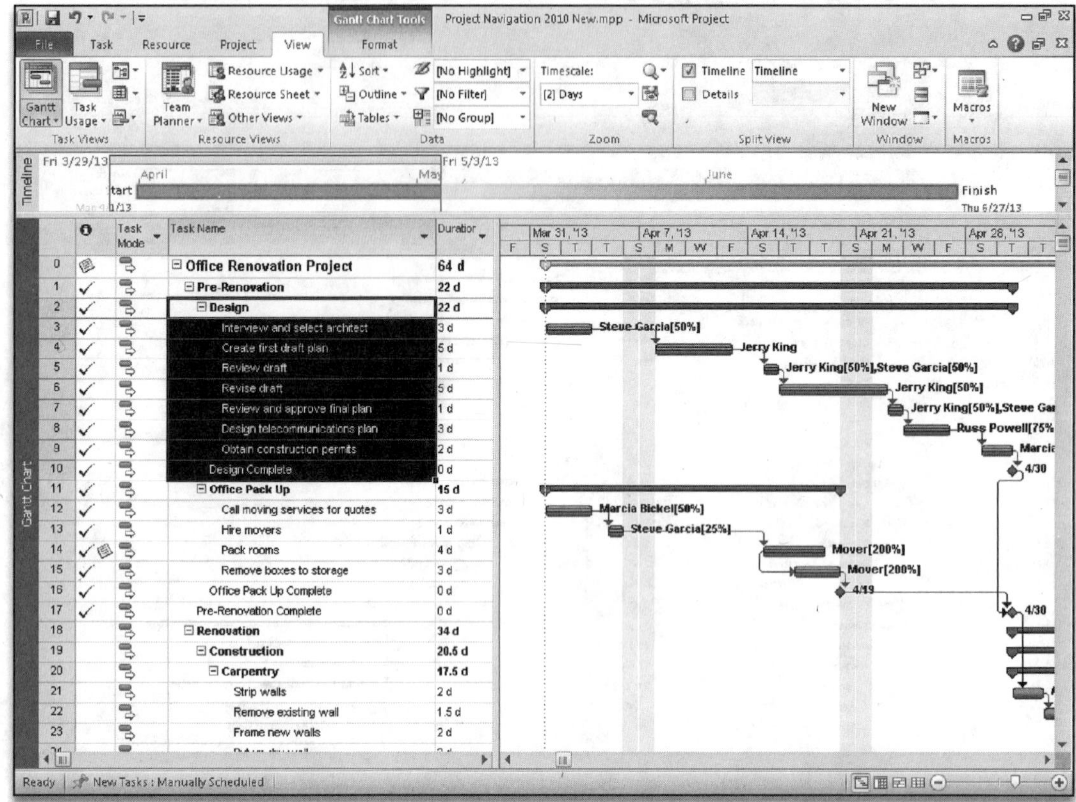

Figure 1 - 33: Gantt Chart view with Timescale zoomed to the selected tasks

In the project shown in Figure 1 - 33, the current level of zoom for the project is "Weeks Over 2-Day Time Periods."

Using the Zoom Slider

Microsoft Project 2010 also provides a handy *Zoom Slider* for zooming the Timescale in your projects. Shown in Figure 1 - 34, the *Zoom Slider* is found in the lower right corner of the Microsoft Project 2010 application window. The *Zoom Slider* allows you to change the current level of zoom quickly by sliding the zoom control manually to the left (to zoom out) or right (to zoom in). You can also click the *Zoom In* button and *Zoom Out* button in the *Zoom Slider* as well.

Figure 1 - 34: Zoom Slider

You can use the *Zoom Slider* in any View with a Gantt Chart, such as the Gantt Chart and Tracking Gantt view, and in the Task Usage, Resource Usage, and Calendar views as well.

Hands On Exercise

Exercise 1-2

Explore the new navigation features in Microsoft Project 2010.

1. Return to your **Project Navigation 2010.mpp** sample file, if necessary.
2. Right-click on task ID #3, *Interview and select architect*, to display the shortcut menu and the *Mini Toolbar*.
3. In the *Mini Toolbar*, click the *Background Color* pick list button and choose the *Blue, Lighter 80%* color in the *Theme Colors* section of the palette.
4. Select task ID #23, *Remove existing wall*, and then click the *Scroll to Task* button on the *Task* ribbon.
5. In the Gantt Chart, right-click on the Gantt bar for the *Strip walls* task and then click the *100% Complete* button in the *Mini Toolbar*.
6. Press the **Alt** ➢ **W** ➢ **Q** ➢ **O** on your computer keyboard to use the built-in KeyTips to select the *View* ribbon and then zoom out one level in the Timescale.
7. In the *Zoom* section of the *View* ribbon, click the *Zoom Entire Project* button.
8. Select all of the tasks in the Carpentry section of the project (task ID #20 - #38) and then click the *Zoom Selected Tasks* button in the *Zoom* section of the *View* ribbon.
9. In the lower right corner of your Microsoft Project 2010 application window, click and hold the slider control in the *Zoom Slider* section, and then zoom the Timescale in and out to see more and less detail in the Gantt Chart.
10. Click the *File* tab, then save and close your **Project Navigation 2010.mpp** sample file.

Customizing the User Interface

Microsoft Project 2010 offers you two ways to customize the user interface by modifying the *ribbon* and the *Quick Access Toolbar*. I discuss each of these topics separately.

Customizing the Ribbon

You can customize the *ribbon* by adding ribbon tabs, ribbon groups, and ribbon buttons. To begin the process of customizing the *ribbon*, complete the following steps:

1. Click the *File* tab.
2. In the *Backstage*, click the *Options* tab.

3. In the *Project Options* dialog, click the *Customize Ribbon* section in the left side of the dialog.

> The fastest way to access the *Customize Ribbon* section of the *Project Options* dialog is to right-click on any ribbon tab and then click the *Customize the Ribbon* item on the shortcut menu.

The system displays the *Project Options* dialog with the *Customize Ribbon* section displayed, as shown in Figure 1 - 35. Notice in the figure that the *Customize Ribbon* section of the *Project Options* dialog contains two sections:

- Use the *Choose Commands From* section to locate the commands you want to add to the ribbon.
- Use the *Customize the Ribbon* section to display the ribbon(s) you want to customize.

Click the *Choose commands from* pick list to choose the type of commands you want to add to the *ribbon*. The pick list offers you the following choices: *Popular Commands* (the default setting), *Commands Not in the Ribbon, All Commands, Macros, File Tab, All Tabs, Main Tabs, Tool Tabs,* and *Custom Tabs* and *Groups*. Select your desired option on the *Choose commands from* pick list.

Click the *Customize the Ribbon* pick list and choose which ribbon tabs to display in the dialog. You have three choices: *Main Tabs* (the default setting), *Tool Tabs* (used for formatting Views), and *All Tabs* (offers both the *Main Tabs* and the *Tool Tabs*). Select your option on the *Customize the Ribbon* pick list.

Figure 1 - 35: Project Options dialog, Customize Ribbon section

After you select your desired options on the *Choose commands from* pick list and the *Customize the Ribbon* pick list, you are ready to customize the *ribbon*. The software offers you multiple choices for customizing the ribbon:

- Show or hide a ribbon tab.
- Create a new ribbon tab.
- Create a ribbon group in a new or existing ribbon tab.
- Add or remove buttons on a default or custom ribbon tab.
- Rename a ribbon tab, a ribbon group, or a button.
- Move buttons, ribbon groups, and ribbon tabs on the ribbon.
- Reset the ribbon to its default settings.
- Import or export the customized ribbon and *Quick Access Toolbar* settings to a file.

Showing and Hiding a Ribbon Tab

To show or hide a ribbon tab, select or deselect the option checkbox to the left of the ribbon tab. For example, if you are a software developer, you might want to show the *Developer* tab so that you can create macros in the Office VBA programming language for Microsoft Project 2010. In this case, select the option checkbox for the *Developer* tab.

Creating a New Ribbon Tab

To create a new ribbon tab, select an existing ribbon tab in the location where you want to insert the new ribbon tab, and then click the *New Tab* button. The system inserts the new ribbon tab **below** the selected ribbon tab, as shown in Figure 1 - 36. Notice in the figure that the new ribbon tab also includes a custom ribbon group as well. Every default and custom ribbon tab **must** contain at least one ribbon group, but you can also create additional ribbon groups.

Figure 1 - 36: Project Options dialog, Customize Ribbon section after inserting a custom ribbon tab below the Project tab

Renaming a Ribbon Tab, Group, or Button

After creating a new ribbon tab or ribbon group, you should immediately rename it. To rename a ribbon tab, click the name of the ribbon tab and then click the *Rename* button. Microsoft Project 2010 displays the *Rename* dialog shown in Figure 1 - 37. Enter the name of the new ribbon tab in the *Display name* field and then click the *OK* button.

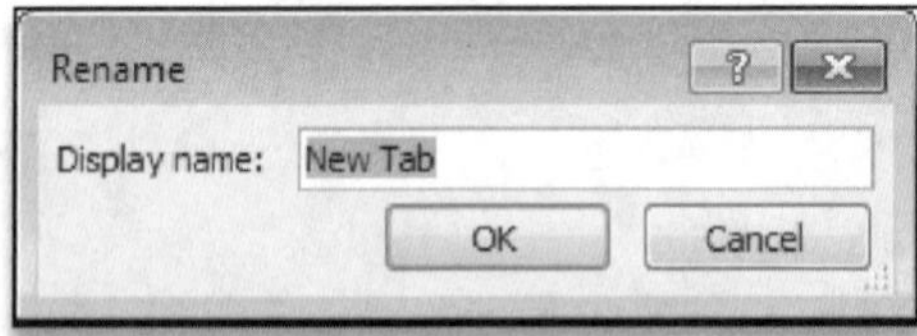

Figure 1 - 37: Rename dialog for a new custom ribbon tab

To rename a ribbon group, click the name of the ribbon group and then click the *Rename* button. Microsoft Project 2010 displays the *Rename* dialog shown in Figure 1 - 38. Enter the name of the new ribbon tab in the *Display name* field and then click the *OK* button.

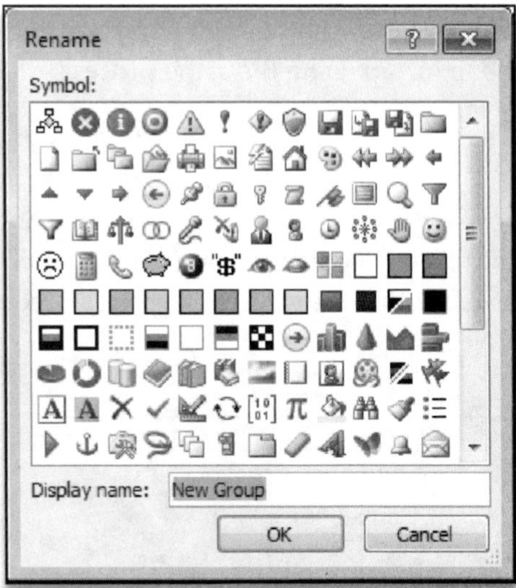

Figure 1 - 38: Rename dialog for a new custom ribbon group

To rename a button, click the name of the button and then click the *Rename* button. Microsoft Project 2010 displays the *Rename* dialog shown previously in Figure 1 - 38. Enter the new name of the button in the *Display name* field, select a symbol for the button in the *Symbol* list, and then click the *OK* button.

When you rename a ribbon group in the *Rename* dialog, selecting a symbol in the *Symbol* list has no effect on the ribbon group. Selecting a symbol in the *Symbol* list applies only to renaming buttons.

Creating a New Ribbon Group

To create a new custom ribbon group, select an existing ribbon tab or ribbon group, and then click the *New Group* button. The system adds the new custom ribbon group **below** the selected ribbon tab or ribbon group. After creating the new ribbon group, you should rename the ribbon group immediately by clicking the *Rename* button and entering a name for the ribbon group. You should create a custom ribbon group for every section of buttons and options you want to display to your custom ribbon tab.

Adding or Removing Buttons on a Ribbon Tab

After creating a new custom ribbon tab and adding custom ribbon groups, you are ready to add buttons to your new custom ribbon tab. To add a button to a ribbon tab, select the button in the list of buttons on the left, select the ribbon group in the list of ribbon tabs and groups on the right, and then click the *Add* button. Microsoft Project 2010 adds the button to the ribbon group.

Warning: You cannot add a button to any default Ribbon tab **unless** you create a custom Ribbon group on that ribbon tab. This means that you cannot add buttons to a default ribbon group on any default ribbon tab.

To remove a button on a ribbon tab, select the button in the list on the right and then click the *Remove* button. You can also remove a custom ribbon tab or ribbon group using the same process.

Moving Items in the Ribbon

Microsoft Project 2010 allows you to move default and custom ribbon tabs, ribbon groups, and buttons to a different location. To move any of these, select the object you want to move and then click the *Move Up* or *Move Down* button. Figure 1 - 39 shows a new custom ribbon tab with multiple ribbon groups. I created this ribbon tab to help me perform the six steps needed to define a new project.

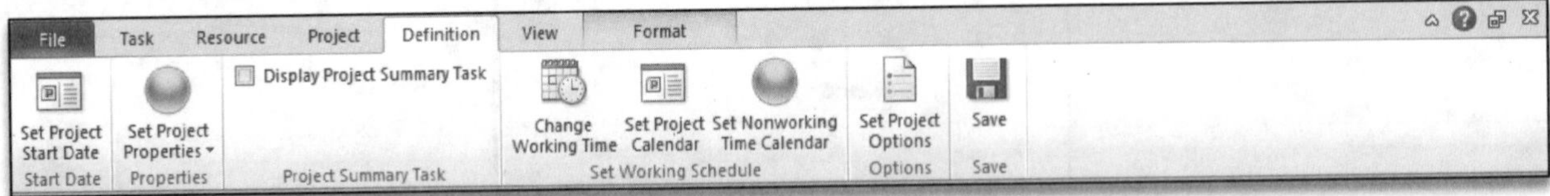

Figure 1 - 39: New custom ribbon tab

Resetting the Ribbon

Microsoft Project 2010 allows you to reset the entire ribbon back to its default settings, or to reset any default ribbon tab to its default settings. To reset only a single ribbon tab, select the ribbon tab in the list on the right, click the *Reset* pick list button and choose the *Reset Only Selected Ribbon Tab* item on the list. The system resets the selected ribbon tab immediately. To reset the entire ribbon, click the *Reset* pick list button and choose the *Reset All Customizations* item on the list. The system displays the warning dialog shown in Figure 1 - 40. Click the *Yes* button to confirm the reset action.

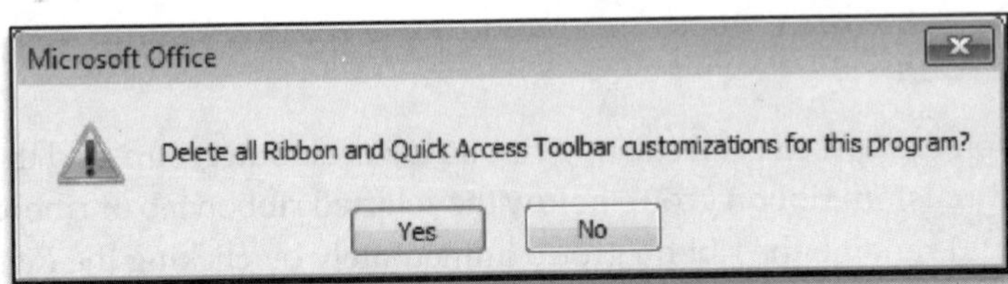

Figure 1 - 40: Warning dialog to reset all customizations to the ribbon

Warning: Notice in the dialog shown in the figure above that the system is about to reset all of the customizations to **both** the Ribbon bar **and** the Quick Access Toolbar. If you do not want to reset customizations to the Quick Access Toolbar, then **do not** select the *Reset All Customizations* option.

Hands On Exercise

Exercise 1-3

Customize the ribbon by adding a new ribbon tab and buttons.

1. Click the *File* tab, click the *New* tab, and then double-click the *Blank Project* icon to open a new blank project.
2. Right-click anywhere in the *ribbon* and choose the *Customize the Ribbon* item on the shortcut menu.
3. In the *Customize Ribbon* section of the *Project Options* dialog, click the *Choose commands from* pick list and select the *All Commands* item on the list.
4. In the list of ribbon tabs on the right side of the dialog, select the *Compare Projects* item and then click the *New Tab* button.
5. Select the *New Tab (Custom)* item, click the *Rename* button, enter *Definition* in the *Display name* field, and then click the *OK* button.
6. Select the *New Group (Custom)* item, click the *Rename* button, enter *Define a New Project* in the *Display name* field, and then click the *OK* button.
7. Add the following buttons to the new *Define a New Project* ribbon group:
    - Project Information
    - Document Properties
    - Project Summary Task
    - Nonworking Time
    - Options
    - Save
8. Click the *OK* button to close the *Project Options* dialog.
9. Click the *Definition* tab to view your new ribbon tab, your new ribbon group, and the buttons you added to the ribbon group.

Customizing the Quick Access Toolbar

Like the ribbon, you can also customize the *Quick Access Toolbar* in Microsoft Project 2010. By default, the *Quick Access Toolbar* appears **above** the ribbon, in the upper left corner of the application window, as shown in Figure 1 - 41. Notice in the figure that the *Quick Access Toolbar* contains only a few buttons, including the *Save, Undo,* and *Redo* buttons.

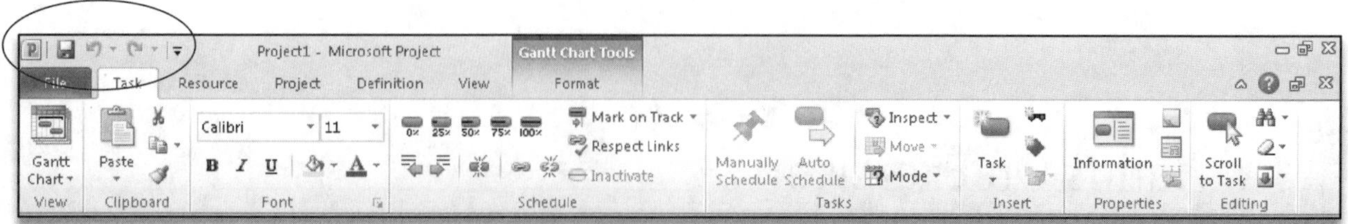

Figure 1 - 41: Quick Access Toolbar above the ribbon

You use the *Quick Access Toolbar* to provide quick access to the buttons you use most often. For example, many users like to add the *Open* and *Print* buttons to the *Quick Access Toolbar*. Microsoft Project 2010 allows you to customize the *Quick Access Toolbar* in two ways:

- Move the *Quick Access Toolbar* below the ribbon.
- Add or remove buttons on the *Quick Access Toolbar*.

To customize the *Quick Access Toolbar*, click the *Customize Quick Access Toolbar* button at the right end of the toolbar, just to the right of the *Redo* button. The system displays the pick list, as shown in Figure 1 - 42.

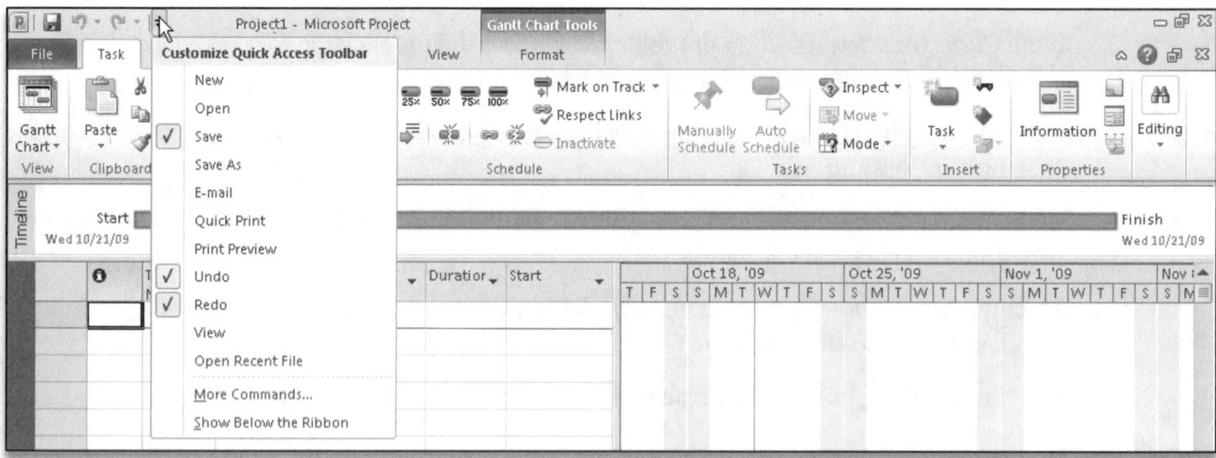

Figure 1 - 42: Click the Customize Quick Access toolbar button to customize the Quick Access Toolbar

To display the *Quick Access Toolbar* below the *ribbon*, click the *Show Below the Ribbon* item on the pick list menu. The system moves the *Quick Access Toolbar* below the ribbon, as shown in Figure 1 - 43.

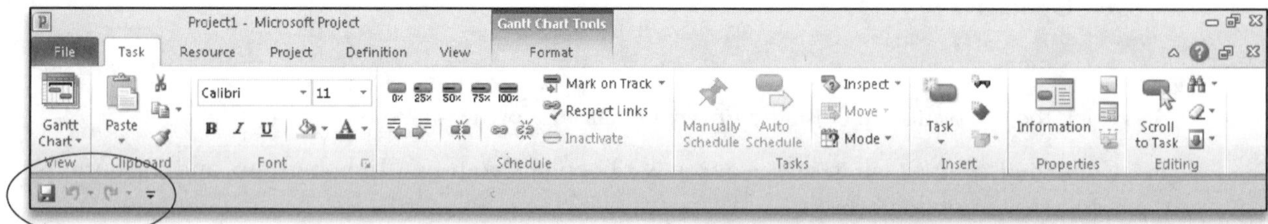

Figure 1 - 43: Quick Access Toolbar displayed below the ribbon

To add or remove buttons on the *Quick Access Toolbar*, click the *Customize Quick Access Toolbar* button again. Notice that the pick list menu contains a number of frequently used buttons, such as the *New*, *Open*, and *Print Preview* buttons. Select any one of these buttons to add it to the *Quick Access Toolbar*. To add other buttons, click the *More Commands* item on the pick list menu. The system displays the *Project Options* dialog with the *Quick Access Toolbar* section selected, as shown in Figure 1 - 44.

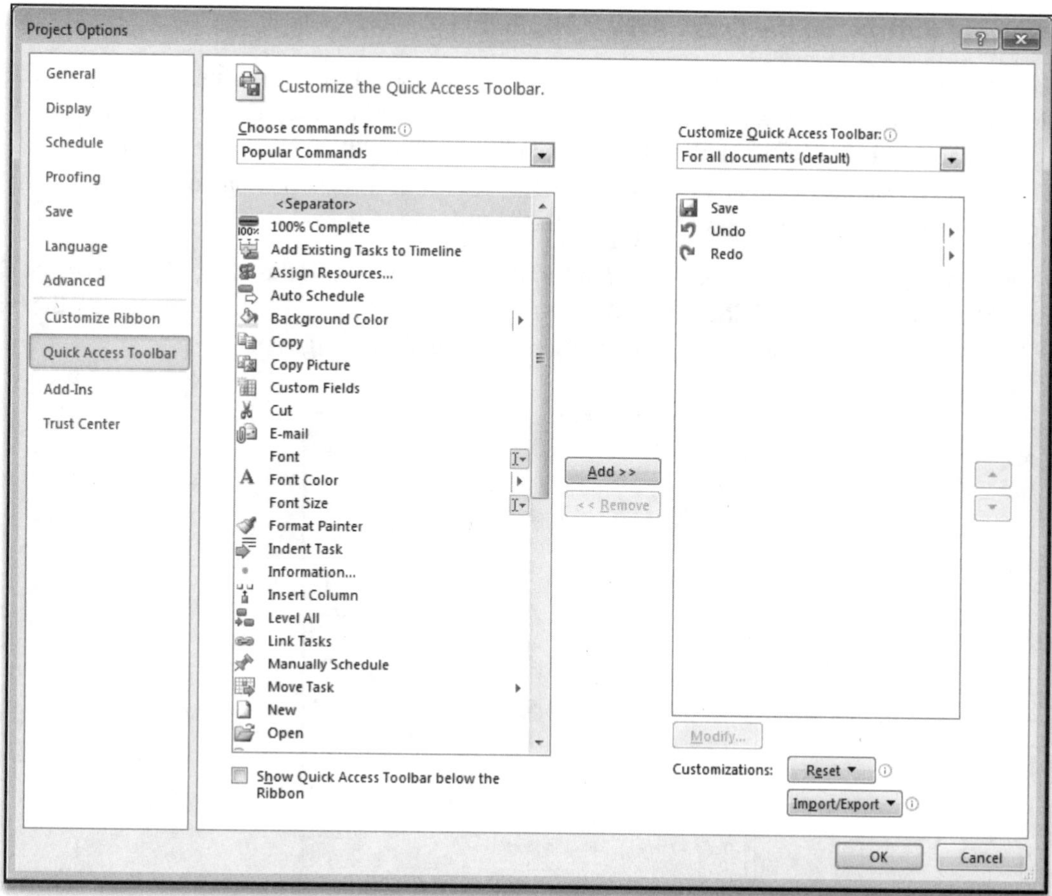

Figure 1 - 44: Project Options dialog, Quick Access Toolbar section

The process of customizing the *Quick Access Toolbar* is very similar to the process of customizing the ribbon. Click the *Choose commands from* pick list to choose the type of commands you want to add to the *Quick Access Toolbar*. The pick list offers you a number of choices, including *Popular Commands* (the default setting), *Commands Not in the Ribbon, All Commands,* and *Macros,* plus the commands found on each of the available ribbon tabs. Select your desired option on the *Choose commands from* pick list.

Click the *Customize Quick Access Toolbar* pick list and choose how to customize the *Quick Access Toolbar*. The choices on the pick list allow you to customize the *Quick Access Toolbar* for all projects or only for the active project. The second option means that you can have a customized *Quick Access Toolbar* for each project, based on your project management needs for each project. Select your desired option on the *Customize Quick Access Toolbar* pick list.

After you select your options on the *Choose commands from* pick list and the *Customize Quick Access Toolbar* pick list, you are ready to customize the *Quick Access Toolbar*. The software offers you only these customization choices:

- Add/remove buttons and Separators on the *Quick Access Toolbar*.
- Change the order of buttons on the *Quick Access Toolbar*.
- Reset the *Quick Access Toolbar* to its default settings.
- Import or export the customized ribbon and *Quick Access Toolbar* settings to a file.

Adding/Removing Buttons on the Quick Access Toolbar

To add a button to the *Quick Access Toolbar*, select the button in the list of buttons on the left. In the list of buttons on the right, select a button representing the location where you want to place the new button, and then click the *Add* button. The system adds the new button **below** the selected button. To add a *Separator* section to organize the buttons into groups, select the <*Separator*> item at the top of the list on the left and click the *Add* button. You place *Separators* in the list to add gridlines between buttons and separate the buttons into groups.

If you add a button for a macro to the *Quick Access Toolbar*, the system activates the *Modify* button on the *Quick Access Toolbar* section of the *Project Options* dialog. Click the *Modify* button to change the icon displayed for the button on the *Quick Access Toolbar*. The system displays the *Modify Button* dialog shown Figure 1 - 45.

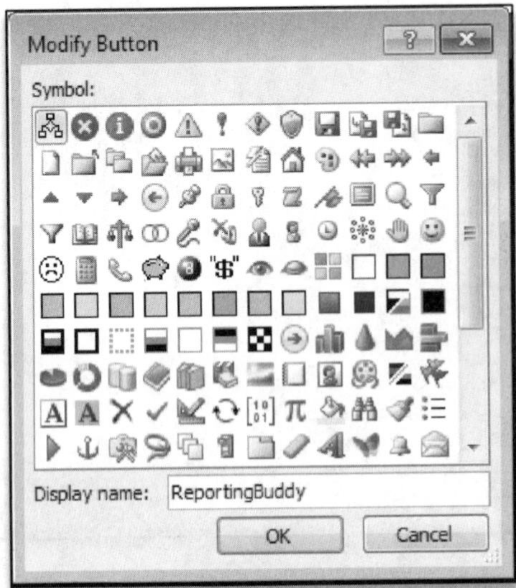

Figure 1 - 45: Modify Button dialog

To remove a button or Separator on the *Quick Access Toolbar*, select the item in the list of buttons on the right, and then click the *Remove* button.

Tip: To add a button to the *Quick Access Toolbar* quickly, you do not need to use the *Project Options* dialog. Instead, right-click on any button on the ribbon and then select the *Add to Quick Access Toolbar* item on the shortcut menu.

Moving Items in the Quick Access Toolbar

Microsoft Project 2010 allows you to move the buttons and *Separators* on the *Quick Access Toolbar* into the order you want to see them. To move any of these, select the item you want to move and then click the *Move Up* or *Move Down* button. Figure 1 - 46 and Figure 1 - 47 shows the custom setup of my *Quick Access Toolbar*. I included the buttons I use most commonly, and then I organized the buttons into groups of similar functionality.

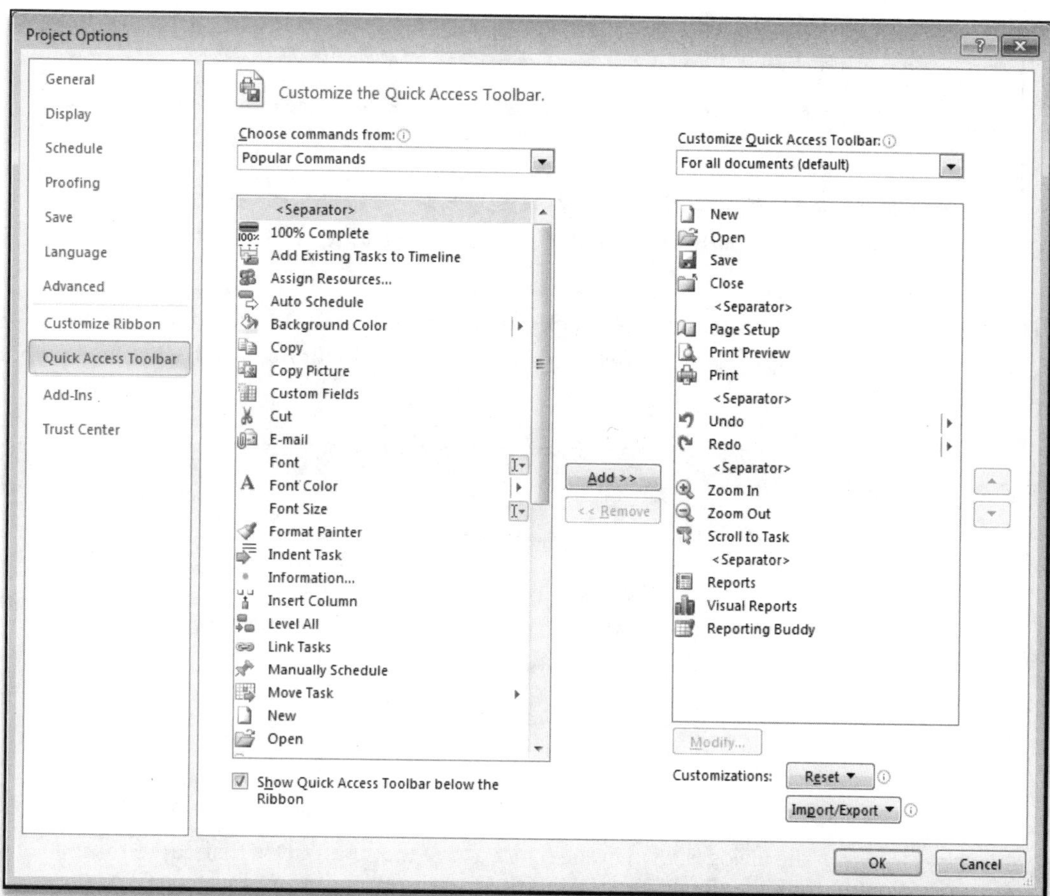

Figure 1 - 46: Project Options dialog, Quick Access Toolbar section after adding, moving, and renaming buttons to the Quick Access Toolbar

Figure 1 - 47: Customized Quick Access Toolbar

Resetting the Quick Access Toolbar

Microsoft Project 2010 allows you to reset the *Quick Access Toolbar* to its default settings, or to reset **both** the *Quick Access Toolbar* and the *ribbon* to their default settings. To reset only the *Quick Access Toolbar*, click the *Reset* pick list button and choose the *Reset Only Quick Access Toolbar* item on the list. The system displays the *Reset Customizations* dialog shown in Figure 1 - 48. Click the *Yes* button to reset the *Quick Access Toolbar* to its default settings.

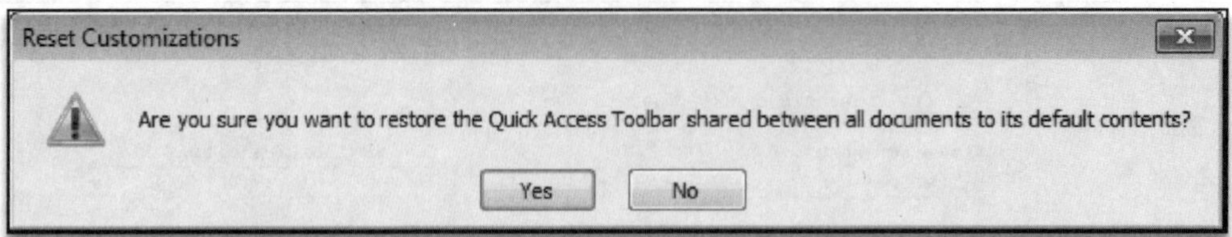

Figure 1 - 48: Confirmation dialog to restore the Quick Access Toolbar

To reset both the *Quick Access Toolbar* and the ribbon, click the *Reset* pick list button and choose the *Reset All Customizations* item on the list. The system displays the confirmation dialog shown in Figure 1 - 49. Click the *Yes* button to confirm the reset action.

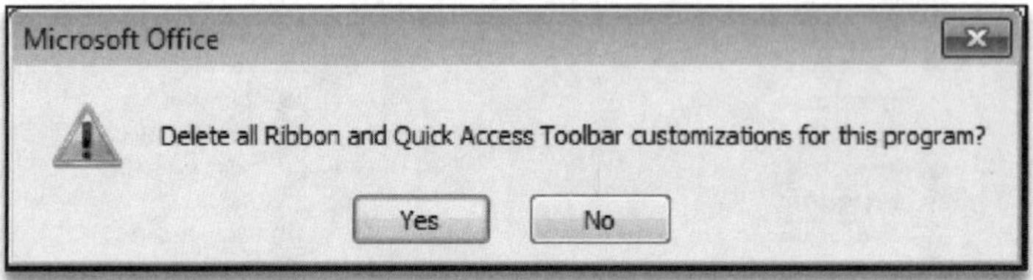

Figure 1 - 49: Confirmation dialog to reset the ribbon and Quick Access Toolbar

Warning: Notice in the dialog shown in the figure above that the system is about to reset all of the customizations to **both** the ribbon **and** the *Quick Access Toolbar*. If you do not want to reset customizations to the ribbon and the *Quick Access Toolbar*, then **do not** select the *Reset All Customizations* option.

Hands On Exercise

Exercise 1-4

Customize the Quick Access Toolbar.

1. At the right end of the *Quick Access Toolbar*, click the *Customize Quick Access Toolbar* pick list button and select the *Show Below the Ribbon* item on the list.
2. Click the *Customize Quick Access Toolbar* pick list button again and select the *More Commands* item on the list.
3. In the *Quick Access Toolbar* section of the *Project Options* dialog, click the *Choose commands from* pick list and select the *All Commands* item on the list.

4. Add the following buttons to your *Quick Access Toolbar* and then move them into the order shown below:

   - New
   - Open
   - Save (already on the Quick Access Toolbar)
   - Close
   - <Separator>
   - Page Setup
   - Print Preview
   - Print
   - <Separator>
   - Undo (already on the Quick Access Toolbar)
   - Redo (already on the Quick Access Toolbar)
   - <Separator>
   - Assign Resources
   - Zoom In
   - Zoom Out
   - Scroll to Task

5. Click the *OK* button to close the *Project Options* dialog, and then examine the new buttons on your *Quick Access Toolbar*.

Importing/Exporting a Custom Ribbon

Microsoft Project 2010 allows you to export the *ribbon* and *Quick Access Toolbar* and customization settings to a file. You can then give the file to other users who can import the customization settings into their own Microsoft Project 2010 application. To export these settings to a file, click the *Import/Export* pick list button and select the *Export All Customizations* item on the pick list. The system displays the *File Save* dialog shown in Figure 1 - 50. In the *File Save* dialog, enter a name for the customization file, select a destination for the file, and then click the *Save* button.

Notice in the following figure that ***.exportedUI** is the file extension for the exported customization file.

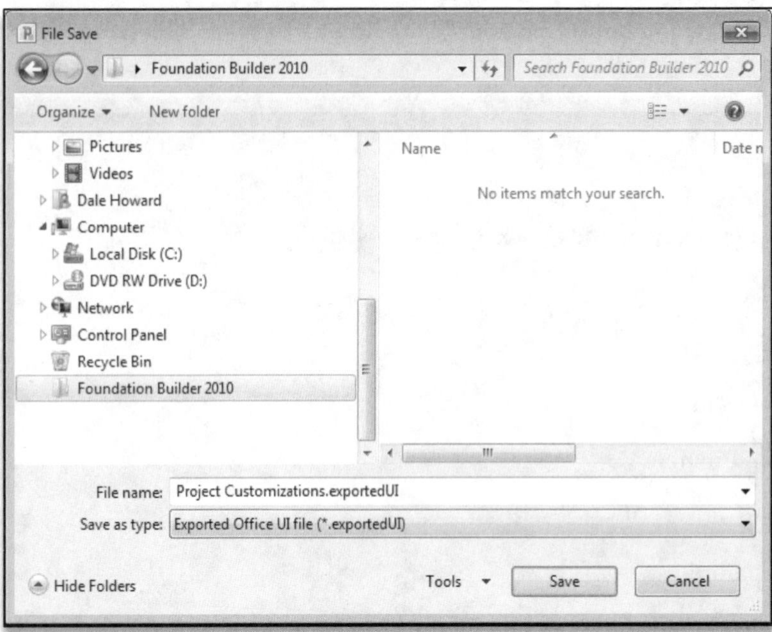

Figure 1 - 50: File Save dialog

To import a customized ribbon, click the *Import/Export* pick list button and select the *Import Customization File* item on the pick list. The system displays the *File Open* dialog shown in Figure 1 - 51. In the *File Open* dialog, navigate to the location of the customization file and select it, and then click the *Open* button.

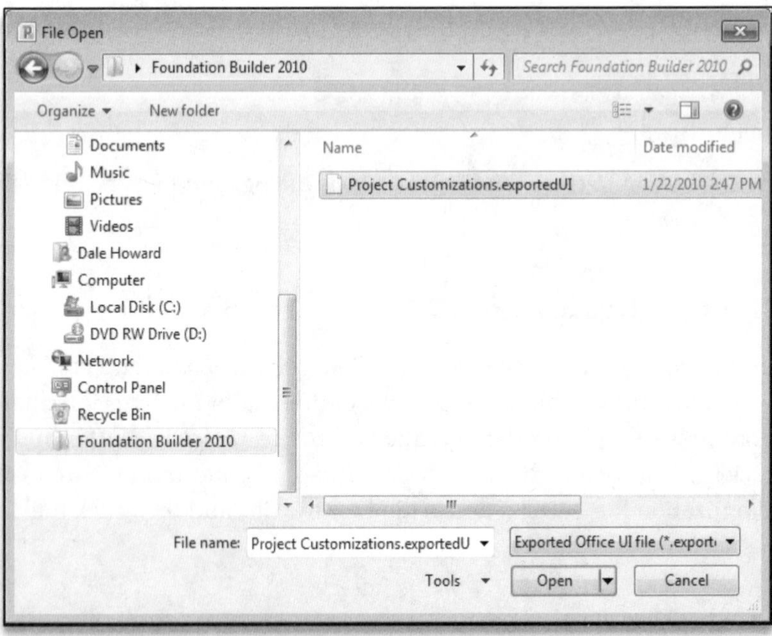

Figure 1 - 51: File Open dialog

The system displays the confirmation dialog shown in Figure 1 - 52. In the confirmation dialog, click the *Yes* button to import the customized *ribbon* and *Quick Access Toolbar* settings, and replace your current *ribbon* and *Quick Access Toolbar.* Click the *OK* button to close the *Project Options* dialog and view your new customized *ribbon* and *Quick Access Toolbar*.

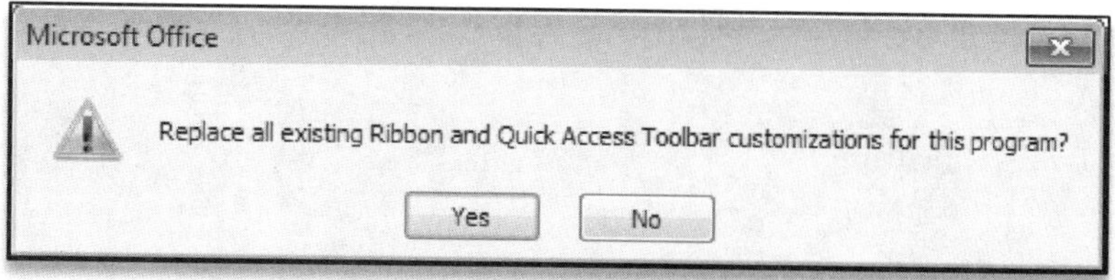

Figure 1 - 52: Warning dialog when importing a customized ribbon

Hands On Exercise

Exercise 1-5

Export the ribbon and *Quick Access Toolbar* customization settings to a file.

1. Right-click anywhere on the ribbon and select the *Customize the Ribbon* item on the shortcut menu.
2. Click the *Import/Export* pick list button and select the *Export all customizations* item on the list.
3. In the *File Save* dialog, leave the default name **Project Customizations.exportedUI** in the *File Name* field, and then click the *Save* button.
4. Click the *Reset* pick list button and select the *Reset All Customizations* item on the list.
5. When prompted in the confirmation dialog, click the *Yes* button to delete all customizations to the ribbon and the *Quick Access Toolbar.*

Notice how the system removed all of your custom settings to the ribbon and the *Quick Access Toolbar.*

6. Click the *Import/Export* pick list button again and select the *Import customization file* item on the list.
7. In the *File Open* dialog, select the **Project Customizations.exportedUI** file, and then click the *Open* button.
8. When prompted in the confirmation dialog, click the *Yes* button to replace all current customization to the ribbon and the *Quick Access Toolbar.*
9. Click the *OK* button to close the *Project Options* dialog.

Notice how the system imported all of your previous custom settings.

Module 02

What's New – Views, Tables, Filters, and Groups

Learning Objectives

After completing this module, you will be able to:

- Understand the new features in the Microsoft Project Data Model
- Use new views in Microsoft Project 2010
- Understand changes to default tables in Microsoft Project 2010
- Apply views and tables
- Work with new filters in Microsoft Project 2010
- Apply standard filters and highlight filters
- Understand the new groups in Microsoft Project 2010
- Apply groups

Inside Module 02

Reviewing the Microsoft Project Data Model **47**
Understanding New Views **47**
Applying a View 49
Understanding Changes to the Default Tables **50**
Applying a Table 51
Understanding New Filters **52**
Applying a Standard Filter 52
Applying a Highlight Filter 53
Understanding New Groups **55**
Applying a Group 56

Reviewing the Microsoft Project Data Model

The Microsoft Project Data Model, shown in Figure 2 - 1, remains unchanged in Microsoft Project 2010. Keep in mind that in the Microsoft Project Data Model, the software maintains and recognizes two separate and distinct types of data: Task data and Resource data. Each type of data has its own unique set of views, tables, filters, and groups.

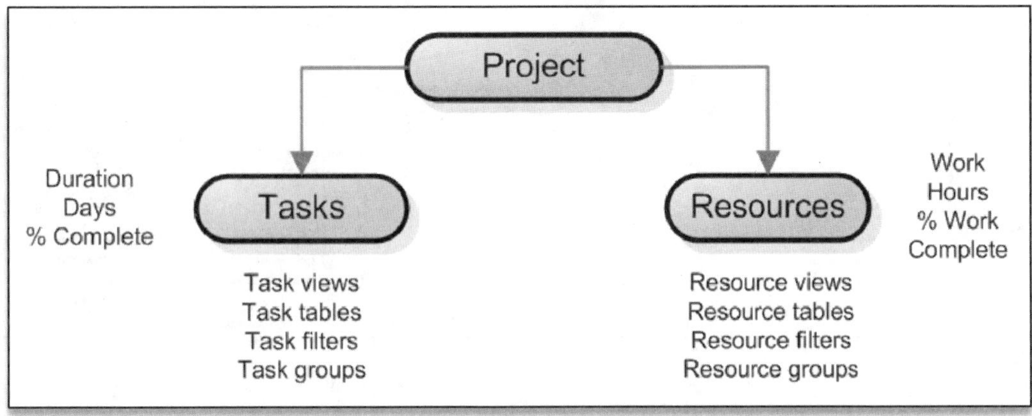

Figure 2 - 1: Simplified Microsoft Project Data Model for Microsoft Project 2010

Microsoft Project 2010 includes a number of new views, tables, filters, and groups that work with other new features in the tool. I document each of these new views, tables, filters, and groups in the remainder of this module.

Understanding New Views

Microsoft Project 2010 includes three new views, along with a new way to apply views. These three new views include the following:

- Gantt with Timeline
- Timeline
- Team Planner

The *Gantt with Timeline* view is the new default view Microsoft Project 2010 displays when you launch the software application. The *Gantt with Timeline* view is a Combination View that consists of two separate views, each displayed in its own pane. The *Gantt with Timeline* view includes the *Timeline* view in the top pane and the *Gantt Chart* view in the bottom pane. Figure 2 - 2 shows the *Gantt with Timeline* view. To apply the *Gantt with Timeline* view, if not already displayed in your Microsoft Project 2010 application, use one of the following methods:

- Click the *Task* tab (or the *Resource* tab or the *View* tab), click the *Gantt Chart* pick list button, and then select the *More Views* item on the pick list. In the *More Views* dialog, select the *Gantt with Timeline* view and click the *Apply* button.
- Click the *View* tab, click the *Gantt Chart* button, and then select the *Timeline* checkbox in the *Split View* section of the Ribbon.

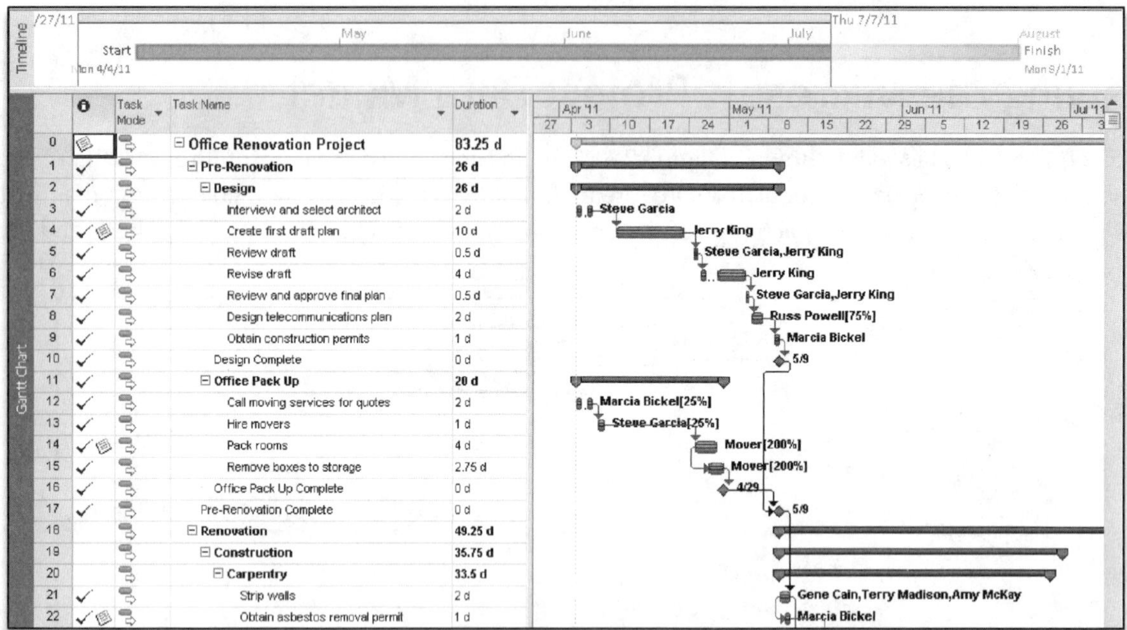

Figure 2 - 2: Gantt with Timeline view

Warning: If you apply any other view after applying the *Gantt with Timeline* view, Microsoft Project 2010 continues to display the *Timeline* view in the top pane. To close the *Timeline* pane, double-click the bottom edge of the pane, or click the *View* tab and deselect the *Timeline* checkbox.

Tip: By default, the *Gantt with Timeline* view does not appear on the view menu. You can change this setting by right-clicking on the *View Bar* on the left edge of the view and then selecting *More Views* from the shortcut menu. Select the *Gant with Timeline* view in the *More Views* dialog and click the *Edit* button. The systems opens the *View Definition* dialog where you can select the *Show on Menu* checkbox. After making this selection, you can select the *Gantt with Timeline* view from the *View* menu that appears when you right-click on the collapsed *View Bar* or click on the *Gantt Chart* button on the *Task* ribbon. You can also select it directly from the expanded *View Bar.*

The *Timeline* view is the second new view included in Microsoft Project 2010. Microsoft designed this view for use in combination with a task view, such as the *Gantt Chart* view, or with a resource view that also displays task or assignment information, such as the *Resource Usage* view. Applied alone, the *Timeline* view makes little sense unless you have already defined the items that appear on it. You need a data grid element to determine which items in the schedule appear on the view. I discuss in detail how to use and customize the *Timeline* view in Module 07, What's New - Reporting.

The third new view in Microsoft Project 2010 is the *Team Planner* view, shown in Figure 2 - 3. To display the *Team Planner* view, click the *Resource* tab and then click the *Team Planner* button. The *Team Planner* view is a new way for you to assign resources to tasks in your projects. This new view is a very special type of resource view that shows the resources in your project team, along with the assigned and unassigned tasks in the project. Notice these details about the *Team Planner* view example shown in Figure 2 - 3:

- I previously assigned the Design task to Calvin Baker.
- I have not assigned the Build task to any team member.
- The Test and Implement tasks are Unscheduled Tasks
- I have not assigned any tasks to David Dyer, Karly Brack, or Mickey Cobb.

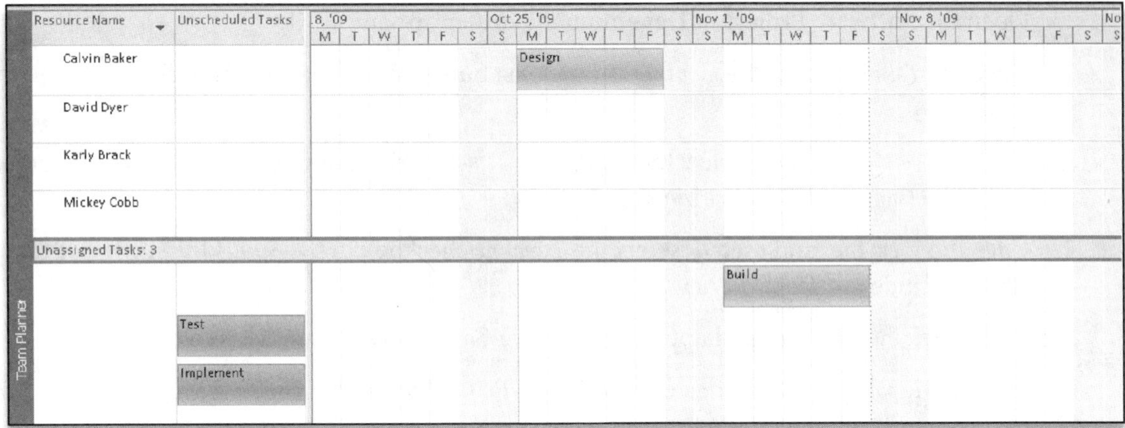

Figure 2 - 3: Team Planner view

I discuss in detail how to use and customize the *Team Planner* view in Module 05, What's New – Resource and Assignment Planning.

Applying a View

In addition to the three new views, Microsoft Project 2010 uses a new method to apply views. You can use any of the following methods to apply a view:

- Select the *Task* tab on the ribbon and click the *Gantt Chart* pick list button, and then either select the view directly from the list if available, or select the *More Views* item on the pick list. In the *More Views* dialog, select a view and click the *Apply* button.
- Click the *Resource* tab, click the *Team Planner* pick list button, and then either select the view directly from the list if available, or select the *More Views* item on the pick list. In the *More Views* dialog, select a view and click the *Apply* button
- Click the *View* tab and then click one of the buttons in the *Task Views* section or *Resource Views* section of the *View* ribbon.
- Right-click on the *View Bar* and either select the view directly from the list if available, or select the *More Views* item on the pick list. In the *More Views* dialog, select a view and click the *Apply* button. The *View Bar* is the gray bar that displays the name of the view on the left side of the screen. For example, you see that the *View Bar* displays the name *Gantt Chart* in Figure 2 - 2, and shows the name *Team Planner* in Figure 2 - 3.

Hands On Exercise

Exercise 2- 1

Explore the new views in Microsoft Project 2010.

1. Open the **Software Project in Development 2010.mpp** sample file.
2. Click the *Task* tab, click the *Gantt Chart* pick list button, and then select the *More Views* item on the pick list.
3. In the *More Views* dialog, select the *Gantt with Timeline* view, and then click the *Apply* button to apply the *Gantt with Timeline* view.
4. Click the *View* tab, and then **deselect** the *Timeline* checkbox in the *Split View* section of the *View* ribbon to hide the *Timeline* view.
5. Right-click the *View Bar* and apply the *Tracking Gantt* view.
6. Click the *Resource* tab and then click the *Team Planner* button in the *View* section.
7. Study the task assignments for each resource, including unscheduled tasks, and study the tasks shown in the *Unassigned Tasks* section as well.
8. Save but do not close the **Software Project in Development 2010.mpp** sample file.

Understanding Changes to the Default Tables

Microsoft Project 2010 does not include any new tables, but several of the default task tables now include the *Task Mode* column, and you apply tables using a new method. The *Task Mode* column allows you to specify whether tasks are *Auto Scheduled* or *Manually Scheduled*. For *Auto Scheduled* tasks, the software calculates the start and finish dates automatically. For *Manually Scheduled* tasks, the software does not specify a default duration value, and does not calculate the start and finish dates. This leaves *Manually Scheduled* tasks as unscheduled.

The default task tables that now include the *Task Mode* column are the *Entry, Rollup, Schedule,* and *Summary* tables. Figure 2 - 4 shows the *Entry* table applied in the *Gantt Chart* view. Notice that I set the *Task Mode* value to *Auto Scheduled* for the first two tasks and to *Manually Scheduled* for the last two tasks. Notice how Microsoft Project 2010 displays the Gantt bars for these tasks in the *Gantt Chart*, as solid bars for *Auto Scheduled* tasks, and as hollow bars for *Manually Scheduled* tasks.

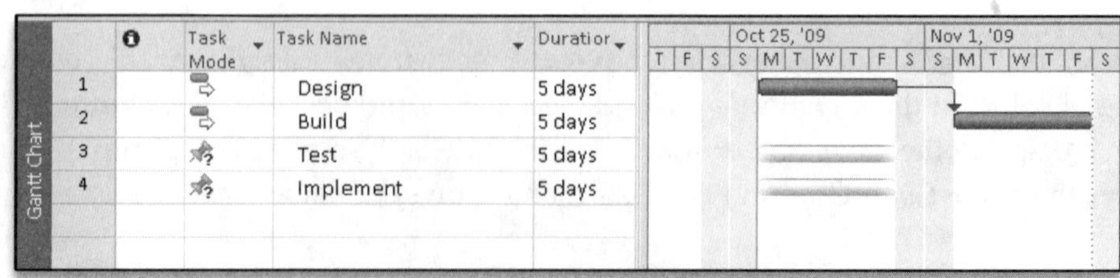

Figure 2 - 4: Entry table shows the Task Mode column

In addition to the tables that now contain the *Task Mode* column, Microsoft also changed one of the default columns displayed in the *Baseline* table. In all previous versions of the software, the *Baseline* table includes the *Baseline Duration* column to the right of the *Task Name* column. In Microsoft Project 2010, the *Baseline* table now includes the *Baseline Estimated Duration* column in place of the *Baseline Duration* column. Do not be confused by the column header of the *Baseline Estimated Duration* column, however, since Microsoft added a *Title* to the column so that *Baseline Duration* appears in the column header instead of *Baseline Estimated Duration.*

Applying a Table

In addition to the changes in several default tables, Microsoft Project 2010 uses a new method to apply a table. To apply any table, use one of the following methods:

- Right-click on the *Select All* button (upper left corner of the *Task Sheet* or *Resource Sheet*) and then choose one of the commonly used tables shown on the shortcut menu.
- Right-click on the *Select All* button and then choose the *More Tables* item on the shortcut menu. In the *More Tables* dialog, select a table and then click the *Apply* button.
- Click the *View* tab and then click the *Table* pick list in the *Data* section of the *View* ribbon. On the *Table* pick list, choose one of the commonly used tables on the list, or select the *More Tables* item on the list.

Hands On Exercise

Exercise 2- 2

Study changes to the default tables in Microsoft Project 2010.

1. Click the *View* tab and click the *Gantt Chart* button in the *Task Views* section.
2. Examine the *Task Mode* column in the current table (the *Entry* table).
3. Click the *Tables* pick list button in the *Data* section and then select the *More Tables* option.
4. In the *More Tables* dialog, select the *Schedule* table and then click the *Apply* button.
5. Notice the *Task Mode* column shown in the *Schedule* table.
6. Right-click on the *Select All* button and select the *Summary* table on the shortcut menu.
7. Notice the *Task Mode* column shown in the *Summary* table.
8. Right-click on the *Select All* button and select the *Entry* table on the shortcut menu.
9. Save and close the **Software Project in Development 2010.mpp** sample file.

Understanding New Filters

Microsoft Project 2010 includes four new task filters, along with a new way to apply standard filters and highlight filters. The four new filters include the following:

- Active Tasks
- Late Tasks
- Manually Scheduled Tasks
- Tasks Without Dates

You use the *Active Tasks* filter in conjunction with the new *Inactivate Task* feature that allows you to cancel tasks no longer needed in the project. The *Active Tasks* filter, therefore, displays all tasks with a *Yes* value in the *Active* field, which allows you to filter out cancelled (*Inactive*) tasks.

The *Inactivate* feature is available **only** in the Professional version of Microsoft Project 2010.

You use the *Late Tasks* filter to identify any task where progress is behind schedule. The *Late Tasks* filter displays only those tasks with a *Late* value in the *Status* field. By default, the software calculates a *Late* value in the *Status* field when the time-phased cumulative percent complete (represented by the black progress line in a Gantt bar) does not reach the status date you specify for the project.

You use the *Manually Scheduled Tasks* filter to locate tasks with this setting in your project. The *Manually Scheduled* filter displays only those tasks with a *Manually Scheduled* value in the *Task Mode* field.

You use the *Tasks Without Dates* filter to locate tasks that do not have a start date or finish date. By default, *Manually Scheduled* tasks do not have a system-calculated start date or finish date, but may contain these date and duration values that you enter manually. At some point during the life of your project, however, you must convert *Manually Scheduled* tasks to *Auto Scheduled* in order for the system to calculate these dates based on dependency links or resource availability. You use the *Tasks Without Dates* filter to locate *Manually Scheduled* tasks that do not yet have a system-calculated start date or finish date.

Note that when you type specific dates into the *Start* and *Finish* fields in a task row when the task is set to *Manually Scheduled,* the filter treats these as *Tasks Without Dates.*

Applying a Standard Filter

In addition to the four new filters, Microsoft Project 2010 introduces a new method for applying filters. To apply any filter as a standard filter, click the *View* tab. In the *Data* section of the *View* ribbon, click the *Filter* pick list and select a standard filter, as shown in Figure 2 - 5.

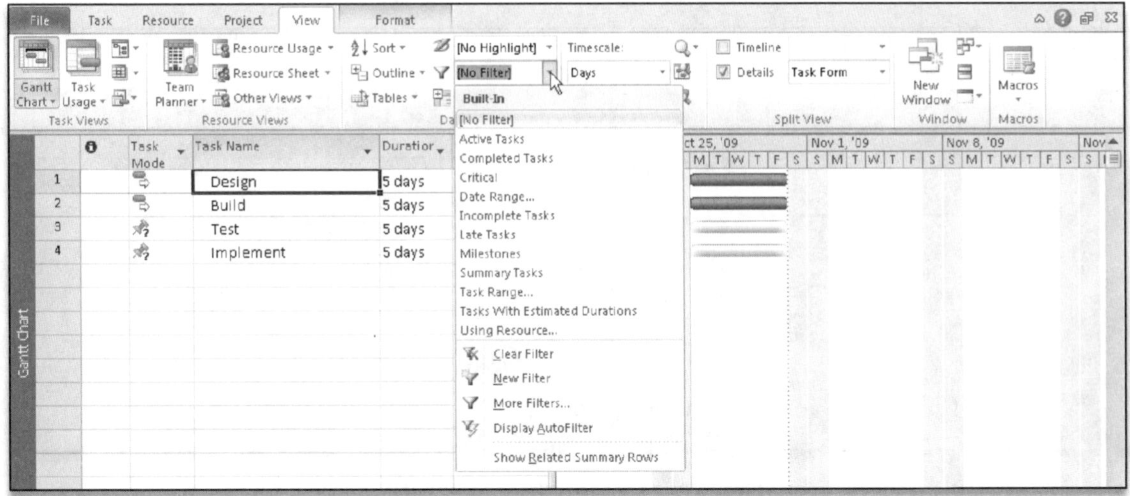

Figure 2 - 5: Apply a Standard filter

Notice in Figure 2 - 5 that the *Filter* pick list allows you to choose from a list of most commonly used filters, and allows you other filtering options such as *Clear Filter* to remove filtering criteria, *New Filter* to create a new filter from scratch, *More Filters* to display the *More Filters* dialog and *Display AutoFilter* to turn on the *AutoFilter* feature in the data grid. On the *Filter* pick list, click the name of the filter you want to apply as a standard filter. When you apply a standard filter, the software displays only those tasks that meet your filtering criteria.

To remove a filter and reapply the *All Tasks* or *All Resources* filter, click the *Filter* pick list again and choose either the *[No Filter]* item or the *Clear Filter* item on the pick list.

Keyboard Shortcut: Press the **F3** function key on your keyboard to apply the *All Tasks* filter in any task View or the *All Resources* filter in any resource View.

Applying a Highlight Filter

In addition to its new approach to standard filters, Microsoft Project 2010 uses a new method for applying highlight filters. To apply any filter as a highlight filter, click the *View* tab. In the *Data* section of the *View* ribbon, click the *Highlight* pick list and select a highlight filter, as shown in Figure 2 - 6.

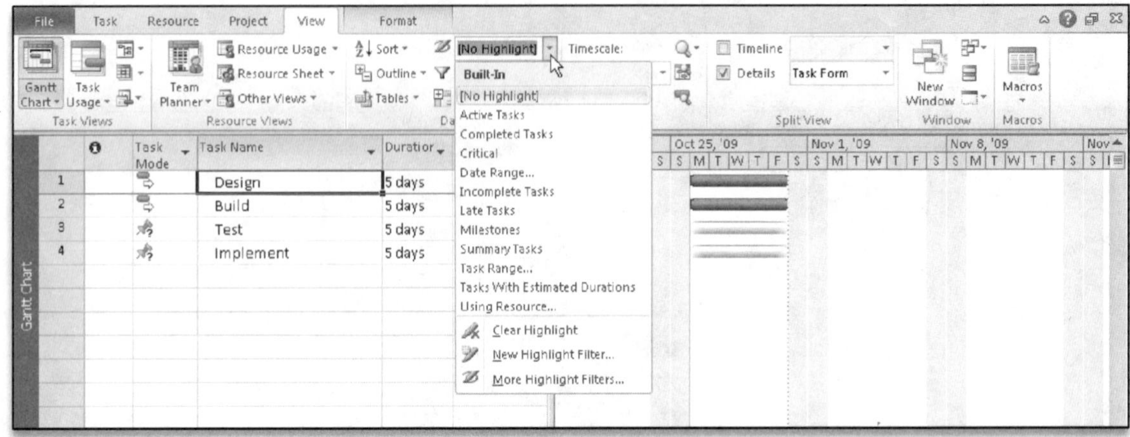

Figure 2 - 6: Apply a Highlight filter

Notice in Figure 2 - 6 that the *Highlight* pick list allows you to choose from a list of most commonly used filters, and allows you other filtering options such as *Clear Highlight*, *New Highlight Filter* to create a new highlight filter, and *More Highlight Filters* that opens the *More Highlight Filters* dialog. On the *Highlight* pick list, click the name of the filter you want to apply as a highlight filter. When you apply a highlight filter, the software displays all tasks and highlights the tasks that meet your filtering criteria using yellow cell background formatting.

The list of Filters shown on the *Highlight* pick list and the *Filter* pick list are identical. When you create a new filter and select the option to show it on the menu, Microsoft Project 2010 displays the new filter on **both** the *Highlight* pick list **and** the *Filter* pick list automatically.

To remove a highlight filter and reapply the *All Tasks* or *All Resources* filter, click the *Highlight* pick list again and choose either the *[No Highlight]* item or the *Clear Highlight* item on the pick list.

You can also use the **F3** keyboard shortcut to to remove the current Highlight Filter and reapply the *All Tasks* or *All Resources* filter.

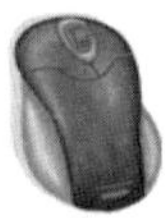

Hands On Exercise

Exercise 2-3

Experiment with the new filters and new filtering techniques in Microsoft Project 2010.

1. Open the **CRM Software Development 2010.mpp** sample file.
2. Click the *View* tab, click the *Filter* pick list in the *Data* section, and click the *Active Tasks* filter.

Notice that the *Active Tasks* filter **excludes** task ID #21, *Re-Test Modified Code,* because this task is an Inactive (cancelled) task.

3. Click the *Filter* pick list and select the *Late Tasks* filter.

Notice that the *Late Tasks* filter displays only task IDs #13 and #14, *Develop Code* and *Developer Testing*. The software considers both tasks late because their progress line falls short of the *Status Date* line, indicated by the red-dashed vertical line in the Gantt Chart.

4. Click the *Highlight* pick list and click the *More Highlight Filters* item on the list.
5. In the *More Filters* dialog, select the *Manually Scheduled Tasks* filter and then click the *Highlight* button.

Notice that when you apply the *Manually Scheduled Tasks* filter as a highlight filter, the software highlights all of the tasks in the Testing phase with the yellow cell background color.

6. Click the *Highlight* pick list and click the *More Highlight Filters* item on the list.
7. In the *More Filters* dialog, select the *Tasks Without Dates* filter and then click the *Highlight* button.

Notice that the software highlights only task ID #20, *Modify Code.*

8. Pull your split bar to the right of the *Finish* column to show that the *Modify Code* task has no *Start* date or *Finish* date.
9. Press the **F3** function key to reapply the *All Tasks* filter.

Understanding New Groups

Microsoft Project 2010 includes four new groups for task data, along with a new method for applying a group. These four new groups include:

- Active v. Inactive
- Auto Scheduled v. Manually Scheduled
- Resource
- Status

The *Active v. Inactive* group organizes tasks into two groups according to each task's value in the *Active* field. Remember that you can set an unneeded task as inactive in your project by selecting a *No* value in the *Active* field.

The *Auto Scheduled v. Manually Scheduled* group organizes tasks into two groups according to each task's value in the *Task Mode* field. Remember that the value you specify in the *Task Mode* field for a task determines whether the software calculates the *Start* date and *Finish* date for the task automatically, or whether you have to enter a *Start* date and *Finish* date manually.

The *Resource* group organizes tasks into groups according to the names of the resource(s) assigned to each task., as listed in the *Resource Names* field. Figure 2 - 7 shows the *Resource* group applied to the *Task Sheet* view in a project.

		Task Mode	Task Name	Duration	Start	Finish	Predecessors	Resource Names	Add New Column
			⊞ **Resource Names: No Value**	**0d**	**Fri 4/29/11**	**Mon 8/1/11**			
			⊟ **Resource Names: Amy McKay,Gene Cain,Terry Madison**	**5d**	**Wed 5/18/1**	**Tue 5/24/11**		**Amy McKay,Gene**	
24			Remove asbestos in ceilings	5 d	Wed 5/18/11	Tue 5/24/11	23,22	Amy McKay,Gene Ca	
			⊟ **Resource Names: Bob Siclari**	**5d**	**Tue 6/7/11**	**Wed 6/15/1**		**Bob Siclari**	
48			Install pipes	5 d	Tue 6/7/11	Mon 6/13/11	40SS+2 d	Bob Siclari	
49			Install sink and faucets	1 d	Tue 6/14/11	Tue 6/14/11	48	Bob Siclari	
50			Connect appliances	0.25 d	Wed 6/15/11	Wed 6/15/11	49	Bob Siclari	
			⊟ **Resource Names: Cher Zall**	**1d**	**Fri 7/1/11**	**Wed 7/13/1**		**Cher Zall**	
64			Order new furniture	1 d	Fri 7/1/11	Tue 7/5/11	63	Cher Zall[50%]	
65			Order Blinds	1 d	Tue 7/5/11	Tue 7/5/11	64SS	Cher Zall[50%]	
66			Install blinds	1 d	Wed 7/13/11	Wed 7/13/11	65FS+5 d	Cher Zall	
			⊟ **Resource Names: Gene Cain**	**2d**	**Tue 6/14/11**	**Mon 6/20/1**		**Gene Cain**	
29			Sand	0.5 d	Tue 6/14/11	Tue 6/14/11	28	Gene Cain	
30			Paint (1st coat)	2 d	Wed 6/15/11	Thu 6/16/11	29	Gene Cain	
31			Paint (2nd coat)	2 d	Fri 6/17/11	Mon 6/20/11	30	Gene Cain	
			⊟ **Resource Names: Gene Cain,Amy McKay**	**2d**	**Wed 6/1/11**	**Fri 6/24/11**		**Gene Cain,Amy Mc**	
26			Frame new walls	2 d	Wed 6/1/11	Thu 6/2/11	25	Gene Cain,Amy McK	
28			Plaster	1 d	Mon 6/13/11	Tue 6/14/11	27	Gene Cain,Amy McK	
35			Lay new flooring	1 d	Wed 6/22/11	Thu 6/23/11	34	Gene Cain,Amy McK	
36			Install appliances	1 d	Thu 6/23/11	Fri 6/24/11	35	Gene Cain,Amy McK	
			⊟ **Resource Names: Gene Cain,Terry Madison,Amy McKay**	**2.5d**	**Tue 5/10/11**	**Mon 6/13/1**		**Gene Cain,Terry M**	
21	✓		Strip walls	2 d	Tue 5/10/11	Wed 5/11/11	17	Gene Cain,Terry Mac	
27			Put up dry wall	2.5 d	Fri 6/3/11	Mon 6/13/11	26	Gene Cain,Terry Mac	
			⊟ **Resource Names: Jerry King**	**10d**	**Mon 4/11/1**	**Tue 5/3/11**		**Jerry King**	
4	✓		Create first draft plan	10 d	Mon 4/11/11	Fri 4/22/11	3	Jerry King	
6	✓		Revise draft	4 d	Tue 4/26/11	Tue 5/3/11	5	Jerry King	

Figure 2 - 7: Resource group applied to the Task Sheet view

The *Status* group organizes tasks into four groups, according to the value in the *Status* field for each task. Microsoft Project 2010 automatically calculates the values in the *Status* field and selects one of four values for each task. The four possible values in the *Status* field include *Future Task, On Schedule, Late,* and *Complete.*

When you apply the *Status* group to a project, this group includes the summary tasks automatically, and maintains the task hierarchy as well. In addition, Microsoft Project 2010 displays the outline number value for each summary task and formats each summary task with a light blue cell background formatting.

Applying a Group

In addition to providing four new groups, Microsoft Project 2010 provides a new method for applying groups. To apply a group to your project data, click the *View* tab. In the *Data* section of the *View* ribbon, click the *Group By* pick list and select a group as shown in Figure 2 - 8.

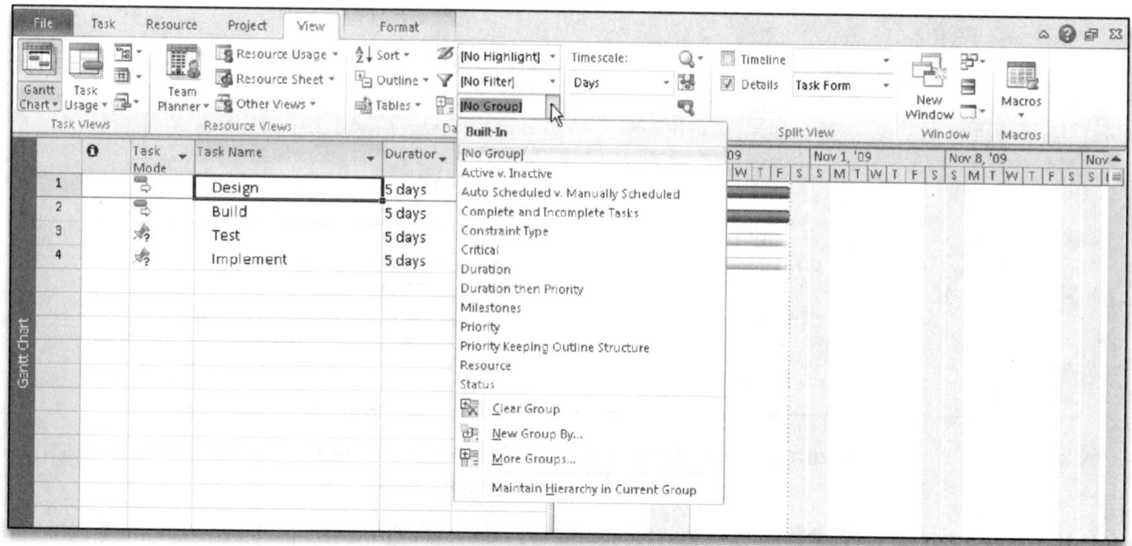

Figure 2 - 8: Apply a group

Another new feature on the *Group By* pick list is the *Maintain Hierarchy in Current Group* item at the bottom of the list. When you apply a group in any task view, most of the default groups do not display the *Work Breakdown Structure* (WBS) of summary tasks for the grouped tasks. This can create a confusing situation when you use same-named tasks in different summary task sections of your project. For example, Figure 2 - 9 shows a list of tasks in a project that includes summary tasks representing the phase and deliverable sections of the project. Notice that the Deliverable 1 and Deliverable 2 summary sections each contain four same-named tasks (Design, Build, Test, and Implement).

		Task	Task Name	Duration	Start	Finish	Predecessors
1			**Phase I**	**29 d**	**11/6/09**	**12/16/09**	
2			**Deliverable 1**	**15 d**	**11/6/09**	**11/26/09**	
3			Design	3 d	11/6/09	11/10/09	
4			Build	5 d	11/11/09	11/17/09	3
5			Test	4 d	11/18/09	11/23/09	4
6			Implement	3 d	11/24/09	11/26/09	5
7			Deliverable 1 Complete	0 d	11/26/09	11/26/09	6
8			**Deliverable 2**	**14 d**	**11/27/09**	**12/16/09**	
9			Design	4 d	11/27/09	12/2/09	7
10			Build	4 d	12/3/09	12/8/09	9
11			Test	3 d	12/9/09	12/11/09	10
12			Implement	3 d	12/14/09	12/16/09	11
13			Deliverable 2 Complete	0 d	12/16/09	12/16/09	12
14			Phase I Complete	0 d	12/16/09	12/16/09	13

Figure 2 - 9: Task list includes same-named tasks

In Figure 2 - 10, I applied the *Auto Scheduled v. Manually Scheduled* group to the task list shown previously in Figure 2 - 9. Notice how each grouping includes only regular tasks and Milestone tasks, and do not include summary tasks at all. This means that I can see two tasks named Design in the *Auto Scheduled* group, but I cannot determine the WBS for either of these Design tasks.

	ℹ	Task	Task Name	Duration	Start	Finish	Predecessors
			⊟ Task Mode: Auto Scheduled	**5d**	**11/6/09**	**12/16/09**	
3			Design	3 d	11/6/09	11/10/09	
4			Build	5 d	11/11/09	11/17/09	3
7			Deliverable 1 Complete	0 d	11/26/09	11/26/09	6
9			Design	4 d	11/27/09	12/2/09	7
10			Build	4 d	12/3/09	12/8/09	9
13			Deliverable 2 Complete	0 d	12/16/09	12/16/09	12
14			Phase I Complete	0 d	12/16/09	12/16/09	13
			⊟ Task Mode: Manually Scheduled	**4d**	**11/18/09**	**12/16/09**	
5			Test	4 d	11/18/09	11/23/09	4
6			Implement	3 d	11/24/09	11/26/09	5
11			Test	3 d	12/9/09	12/11/09	10
12			Implement	3 d	12/14/09	12/16/09	11

Figure 2 - 10: Auto Scheduled v. Manually Scheduled group does not include summary tasks

To eliminate the confusion about the WBS for each Design task, I click the *Group By* pick list again and select the *Maintain Hierarchy in Current Group* item. Figure 2 - 11 shows the result. Notice in the figure that the groupings now include the Phase and Deliverable summary sections for each regular task and milestone task. Because of this, I can now determine the WBS for each Design task in the *Auto Scheduled* group.

	ℹ	Task	Task Name	Duration	Start	Finish	Predecessors
			⊟ Task Mode: Auto Scheduled	**5d**	**11/6/09**	**12/16/09**	
			⊟ 1 Phase I	**5d**	**11/6/09**	**12/16/09**	
14			Phase I Complete	0 d	12/16/09	12/16/09	13
			⊟ 1.1 Deliverable 1	**5d**	**11/6/09**	**11/26/09**	
3			Design	3 d	11/6/09	11/10/09	
4			Build	5 d	11/11/09	11/17/09	3
7			Deliverable 1 Complete	0 d	11/26/09	11/26/09	6
			⊟ 1.2 Deliverable 2	**4d**	**11/27/09**	**12/16/09**	
9			Design	4 d	11/27/09	12/2/09	7
10			Build	4 d	12/3/09	12/8/09	9
13			Deliverable 2 Complete	0 d	12/16/09	12/16/09	12
			⊟ Task Mode: Manually Scheduled	**4d**	**11/18/09**	**12/16/09**	
			⊟ 1 Phase I	**4d**	**11/18/09**	**12/16/09**	
			⊟ 1.1 Deliverable 1	**4d**	**11/18/09**	**11/26/09**	
5			Test	4 d	11/18/09	11/23/09	4
6			Implement	3 d	11/24/09	11/26/09	5
			⊟ 1.2 Deliverable 2	**3d**	**12/9/09**	**12/16/09**	
11			Test	3 d	12/9/09	12/11/09	10
12			Implement	3 d	12/14/09	12/16/09	11

Figure 2 - 11: Auto Scheduled v. Manually Scheduled group with "Maintain Hierarchy" applied

After you select the *Maintain Hierarchy in Current Group* item for any task group, the software continues to show the task hierarchy automatically each time you reapply that group in the current project. If you do not want to see the task hierachy, you must click the *Group By* pick list again and then click the *Maintain Hierarchy in Current Group* item again to deselect this option.

If you want to create your own custom groups, Microsoft Project 2010 offers you the option to include the hierarchy as a part of the group definition. To create a new custom group, click the *Group By* pick list and select the *New Group By* item on the list. The software displays the *Group Definition* dialog shown in Figure 2 - 12.

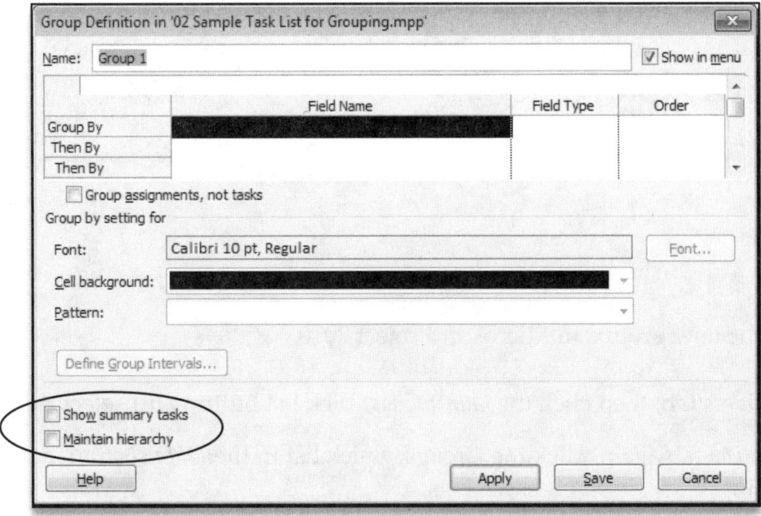

Figure 2 - 12: Group Definition dialog offers the Maintain Hierarchy option

In Figure 2 - 12, notice the *Maintain Hierarchy* option in the lower left of the *Group Definition* dialog. If you want to display the WBS for the tasks in a new task group, select the *Maintain Hierarchy* option when you create your custom group.

The *Maintain Hierachy* option is available only for task groups. You cannot display the hierarchy information for resource groups because resources do not have any Work Breakdown Structure information. This means that the software disables the the *Maintain Hierarchy in Current Group* item on the *Group By* pick list in any resource view, and disables the *Maintain Hierarchy in Current Group* option in the *Group Definition* dialog when creating a resource group.

When you have a group applied in any task or resource view, you can remove the group by clicking the *Group By* pick list and selecting either the *[No Group]* item or the *Clear Group* item on the pick list.

Keyboard Shortcut: Press **Shift + F3** on your keyboard to remove the current group and reapply the group called *No Group*.

Hands On Exercise

Exercise 2- 4

Experiment with the new groups in Microsoft Project 2010.

1. Click the *Tasks* tab, then click the *Gantt Chart* pick list button and select the *Task Sheet* view.
2. Click the *View* tab again, click the *Group By* pick list in the *Data* section, and select the *Active v. Inactive* group.

Notice how the software groups the tasks in the project into the *Active* (Active: Yes) and *Inactive* (Active: No) groups.

3. Click the *Group By* pick list in the *Data* section, and select the *Auto Scheduled v. Manually Scheduled* group.

Notice how the software groups the tasks in the project into the *Auto Scheduled* and *Manually Scheduled* groups, but does not display the task hierarchy of summary tasks to reveal the WBS of each task.

4. Click the *Group By* pick list again and select the *Maintain Hierarchy in Current Group* item at the bottom of the list.
5. Click the *Group By* pick list in the *Data* section, and select the *Resource* group.

Notice how the software groups the tasks in the project into groups corresponding with the resource(s) assigned to each task, but does not display the task hierarchy of summary tasks to reveal the WBS of each task.

6. Click the *Group By* pick list again and select the *Maintain Hierarchy in Current Group* item at the bottom of the list.
7. Click the *Group By* pick list in the *Data* section, and select the *Status* group.

Notice how the software groups the tasks by their status and displays the task hierarchy of summary tasks to reveal the WBS of each task.

8. Click the *Group By* pick list and select the *[No Group]* item on the list.
9. Save and close the **CRM Software Development 2010.mpp** sample file.

Module 03

What's New – Project Planning

Learning Objectives

After completing this module, you will be able to:

- Create a new project from a SharePoint task list or an Office.com template
- Define a new project using the Six-Step Method
- Specify the Task Mode setting for new tasks
- Specify Options settings for a project
- Save your project using an alternate file type
- Save your project to a SharePoint workspace
- Share your project with others via e-mail

Inside Module 03

Creating a New Project from a Template **63**

Creating a New Project from a SharePoint Task List 63

Creating a New Project Using an Office.com Template 66

Defining a New Project **68**

Setting Project Options **69**

Setting the Task Mode Option 69

Setting Options in the Project Options Dialog 70

Setting General Options 71

Setting Display Options 72

Setting Schedule Options 74

Setting Proofing Options 79

Setting Save Options 81

Setting Language Options 82

Setting Advanced Options 83

Setting Add-Ins Options 86

Setting Trust Center Options 87

Saving a Project as an Alternate File Type **92**

Saving a Project File as a PDF or XPS Document 94
Understanding Reduced Functionality with Older Project File Formats 96
Opening a Project Created in an Older Version of Microsoft Project 98
Saving a Project to SharePoint 100
Sharing a Project via E-Mail 105

Creating a New Project from a Template

As I noted previously in Module 01, Microsoft Project 2010 offers you a number of ways to create a new project from the *New Templates* page in the *Backstage*, including each of the following:

- Click the *Blank Project* button to create a new blank project.
- Click the *Recent Templates* button to create a new project from a recent template.
- Click the *My Templates* button to create a new project from a custom project template you created.
- Click the *New from Existing Project* button to create a new project from an existing project.
- Click the *New from Excel Workbook* button to create a new project from an existing Microsoft Excel workbook file using the Import/Export Wizard.
- Click the *New from SharePoint Task List* button to create a new project from a Task list in an existing SharePoint site (available **only** in the Professional version of Microsoft Project 2010).
- Click one of the icons in the *Office.com Templates* section to search Office.com for customized project templates.

In the preceding list, only the last two items offer new functionality in Microsoft Project 2010, and I discuss each of these separately.

Creating a New Project from a SharePoint Task List

If your organization uses Microsoft SharePoint Foundation 2010 or Microsoft SharePoint Server (MSS) 2010, but does not use the enterprise tool Microsoft Project Server 2010, you can leverage the power of SharePoint by creating a new project in Microsoft Project 2010 from a list of tasks in a SharePoint site. This feature can be useful to your organization if you need to create a new project from a standard list of tasks defined by your organization. Before you can create a new project from a task list in SharePoint, your organization must meet the following requirements:

- You or your SharePoint administrator must create a SharePoint site for you and add you to the list of Users in the SharePoint site.
- Your SharePoint administrator must supply you with the URL of the site.
- You must create a new *Task list* containing the names of tasks for a standard project. Ideally, the *Task list* should include task dependencies, if possible.
- You must navigate to the SharePoint site and copy the URL to your Clipboard.

Warning: Your organization **must** use either Microsoft SharePoint Foundation 2010 or Microsoft SharePoint Server 2010 before you can create a new project from a Task List in SharePoint. You cannot use any previous version of Windows SharePoint Services for this functionality. Furthermore, your organization must create a new *Task List* item rather than a *List* item only for this purpose.

Figure 3 - 1 shows a Microsoft SharePoint Server 2010 site with a custom Task List named Project Tasks. Notice that the Project Tasks list includes four standard tasks including Design, Build, Test, and Implement, plus one Milestone task called Project Complete.

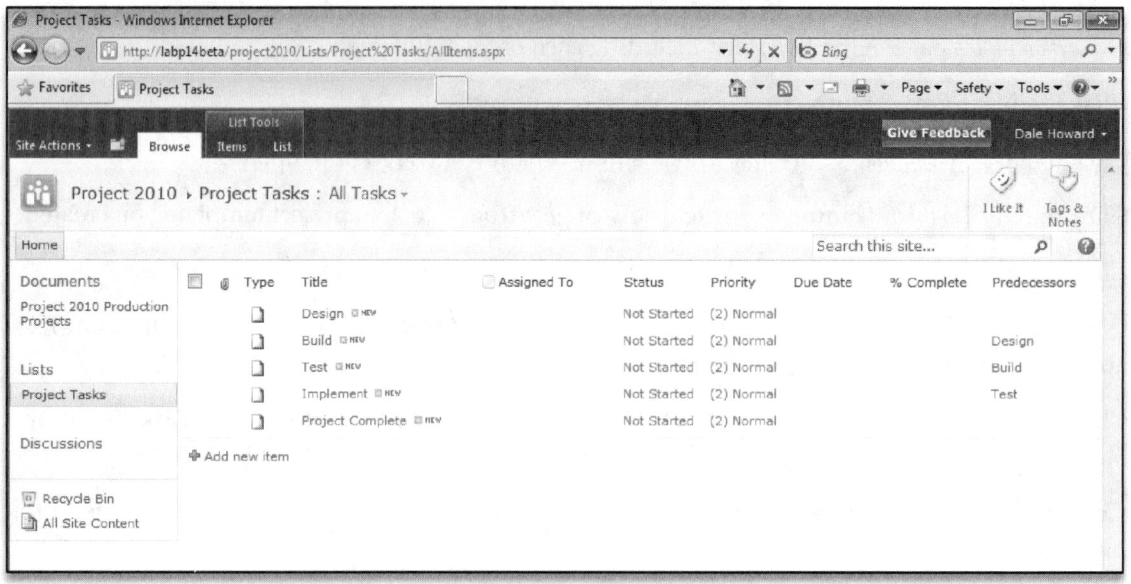

Figure 3 - 1: SharePoint site includes custom Task List

To create a new project from a list of Tasks in a SharePoint site, complete the following steps:

1. Click the *File* tab and then click the *New* tab in the *Backstage.*

2. On the *Available Templates* page in the *Backstage,* click the *New from SharePoint Task List* button. Microsoft Project 2010 displays the *Import SharePoint Tasks List* dialog shown in Figure 3 - 2.

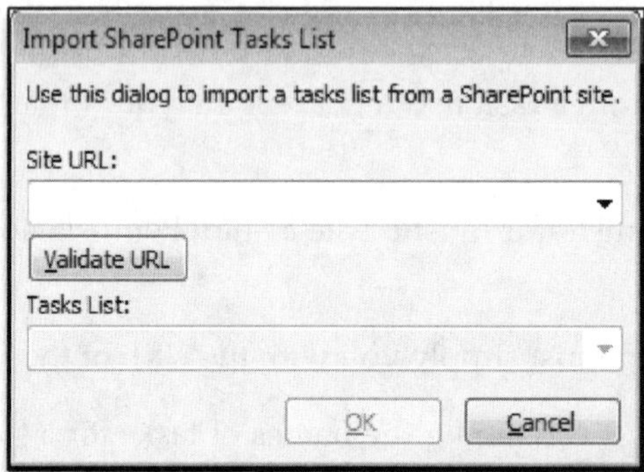

Figure 3 - 2: Import SharePoint Tasks List dialog

3. In the *Import SharePoint Tasks List* dialog, enter the URL of the SharePoint site in the *Site URL* field.

After you create at least one new project from a Task List in SharePoint, Microsoft Project 2010 populates the *Site URL* field automatically by adding the URL of the SharePoint site to the pick list. When you create new projects from multiple SharePoint sites, the *Site URL* field displays a pick list containing the entire URL history.

4. Click the *Validate URL* button in the *Import SharePoint Tasks List* dialog. If your URL is valid, the system activates the *Tasks List* pick list with a list of Task List items, such as shown in Figure 3 - 3.

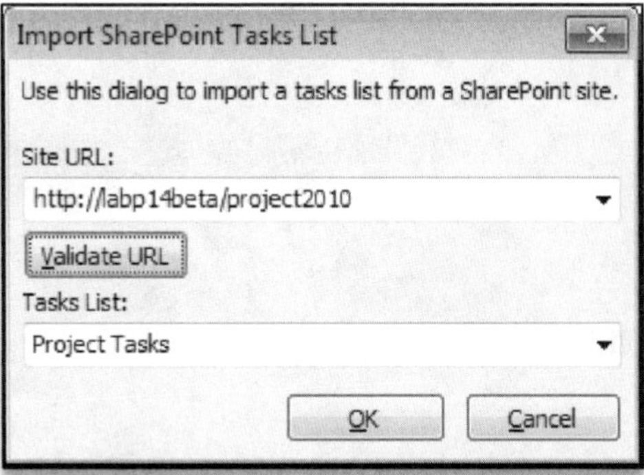

Figure 3 - 3: Tasks List populated with available Task List items

5. Click the *Tasks List* pick list and choose an available Task List item, if needed, and then click the *OK* button. As Microsoft Project 2010 collects the Task List information, the system displays the *SharePoint Synchronization* dialog shown in Figure 3 - 4.

Figure 3 - 4: SharePoint Synchronization dialog

After Microsoft Project 2010 completes the process of creating a new project from a Task list in SharePoint, you see the new project in the application, including the list of tasks defined in the SharePoint site. Figure 3 - 5 shows a new project created from the Task List shown previously in Figure 3 - 1.

Warning: When you create a new project from a Task List in SharePoint, the process creates a new project with Manually Scheduled tasks sorted in alphabetical order, even if you specified the Task List in order by Start date in the SharePoint site. After you create your project, you may want to convert the tasks to Auto Scheduled tasks and sort the tasks by Start date.

MsProjectExperts recommends that you prefix your task names with numbers to force the sort order of your tasks if you choose to use this feature in its first version.

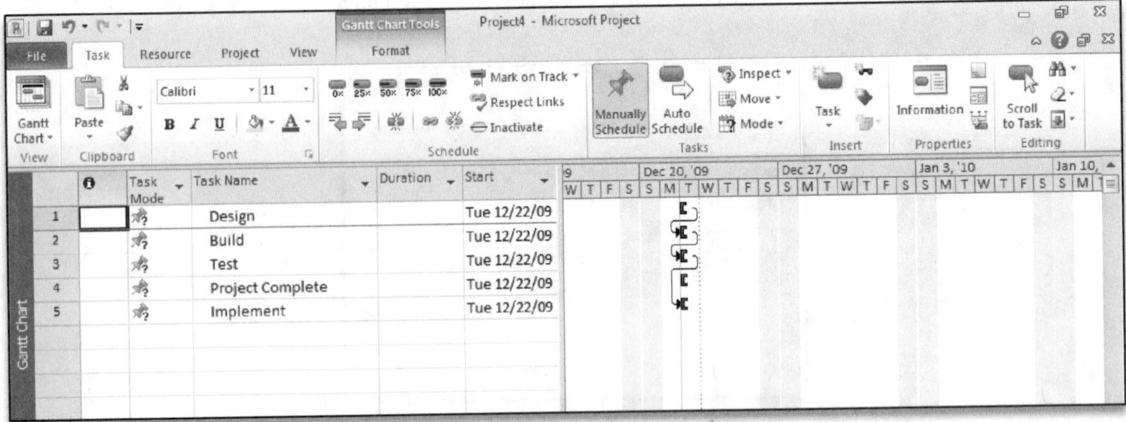

Figure 3 - 5: New project created from a Task List in SharePoint

Creating a New Project Using an Office.com Template

Unlike with previous versions of the software, Microsoft Project 2010 **does not** ship with default project templates. Instead, Microsoft offers a continuously-updated list of project templates through its Office.com web site. To create a new project from an Office.com template, complete the following steps:

1. Click the *File* tab and then click the *New* tab in the *Backstage*.

On the *Available Templates* page in the Backstage, the system displays the current list of template types and categories in the *Office.com Templates* section of the page. Microsoft updates this section continuously so that you always have the "latest and greatest" project templates available to you.

2. In the *Office.com Template* section of the *Available Templates* page, select the name of a template type or template category.

The system displays the current list of projects of that type, such as the *Schedules* type of templates I selected in Figure 3 - 6. Notice that the *Schedules* list currently includes four project templates as of this writing. I expect that more will be available by the time you read this. Notice also that the system shows a preview of the selected template on the right side of the page and that it was not created by Microsoft. Rather, it was contributed by P-Cubed, a Microsoft Partner.

The Changing Face of Help Content in Project 2010

As part of a larger initiative that blankets the entire Microsoft product stack, users of Office, Visio, and Project 2010 will see a steady evolution toward community-authored content when they access Help or other application content, such as templates. Microsoft's new model of enriching connected-Help sources with continuously evolving content from both Microsoft and non-Microsoft sources is a compelling reason to always favor using connected Help over the static help files that ship with the products.

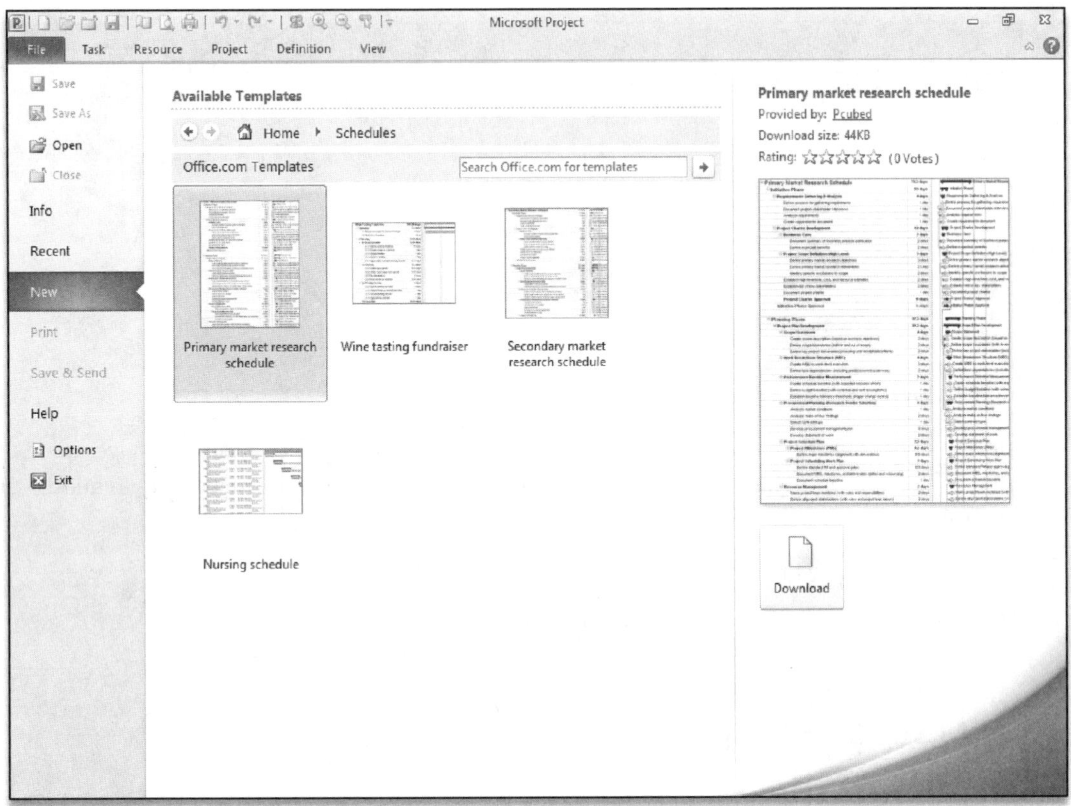

Figure 3 - 6: Office.com templates in the Schedules section

3. Click the *Download* button in the preview section on the right side of the *Available Templates* page.

Microsoft Project 2010 downloads the template from the Office.com web site and creates a new project from the template. In addition, the software saves the template in your *Templates* folder and makes it available for future use by clicking the *My Templates* button on the *Available Templates* page of the *Backstage*. When you click the *My Templates* button, the system displays the *New* dialog. This dialog contains the list of project templates you created and saved previously, as well as the templates you downloaded from the Office.com web site. Notice in Figure 3 - 7 that I downloaded the *Primary Market Research Schedule* template.

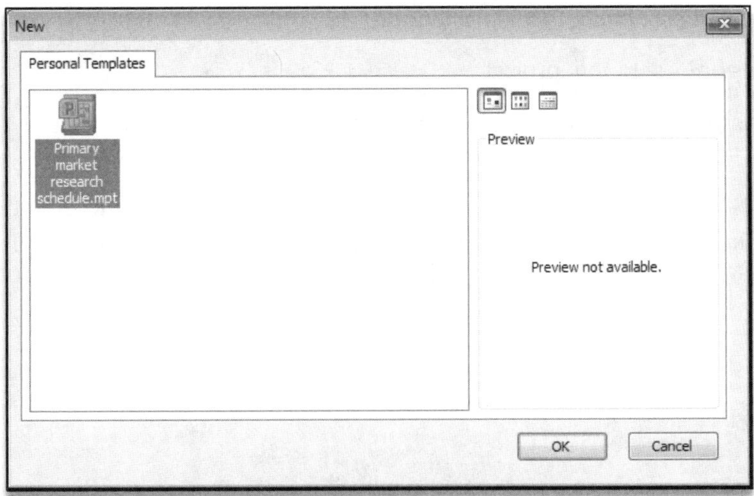

Figure 3 - 7: New dialog contains the template I downloaded from Office.com

Hands On Exercise

Exercise 3-1

Create a new project from an Office.com template.

1. Click the *File* tab and then click the *New* tab in the *Backstage*.
2. In the *Office.com Templates* section of the *Available Templates* page in the *Backstage*, search for and then select the *Annual Report Preparation* template (if not available, select any available project template).
3. Click the *Download* button.
4. Drag the split bar on the right edge of the *Duration* column.

Defining a New Project

After you create the new project, you are ready to define the project in Microsoft Project 2010 using the Six-Step Method recommended by MSProjectExperts. You should use this Six-Step Method whether you begin the new project from a blank project or create a new project from a project template. The Six-Step Method includes the following:

1. Set the project start date.
2. Enter the project properties.
3. Display the Project Summary Task (also known as Row 0 or Task 0).
4. Set the project working schedule using a calendar.
5. Set project options unique to this project.
6. Save the project according to your company's naming standards.

These six steps are exactly the same steps used in Microsoft Project 2007, but the method you use to access the functionality is different in Microsoft Project 2010. Table 3 - 1 documents how to complete each step in the Six-Step Method using the new Microsoft Project 2010 user interface.

Step	Project 2007	Project 2010
1) Set the project start date	Project ➢ Project Information	Project ribbon ➢ Project Information button
2) Enter the project properties	File ➢ Properties	File tab ➢ Info ➢ Project Information ➢ Advanced Properties
3) Display the Project Summary Task	Tools ➢ Options ➢ View	Format ribbon ➢ Project Summary Task
4) Set the project working schedule	1. Tools ➢ Change Working Time 2. Project ➢ Project Information 3. Format ➢ Timescale ➢ Non-Working Time	1. Project ribbon ➢ Change Working Time 2. Project ribbon ➢ Project Information 3. View ribbon ➢ Timescale ➢ Timescale ➢ Non-Working Time
5) Set project options	Tools ➢ Options	File tab ➢ Options
6) Save the project	File ➢ Save	File tab ➢ Save

Table 3 - 1: Six-Step Definition Process Comparison between Microsoft Project 2010 and 2007

During the first four steps, the dialogs you use in Microsoft Project 2010 are identical to in the dialogs you use in Microsoft Project 2007, so I do not discuss these steps. On the other hand, step #5 includes a number of new options settings, and step #6 offers new file types. I discuss these two steps in detail.

Setting Project Options

You need to specify two types of options for your new project. I discuss each of these types of options individually:

- Set the *Task Mode* option.
- Set options in the *Project Options* dialog.

Setting the Task Mode Option

One of the major changes to Microsoft Project 2010 is the *Task Mode* setting that allows you to specify tasks as either *Auto Scheduled* or *Manually Scheduled. Auto Scheduled* tasks were the default type of tasks in all previous versions of the software. *Manually Scheduled* tasks are a new feature in Microsoft Project 2010. You can use this new feature for tasks that you know you need to include in the project, but for which you may not have enough information to properly schedule, and you can use these for Top-down planning exercises. Other potential purposes for this feature include more relaxed scheduling approaches that agile methodology practitioners desire when, for example, modeling schedules for sprints in the SCRUM methodology

The default *Task Mode* setting in Microsoft Project 2010 is the *Manually Scheduled* option, which specifies all new tasks as *Manually Scheduled* tasks. Every time you launch the software, you see this default *Task Mode* setting as a ScreenTip on the Status bar in the lower left corner of the application window, as shown in Figure 3 - 8.

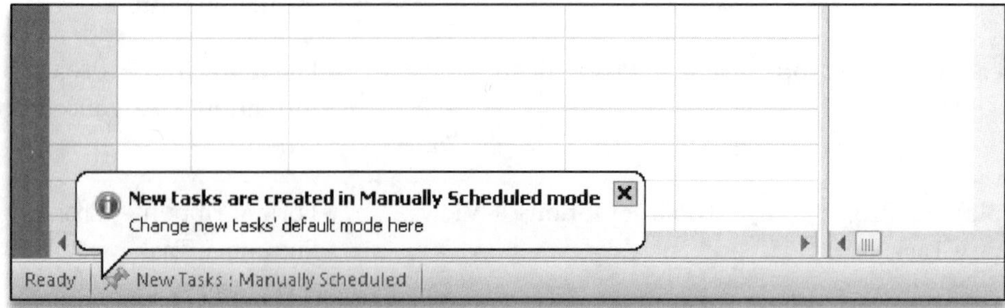

Figure 3 - 8: Task Mode option set to Manually Scheduled for all new tasks

To change the *Task Mode* setting and specify that all tasks must be *Auto Scheduled* in your new project, use either of the following methods:

- Click the *New Tasks* button on the Status bar and select the *Auto Scheduled* option.
- In the *Tasks* section of the *Task* ribbon, click the *Task Mode* pick list button and choose the *Auto Schedule* item on the pick list, as shown in Figure 3 - 9.

After selecting this option, when you create new tasks in your new project, Microsoft Project 2010 creates them as *Auto Scheduled* tasks. If you want to specify the default *Task Mode* setting for all new blank projects, you must specify this setting in the *Project Options* dialog. I discuss this setting in the next section of this module.

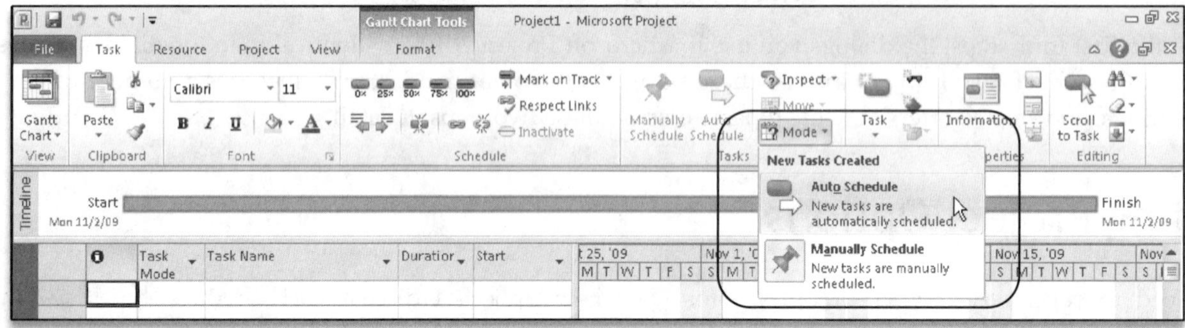

Figure 3 - 9: Task Mode pick list

Setting Options in the Project Options Dialog

After you specify the *Task Mode* setting for your new project, you are ready to specify options in the *Project Options* dialog. Microsoft Project 2010 allows you to specify three types of options settings in the *Project Options* dialog as follows:

- Application options that control how the software looks and works.
- Options specific to any project currently open.
- Options for all new projects created from a blank project.

To specify all three types of options settings, click the *File* tab and then click the *Options* tab. The software displays the *General* page of the *Project Options* dialog shown in Figure 3 - 10.

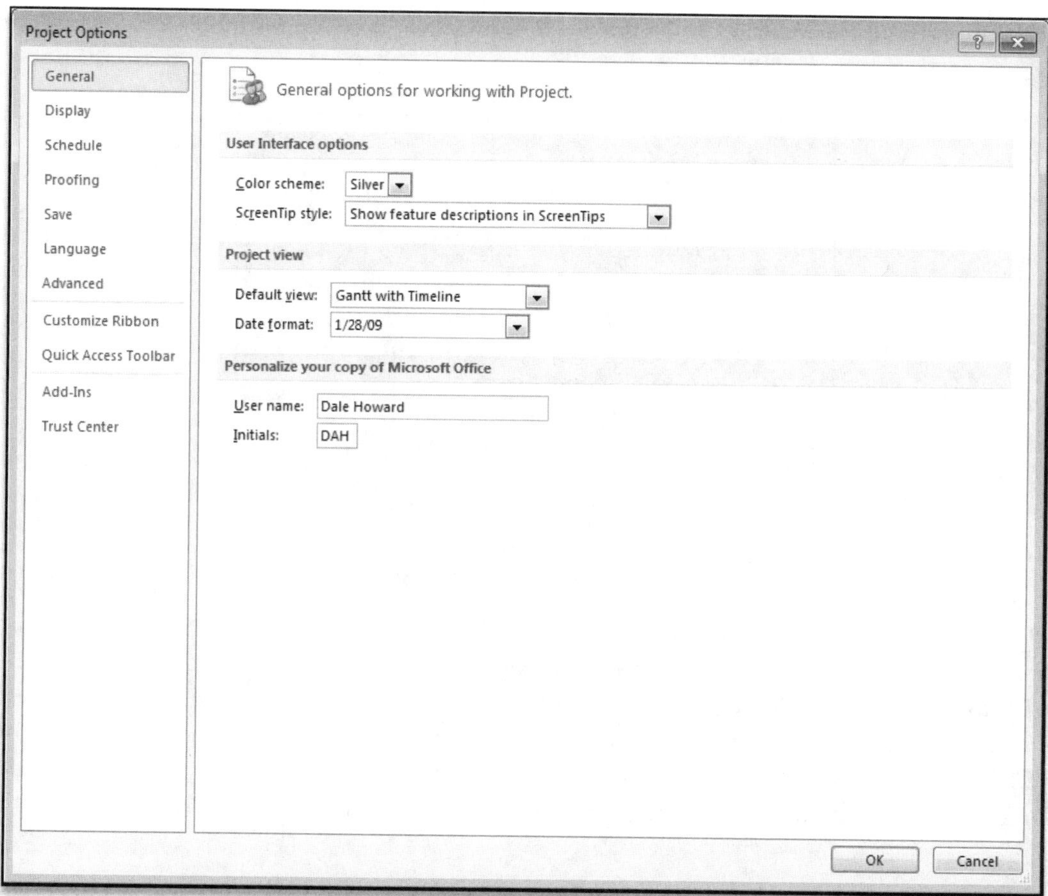

Figure 3 - 10: Project Options dialog, General page

Notice in Figure 3 - 10 that the *Project Options* dialog includes tabs for the following eleven pages of options: *General, Display, Schedule, Proofing, Save, Language, Advanced, Customize Ribbon, Quick Access Toolbar, Add-Ins,* and *Trust Center*. With the exception of the *Customize Ribbon* and *Quick Access Toolbar* pages, which I discussed previously in Module 01, I discuss all of the other pages in detail below.

Setting General Options

The *Project Options* dialog *General* page, shown previously in Figure 3 - 10, contains application options only. Remember that these options control how the software looks, works, and displays every project you open. The *User Interface options* section of the *General* page includes two new options for Microsoft Project 2010, the *Color Scheme* and *ScreenTip Style* options.

Use the *Color Scheme* option to control the color scheme that the system applies to all display elements in the Microsoft Project 2010 application window. These elements include the Title Bar, Quick Access Toolbar, Ribbon, column headers and row headers, Timescale bar, vertical and horizontal scroll bars, View bar (displayed along the left side of every View), and Status bar. Click the *Color Scheme* pick list and choose the *Blue, Silver,* or *Black* item. The *Silver* item is the default setting for the *Color Scheme* option.

When you float your mouse pointer over an object in the Microsoft Project 2010 application window, the software displays a *ScreenTip* to give you more information about that object. For example, the system displays *ScreenTips* for objects in the Gantt Chart, such as Gantt Bars or link lines, column headers for the columns shown in the current table, and buttons on the active ribbon. Figure 3 - 11 shows the *ScreenTip* for the *Project Information* button in the *Properties* section of the *Project* ribbon.

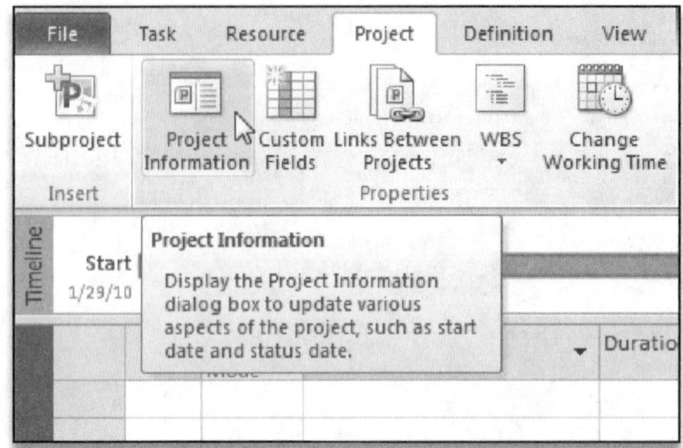

Figure 3 - 11: ScreenTip for the Project Information button

When you click the *ScreenTip Style* pick list in the *Project Options* dialog, the software offers you three settings. Leave the default *Show Feature Descriptions in ScreenTips* setting selected to show the most information possible in every *ScreenTip*, as shown for the *Project Information* button in Figure 3 - 11. Choose the *Don't Show Feature Descriptions in ScreenTips* setting to display only a minimum amount of information in the ScreenTip. Choose the *Don't Show ScreenTips* setting to disable the display of *ScreenTips*. When you chose the last setting, you **do not** see a ScreenTip for any object when you float your mouse pointer over it in the Microsoft Project 2010 application window.

Table 3 - 2 shows the options on the *General* page of the *Project Options* dialog in Microsoft Project 2010 and the corresponding location in Microsoft Project 2007.

Project 2010 Option	Project 2007 Option Location
Project View section Default View Date Format	*Options* dialog, *View* page
Personalize Your Copy of Microsoft Office section User Name Initials	*Options* dialog, *General* page, *General Options for Microsoft Office Project* section (no corresponding option for *Initials*)

Table 3 - 2: General Options comparison between Microsoft Project 2010 and 2007

Setting Display Options

Click the *Display* tab in the *Project Options* dialog to view the options on the *Display* page shown in the Figure 3 - 12. As indicated at the top of the *Display* page, use the options on this page to control how Microsoft Project 2010 displays project data on the screen.

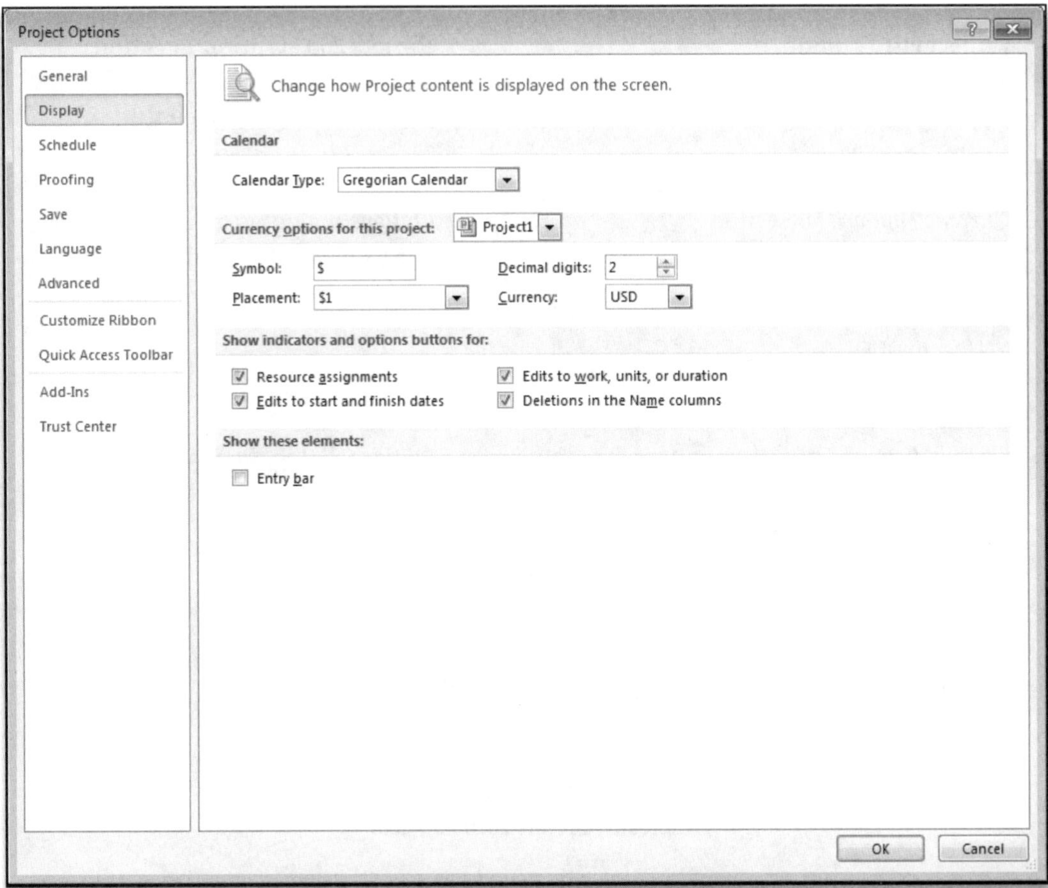

Figure 3 - 12: Project Options dialog, Display page

A new feature in Microsoft Project 2010 allows you to specify option settings for any project you have currently open, regardless of whether that project is the active project or not. You see this new feature on the *Display* page in the *Currency options for this project* section. Click the *Currency options for this project* pick list to view a list of projects currently open, and then select one of the open projects. By default, the pick list pre-selects the active project, but you can choose any other open project and then specify the *Currency options for this project* setting for that project. This new functionality means that you can specify a unique set of Options settings for each open project without the nuisance of continually selecting a new active project and opening and closing the *Project Options* dialog for each project.

Beyond this new convenience, there are no other new options in Microsoft Project 2010 on the *Display* page of the *Project Options* dialog. Table 3 - 3 shows the corresponding location in Microsoft Project 2007 for each of the options on the *Display* page of the *Project Options* dialog in Microsoft Project 2010.

Project 2010 Option	Project 2007 Option Location
Calendar section Calendar Type	*Options* dialog, *View* page
Currency options for section Symbol Placement Decimal Digits Currency	*Options* dialog, *View* page, *Currency Options For* section
Show indicators and options buttons for section Resource Assignments Edits to Start and Finish dates Edits to Work, Units, or Duration Deletions in the Name Columns	*Options* dialog, *Interface* page
Show these elements section Entry Bar	*Options* dialog, *View* page, *Show* section

Table 3 - 3: Display Options comparison between Microsoft Project 2010 and 2007

Setting Schedule Options

Click the *Schedule* tab in the *Project Options* dialog to view the options on the *Schedule* page shown in the Figure 3 - 13. As indicated at the top of the *Schedule* page, you use the options on this page to control scheduling, calendars, and calculations in Microsoft Project 2010. Notice in Figure 3 - 13 that the *Schedule* page includes sections in which you may specify the following types of options: Calendar, Schedule, Scheduling, and Schedule Alerts, along with two sections for Calculation options.

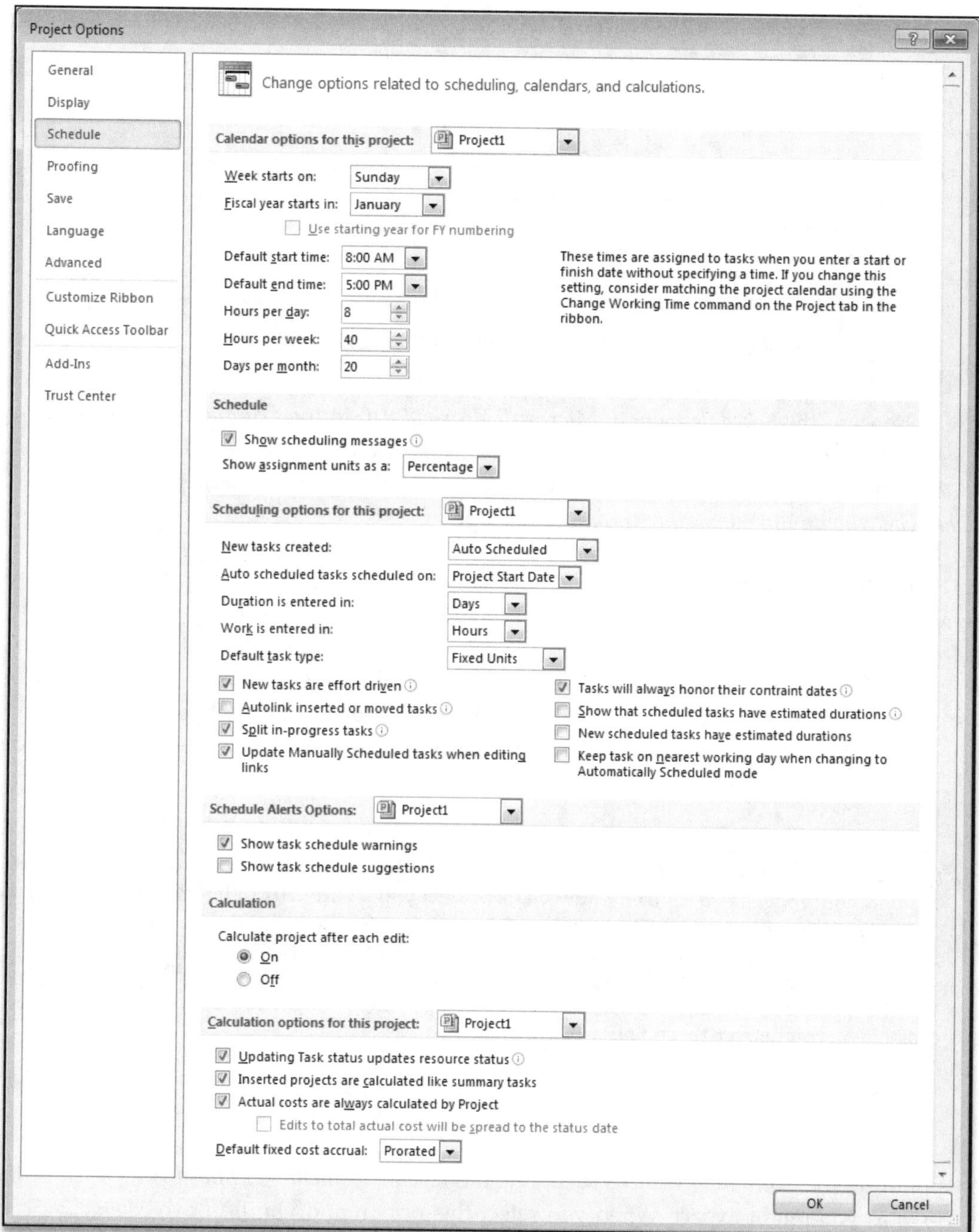

Figure 3 - 13: Project Options dialog, Schedule page

Notice in Figure 3 - 13 that four of the six sections include the new ability to select any open project from a pick list. The pick lists on the *Schedule* page, however, differ slightly from the pick list shown on the *Display* page. For example, if you click the *Calendar options for this project* pick list, the list includes all projects currently open, plus an *All New Projects* item as well. If you select the *All New Projects* item, the system allows you to specify an options setting for all future projects created from a new blank project. Figure 3 - 14 shows the *calendar options for this project* pick list, with two projects open currently.

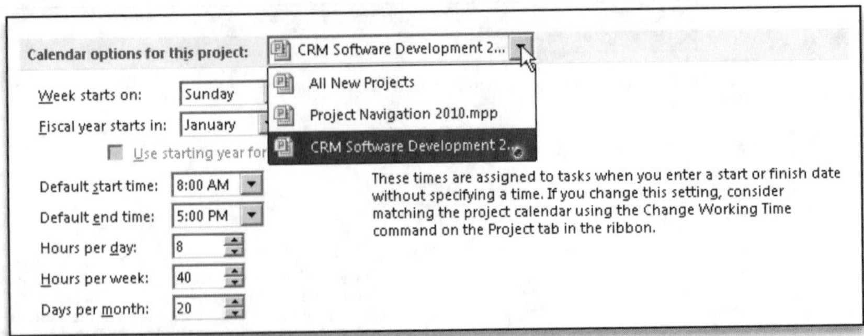

Figure 3 - 14: Calendar Options for this Project pick list

There are new options on the *Schedule* page in Microsoft Project 2010 in the *Scheduling options for this project* section and the *Schedule Alerts Options* section. In the *Scheduling options for this project* section, new options include the *New tasks created* option, the *Update Manually Scheduled tasks when editing links* option, and the *Keep task on nearest working day when changing to Automatically Scheduled mode* option.

The *New tasks created* option affects the default *Task Mode* setting for new tasks that you add to your project. When you click the *New tasks created* pick list, the system offers you two ways to set the task mode for new tasks, *Manually Scheduled* and *Auto Scheduled*. On the *Auto scheduled tasks scheduled on* pick list, you can select the *Project Start Date* or *Current Date* options. These are not new, and existed with the *New Tasks* option in Microsoft Project 2007. The system creates *Auto Scheduled* tasks with Start and Finish dates and with a default Duration of 1 day, while the system creates all *Manually Scheduled* tasks with no Duration, Start date, and Finish date values.

Although not entirely obvious, you can use the *New Tasks Created* pick list to set the default *Task Mode* option to *Auto Scheduled* for **every new blank project** you create. To do this, click the the *Scheduling options for this project* pick list and select the *All New Projects* item. Then click The *New tasks created* pick list and select the *Auto Scheduled* item. Click the *Auto scheduled tasks scheduled on* pick list and select either the *Project Start Date* or the *Current Date* option. When you click the *OK* button, Microsoft Project 2010 sets the default *Task Mode* option to *Auto Scheduled* for every new blank project you create from this point forward.

Another new option in the *Scheduling Options* section is the *Update manually scheduled tasks when editing links* option, which works as you might expect. When you select this option and you link two *Manually Scheduled* tasks with a task dependency, the system reschedules the successor task automatically. If you deselect this option, and you link two *Manually Scheduled* tasks with a task dependency, the system **does not** reschedule the successor task but leaves it at its original Start date instead.

The final change in the *Scheduling Options* section is the *Keep task on the nearest working day when changing to Automatically Scheduled mode* option. You can see how this option affects a task when you convert it from *Manually Scheduled* to *Auto Scheduled* in the example, I show you in Figure 3 - 15. Notice that I have two *Manually Scheduled* tasks, Task A and Task B. In this example, I manually scheduled Task A to start on Monday and Task B to start on Wednesday.

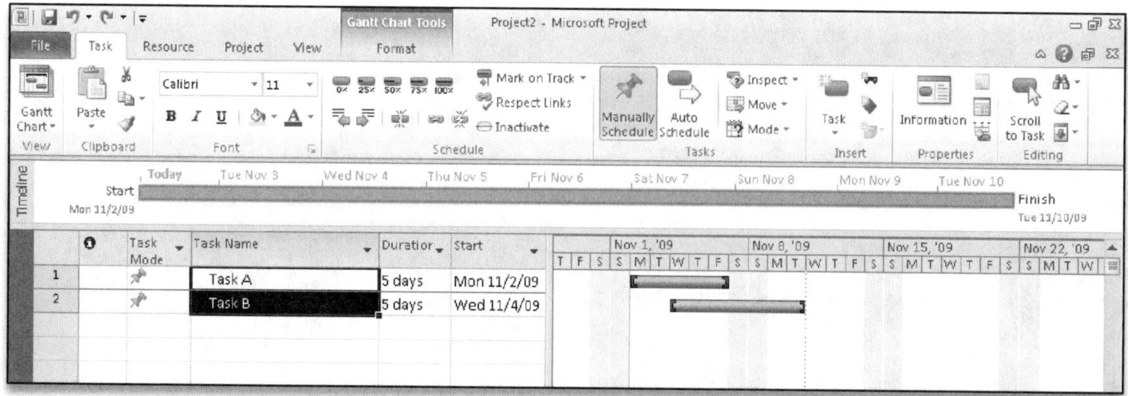

Figure 3 - 15: Two Manually Scheduled Tasks

Figure 3 - 16 shows the result of the operation when I change the *Task Mode* setting to *Auto Schedule* for both Task A and Task B with the *Keep task on the nearest working day when changing to Automatically Scheduled mode* option **deselected** (the default setting). Notice that Microsoft Project 2010 schedules Task A and Task B to start on Monday, in spite of the fact that I indicated I want Task B to start on Wednesday.

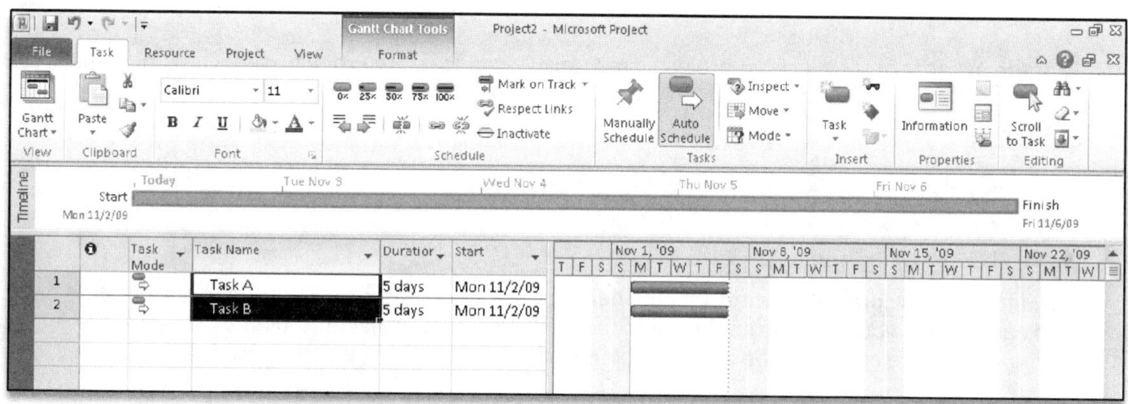

Figure 3 - 16: Convert Manually Scheduled Tasks to Auto Scheduled tasks with the Option DESELECTED

Figure 3 - 17 shows the result of changing the *Task Mode* setting to *Auto Schedule* for these two tasks after **selecting** the *Keep task on the nearest working day when changing to Automatically Scheduled mode* option. Notice in the figure that there is an indicator showing to the left of each task in the *Indicators* column. This indicator represents a Start No Earlier Than (SNET) constraint placed by Microsoft Project 2010 on each task to enforce my start dates. This means that Task A continues to start on Monday and Task B continues to start on Wednesday, as I specified when I created these tasks in *Manually Scheduled* mode.

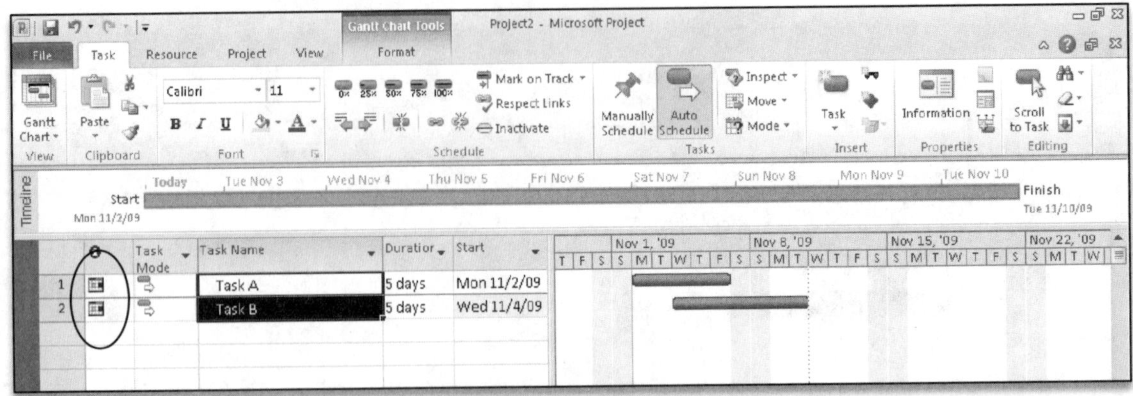

Figure 3 - 17: Convert Manually Scheduled Tasks to Auto Scheduled tasks with the Option SELECTED

Two other options in the *Scheduling Options* section change their default settings from selected to deselected in Microsoft Project 2010. These options are the *New tasks are effort driven* option and the *Autolink inserted or moved tasks* option. In Microsoft Project 2007, these two options were selected by default.

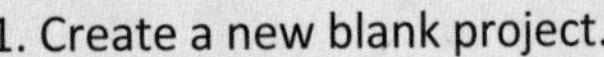
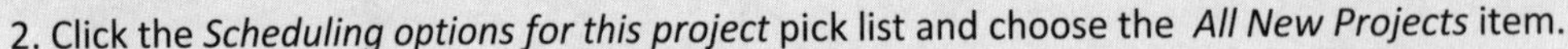

If the majority of tasks in your projects are Effort Driven tasks, MsProjectExperts recommends that you do the following early in your use of Microsoft Project 2010:

1. Create a new blank project.
2. Click the *Scheduling options for this project* pick list and choose the *All New Projects* item.
3. Select the *New tasks are effort driven* option.
4. Click the *OK* button.

Completing the preceding steps sets the default value for all tasks to *Effort Driven* in all of the new blank projects you create from this point forward. If you use project templates to create new projects, you should also complete the above steps in each of your existing project templates.

The remaining new options you find on the *Schedule* page of the *Project Options* dialog are the two options in the *Schedule Alerts Options* section of the page. Both of these options control the information shown in the *Task Information* pane when you use the *Task Inspector* tool to analyze schedule problems. The *Task Inspector* pane, which started as the *Task Drivers* feature in Project 2007, shows the factors controlling the Start date of any task, along with Warnings and Suggestions for correcting task schedule problems. By default, the system selects the *Show task schedule warnings* option and deselects the *Show task schedule suggestions* option. To take maximum advantage of the new *Schedule Alerts* feature, I recommend you select **both options** for the current project and for all new projects. I discuss the *Task Inspector* tool in detail in Module 04, "What's New - Task Planning." Table 3 - 4 shows the Microsoft Project 2010 option and corresponding location in Microsoft Project 2007 for each of the options on the *Schedule* page of the *Project Options* dialog.

Project 2010 Option	Project 2007 Option Location
Calendar options section	*Options* dialog, *Calendar* page
Schedule section	*Options* dialog, *Schedule* page, *Schedule Options for Microsoft Office Project* section
Scheduling options for this project section	*Options* dialog, *Schedule* page, *Scheduling Options* section for the active project
Calculation section Calculate project after each edit	*Options* dialog, *Calculation* page, *Calculation Options for Microsoft Office Project* section
Calculation options for this project section	*Options* dialog, *Calculation* page, *Calculation Options* section for the active project

Table 3 - 4: Schedule Options comparison between Microsoft Project 2010 and 2007

Setting Proofing Options

Click the *Proofing* tab in the *Project Options* dialog to view the options on the *Proofing* page shown in Figure 3 - 18. As indicated at the top of the *Proofing* page, use the options on this page to control how Microsoft Project 2010 corrects and formats text in your projects.

The only new option on this page is the *Spanish modes* option, set to the *Tuteo verb forms only* option by default. If you use the Spanish version of Microsoft Project 2010, click the *Spanish modes* pick list and choose your preferred option for working with the Spanish language. Your options are as follows:

- Tuteo Verb Forms Only (the default option)
- Tuteo and Voseo Verb Forms
- Voseo Verb Forms Only

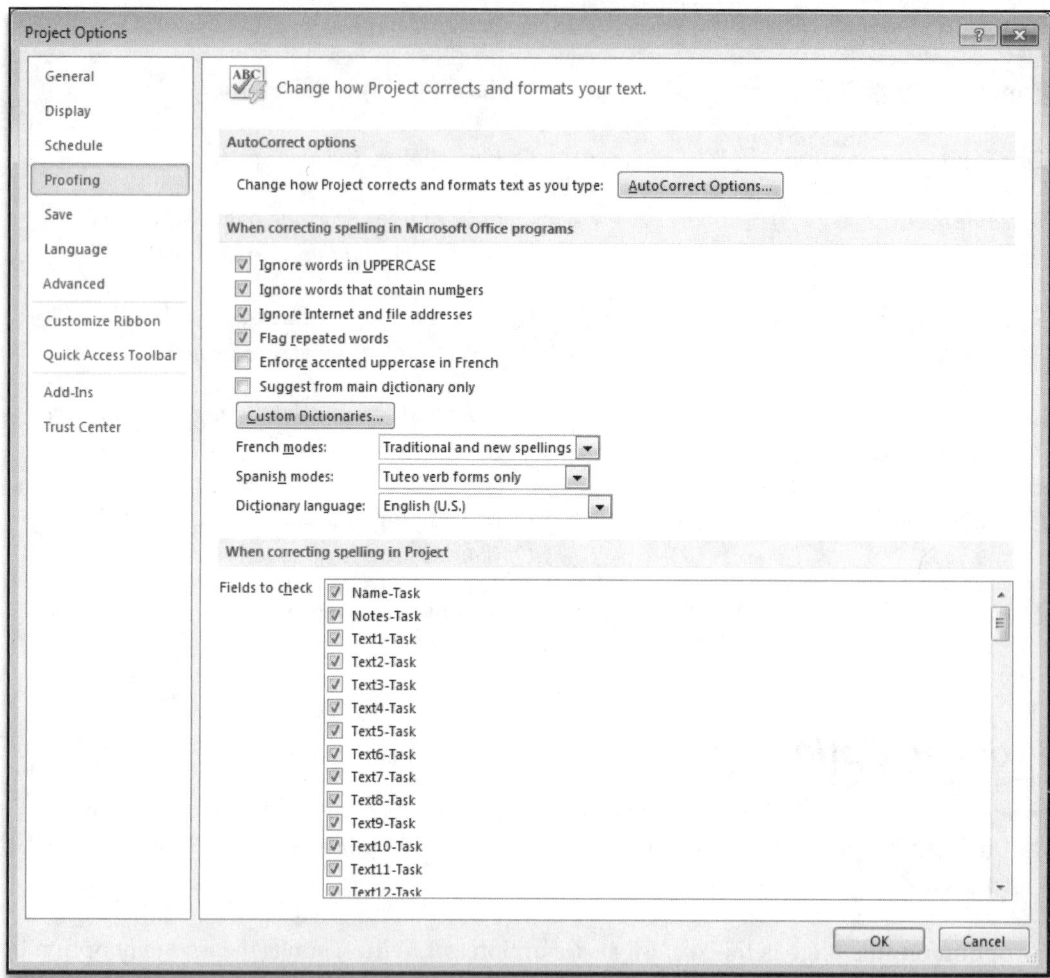

Figure 3 - 18: Project Options dialog, Proofing page

Table 3 - 5 shows the Microsoft Project 2010 option and corresponding location in Microsoft Project 2007 for each of the options on the *Proofing* page of the *Project Options* dialog.

Project 2010 Option	Project 2007 Option Location
AutoCorrect options section	Tools ➤ AutoCorrect Options
When correcting spelling in Microsoft Office programs section	*Options* dialog, *Spelling* page, *More Spelling Options* button
When correcting spelling in Project section	*Options* dialog, *Spelling* page, *Fields to Check* section

Table 3 - 5: Proofing Options comparison between Microsoft Project 2010 and 2007

Setting Save Options

Click the *Save* tab in the *Project Options* dialog to view the options on the *Save* page shown in Figure 3 - 19. As indicated at the top of the *Save* page, use the options on this page to determine options for saving a project in Microsoft Project 2010.

The only new options on the *Save* page are those found in the *Cache* section at the bottom of the page. These options are available **only** in the Professional version of Microsoft Project 2010, and for use only with Microsoft Project Server 2010. If you have the Standard version of the software, you do not see a *Cache* section on this page.

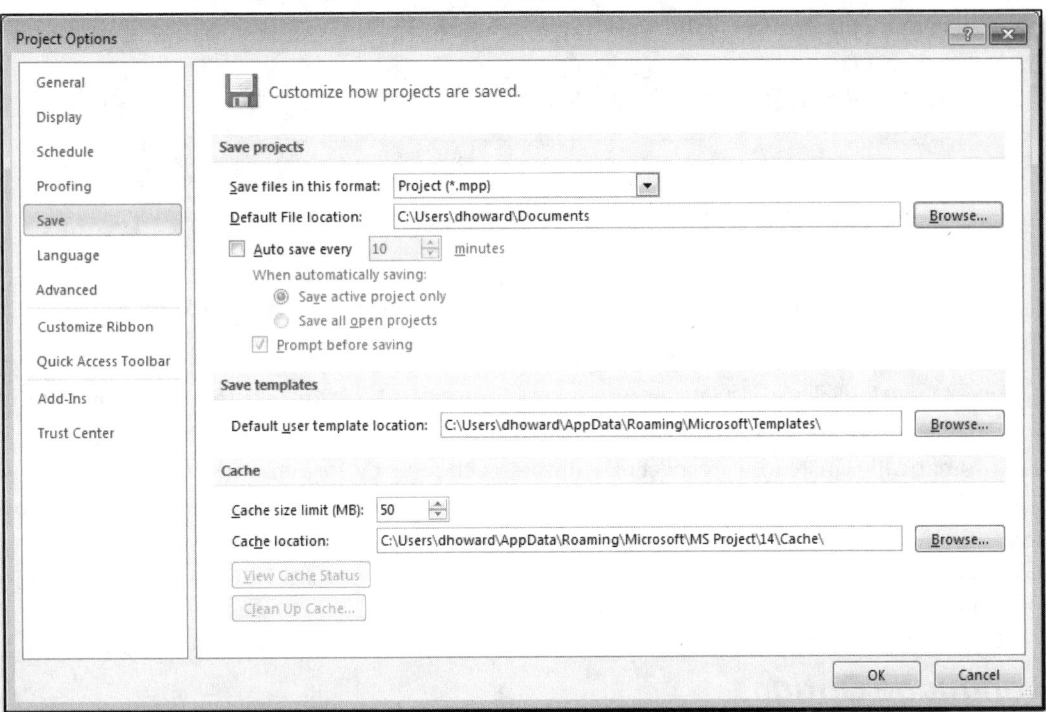

Figure 3 - 19: Project Options dialog, Save page

Table 3 - 6 shows the Microsoft Project 2010 option and the corresponding location in Microsoft Project 2007 for each of the options on the *Save* page of the *Project Options* dialog.

Project 2010 Option	Project 2007 Option Location
Save projects section	*Options* dialog, *Save* page, *File Locations* section and *Auto Save* section
Save templates section	*Options* dialog, *Save* page, *File Locations* section
Cache section (Microsoft Project Professional 2010 only)	Tools ➢ Local Project Cache

Table 3 - 6: Save Options comparison between Microsoft Project 2010 and 2007

Backward Compatibility and Save Option Behavior

As with prior versions, Microsoft designed Project 2010 to be backward compatible through at least two generations. Microsoft Project 2010 is capable of saving projects in both 2007 and 2000-2003 formats. Although the *Save files in this format* pick list in the *Save Projects* section is not a new option, it has a profoundly different affect on the behavior of your project client when you choose to save in an older project format as your default save option.

When you select either of the older project formats as the default, the system creates all new blank projects in your selected format, and disables many of the new features in Microsoft Project 2010, including the ability to schedule tasks manually. When you create a new blank project the system presents the project in *Compatibility Mode,* which the system displays rather subtly as shown in Figure 3 - 20.

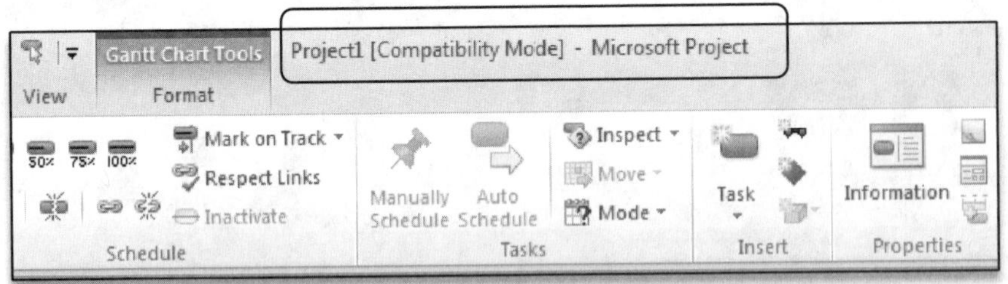

Figure 3 - 20: Compatibility Mode display

You cannot create *Manually Scheduled* tasks in new blank projects when your system is set by default to save in older formats. The same is true when you open projects saved in legacy formats. The system does not convert these for you automatically. Instead, it respects the limits of the legacy format and disables new scheduling features in Project 2010 for those projects. You can, however, continue to use these features when you open projects previously saved in the new Project 2010 .mpp format and for new blank projects and existing projects saved in a legacy format after you deliberately save the project to the new 2010 format. I discuss these limitations in more depth later in this module.

Setting Language Options

Click the *Language* tab in the *Project Options* dialog to view and set options on the *Language* page shown in Figure 3 - 21. As indicated at the top of the *Language* page, use the options on this page to specify your language preference(s) for all of your Microsoft Office 2010 applications and Microsoft Project 2010. The *Language* page is common to all Microsoft Office applications, as well as to Microsoft Visio and Microsoft Project.

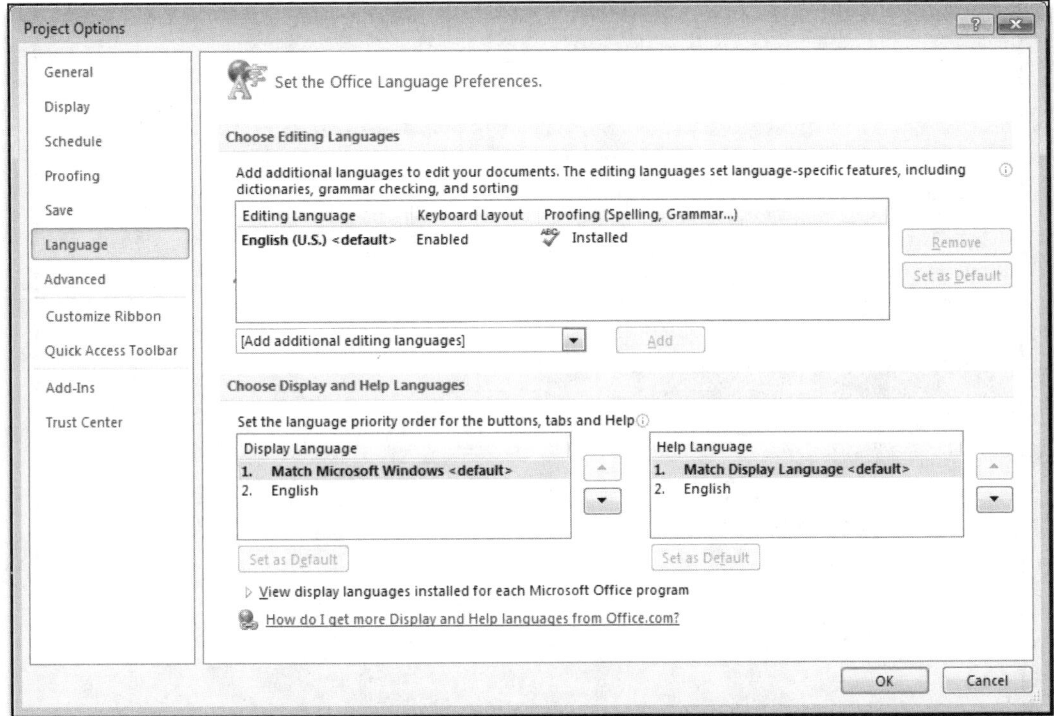

Figure 3 - 21: Project Options dialog, Language page

Before you can use the *Language* page, you must install one or more *Language Packs* for Microsoft Office 2010 applications. After installing at least one *Language Pack,* you can specify the language you want use for editing your projects, and choose the language the software uses to display your application and to display *Help* dialogs. If you do not install at least one *Language Pack,* the software limits you to the default options shown on the *Language* page. The corresponding Language options in Microsoft Project 2007 are located at Start ➤ Programs ➤ Microsoft Office ➤ Microsoft Office Tools ➤ Microsoft Office 2007 Language Tools.

Setting Advanced Options

Click the *Advanced* tab in the *Project Options* dialog to view the options on the *Advanced* page shown in Figure 3 - 22. As indicated at the top of the *Advanced* page, use the options on this page to specify advanced settings for Microsoft Project 2010.

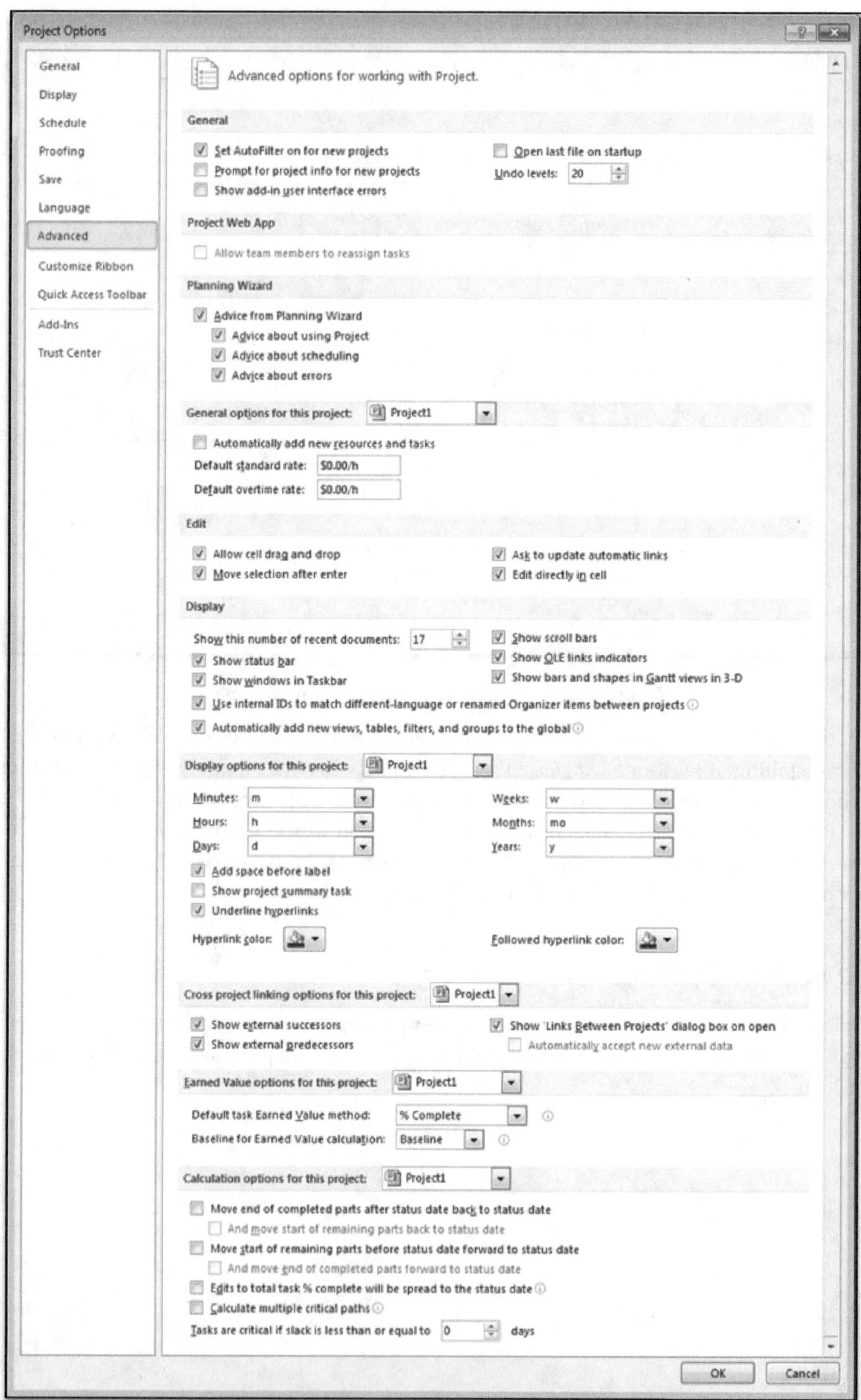

Figure 3 - 22: Project Options dialog, Advanced page

Notice in Figure 3 - 22 that the *Advanced* page includes sections where you specify the following types of options: *General, Project Web App, Planning Wizard, General options for this project, Edit, Display, Display options for this project, Cross project linking, Earned Value,* and *Calculation*. The *Project Web App* section is available **only** in the Professional version of Microsoft Project 2010. If you have the Standard version of the software, you do not see the *Project Web App* section.

Microsoft Project 2010 includes two new options on the *Advanced* page: the *Show add-in user interface errors* option in the *General* section, and the *Automatically add new views, tables, filters, and groups to the global* option in the *Display* section. The first option displays errors originating from Project Add-ins in the project client interface. When you select the *Automatically add new views, tables, filters, and groups to the global* option (the default), the software automatically adds new views, tables, filters, and groups, to your Global.mpt file when you create them, making them available to all current and future projects. If you want to create custom views, tables, filters, and groups on a per-project basis, or if you want to manually control the content available in the Global.mpt file using the *Organizer* dialog, you should **deselect** the *Automatically add new views, tables, filters, and groups to the global* option.

Table 3 - 7 shows the location for options on the *Advanced* page of the *Project Options* dialog and their corresponding locations in Microsoft Project 2007.

Project 2010 Option	Project 2007 Option Location
General section	*Options* dialog, *General* page, *General Options for Microsoft Office Project* section
Project Web App section	*Options* dialog, *Collaborate* tab
Planning Wizard section	*Options* dialog, *General* page, *Planning Wizard* section
General options for this project section	*Options* dialog, *General* page, *General* section for the active project
Edit section	*Options* dialog, *Edit* page, *Edit Options for Microsoft Office Project* section
Display section	*Options* dialog, *General, View,* and *Interface* pages
Display options for this project section	*Options* dialog, *Edit* and *View* pages
Cross project linking section	*Options* dialog, *View* page, *Cross Project Linking* section
Earned Value section	*Options* dialog, *Calculation* page, *Earned Value* button
Calculation section	*Options* dialog, *Calculation* page

Table 3 - 7: Advanced Options comparison between Microsoft Project 2010 and 2007

Although not a new option, the *Show Project Summary Task* option offers a new setting state. To display the Project Summary Task in all new blank projects, click the *Display options for this project* pick list and choose the *All New Projects* item, and then select the *Show Project Summary Task* option. In prior versions of Microsoft Project, you must select this option for each project individually.

Setting Add-Ins Options

Click the *Add-Ins* item in the *Project Options* dialog to view the options on the *Add-Ins* page shown in Figure 3 - 23. As indicated at the top of the *Add-Ins* page, use the options on this page to view and manage COM Add-Ins for Microsoft Office 2010.

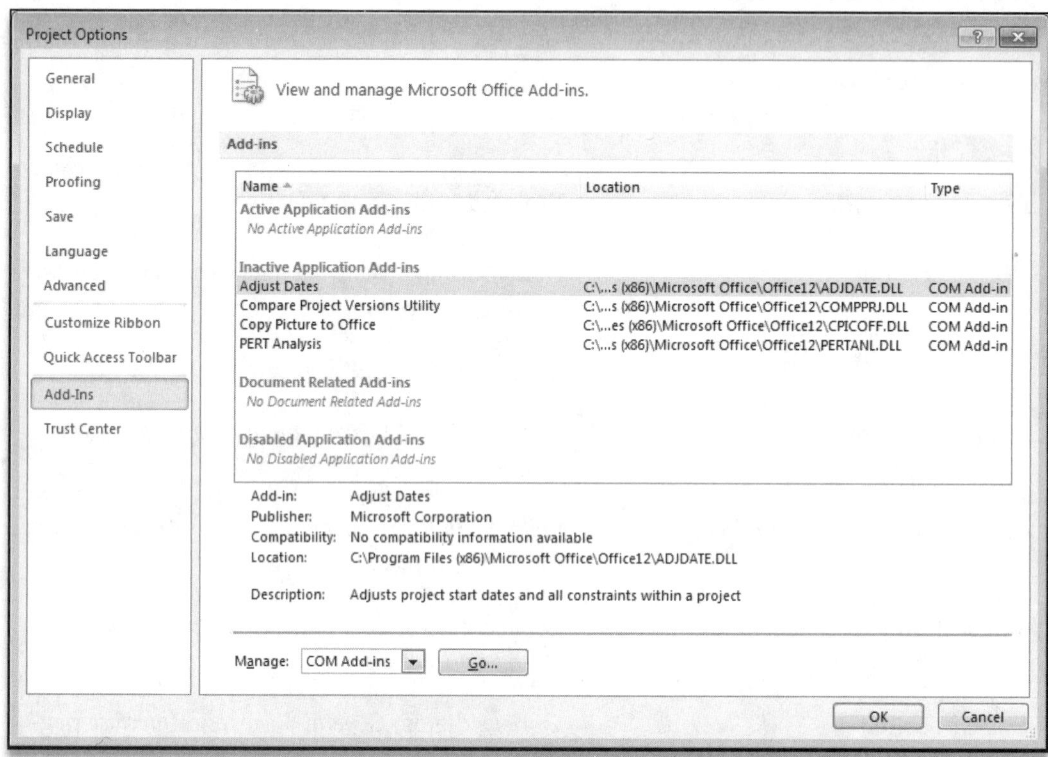

Figure 3 - 23: Project Options dialog, Add-Ins page

Microsoft Project 2010 **does not** include any of the pre-built macros found in previous versions. Note in the *Inactive Application Add-ins* section of the *Add-Ins* page, that the familiar macros from Project 2007 display in this section because I also have Project 2007 installed on my system.

Setting Trust Center Options

Click the *Trust Center* tab in the *Project Options* dialog to view the options on the *Trust Center* page shown in Figure 3 - 24. As indicated at the top of the *Trust Center* page, use the options on this page to provide security for your project and for your computer. The *Trust Center* page in the *Project Options* dialog provides three sections of security-related information:

- Protecting your privacy
- Security & more
- Microsoft Office Project Trust Center

The *Protecting your privacy* section includes three links, the *Show the Microsoft Office Project privacy statement*, the *Office.com privacy statement*, and the *Customer Experience Improvement Program* links. I do not discuss these options, as they are self-explanatory. The *Security & more* section includes the *Microsoft Trustworthy Computing* link that displays the Microsoft Trustworthy Computing web site. Again, I do not discuss this option, as it self-explanatory.

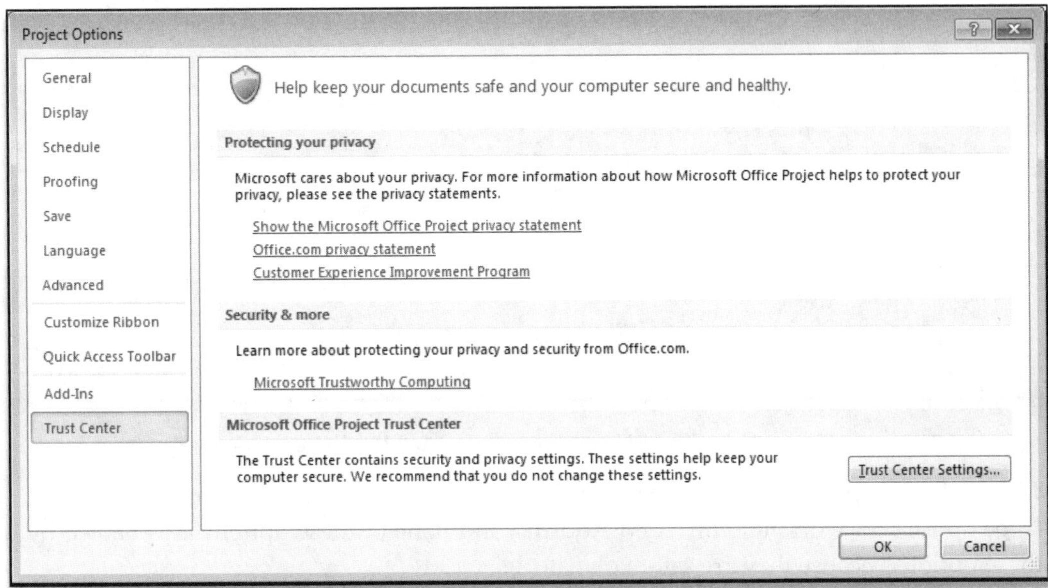

Figure 3 - 24: Project Options dialog, Trust Center page

In the *Microsoft Office Project Trust Center* section, click the *Trust Center Settings* button to specify a range of security settings. The system displays the *Macro Settings* page of the *Trust Center* dialog shown in Figure 3 - 25. Use the *Macro Settings* page to set your level of macro security. By default, Microsoft Project 2010 selects the *Disable all macros with notification* option, which prevents you from running macros in the application. The software notifies you in a warning dialog about this limitation when you attempt to run a macro. To avoid the security warnings, select the *Disable all macros without notification* option. To specify a lower level of macro security, select either the *Disable all macros except digitally signed macros* option or the *Enable all macros* option. Notice in the dialog shown in Figure 3 - 25 that Microsoft does not recommend selecting *Enable all macros* option.

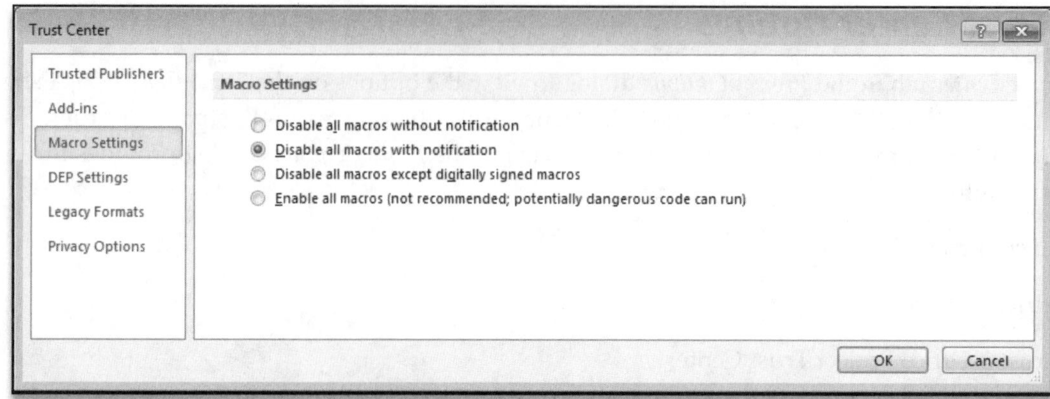

Figure 3 - 25: Trust Center dialog, Macro Settings page

Select the *Trusted Publishers* tab to display the *Trusted Publishers* page in the *Trust Center* dialog shown in Figure 3 - 26. The *Trusted Publishers* page shows macro authors whose VBA code you trust. Notice in the dialog shown in Figure 3 - 26 that I do not currently have a formal macro trust relationship with any macro authors.

Figure 3 - 26: Trust Center dialog, Trusted Publishers page

Click the *Add-Ins* tab to display the *Add-Ins* page in the *Trust Center* dialog shown in Figure 3 - 27. The *Add-Ins* page offers three options for working with COM Add-Ins, and none of these options are enabled by default. I do not discuss these options because they are self-explanatory.

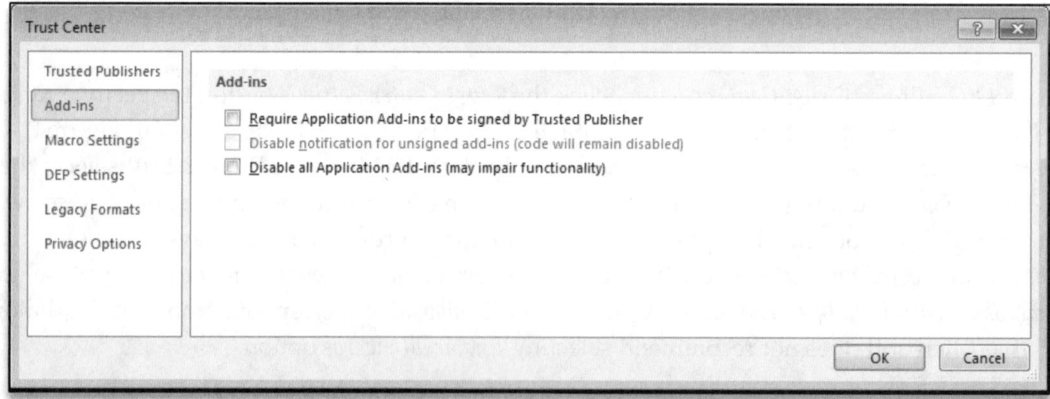

Figure 3 - 27: Trust Center dialog, Add-Ins page

Click the *DEP Settings* tab to display the *Data Execution Prevention* page in the *Trust Center* dialog shown in Figure 3 - 28. Data Execution Prevention (DEP) is a set of hardware and software technologies that protect your computer memory from malicious software code exploits. By default, the single option on the page enables Data Execution Prevention.

If you use Microsoft Project 2010 while connected to Project Server 2010, the *Trust Center* dialog does not contain a *DEP Settings* tab.

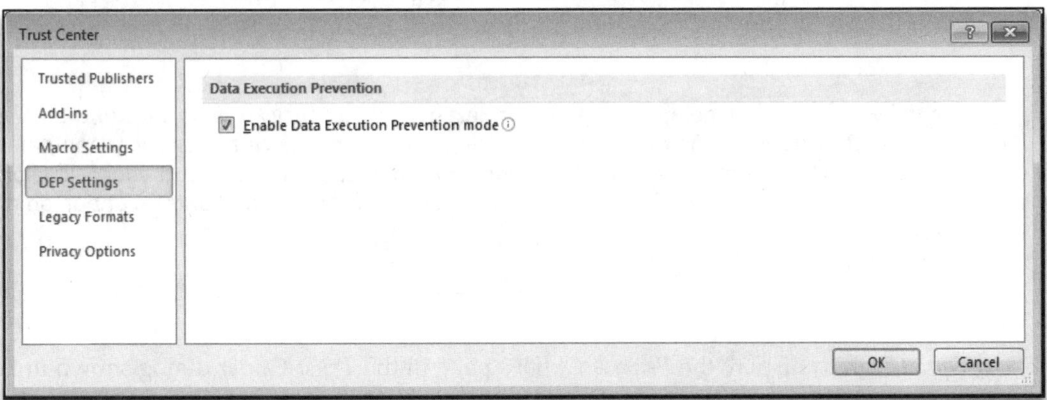

Figure 3 - 28: Trust Center dialog, Data Execution Prevention page

Click the *Legacy Formats* tab to display the *Legacy Formats* page in the *Trust Center* dialog shown in Figure 3 - 29. The options on the *Legacy Formats* page control how Microsoft Project 2010 works with non-default and legacy file formats. Legacy formats controlled by this setting include:

- Microsoft Project Database files
- Microsoft Excel .XLS workbook files
- Microsoft Access databases
- Project Exchange Format .MPX files
- Text files .TXT
- Comma Delimited .CSV files

The default *Do not open/save file with legacy or non-default file formats in Project* option prevents you from opening or closing files that are non-default or legacy format. If you need to work with non-default or legacy files, select either the *Prompt when loading files with legacy or non-default file format* option or the *Allow loading files with legacy or non-default file format* option in the dialog.

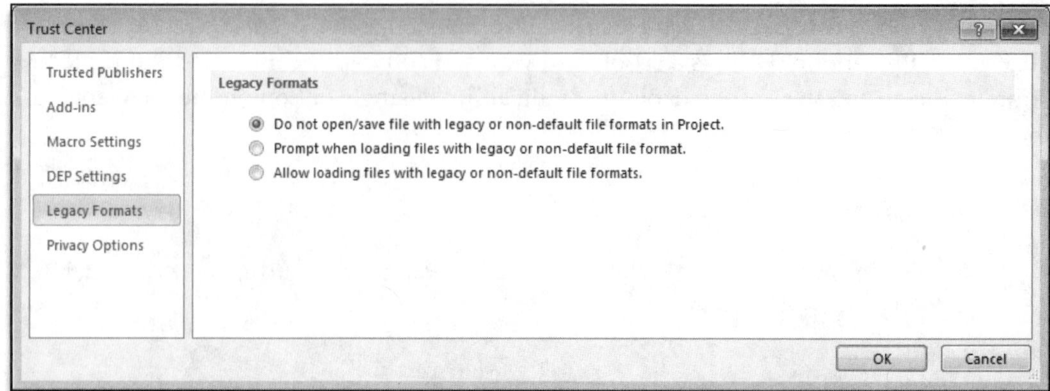

Figure 3 - 29: Trust Center dialog, Legacy Formats page

Warning: If you do not change the default option setting in the *Legacy Formats* page of the *Trust Center* dialog, the system prevents you from either exporting to or importing with a legacy or non-default file format such as the Microsoft Office Excel workbook format. If you want to export your Microsoft Project 2010 data to an Excel workbook, be sure to select either the second or third option on the *Legacy Formats* page.

Click the *Privacy Options* tab to display the *Privacy Options* page in the *Trust Center* dialog shown in Figure 3 - 30. As the name of the page implies, use the settings on the *Privacy Options* page to control how much information Microsoft Project 2010 shares with Microsoft and other outside organizations. The *Privacy Options* page contains six application options and one project-specific option. The names of the six application options reveal their function, so I do not discuss them individually. If you select the *Remove personal information from file properties on save* option, the single project-specific option, the system clears the *Author, Manager, Company* and *Last Saved By* fields in the *Properties* dialog each time you save the project.

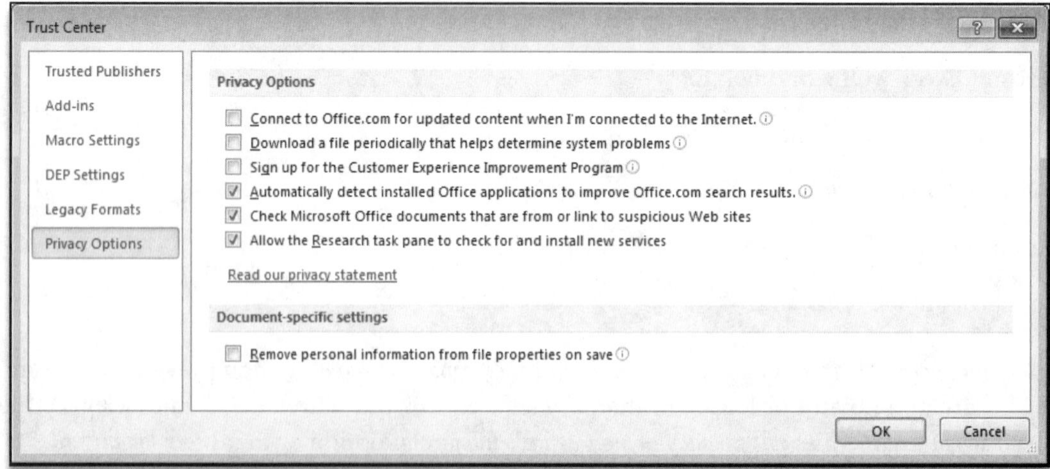

Figure 3 - 30: Trust Center dialog, Privacy Options page

After selecting your Trust Center options, click the *OK* button to close the *Trust Center* dialog and then click the *OK* button to close the *Project Options* dialog as well.

Hands On Exercise

Exercise 3-2

In your new project, specify Project Options settings recommended by MSProjectExperts.

1. Click the *File* tab and then click the *Options* tab in the *Backstage.*
2. On the *General* page of the *Project Options* dialog, click the *Date Format* pick list and select the *1/28/09* setting.
3. On the *Schedule* page, set the following options for the new project in the *Scheduling options for this project* section:

Autolink inserted or moved tasks	Deselected
Show that scheduled tasks have estimated durations	Deselected
New scheduled tasks have estimated durations	Deselected

4. On the *Schedule* page, click the *Scheduling options for this project* pick list, select the *All New Projects* item, and then set the following options for all new projects:

New tasks are effort driven	Selected
Show that scheduled tasks have estimated durations	Deselected
New scheduled tasks have estimated durations	Deselected

5. On the *Schedule* page, select the *Show task schedule suggestions* option in the *Schedule Alert Options* section.
6. On the *Schedule* page, click the *Schedule Alert Options* pick list, select the *All New Projects* item, and then select the *Show task schedule suggestions* option again for all new projects.
7. On the *Advanced* page, deselect the *Automatically Add New Resources and Tasks* option in the *General Options for this Project* section.
8. On the *Advanced* page, click the *General options for this project* pick list, select the *All New Projects* item, and then deselect the *Automatically add new resources and tasks* option for all new projects.
9. On the *Advanced* page, set the following options for the new project in the *Display options for this project* section:

Minutes	m
Hours	h
Days	d
Weeks	w
Months	mo
Years	y
Show Project Summary Task	Selected

10. On the *Advanced* page, click the *Display options for this project* pick list, select the *All New Projects* item, and then specify the same settings for all new projects as those selected in the previous step.
11. On the *Trust Center* page, click the *Trust Center Settings* button.
12. On the *Legacy Formats* page of the *Trust Center* dialog, select the *Allow loading files with legacy or non-default file formats* option.
13. Click the *OK* button to close the *Trust Center* dialog.
14. Click the *OK* button to close the *Project Options* dialog as well.

Saving a Project as an Alternate File Type

As with Microsoft Project 2007, Microsoft Project 2010 allows you to save your project using alternate file types. When you save a new project file for the first time, the system selects the *Project (*.mpp)* option as the default file type, which saves the project file in the native Microsoft Project 2010 file format. If you want to save all of your projects using a backwards compatible file type, remember that you can specify an alternate file type as the default file type on the *Save* page of the *Project Options* dialog.

As with Microsoft Project 2007, you can continue to save your projects using a number of other file types, but Microsoft Project 2010 offers several new file types. The file types available in Microsoft Project 2010 include the following:

Warning: In order to work with some of the file types below, you must change the settings on the *Legacy Formats* page in the *Trust Center* as discussed in the previous topic.

Microsoft Project 2007 – This file type maintains backwards compatibility with only Microsoft Project 2007 and Microsoft Project 2003 only with Service Pack 3 (SP3) applied.

- **Microsoft Project 2000-2003** – This file type maintains backwards compatibility with Microsoft Project 2000, 2002, and 2003.

- **Project Template (*.mpt)** – Only users with Microsoft Project 2010 can create a new project from project templates saved with this file type.

- **Microsoft Project 2007 Template (*.mpt)** – Users of both Microsoft Project 2007 and 2010 can create a new project from project templates saved with this file type.

- **PDF Files (*.pdf)** – Select this file type to save a project file as a Portable Document Format (PDF) file. Using the PDF file type allows you to share project information with users who do not have Microsoft Project 2010 installed on their workstations.

- **XPS Files (*.xps)** – Select this file type to save a project file as an XML Paper Specification file.

- **Excel Workbook (*.xlsx)** - Select this file type to save a project file as a Microsoft Excel workbook using a format that allows only Microsoft Excel 2007 and 2010 to open the workbook.

- **Excel Binary Workbook (*.xlsb)** – Select this file type to save the project file as a Macro-Enabled Excel workbook file stored in Binary format rather than XLSX format. Use this file format to save a very large Microsoft Project file quickly and efficiently. This file type is compatible with versions of Microsoft Excel earlier than the 2007 version; however, users must download and install a converter for their version of Microsoft Excel before they can open this file type.

- **Excel 97-2003 Workbook (*.xls)** – Select this file type to save a project file as a Microsoft Excel workbook using a format that allows Excel 97 through Excel 2003 to open the workbook directly without using a converter.

- **Text (Tab delimited) (*.txt)** and **CSV (Comma delimited) (*.csv)** – Select one of these two file types to save your project file as a text file.

- **XML Format** – Select this file type to save your project file as an Extensible Markup Language (XML) file.

To save a Microsoft Project 2010 file using an alternate file type, click the *File* tab and then click the *Save As* tab in the *Backstage*. In the *Save As* dialog, click the *Save as type* pick list and select an alternate file type, as shown in Figure 3 - 31.

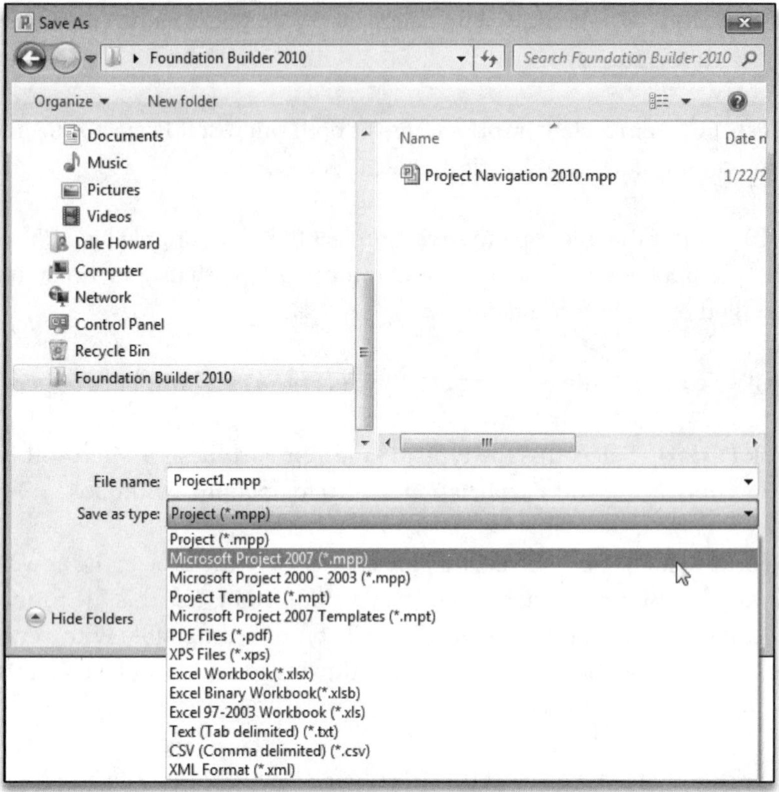

Figure 3 - 31: Select an alternate file type on the Save as type pick list

Saving a Project File as a PDF or XPS Document

Before you save a Microsoft Project 2010 file as a PDF or XPS file, apply the view you want to display in the resulting file, such as the *Gantt Chart* view. Click the *File* tab and then click the *Save As* tab in the *Backstage*. In the *Save As* dialog, click the *Save as type* pick list, and then select either the *PDF Files (*.pdf)* item or the *XPS Files (*.xps)* item. Click the *Save* button and Microsoft Project 2010 displays the *Document Export Options* dialog shown in Figure 3 - 32.

Figure 3 - 32: Document Export Options dialog

In the *Publish Range* section, select the *All* option to export all tasks in the project, along with the entire Gantt Chart timeline if you applied the *Gantt Chart with Timeline* view in the project. Select the *From* option and select a date range to print the task list on the left side with the date range specified for the Gantt Chart.

In the *Include Non-Printing Information* section of the dialog, leave the *Document Properties* option and the *Document Showing Markup* option selected to include this information in the PDF or XPS file. Users can view this non-printing information in the PDF file by clicking File ➤ Properties in the Adobe Acrobat Reader software. Deselect one or both of these options to remove the non-printing information from the PDF or XPS file.

In the PDF Options section, select the *ISO 19500-1 Compliant (PDF/A)* option to save a PDF document in ISO compliant format. Do not select this option if you do not need an ISO compliant PDF file. Click the *OK* button to save the project file as a PDF file. Figure 3 - 33 shows a Microsoft Project 2010 project file saved as a PDF document and displayed in the Adobe Acrobat Reader software. Figure 3 - 34 shows the same project file saved as an XPS document and displayed in the Microsoft XPS Viewer application.

Companies use the PDF/A file format for the long-term archiving of electronic documents. This file format guarantees that users can reproduce the original document in exactly the same way years later.

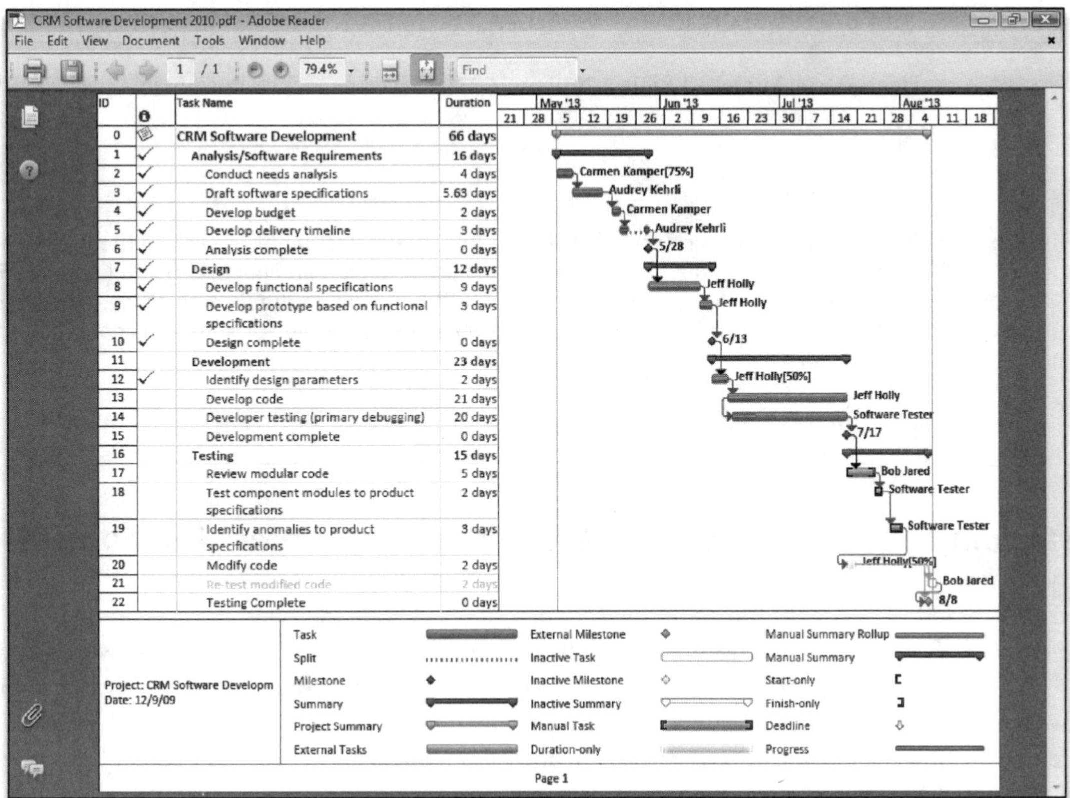

Figure 3 - 33: Microsoft Project 2010project file saved as a PDF document

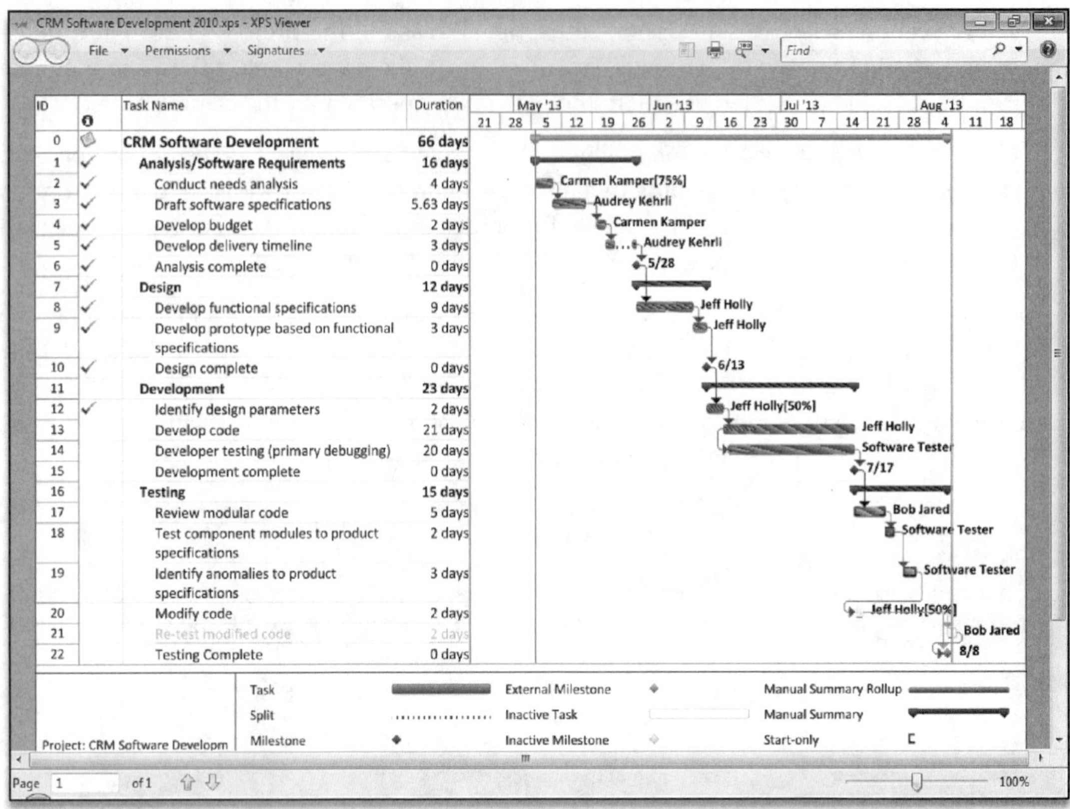

Figure 3 - 34: Microsoft Project 2010 project file saved as an XPS document

You can also save a Microsoft Project 2010 file as a PDF or XPS document by clicking the *File* tab and then clicking the *Save & Send* tab in the *Backstage*. On the *Save & Send* page, click the *Create PDF/XPS Document* menu item and then click the *Create a PDF/XPS* button. In the *Browse* dialog, browse to the location where you want to save the file and then click the *Save as type* pick list and choose your file type.

Understanding Reduced Functionality with Older Project File Formats

If you save a Microsoft Project 2010 file using the Microsoft Project 2007 file type, the system displays the *Saving to Previous Version – Compatibility Checker* warning dialog shown in Figure 3 - 35. The dialog warns you of Microsoft Project 2010 features not supported in the 2007 version of the software application. Notice that the warning dialog shown in Figure 3 - 35 warns about *Manually Scheduled* tasks and *Manually Scheduled Summary Tasks* in the project, and reveals how the software converts these features to work with the 2007 version of the software.

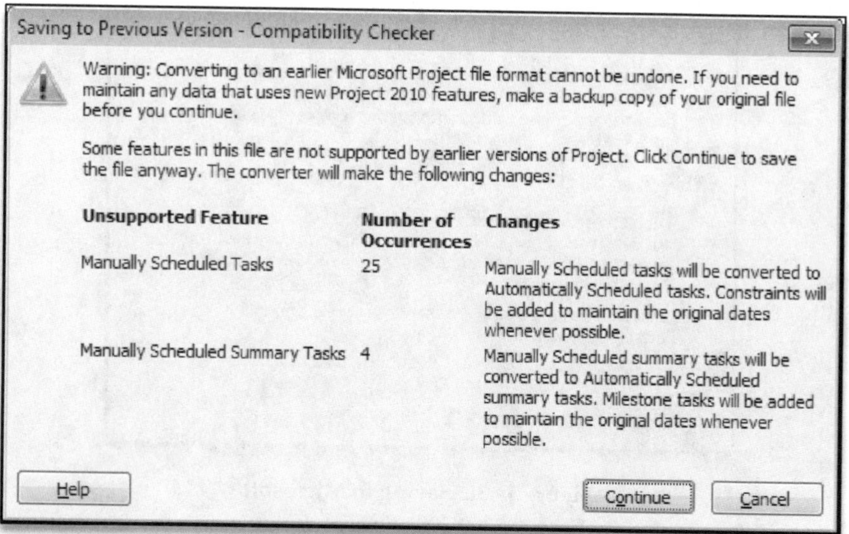

Figure 3 - 35: Saving to Previous Version – Compatibility Checker dialog

When you click the *Continue* button in the *Saving to Previous Version – Compatibility Checker* dialog, the system converts the data that relies on new features as follows:

- The system changes *Manually Scheduled* tasks to *Auto Scheduled* tasks, and adds Start No Earlier Than (SNET) constraints to the tasks to preserve current dates in the schedule.
- The system changes *Manually Scheduled* summary tasks to *Auto Scheduled* summary tasks.
- After converting *Manually Scheduled* summary tasks to *Auto Scheduled* summary tasks, the system adds two milestone tasks immediately after the summary task to indicate the original start date and finish date for the summary task. The system adds a Must Start On (MSO) constraint to these milestone tasks as well.
- The system deletes *Inactive* tasks.
- The system removes *Strikethrough* font formatting on any tasks manually formatted by the user.
- If you apply custom formatting to the *Team Planner* view, save the file as an earlier version, then close and re-open the file, you lose the custom formatting in the *Team Planner* view.
- The system converts 32-bit colors to the 16 colors used in all previous versions of Microsoft Project. These colors apply to font formatting, Gantt bar colors, and cell background formatting (Microsoft Project 2007 only).
- Previous versions of Microsoft Project do not display the *Timeline* view.
- The system applies AutoFilter to the data in the project.

If you save a Microsoft Project 2010 file using the Microsoft Project 2003 file type, the system displays the *Saving to Microsoft Project 2000-2003 format* dialog shown in Figure 3 - 36. The dialog warns you of Microsoft Project 2010 features not supported in the earlier version of the software application.

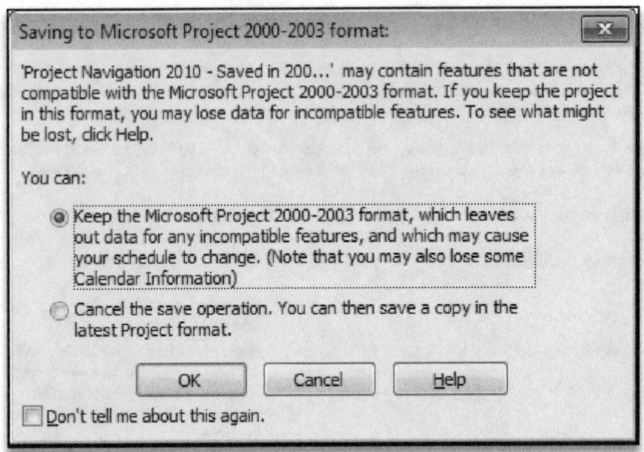

Figure 3 - 36: Saving to Microsoft Project 2000-2003 Format dialog

When you save a Microsoft Project 2010 file in the Microsoft Project 2000-2003 file format, the system converts the data that relies on new features the same way as with the 2007 file format, and impacts your saved file as follows:

- You lose any information contained in *Budget* fields, such as in the *Budget Cost* field.
- The system converts each *Cost* resource to a same-named *Material* resource, but you do not lose information contained in the *Cost* fields for the *Cost* resources.
- The system removes cell background formatting applied to tasks, but you do not lose font formatting.
- The system removes information contained in the *Assignment Owner* field and other fields added to Project since the 2003 version.
- The system converts recurring calendar exceptions to a series of multiple individual exceptions.
- The system removes all information related to enterprise custom fields.

Opening a Project Created in an Older Version of Microsoft Project

In Microsoft Project 2010, when you open a project file created in an earlier version of the software, the system opens the file in *Compatibility Mode,* discussed previously in the *Save* options section in this module. The system displays this information to the right of the file name in the Title bar of the application window as shown previously in Figure 3 - 20. While you have a project file open in Compatibility Mode, you cannot use any of the new features of the software, such as *Manually Scheduled* tasks or *Inactive* tasks. If you save the project file as a Microsoft Project 2010 file, the system enables all of the new features in the software, but handles existing tasks and new tasks as follows:

- The system sets existing tasks and new tasks to *Auto Scheduled*. You can then set any existing or new tasks to Manually Scheduled.
- The system does not show the *Task Mode* column automatically. You must add this column manually, if you want it exposed.
- The system does not display the *Gantt with Timeline* view automatically. To display this view, apply the *Gantt with Timeline* view manually.

Hands On Exercise

Exercise 3-3

Save your project using several file types.

1. Save your new project in the *My Documents* folder using the name *My Company Annual Report* and using the default *Project (*.mpp)* file format.
2. Click the *File* tab and then click the *Save As* item.
3. In the *Save As* dialog, click the *Save as type* pick list, select the *PDF Files (*.pdf)* item, and then click the *Save* button.
4. In the *Document Export Options* dialog, leave all of the default options selected and then click the *OK* button.
5. Click the *File* tab and then click the *Save As* tab.
6. In the *Save As* dialog, change the file name to *My Company Annual Report – 2007 Format.*
7. In the *Save As* dialog, click the *Save as type* pick list, select the *Microsoft Project 2007 (*.mpp)* item, and then click the *Save* button.
8. If you see a *Compatibility Checker* dialog, click the *Continue* button.
9. Notice the **[Compatibility Mode]** label appended to the file name on the Title bar at the top of the Microsoft Project 2010 application window.
10. On the *Task* ribbon, notice that the system disables the *Inactivate, Manually Schedule,* and *Auto Schedule* buttons.

Exercise 3-4

Convert a project file saved in the 2007 format to the default Microsoft Project 2010 format.

1. Close and then reopen the **My Company Annual Report – 2007 Format** project.
2. On the *Task* ribbon, click the *View* pick list button and select the *Reset to Default* item.
3. When prompted in a warning dialog, click the *Yes* button to reset the *Gantt Chart* view.
4. Widen the *Task Name* column and then drag the split bar on the right side of the *Duration* column.
5. On the *Task* ribbon, click the *View* pick list button again and select the *More Views* item.
6. In the *More Views* dialog, select the *Gantt with Timeline* view and then click the *Apply* button.
7. Save and close the **My Company Annual Report– 2007 Format** project.
8. In the confirmation dialog, click the *No* button to save the project in the 2007 format.

Saving a Project to SharePoint

If your organization uses Microsoft SharePoint Foundation 2010 or Microsoft SharePoint Server (MSS) 2010, you can save your Microsoft Project 2010 project files to a SharePoint site in a document library. Before you can save your project file to a SharePoint site, however, your organization must meet the following requirements:

- Your SharePoint administrator must create a SharePoint site for you.
- Your SharePoint administrator must supply you with the URL of the site.
- Either you or your SharePoint administrator must create a document library for your project.
- You must navigate to the SharePoint site and copy the URL to your Windows clipboard.

Warning: Your organization **must** use Microsoft SharePoint Foundation 2010 or Microsoft SharePoint Server 2010 before you can save your Microsoft Project 2010 files in a document library in SharePoint. You cannot use any previous version of SharePoint for this functionality.

Figure 3 - 37 shows a Microsoft SharePoint Server 2010 site containing a document library called Project 2010 Production Projects.

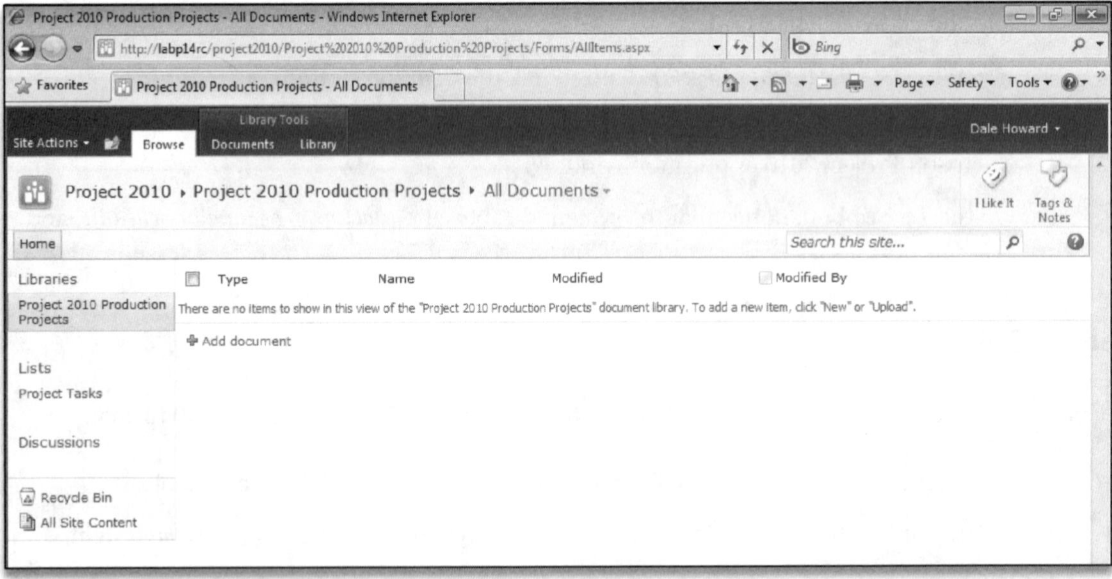

Figure 3 - 37: Document Library created in Microsoft SharePoint Server 2010

After meeting the previous set of conditions, you can save a Microsoft Project 2010 file to the SharePoint site by completing the following steps:

1. Click the *File* tab and then click the *Save & Send* tab.
2. On the *Save & Send* page, click the *Save to SharePoint* tab.

Microsoft Project 2010 displays the *Save & Send* page with the *Save to SharePoint* section shown in Figure 3 - 38.

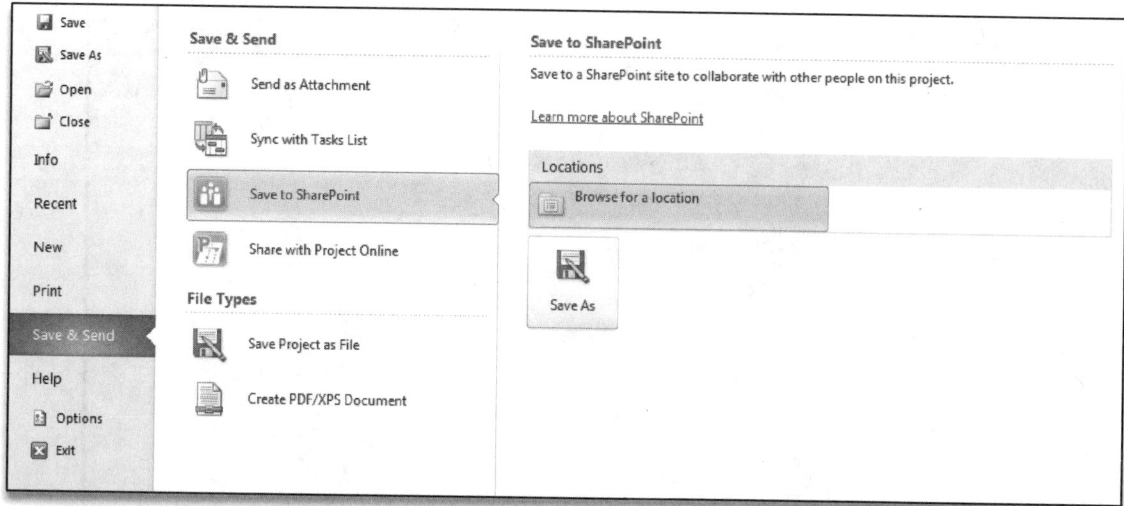

Figure 3 - 38: Save to SharePoint page in the Backstage

3. In the *Save to SharePoint* section, double-click the *Browse for a location* button. Microsoft Project 2010 displays the *Save As* dialog.

4. In the *Save As* dialog, paste the URL of the SharePoint site into the address field at the top of the dialog, such as shown in Figure 3 - 39.

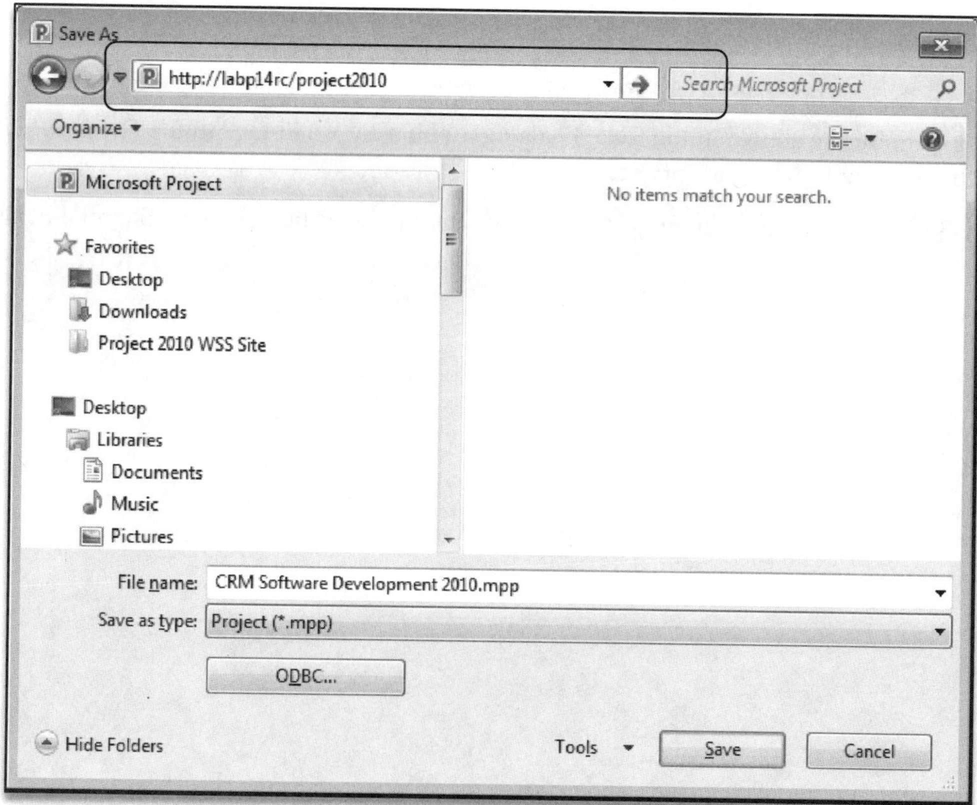

Figure 3 - 39: Paste the SharePoint URL into the address field at the top of the Save As dialog

5. Press the *Enter* key on your computer keyboard and allow the *Save As* dialog to access the SharePoint site, as shown in Figure 3 - 40.

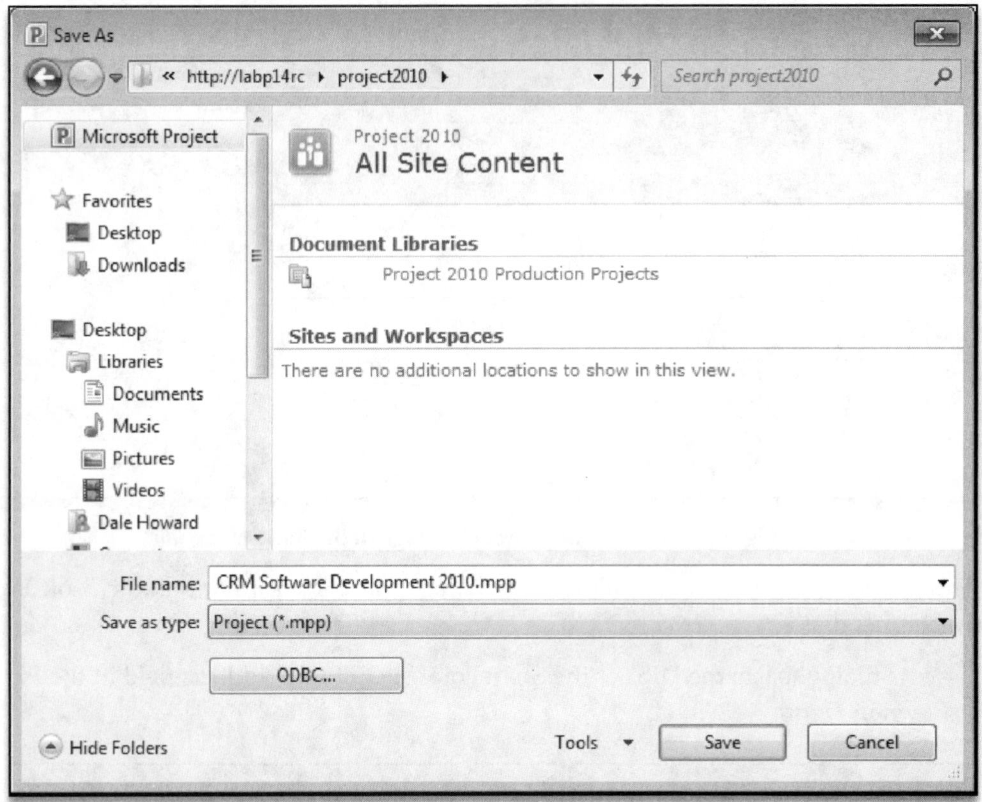

Figure 3 - 40: Save As dialog shows the SharePoint site

6. In the SharePoint site shown in the *Save As* dialog, double-click a library in the *Document Libraries* section in which you want to save your project.

Notice in Figure 3 - 41 that I selected the Project 2010 Production Projects library in the SharePoint site.

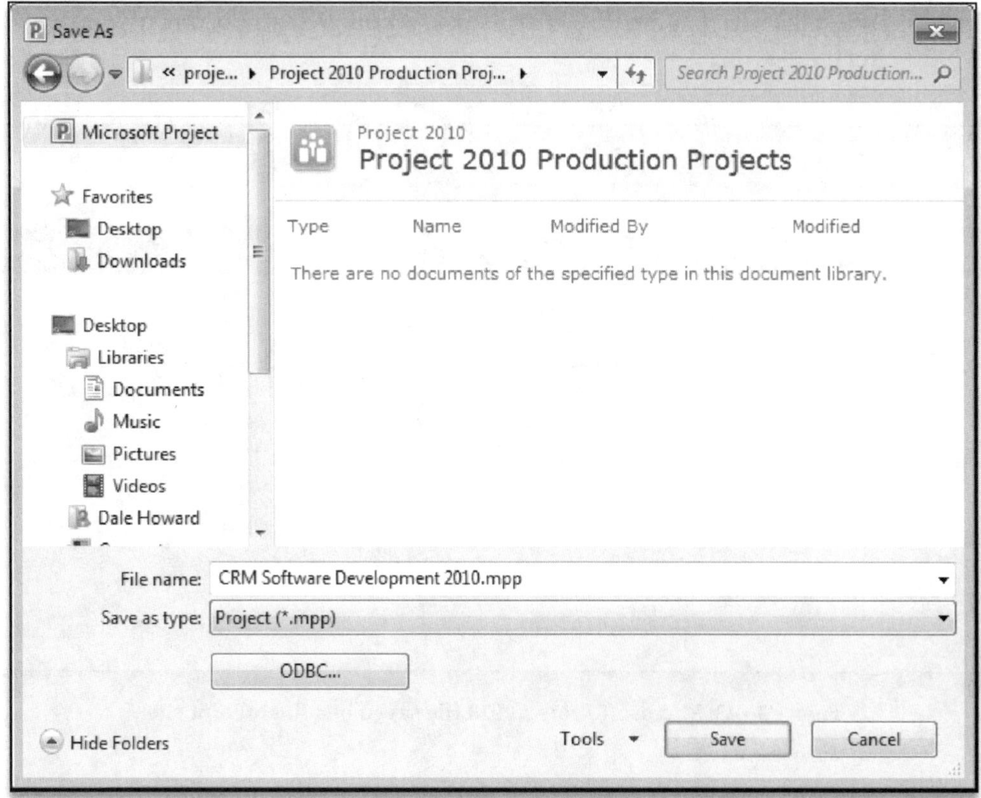

Figure 3 - 41: Document Library accessed in the Save As dialog

7. Click the *Save* button in the *Save As* dialog.

As Microsoft Project 2010 saves the project file to the SharePoint site, the system displays a progress meter in a *Saving* dialog as shown in Figure 3 - 42.

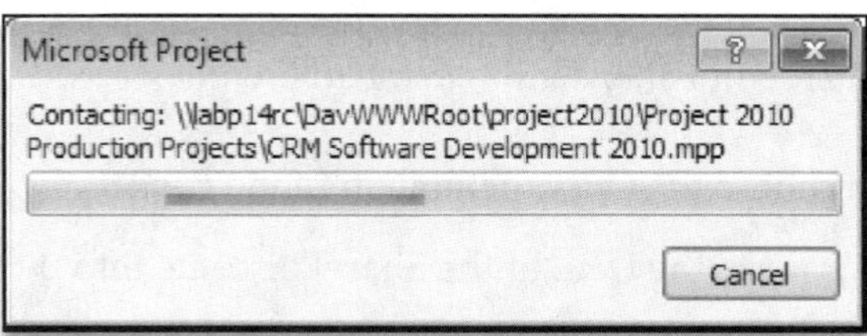

Figure 3 - 42: Saving dialog

Figure 3 - 43 shows a project file saved in the Project 2010 Production Projects document library in the SharePoint site shown previously in Figure 3 - 37.

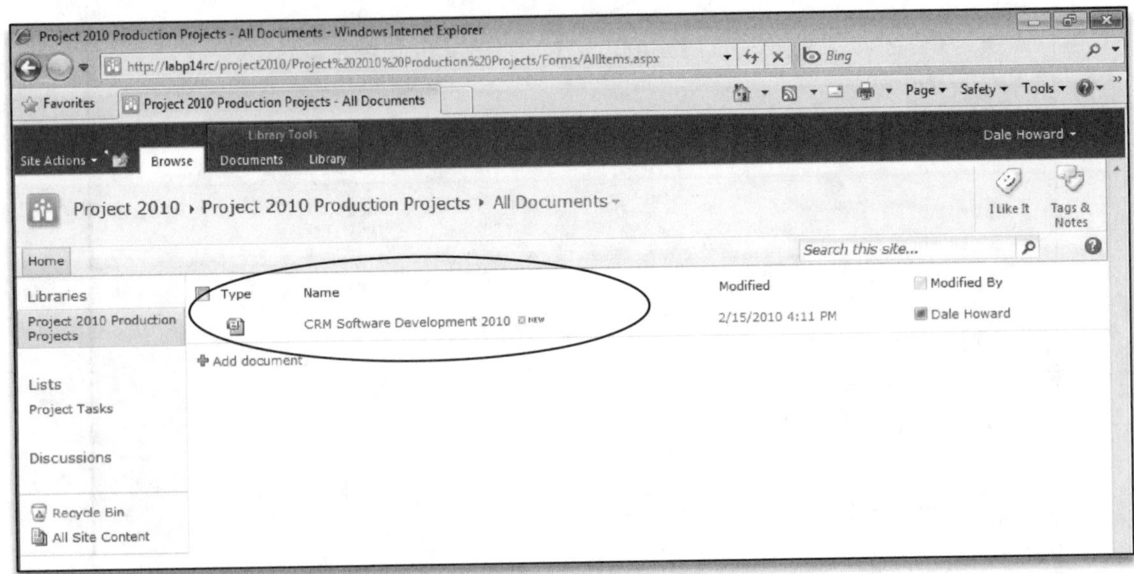

Figure 3 - 43: Microsoft Project 2010 file saved in a SharePoint site

Warning: After you save your project to a document library in SharePoint, Microsoft Project 2010 is designed to save the URL of the SharePoint site in the *Locations* section of the *Save to SharePoint* page in the *Backstage*. Because of a bug prior to Server Pack 1 (SP1) in the software, however, the system does not work as designed and **does not** save the URL of the SharePoint site for you.

To open a project file saved in a SharePoint site, complete the following steps:

1. Click the *File* tab and then choose the *Open* menu item in the *Backstage*.
2. In the *Open* dialog, enter or paste the URL of the SharePoint site into the address field at the top of the dialog and then press the *Enter* key.
3. In the *Document Library* section of the SharePoint site, double-click the name of the library containing the project, and then select the project, as shown in Figure 3 - 44.
4. Click the *Open* button in the *Open* dialog.

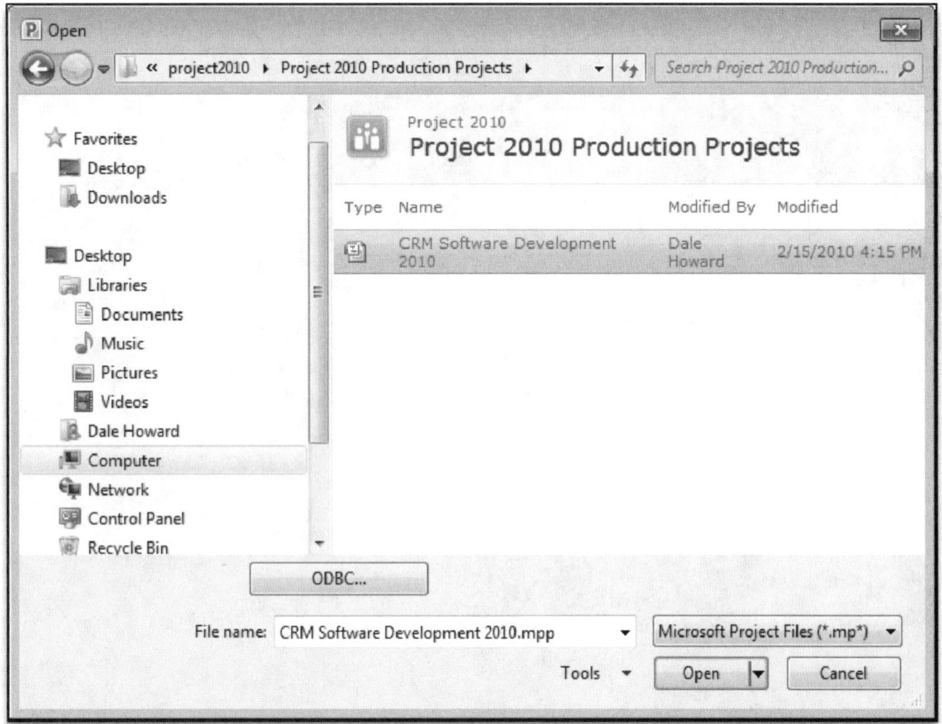

Figure 3 - 44: Open a project in a SharePoint document library

To provide you with faster access to the SharePoint site, save the URL of the site in the *Favorites* list in the left side of the *Save As* dialog or the *Open* dialog.

Sharing a Project via E-Mail

Microsoft Project 2010 allows you to send a project file via e-mail to multiple users. Each user receives an individual copy of the project and can comment on the file. To send a file via e-mail, click the *File* tab and then click the *Save & Send* tab. On the *Save & Send* page, click the *Send as Attachment* button. The system opens a new blank e-mail message with the project file attached, as shown in Figure 3 - 45.

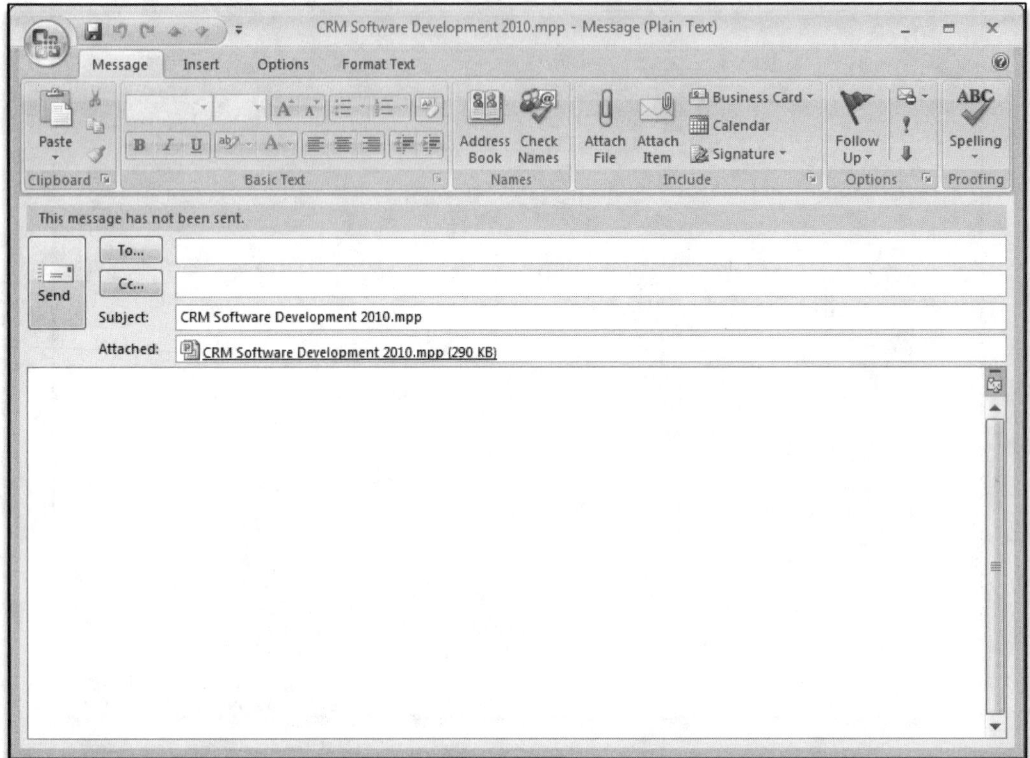

Figure 3 - 45: E-mail message with Microsoft Project 2010 file attached

Notice in Figure 3 - 45 that Microsoft Project 2010 enters the name of the attached project file in the *Subject* field of the outgoing e-mail message. Select one or more recipients and enter e-mail message text as needed. Click the *Send* button to send your email.

Warning: If you do not have your e-mail application running when you send the e-mail message with the attachment, your e-mail application does not send the outgoing e-mail message until the next time you launch the application.

Module 04

What's New – Task Planning

Learning Objectives

After completing this module, you will be able to:

- Use the auto-wrap feature to wrap the text of long task names
- Insert summary tasks and milestone tasks
- Use Manually Scheduled and Auto Scheduled tasks
- Understand warning and suggestion messages about Manually Scheduled tasks
- Use the Task Inspector

Inside Module 04

Auto-Wrapping Task Names **109**

Inserting Summary Tasks **109**

Inserting a Summary Task for Selected Tasks 110

Inserting a Milestone Task **111**

Using Manually Scheduled Tasks **112**

Linking Manually Scheduled Tasks 114

Understanding Schedule Warnings and Suggestions 117

Using the Respect Links Feature 118

Using the Task Inspector 118

Creating a Manually Scheduled Summary Task 120

Understanding Task Scheduling Changes **122**

Auto-Wrapping Task Names

During the task planning process, you see the new *Auto-Wrap Task Names* feature in Microsoft Project 2010 when you enter a task name that exceeds the width of the *Task Name* column. In all previous versions of the tool, the only way to auto-wrap task names was to manually increase the height of the task row until the task name wrapped completely within the cell. In Microsoft Project 2010, the software auto-wraps task names in cells when one of several events occurs:

- You manually type a task name that exceeds the width of the *Task Name* column and then press the *Enter* key to complete the data entry. The software automatically increases the row height for that task to wrap the task name within the cell.
- You paste a task name that exceeds the width of the *Task Name* column. The software automatically increases the row height for that task to wrap the task name within the cell.
- You manually decrease the width of the *Task Name* column. The software automatically increases the row height for **every** task with a name exceeding the width of the *Task Name* column.
- You manually increase the width of the *Task Name* column. The software automatically decreases the row height for that task and un-wraps the text.

Inserting Summary Tasks

Many organizations like to do "top down" task planning by creating summary tasks initially to represent Phase and Deliverable sections in the project, and then they add regular tasks to each summary section. In previous versions of Microsoft Project, "top down" task planning was difficult. In Microsoft Project 2010, however, "top down" task planning is made easier by using the new *Insert Summary Task* feature, particularly in combination with *Manually Scheduled* tasks.

To perform "top down" task planning in Microsoft Project 2010, click the *Insert Summary Task* button in the *Insert* section of the *Task* ribbon. The software inserts a new unnamed summary task and subtask, such as shown in Figure 4 - 1.

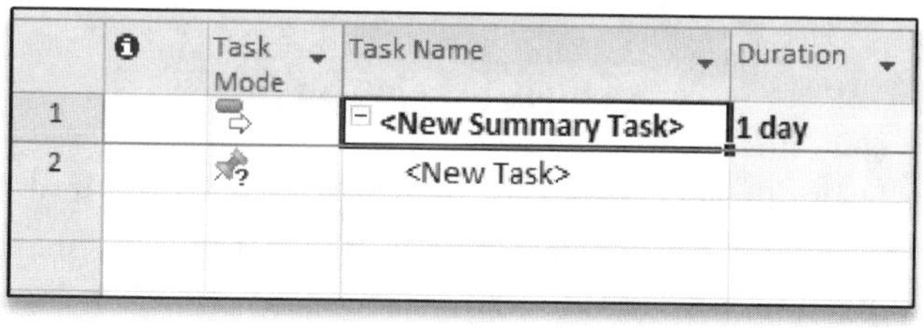

		Task Mode	Task Name	Duration
1			<New Summary Task>	1 day
2			<New Task>	

Figure 4 - 1: Newly Inserted Summary Task during "top down" task planning process

After inserting the new summary task and subtask pair, you should edit the name of the summary task, replacing the default value with the name of the Phase or Deliverable section it represents. Similarly, you eventually edit the name of the subtask and add additional subtasks as needed. You can leave the name of the subtask with its original <New Task> name as a placeholder for a future subtask until you are ready to add detail tasks to the summary section.

If you insert a summary task below another summary task or a subtask, Microsoft Project 2010 automatically indents the new summary task at the same level of indenture as the task immediately preceding it. This is the default behavior of the tool, and you cannot change it. For example, Figure 4 - 2 shows a new summary task and subtask pair inserted after the Design task. Notice that the system indented the new summary task at the same level as the Design task preceding it.

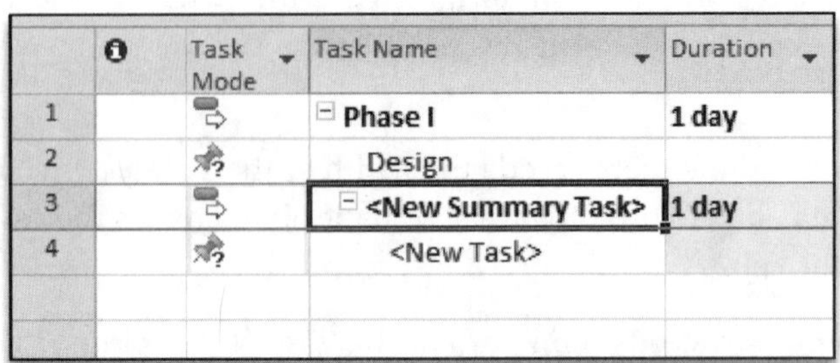

		Task Mode	Task Name	Duration
1			Phase I	1 day
2			Design	
3			<New Summary Task>	1 day
4			<New Task>	

Figure 4 - 2: New summary task indented at same level as the Design task preceding it

To resolve the indenting situation shown in Figure 4 - 2, select the new summary task and then click the *Outdent Task* button in the *Schedule* section of the *Task* ribbon.

Inserting a Summary Task for Selected Tasks

In addition to inserting summary tasks during "top down" task planning, Microsoft Project 2010 makes it easier to insert a summary task for a selected group of subtasks. For example, consider the set of four tasks shown in Figure 4 - 3. I want to show that each of these four tasks is a subtask in the Phase I section of the project.

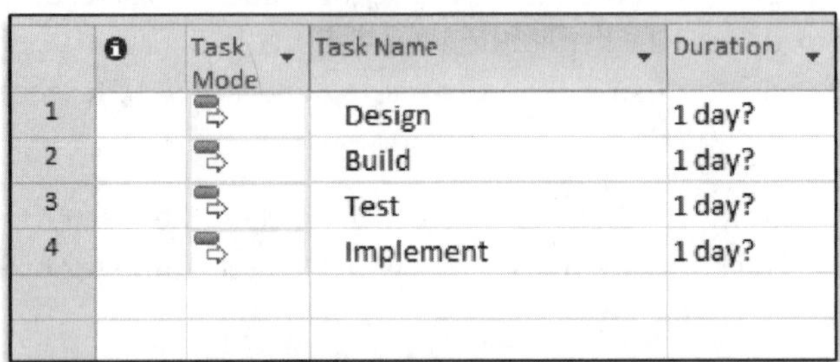

		Task Mode	Task Name	Duration
1			Design	1 day?
2			Build	1 day?
3			Test	1 day?
4			Implement	1 day?

Figure 4 - 3: Four tasks ready for inclusion as subtasks of Phase I

To make these tasks a subtask in the Phase I section of the project, select the four tasks and then click the *Insert Summary Task* button on the *Task* ribbon. Microsoft Project 2010 automatically inserts a new unnamed summary task and indents the four tasks as subtasks of the summary section, as shown in Figure 4 - 4. You can then rename the new summary task as desired.

	Task Mode	Task Name	Duration
1		**<New Summary Task>**	**1 day?**
2		Design	1 day?
3		Build	1 day?
4		Test	1 day?
5		Implement	1 day?

Figure 4 - 4: Four tasks inserted as subtasks below the new unnamed summary task

Inserting a Milestone Task

To create a Milestone task in any previous version of Microsoft Project, users first added the task and then set the task Duration to 0 days, which caused the software to convert the task to a Milestone task. To create a Milestone task in Microsoft Project 2010, click the *Milestone* button in the *Insert* section of the *Task* ribbon. The software automatically inserts an unnamed milestone task with a duration value of 0 days, as shown in Figure 4 - 5.

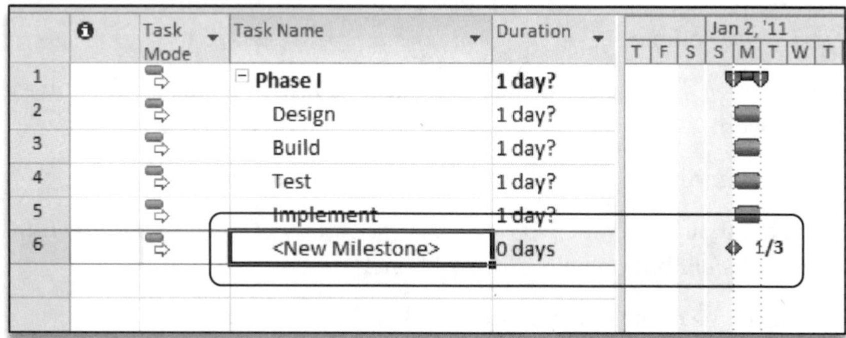

	Task Mode	Task Name	Duration
1		**Phase I**	**1 day?**
2		Design	1 day?
3		Build	1 day?
4		Test	1 day?
5		Implement	1 day?
6		<New Milestone>	0 days

Figure 4 - 5: New inserted Milestone task

After inserting a new milestone task, you should rename it. For the new milestone I inserted in the project shown Figure 4 - 5, I might rename the milestone task as Phase I Complete, for example.

Hands On Exercise

Exercise 4-1

Work with auto-wrapping task names and insert top-down Summary Tasks and Milestones.

1. Navigate to your student folder and open the **Task Planning 1.mpp** sample file.
2. Select task IDs #1-4 (from the *Conduct Needs Analysis* task to the *Develop Delivery Timeline* task).

3. Click the *Task* tab and then click the *Insert Summary Task* button in the *Insert* section of the *Task* ribbon.

Notice how Microsoft Project 2010 inserts a new unnamed summary task and indents the selected tasks as subtasks automatically.

4. Change the name of the new summary task to *Analysis and Software Requirements.*
5. Select the first blank row after the *Develop Delivery Timeline* task and then click the *Insert Summary Task* button on the *Task* ribbon.

Notice how Microsoft Project 2010 inserts a new unnamed summary task with an unnamed subtask as well. Notice that the new summary task is indented at the same level as the *Develop Delivery Timeline* Task.

6. Click the *Outdent Task* button in the *Schedule* section of the *Task* ribbon.
7. Change the name of the new summary task to *Design.*
8. Change the name of the new subtask to *Develop Design Specifications.*
9. On the blank line after the *Develop Specifications* task, add a new task called *Develop Prototype Based on Design Specifications.*

Notice how Microsoft Project 2010 auto-wrapped the task name of the new task because it exceeded the width of the *Task Name* column.

10. Select the *Design* summary task and then click the *Insert Milestone* button in the *Insert* section of the *Task* ribbon.
11. Change the name of the new milestone task to *Analysis Complete.*
12. Select the blank line after the *Develop Prototype Based on Design Specifications* task and then click the *Insert Milestone* button on the *Task* ribbon.
13. Change the name of the new milestone task to *Design Complete.*
14. Save and close your **Task Planning 1.mpp** sample file.

Using Manually Scheduled Tasks

By now you must be more than a little curious about how you actually use what is probably the most important change to Microsoft Project 2010 in many years, *Manually Scheduled* tasks. You may also be wondering why Microsoft chose to introduce manual scheduling, and if you are a dynamic scheduling purist, you might even be close to convulsions when you think about how uncontrollable a schedule can be using this feature.

One of Microsoft's goals in introducing *Manually Scheduled* tasks is to lower the barrier to entry for users making the transition from managing their projects in Excel so that they can start to learn how to use a scheduling tool. The thinking is that this at least gets them into the correct environment. When tasks are set to *Manually Scheduled* mode, entering task data into a project doesn't cause dates to move unless the user specifies them. Users who are untrained in the behaviors of the Microsoft Project scheduling engine are typically put off by the scheduling engine's insistence on remaining in control of dates in all prior versions of Microsoft Project.

This change also addresses another previously unmet Microsoft Project user need by providing a way to represent tasks where scheduling information is unavailable such as during early phase planning, and it also helps Project apply better to real-world scenarios such as scheduling projects where agile methodologies are in use. Tasks that are *Manually Scheduled* do not require duration, start date, or finish date data, thereby providing complete flexibility. As you learned in Module 03, among your first steps in specifying options settings for a new project is to set the *Task Mode* setting to either the *Manually Scheduled* or *Auto Scheduled* option. Unless you specify otherwise, Microsoft Project 2010 sets the *Task Mode* to the *Manually Scheduled* option for all tasks in every new project. As you create your task list, the software sets each new task to the *Task Mode* setting you specified.

During the task planning process, you can designate any task as either a *Manually Scheduled* task or an *Auto Scheduled* task. To specify the *Task Mode* setting for any task, complete the following steps:

1. Click the *Task* tab to display the *Task* ribbon.
2. Select the task(s) whose *Task Mode* setting you want to change.
3. Click the *Manually Schedule* button or the *Auto Schedule* button on the *Task* ribbon.

> To specify the *Task Mode* setting for an individual task, you can also select a cell in the *Task Mode* column for the task, click the pick list in the *Task Mode* cell, and choose either *Manually Scheduled* or *Auto Scheduled* from the list.

Figure 4 - 6 shows a project in which I included four *Auto Scheduled* tasks (Design, Build, Test, and Implement) and two *Manually Scheduled* tasks (Rebuild and Retest). Notice the following:

- Microsoft Project 2010 displays a unique indicator to the left of each task in the *Indicators* column to identify the *Task Mode* setting for each task.
- The Rebuild and Retest tasks have no values in the *Duration, Start,* or *Finish* columns.
- The *Gantt Chart* view does not include Gantt bars for these two *Manually Scheduled* tasks.

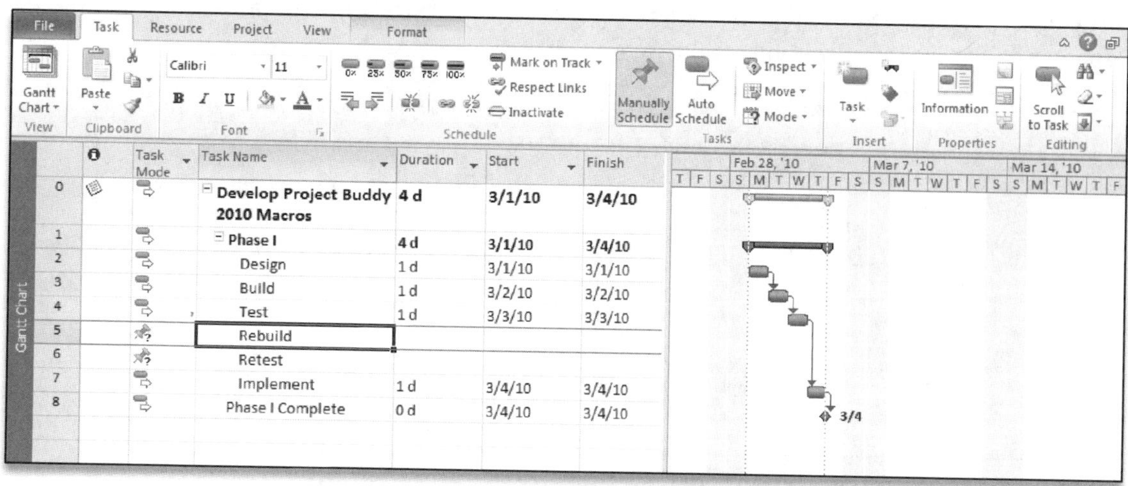

Figure 4 - 6: New project includes both Manually Scheduled tasks and Auto Scheduled tasks

When you specify any task as a *Manually Scheduled* task, Microsoft Project 2010 allows you to specify values in the *Duration, Start,* and *Finish* columns in a number of ways, including:

- Specify no duration, start, or finish values until you have an estimated duration, start, or finish date.

- Enter text information in the *Duration* column about an approximate duration, and enter text information in the *Start* and *Finish* columns about approximate start and finish dates.
- Enter an estimated duration in the *Duration* column, and/or estimated dates in the *Start* and *Finish* columns.

In addition to typing text to enter an approximate Duration, Start date, or Finish date, you can enter other textual information, such as "TBD" or "Decision by 11/01/10."

In Figure 4 - 6 shown previously, you can see an example of two *Manually Scheduled* tasks with no duration, start, or finish date information. When you create a new *Manually Scheduled* task, Microsoft Project 2010 leaves the *Duration, Start,* and *Finish* columns blank. In Figure 4 - 7, you see an example of two *Manually Scheduled* tasks with approximate duration values (entered as "About 1w" and "About 2d") and approximate start dates (entered as "Late May" and "Early June").

4			Test	1 d	3/3/10	3/3/10
5			Rebuild	About 1w	Late May	
6			Retest	About 2d	Early June	
7			Implement	1 d	3/4/10	3/4/10

Figure 4 - 7: Approximate Duration and Start values for Manually Scheduled tasks

If you enter a valid duration value (versus an approximate duration) for a *Manually Scheduled* task, Microsoft Project 2010 displays a "highlighted" Gantt bar for the task. If you also enter a valid date value in the *Start* or *Finish* columns, the software displays a silhouetted teal-colored Gantt bar for the task. In Figure 4 - 8, notice that I entered a valid duration value for the Rebuild and Retest tasks, and specified a valid date value in the *Start* column for only the Retest task. Notice the two different types of Gantt bars for these tasks. Notice also the different indicators shown in the *Indicators* column for the Rebuild and Retest tasks.

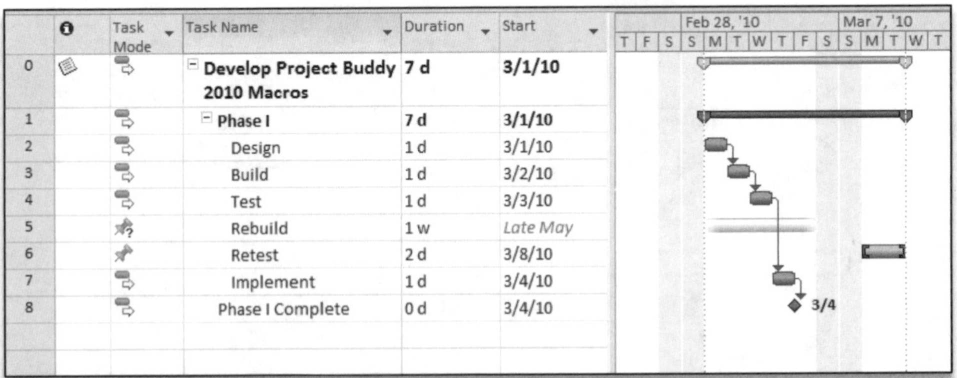

	Task Mode	Task Name	Duration	Start
0		Develop Project Buddy 2010 Macros	7 d	3/1/10
1		Phase I	7 d	3/1/10
2		Design	1 d	3/1/10
3		Build	1 d	3/2/10
4		Test	1 d	3/3/10
5		Rebuild	1 w	Late May
6		Retest	2 d	3/8/10
7		Implement	1 d	3/4/10
8		Phase I Complete	0 d	3/4/10

Figure 4 - 8: Manually Scheduled tasks with Duration and Start date values specified

Linking Manually Scheduled Tasks

If you specify task dependencies by linking *Manually Scheduled* tasks with predecessor and successor tasks, Microsoft Project 2010 **initially schedules** each *Manually Scheduled* task as follows:

- If you do not enter duration, start, or finish values for a *Manually Scheduled* task, the software sets the duration of the task to the default value of 1d and then calculates the start and finish dates accordingly, based on its dependency relationship with its Predecessor task.
- If you enter an approximate duration on a *Manually Scheduled* task, the software maintains the approximate duration, but treats the task as if it has a duration value of 1 day, and then calculates the start and finish dates accordingly.
- If you enter a valid duration value on a *Manually Scheduled* task, the software maintains the valid duration, and then calculates the start and finish dates accordingly.
- If you enter an approximate start and/or finish date on a *Manually Scheduled* task, the software replaces the approximate date values for calculated dates in the *Start* and *Finish* columns.
- If you enter a valid start date on a *Manually Scheduled* task, the software **ignores** the start date and calculates the start date based on based on its dependency relationship with its predecessor task.
- If you enter a valid finish date on a *Manually Scheduled* task, the software honors the finish date, calculates the duration of the task based on the scheduled start date and the valid finish date, and then schedules the task accordingly.

To understand how the system initially schedules *Manually Scheduled* tasks when you link them with predecessor and successor tasks, first examine the *Manually Scheduled* tasks shown in Figure 4 - 9. Notice that Task A contains no duration, start, or finish information. Notice that Task B has an approximate duration while Task C has a valid duration value. Notice that Task D has an approximate start date, while Task E has a valid start date value. Notice that Task F has an approximate finish date, while Task G has a valid finish date value. Also notice the unusual bracket-shaped Gantt bars for the two tasks that have a valid start or finish date.

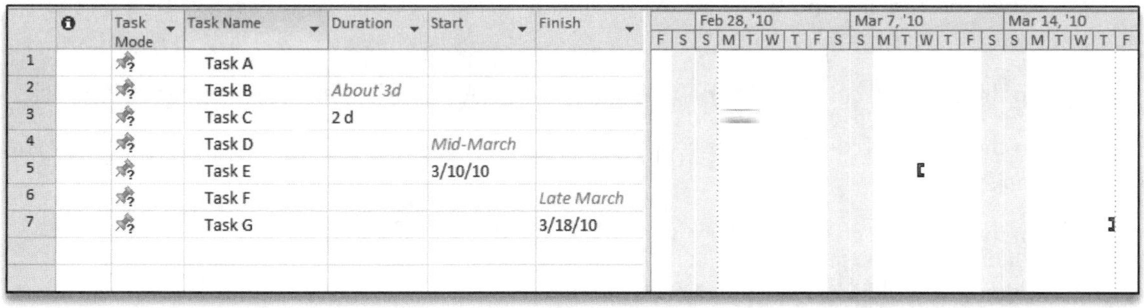

	Task Mode	Task Name	Duration	Start	Finish
1		Task A			
2		Task B	*About 3d*		
3		Task C	2 d		
4		Task D		*Mid-March*	
5		Task E		3/10/10	
6		Task F			*Late March*
7		Task G			3/18/10

Figure 4 - 9: Manually Scheduled tasks BEFORE setting task dependencies

Now examine the same set of *Manually Scheduled* tasks after I link them with Finish-to-Start (FS) dependencies in Figure 4 - 10.

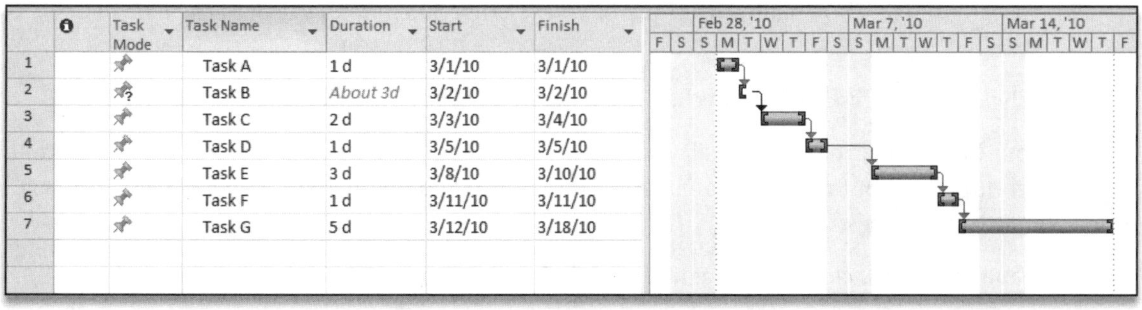

	Task Mode	Task Name	Duration	Start	Finish
1		Task A	1 d	3/1/10	3/1/10
2		Task B	*About 3d*	3/2/10	3/2/10
3		Task C	2 d	3/3/10	3/4/10
4		Task D	1 d	3/5/10	3/5/10
5		Task E	3 d	3/8/10	3/10/10
6		Task F	1 d	3/11/10	3/11/10
7		Task G	5 d	3/12/10	3/18/10

Figure 4 - 10: Manually Scheduled tasks AFTER setting task dependencies

In Figure 4 - 10, notice that the software behaved exactly as I described in the previous bulleted list. Take special notice of how the software scheduled Task G. The software calculated the start date of the task, honored the finish date of the task, and calculated a 5-day duration between these two dates.

When you link *Manually Scheduled* tasks using task dependencies, the software calculates the **intial schedule** of each task. If you later change the duration, start, or finsh date of a *Manually Scheduled* task, Microsoft Project 2010 **does not** recalculate the schedule of the *Manually Scheduled* task. I discuss this behavior in the next section of this Module.

Hands On Exercise

Exercise 4-2

Work with Manually Scheduled tasks.

1. Navigate to your student folder and open the **Task Planning 2.mpp** sample file.
2. Select task IDs #8-11 (from the *Develop Design Specifications* task to the *Design Complete* milestone).
3. Click the *Task* tab and then click the *Manually Schedule* button in the *Tasks* section of the *Task* ribbon.
4. In the *Duration* column, enter a value of *About 5d* for the *Develop Design Specifications* task.
5. In the *Duration* column, enter a value of *5d* for the *Develop Prototype Based on Design Specifications* task.
6. In the *Duration* column, enter a value of *5d* for the *Review Prototype with Client* task.
7. Pull the split bar to the right edge of the *Start* column.
8. In the *Start* column, enter a value of *Early February* for the *Review Prototype with Client* task.

Notice the different types of Gantt bars drawn by Microsoft Project 2010 for each type of *Manually Scheduled* task.

9. Select task IDs #8-11 again (from the *Develop Design Specifications* task to the *Design Complete* milestone).
10. Click the *Link Tasks* button in the *Schedule* section of the *Task* ribbon.

Notice how Microsoft Project 2010 calculates start and finish dates for the two *Manually Scheduled* tasks with valid durations, but does not calculate a start or finish date for the *Manually Scheduled* task with an approximate duration

11. Save but do not close your **Task Planning 2.mpp** sample file.

Understanding Schedule Warnings and Suggestions

When you link *Manually Scheduled* tasks and then later change the project schedule, Microsoft Project 2010 recalculates the schedule for **only** *Auto Scheduled* tasks. It **does not** recalculate the schedule of *Manually Scheduled* tasks. Instead, the software calculates a likely start and finish date in the background, and then compares the current start and finish dates with the likely start and finish dates. If there is a schedule discrepancy, the software displays a *Warning* on that task by applying a red wavy underline to the date in the *Finish* column and by formatting the Gantt bar with a dotted outline. For example, in the schedule shown in Figure 4 - 11, I manually entered a duration value on the Design, Build, and Test tasks. This resulted in a schedule discrepancy on the Rebuild task, and the warnings from Microsoft Project 2010.

	Task Name	Duration	Start	Finish
0	Develop Project Buddy 2010 Macros	11 d	3/1/10	3/15/10
1	Phase I	11 d	3/1/10	3/15/10
2	Design	2 d	3/1/10	3/2/10
3	Build	3 d	3/3/10	3/5/10
4	Test	1 d	3/8/10	3/8/10
5	Rebuild	1 w	3/4/10	3/10/10
6	Retest	2 d	3/11/10	3/12/10
7	Implement	1 d	3/15/10	3/15/10
8	Phase I Complete	0 d	3/15/10	3/15/10

Figure 4 - 11: Schedule discrepancy Warning on a Manually Scheduled task

By default, Microsoft Project 2010 shows *Warnings* about schedule discrepancies on *Manually Scheduled* tasks; however, you can configure the software to show *Suggestions* about how to optimize your schedule as well. As I noted in Module 03, you can enable *Suggestions* by selecting the *Show task schedule suggestions* option on the *Schedule* page of the *Project Options* dialog. Remember that you can select to apply this option only to the current project or for all new projects. If you did not select this option in the *Project Options* dialog, you can select this option for the current project by clicking the *Inspect* pick list button on the *Task* ribbon and then selecting the *Show Suggestions* item, as shown in Figure 4 - 12.

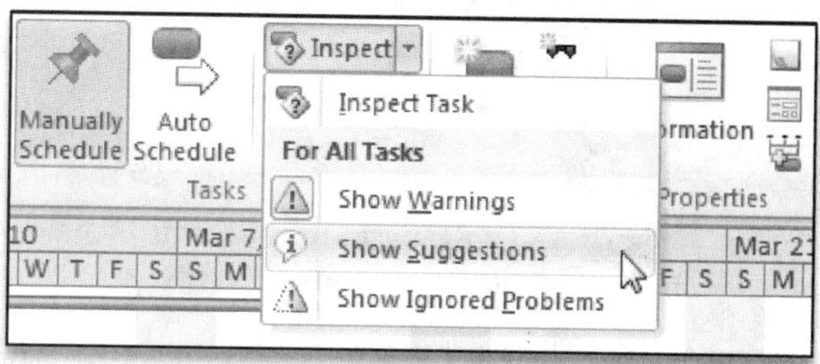

Figure 4 - 12: Enable optimization Suggestions for Manually Scheduled tasks

When you enable optimization *Suggestions*, Microsoft Project 2010 examines the current Start and Finish date for each *Manually Scheduled* task and looks for opportunities to optimize the schedule with an earlier start or finish date. If the software finds an opportunity for you to improve your schedule, the system displays a *Suggestion* for that task by applying a green wavy underline to the date in the *Finish* column. For example, in the schedule shown in Figure 4 - 13, I manually entered a start date of Wednesday, March 10 on the Rebuild task. This caused a gap between the finish date of the Test task and the start date of the Rebuild task, and resulted in an optimization *Suggestion* from Microsoft Project 2010.

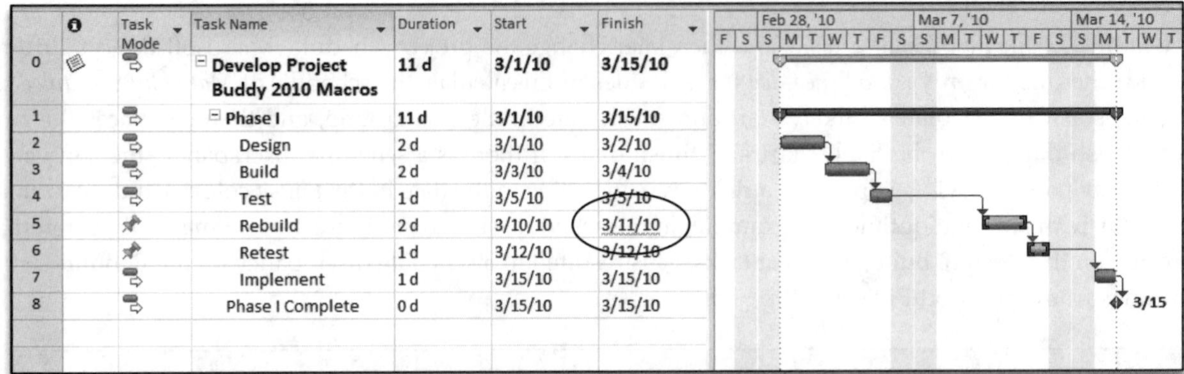

Figure 4 - 13: Optimization Suggestion on a Manually Scheduled task

When you float your mouse pointer over an optimization *Suggestion,* the system displays a tool tip "Potential scheduling optimization. Right-click to see options." The shortcut menu provides three options for acting on the *Suggestion,* including the *Fix in Task Inspector, Respect Links* and *Ignore Problems for this Task* selections as shown in Figure 4 - 14.

Using the Respect Links Feature

Microsoft Project 2010 allows you to respond to schedule *Warnings* and optimization *Suggestions* using the new *Respect Links* feature. To use this feature, right click in any cell containing a *Warning* or a *Suggestion.* The system displays the shortcut menu shown in Figure 4 - 14.

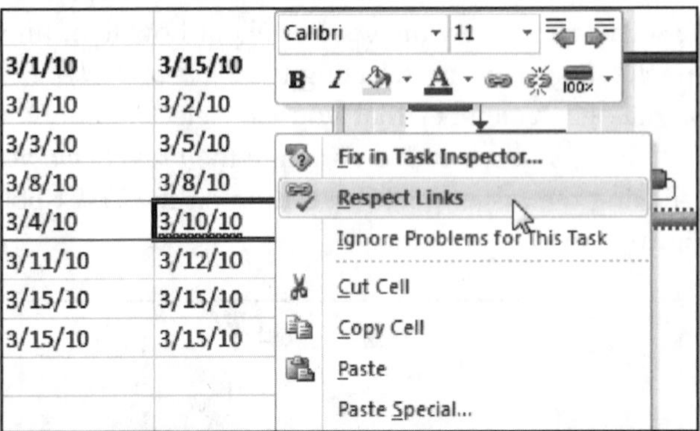

Figure 4 - 14: Respect Links item in shortcut menu for a schedule Warning

When you click the *Respect Links* item on the shortcut menu for a schedule *Warning* or optimization *Suggestion,* Microsoft Project 2010 changes the start and finish dates for the task to calculated start and finish dates, and then removes the schedule *Warning* or *Suggestion.* Keep in mind that this action might result in a new schedule *Warning* or optimization *Suggestion* on other *Manually Scheduled* tasks linked to the rescheduled task!

Using the Task Inspector

The *Task Inspector* is a newly revamped feature of Microsoft Project 2010 evolving from the *Task Drivers Pane* found in Microsoft Project 2007. The *Task Inspector* offers more functionality than its 2007 predecessor. You can use the *Task Inspector* to examine both *Manually Scheduled* tasks and *Auto Scheduled* tasks to resolve schedule problems and to determine the reason for the current scheduled Start date of any task. To display the *Task Inspector,* click the *Inspect* button in the *Tasks* section of the *Task* ribbon. The system displays the *Task Inspector* on the left side of the application window.

Depending on the type of task you select, the *Task Inspector* includes either three sections or one section only. For example, Figure 4 - 15 shows the *Task Inspector* for a *Manually Scheduled* task with a schedule *Warning*. Notice that first section displays the reason for the schedule *Warning* (the task needs to be delayed by 3 days). The *Repair Options* section offers the *Respect Links* button and the *Auto Schedule* button to resolve the schedule problem. The *Factors Affecting Task* section reveals the reason for the scheduled start date of the selected task.

Figure 4 - 16 shows the *Task Inspector* for a task with an optimization *Suggestion*. Notice that only the first section differs from the *Task Inspector* shown in Figure 4 - 15, and reveals the reason for the optimization *Suggestion* (the task can start 2 days earlier than currently scheduled). Figure 4 - 17 shows the *Task Inspector* for an *Auto Scheduled* task and contains only a single section, the *Factors Affecting Task* section. To close the *Task Inspector* click the *Close* (**X**) button in the upper right corner of the pane.

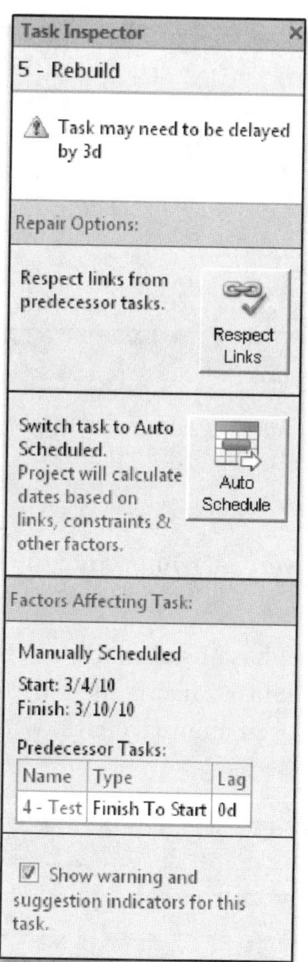

Figure 4 - 15: Task Inspector for a task with a Warning

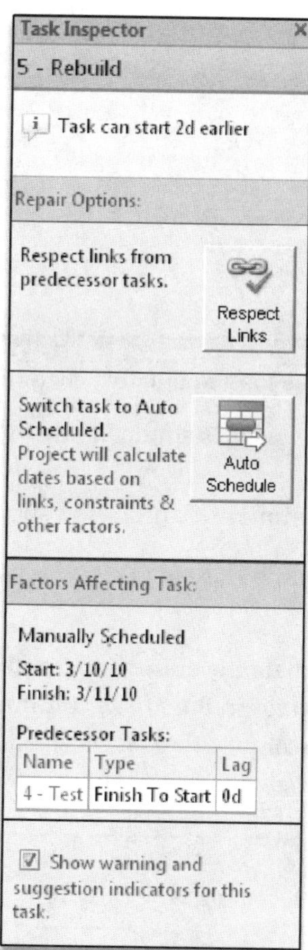

Figure 4 - 16: Task Inspector for a task with a Suggestion

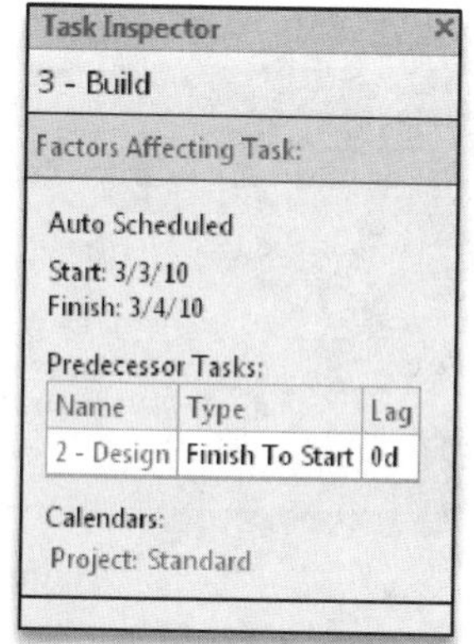

Figure 4 - 17: Task Inspector for an Auto Scheduled task

For *Auto Scheduled* tasks, the *Task Inspector* tool reveals the reason for the current scheduled start date of any task. Possible reasons can include task dependencies, non-working time on a calendar, a task calendar applied to the task, constraints, and even leveling delays.

Creating a Manually Scheduled Summary Task

In addition to creating *Manually Scheduled* tasks, Microsoft Project 2010 also allows you to create Manually Scheduled summary tasks. For example, Figure 4 - 18 shows a project with a *Manually Scheduled* summary task with *Manually Scheduled* subtasks. Notice in Figure 4 - 18 that the software displays a different type of summary Gantt bar for *Manually Scheduled* summary tasks than it does for *Auto Scheduled* summary tasks.

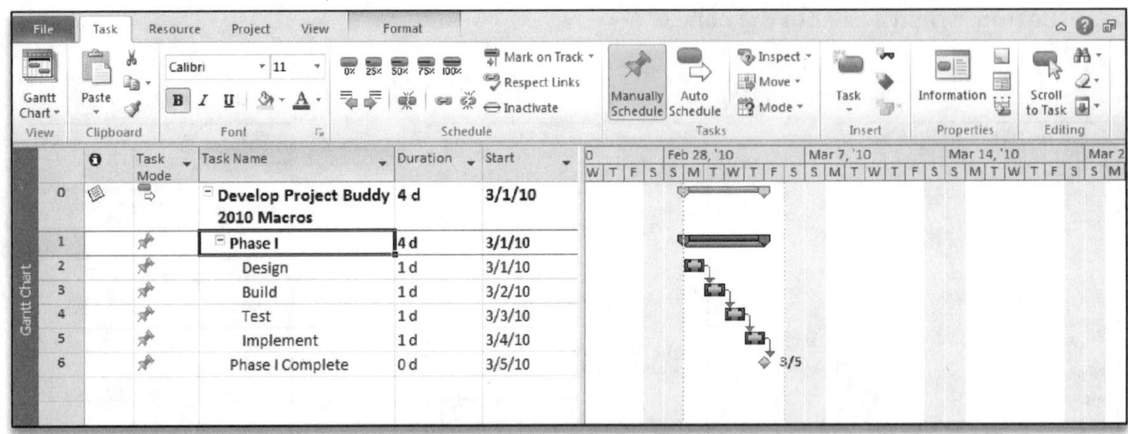

Figure 4 - 18: Phase I is a Manually Scheduled summary task

The behavior of *Manually Scheduled* summary tasks is similar to the behavior of *Manually Scheduled* tasks, but with a few differences, including:

- Microsoft Project 2010 formats the summary Gantt bar to show schedule *Warnings*.
- Microsoft Project 2010 shows a schedule *Warning* on the finish date of every task impacting the *Manually Scheduled* summary task.

Notice in Figure 4 - 19 that the software formats the summary Gantt bar for the Phase I summary task to show a schedule *Warning*, and shows schedule *Warnings* in the *Finish* column for each subtask causing the schedule problem. To resolve the schedule problems, you can use the *Task Inspector* on the Phase I summary task, which offers the option to extend the duration of the *Manually Scheduled* summary task.

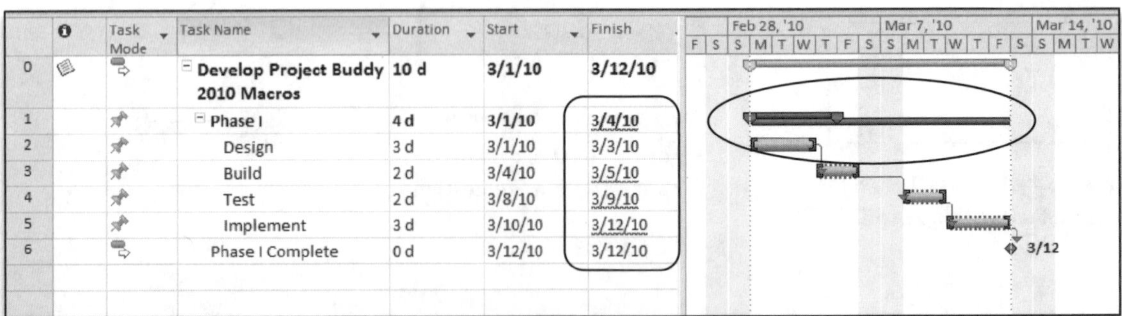

Figure 4 - 19: Schedule Warnings on a Manually Scheduled summary task and subtasks

Hands On Exercise

Exercise 4-3

Study schedule Warnings and use the Task Inspector.

1. Return to your **Task Planning 2.mpp** sample file.
2. Pull your split bar to the right edge of the *Finish* column.
3. Change the duration of the *Develop Design Specifications* task to *5d.*

Notice the schedule *Warning* (red wavy underline) on the finish date of the *Develop Prototype Based on Design Specifications* task.

4. Select the *Develop Prototype Based on Design Specifications* task and then click the *Inspect* button in the *Tasks* section of the *Task* ribbon.
5. In the *Task Inspector* pane, click the *Respect Links* button to resolve the scheduling problem.
6. Select the *Review Prototype with Client* task and then click the *Respect Links* button to resolve the new scheduling problem on this task.
7. Select the *Design Complete* task and then click the *Respect Links* button to resolve the new scheduling problem on this milestone task.
8. Click the *Close* button (**X**) in the upper right corner of the *Task Inspector* pane to close it.
9. Select the *Analysis and Software Requirements* summary task and then click the *Manually Schedule* button in the *Task* ribbon.
10. Change the duration of the *Develop Delivery Timeline* task to *3d.*

Notice the schedule *Warning* (red wavy underline) on the finish date of the *Analysis and Software Requirements* summary task, and notice its unusual Gantt bar as well.

11. Select the *Analysis and Software Requirements* summary task and then click the *Inspect* button on the *Task* ribbon.
12. In the *Task Inspector* pane, click the *Extend Finish* button to resolve the scheduling problem.
13. Click the *Close* button (**X**) in the upper right corner of the *Task Inspector* pane to close it.
14. Save and close your **Task Planning 2.mpp** sample file.

Understanding Task Scheduling Changes

One of the major changes in Microsoft Project 2010 is the way the software responds when you manually enter a start date and/or finish date on a task. In previous versions of the software, when you manually entered a start date on a task, the system added a *Start No Earlier Than* (SNET) constraint on the task, using the date you entered as the constraint date. When you manually entered a finish date on a task, the system added a *Finish No Earlier Than* (FNET) constraint, using the date you entered as the constraint date. If you manually entered both a Start date and a Finish date on a task, the software sets either a SNET constraint or a FNET constraint, depending on which date you entered last.

In Microsoft Project 2010, when you manually enter only a start date on a task, the system continues to add a *Start No Earlier Than* (SNET) constraint on the task, using the date you entered as the constraint date. Likewise, when you manually enter only a finish date on a task, the system continues to add a *Finish No Earlier Than* (FNET) constraint on the task, using the date you entered as the Constraint Date.

The major change in behavior happens when you manually enter **both** a start date and a finish date on a task: Microsoft Project 2010 automatically calculates the duration of the task. This behavior is a radical change from all previous versions of the software. In addition, when you manually enter both a start date and a finish date on a task, the software sets either a SNET constraint or a FNET constraint, depending on which date you entered last.

Hands On Exercise

Exercise 4-4

Learn more about task scheduling changes in Microsoft Project 2010.

1. Navigate to your student folder and open the **Task Planning 3.mpp** sample file.
2. For the *Develop Delivery Timeline* task, enter *01/20/2014* in the *Start* column.
3. When warned in a *Planning Wizard* dialog, select the **second option**, *Move the task and keep the link,* and then click the *OK* button.
4. For the *Develop Delivery Timeline* task, enter *01/22/2014* in the *Finish* column.

Notice how Microsoft Project 2010 calculates the duration of the task automatically.

5. Save and close your **Task Planning 3.mpp** sample file.

Module 05

What's New – Resource and Assignment Planning

Learning Objectives

After completing this module, you will be able to:

- Insert a Work, Material, or Cost resource in the Resource Sheet
- Assign resources to tasks using the Task Entry view and the Assign Resources dialog
- Analyze resource allocation in the Team Planner view
- Use the Team Planner view to locate and level resource overallocations
- Move tasks in the Team Planner view
- Customize the Team Planner view
- Print the Team Planner view
- Locate and resolve resource overallocations

Inside Module 05

Inserting New Resources in the Resource Sheet View 125

Assigning Resources to Tasks 126

Using the Task Entry View 126

Using the Assign Resources Dialog 127

Using the Team Planner View 131

Leveling an Overallocated Resource in the Team Planner View 133

Dragging Tasks in the Team Planner View 135

Changing Schedule Information in the Team Planner View 137

Customizing the Team Planner View 140

Printing the Team Planner View 144

Detecting and Resolving Resource Overallocations 146

Inserting New Resources in the Resource Sheet View

After you complete task planning, you are ready to begin resource planning. During the resource planning process, you first build the team of resources to work on tasks in your project. Microsoft Project 2010, like its 2007 predecessor, offers Work, Material, and Cost resource types. A new feature in the software, the *Add Resources Picklist,* allows you to insert a new resource in the *Resource Sheet* view, by selecting a resource Type. To insert a new resource in your project, complete the following steps:

1. Click the *Resource* tab to display the *Resource* ribbon.
2. In the *View* section of the *Resource* ribbon, click the *View* pick list button and select the *Resource Sheet* view.
3. In the *Insert* section of the *Resource* ribbon, click the *Add Resources* pick list button shown in Figure 5 - 1.

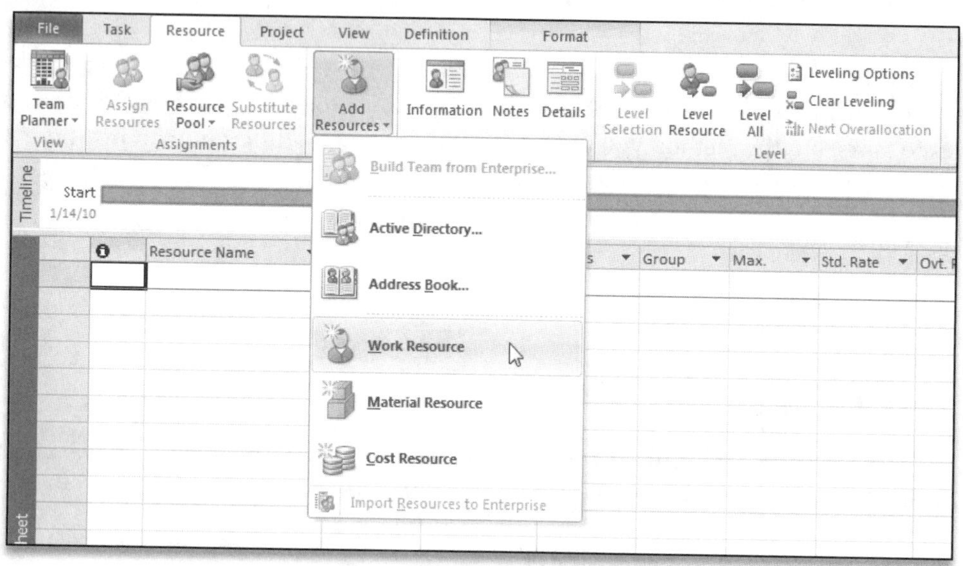

Figure 5 - 1: Add Resources pick list

4. On the *Add Resources* pick list, select the *Work Resource, Material Resource,* or *Cost Resource* item. Microsoft Project 2010 inserts a new resource of the type you selected. Notice in Figure 5 - 2 that I created one new resource of each type (Work, Material, and Cost).

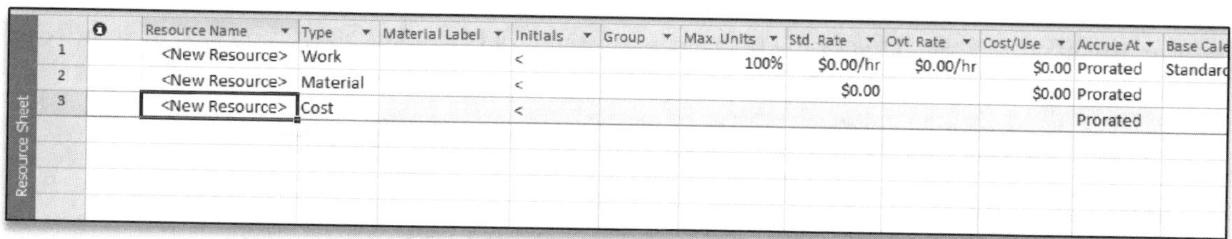

	Resource Name	Type	Material Label	Initials	Group	Max. Units	Std. Rate	Ovt. Rate	Cost/Use	Accrue At	Base Cale
1	<New Resource>	Work		<		100%	$0.00/hr	$0.00/hr	$0.00	Prorated	Standard
2	<New Resource>	Material		<			$0.00		$0.00	Prorated	
3	<New Resource>	Cost		<						Prorated	

Figure 5 - 2: Work, Cost, and Material resources inserted in a project

When you insert a new resource using the *Add Resources* pick list, Microsoft Project 2010 creates the new resource by inserting the name *<New Resource>* in the *Resource Name* field, inserting the < symbol in the *Initials* field, and selecting the *Prorated* value in the *Accrue At* field for all three types of resources. For a *Work Resource,* the system also selects the *Work* value in the *Type* field, defaults the *Max. Units* field value to *100%*, enters *$0.00/hr* in the *Std. Rate* and *Ovt. Rate* fields, enters *$0.00* in the *Cost/Use* field, and selects the *Standard* calendar in the *Base Calendar* field. For a *Material Resource,* the system selects the *Material* value in the *Type* field and enters *$0.00* in the *Std. Rate* and *Cost/Use* fields. For a *Cost Resource,* the system selects the *Cost* value in the *Type* field. After you insert any of the three types of resources, you must rename the resource and provide any other basic and custom resource information you want to record for the selected resource.

When you insert a new *Cost Resource*, the system creates an *Expense Cost Resource* automatically. If you need to create a new *Cost Resource* as a *Budget Cost Resource*, double-click the name of the *Cost Resource* and select the *Budget* option on the *General* page of the *Resource Information* dialog.

Assigning Resources to Tasks

After you enter project team members in the *Resource Sheet* view of your project, you are ready to assign team members to tasks. Like all previous versions of the tool, Microsoft Project 2010 offers two powerful tools for assigning resources to tasks, but the method you use to apply these tools is different than in all previous versions of the software. These two powerful resource assignment tools are:

- *Task Entry* view
- *Assign Resources* dialog

Using the Task Entry View

The *Task Entry* view is the most powerful way to assign resources to tasks because it allows you to control all of the following assignment actions and attributions in a single location:

- Assigning multiple resources simultaneously, and specify different *Units* and *Work* values for each resource.
- Specifying the *Duration* of the task.
- Setting the *Task Type* for the task to determine whether the software fixes or "locks" the *Units, Work,* or *Duration* value for the task.
- Setting the *Effort Driven* status of the task to determine what happens when you add or remove resources on the task.
- Setting the Task Mode for the task as either *Manually Scheduled* or *Auto Scheduled.*

To apply the *Task Entry* view, complete the following steps:

1. Click the *Task* tab and then click the *Gantt Chart* button if you do not have the *Gantt Chart* view displayed currently.
2. Click the *View* tab and select the *Details* checkbox in the *Split View* section of the *View* ribbon. Microsoft Project 2010 displays the *Task Entry* view, shown in Figure 5 - 3.

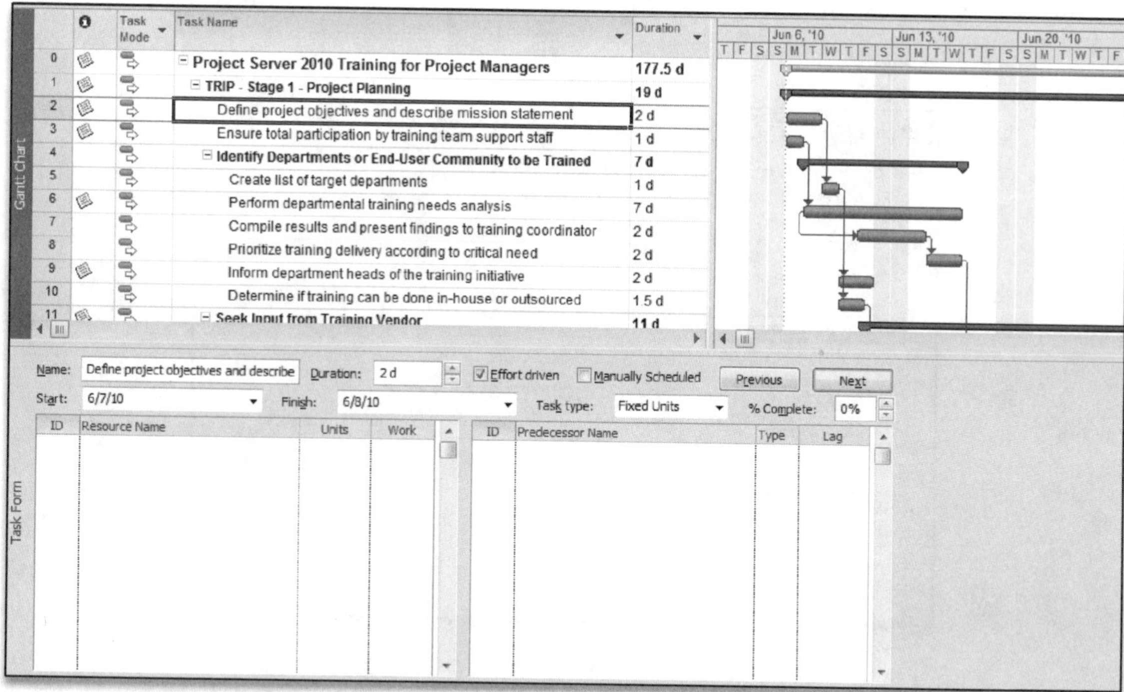

Figure 5 - 3: Task Entry view

As with all previous versions of Microsoft Project, the *Task Entry* view is a combination view consisting of two other views, each displayed in a separate pane. The *Task Entry* view includes the *Gantt Chart* view in the top pane and the *Task Form* view in the bottom pane. To assign resources to tasks using the *Task Entry* view, select a task in the top pane (the *Gantt Chart*), and then specify resource assignment information in the bottom pane (the *Task Form*). When you specify assignment information, the software allows you to select one or more resources, and to specify *Units* and *Work* values for each resource. After entering assignment information, click the *OK* button to assign the resources to the selected task.

Using the Assign Resources Dialog

The *Assign Resources* dialog is the second tool you use in the assignment process. The *Assign Resources* dialog is ideal for assigning resources to recurring tasks, such as meetings, because it allows you to select and assign multiple resources to the recurring task. The *Assign Resources* dialog is also ideal for assigning one or more resources to multiple tasks simultaneously. Finally, the *Assign Resources* dialog is ideal for replacing one resource with another, especially if the original resource completed some actual work on the task and you want to preserve the historical record. Although the *Assign Resources* dialog offers you a simple interface to assign resources to tasks quickly, keep in mind that it does not have all of the options available in the *Task Entry* view. Using the *Assign Resources* dialog, you cannot specify a the *Task Type*, specify the *Effort Driven* status, or set the *Task Mode* for a task; however, you can set up a task view that works as a companion to the *Assign Resources* dialog, exposing the data you need for your resourcing efforts.

To display the *Assign Resources* dialog, click the *Resource* tab and then click the *Assign Resources* button in the *Assignment* section of the *Resource* ribbon. Microsoft Project 2010 displays the *Assign Resources* dialog, as shown in Figure 5 - 4.

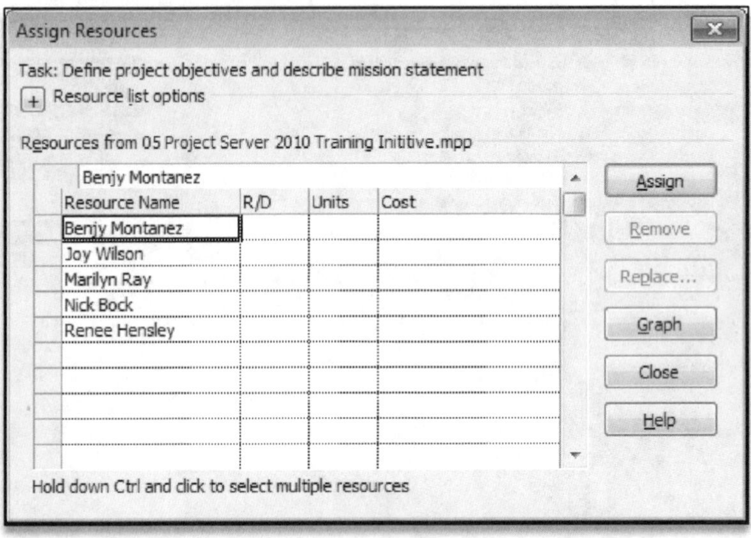

Figure 5 - 4: Assign Resources dialog

To assign resources using the *Assign Resources* dialog, select one or more tasks, select a single resource in the list of resources shown in the dialog, specify a *Units* value (if different than 100% Units), and then click the *Assign* button. If you want to assign multiple resources to one or more selected tasks, then select the resources while pressing the Control key or Shift key, and then click the *Assign* button.

You can also use the *Units* field to enter work values. When you enter a numeric value without following it with a symbol, the system assumes that you want to specify the *Units* value. When you enter a numeric value followed by the letter "h" or "d" with the quotes, the system interprets this as a work value. If your system is set to 8-hours of work per day, entering "1d" is the same as entering "8h" into the *Units* field.

Warning: Remember that when you use the Assign Resources dialog to assign multiple resources to a task, do not attempt to specify a different *Units* value for each individual resource. Doing so can lead to negative and unintended consequences!

Hands On Exercise

Exercise 5-1

Insert new Work, Material, and Cost resources in a project.

1. Navigate to your student folder and open the **Resource and Assignment Planning 1.mpp** sample file.
2. Click the *View* tab and then click the *Resource Sheet* button in the *Resource Views* section of the *View* ribbon.
3. Click the *Resource* tab to display the *Resource* ribbon.
4. Select the first blank row after the resource named Terry Uland.
5. Click the *Add Resources* pick list button in the *Insert* section of the *Resource* ribbon and select the *Work Resource* item on the list.
6. Change the name of the new Work resource to *Vicky Joslyn*, enter *VJ* in the *Initials* column, and enter *Test* in the *Group* field.
7. For Vicky Joslyn, enter *$50/h* in the *Std. Rate* column and *$75/h* in the *Ovt. Rate* column.
8. Select the first blank row after Vicky Joslyn.
9. Click the *Add Resources* pick list button in the *Resource* ribbon and select the *Material Resource* item.
10. Change the name of the new Material resource to *Training Supplies*, enter *Sets* in the *Material Label* column, and enter *TS* in the *Initials* column.
11. For the Training Supplies resource, enter *Supplies* in the *Group* column, and enter *$50* in the *Std. Rate* column.
12. Select the first blank row after the Training Supplies material resource.
13. Click the *Add Resources* pick list button in the *Resource* ribbon and select the *Cost Resource* item.
14. Change the name of the new Cost resource to *Software Licenses*, enter *SL* in the *Initials* column, and enter *Acct$* in the *Group* column.
15. Save but **do not** close your **Resource and Assignment Planning 1.mpp** sample file.

Exercise 5-2

Assign resources to tasks using the Assign Resources dialog.

1. Return to your **Resource and Assignment Planning 1.mpp** sample file.

2. In the *View* section of the *Resource* ribbon, click the *Team Planner* pick list button and select the *Gantt Chart* item on the list.

3. Select task ID #4, the *Load and Configure Software* task, and then click the *Assign Resources* button in the *Resource* ribbon.

4. In the *Assign Resources* dialog, select the *Software Licenses* resource and then click the *Assign* button.

5. In the *Assign Resources* dialog, enter **$15,000** in the *Cost* column for the Software Licenses resource and then press the **Enter** key on your computer keyboard.

The $15,000 amount you just entered for the Software Licenses cost resource represents the planned cost of the software licenses needed for this task.

6. Click outside of the *Assign Resources* dialog and select task IDs #15-17 (the *Create Training Module 01, Create Training Module 02,* and *Create Training Module 03* tasks).

7. In the *Assign Resources* dialog, select *Ruth Andrews* and click the *Assign* button.

Notice that Microsoft Project 2010 assigned Ruth Andrews at 100% Units to each of the three tasks. If you do not supply a *Units* value when assigning a resource, the system defaults to the *Max. Units* value specified for the resource in the *Resource Sheet* view of your project.

8. Click the *Close* button to close the *Assign Resources* dialog.

Exercise 5-3

Assign resources to tasks using the Task Entry view.

1. Click the *View* tab and then select the *Details* checkbox in the *Split View* section of the *View* ribbon to apply the *Task Entry* view.

2. In the top pane (Gantt Chart), scroll down and select task ID #19, the *Conduct Skills Assessment* task.

3. In the bottom pane (Task Form), select Chuck Kirkpatrick and Kent Bergstrand, set the *Units* value to *50%* for each of them, enter *40h* in the *Work* field for each of them, and then click the *OK* button to complete the assignment.

Notice how Microsoft Project 2010 calculated the *Duration* value when you supplied the *Units* and *Work* values. This is the default behavior for *Fixed Units* tasks.

4. In the *Task Form,* click the *Next* button to select the *Create Training Schedule* task.

5. In the *Task Form,* select Kent Bergstrand, enter *25%* in the *Units* field, and then click the *OK* button.

Notice how Microsoft Project 2010 calculated the *Work* value when you supplied the *Units* and *Duration* values. Again, this is the default behavior for *Fixed Units* tasks.

6. In the *Task Form,* click the *Next* button to select the *Provide Training* task.

7. In the *Task Form,* select Kent Bergstrand, Chuck Kirkpatrick, and Ruth Andrews and then click the *OK* button.

8. Below the name of Ruth Andrews in the Task Form, select the Training Supplies material resource, enter *36/d* in the *Units* field, and then click the *OK* button.
9. Save and close the **Resource and Assignment Planning 1.mpp** sample file.

Using the Team Planner View

Warning: Only the **Professional** version of Microsoft Project 2010 includes the *Team Planner* view. If you use the Standard version of the software, the *Team Planner* view **is not** an available View.

At any point during the assignment process, you may want to display the new *Team Planner* view in Microsoft Project 2010. This new view allows you to analyze the current state of resource assignments in your project using a friendly graphical display. To apply the *Team Planner* view, click the *Resource* tab and then click the *Team Planner* button. The system displays the *Team Planner* view for your project, as shown in Figure 5 - 5.

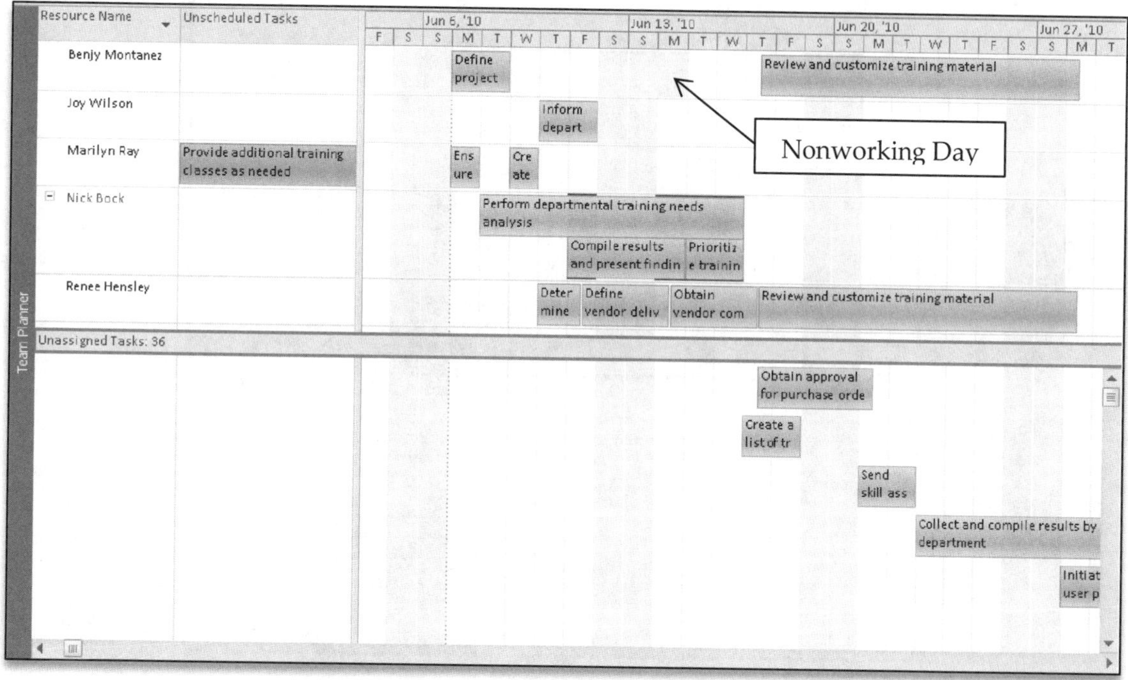

Figure 5 - 5: Team Planner view

Warning: The first time you apply the Team Planner view in a project, the software always scrolls to the **current date** in the Gantt Chart area on the right side of the view. If you scheduled your project to start in the future, this means you may not see any tasks in the *Unassigned Tasks* pane. To see tasks in the *Unassigned Tasks* pane, you must scroll the the Gantt Chart to the Start Date of your project.

The *Team Planner* view consists of two viewing panes. The top pane is the *Resource* pane and shows resources from the *Resource Sheet* view of your project, sorted by ID number. Assigned tasks appear in the Gantt Chart area on the right side of the pane for each resource. Unlike the *Gantt Chart* view, the *Team Planner* view displays the Gantt bars arranged horizontally on a single line for each resource. *Unscheduled Tasks* (*Manually Scheduled* tasks with no *Duration, Start,* or *Finish* date) already assigned to a resource appear in the *Unscheduled Tasks* column to the right of the resource name.

The Gantt Chart portion of the *Resource* pane also shows nonworking time for each resource, displayed as a gray shaded band for each time period. Nonworking time includes weekends and company holidays for all resources, plus vacation and planned sick leave for each resource individually. In the Gantt Chart portion of the *Resource* pane shown previously in Figure 5 - 5, you can also see than Benjy Montanez has one day of nonworking time scheduled on Monday, June 14, indicated by the gray shaded band in the Gantt Chart area for this resource. To learn more about any person's nonworking time for any time period, double-click the gray shaded band for that time period. Microsoft Project 2010 displays the *Change Working Time* dialog shown in Figure 5 - 6. Notice in the *Change Working Time* dialog shown in Figure 5 - 6 that Benjy Montanez scheduled a Personal Day Off on June 14.

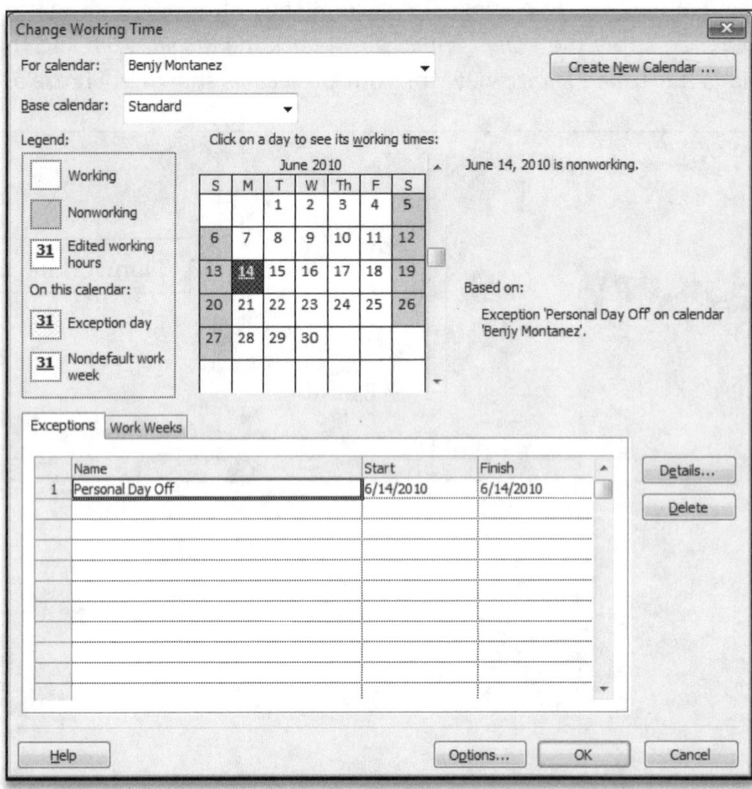

Figure 5 - 6: Change Working Time dialog, Personal Day Off for Benjy Montanez

The bottom pane of the *Team Planner* view is the *Unassigned Tasks* pane and shows the list of tasks not yet assigned to any resource, sorted by their ID number. The *Gantt Chart* on the right side of the *Unassigned Tasks* pane shows the current schedule for each unassigned task, based on the schedule specified in the *Gantt Chart* view of the project. The system zooms the *Gantt Chart* to the *Weeks Over Days* level of zoom by default.

In the *Team Planner* view shown previously in Figure 5 - 5, notice that I already assigned tasks to each team member in the project, including one *Unscheduled Task* assigned to Marilyn Ray. To view additional information about any task, float your mouse pointer over the Gantt bar of the task. Microsoft Project 2010 displays a screen tip for the selected Gantt bar, as shown in Figure 5 - 7.

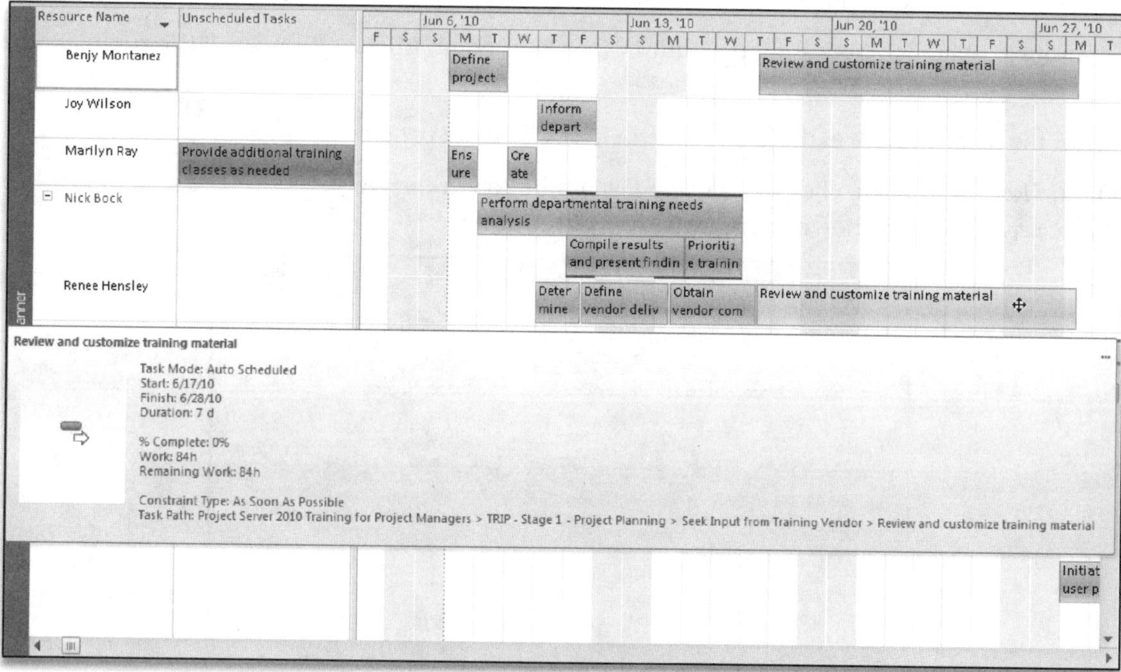

Figure 5 - 7: Schedule information for the selected task

The *Team Planner* view uses special colors and formatting to display task information for each assigned and unassigned task. The key to understanding the color formatting is as follows:

- Light blue Gantt bars represent unstarted *Auto Scheduled* tasks.
- Teal (turquoise) Gantt bars represent *Manually Scheduled* tasks.
- Dark blue in a Gantt bar represents task progress for both *Auto Scheduled* tasks and *Manually Scheduled* tasks.
- Gray Gantt bars represent external tasks in another project.
- Black Gantt bars with white text represent late tasks (tasks where the current % Complete progress does not extend to the *Status Date* of the project).
- Resource names formatted in red represent overallocated resources.
- Red borders on a Gantt bar represent the overallocated time periods for a resource.

For example, in Figure 5 - 5 and Figure 5 - 7 shown previously, the system formats Nick Bock's name in red, and displays red borders on his three assigned tasks. This indicates that Nick Bock is overallocated on these three tasks. In fact, he is overallocated specifically on June 11, 14, 15, and 16 on these three tasks.

Leveling an Overallocated Resource in the Team Planner View

While in the *Team Planner* view, Microsoft Project 2010 allows you to resolve resource overallocations using several different methods, including the following:

- Level the resource overallocation using the built-in *Leveling* tool in the software.

- Reschedule a task that is causing an overallocation by dragging it to a different time period.
- Reassign a task that is causing an overallocation by dragging the task to a different resource.

To level a resource overallocation using the built-in Leveling tool in Microsoft Project 2010, complete the following steps:

1. Select the name of an overallocated resource in the *Resource* pane.
2. On the *Resource* ribbon, click the *Leveling Options* button in the *Level* section. The system displays the *Resource Leveling* dialog shown in Figure 5 - 8.

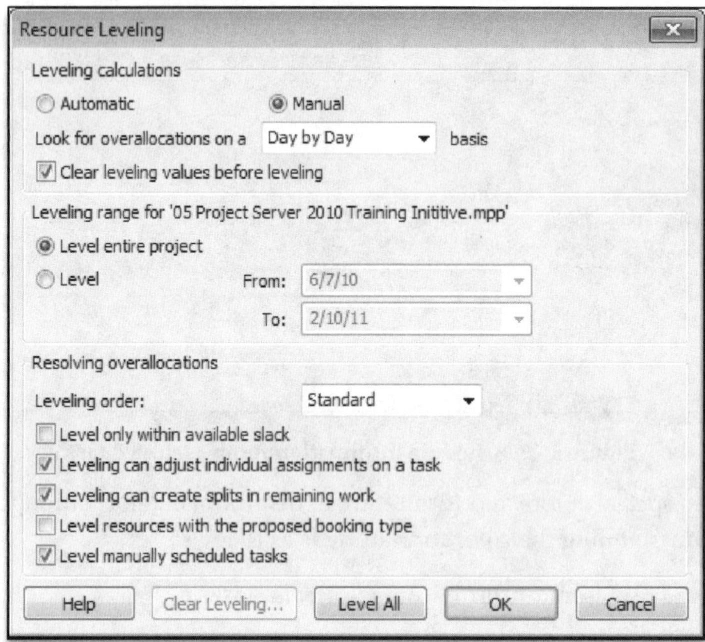

Figure 5 - 8: Resource Leveling dialog

3. In the *Resource Leveling* dialog, select the options you want to use for leveling the selected resource and then click the *OK* button.

The *Resource Leveling* dialog in Microsoft Project 2010 contains all of the leveling options available in the 2007 version of the software, plus one new option: the *Level Manually Scheduled Tasks* option. The system selects this option by default, and you must deselect it if you do not want the leveling operation to level *Manually Scheduled* tasks.

Warning: Do not click the *Level All* button in the *Resource Leveling* dialog. If you click the *Level All* button, you lose control over the leveling process because the software levels **all** of the overallocated resources in your project in a single operation.

4. Click the *Level Resource* button in the *Level* section of the *Resource* ribbon.

When you use the built-in leveling tool to level an overallocated resource, as with all previous versions of the software, Microsoft Project 2010 resolves the overallocation using one or both of the following methods:

- The software delays tasks or assignments.
- The software splits tasks or assignments.

Figure 5 - 9 shows the *Team Planner* view after leveling the resource overallocations for Nick Bock using the built-in leveling tool in Microsoft Project 2010. Notice that the software delayed several of the tasks assigned to Nick Bock to resolve the overallocation.

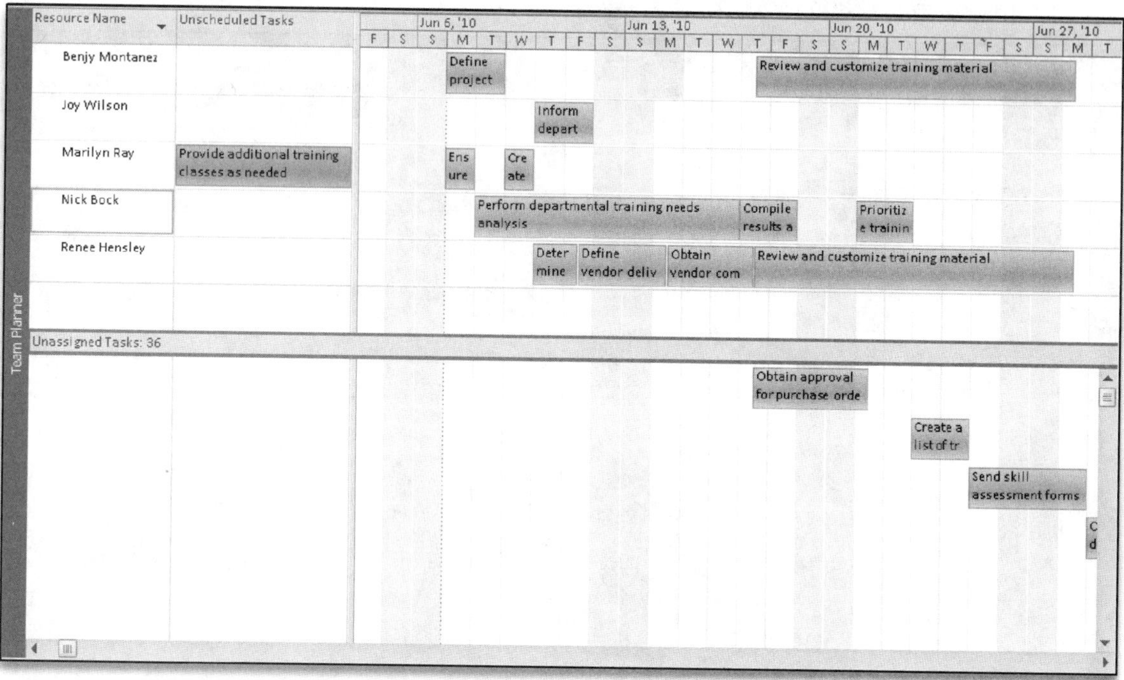

Figure 5 - 9: Team Planner view after leveling Nick Bock's overallocations

If you prefer to use a manual approach to level a resource overallocation, Microsoft Project 2010 allows you to reschedule a task by dragging it to a different time period, or dragging tasks to a different resource.

Dragging Tasks in the Team Planner View

You can use the "drag and drop" functionality of the *Team Planner* view to do any of the following:

- Drag an assigned task to a different time period to reschedule the task.
- Drag an assigned task to a different resource.
- Drag an unassigned task to a resource.

To reschedule a task to a different time period, simply drag the task's Gantt bar to the new time period. Keep in mind, however, that when you reschedule a task by dragging it to a new time period, Microsoft Project 2010 sets a *Start No Earlier Than* (SNET) constraint on the task. If you drag a task beyond the right edge of the *Team Planner* view, the system scrolls the view automatically so that you do not need to release the mouse button and scroll manually.

Warning: Microsoft Project's use of SNET constraints in the *Team* Planner view may be contrary to the best interests of your schedule model if you want to maintain a fully dynamic model. These prevent a task from moving to an earlier start date if an earlier start became available. You can easily clear delays added by the built-in leveling tool with a press of a button, while you must manually manage constraints added by the *Team Planner*.

To reassign a task to another resource, simply drag the task's Gantt bar from the assigned resource to the new resource and drop it on the desired time period. For example, Figure 5 - 10 shows the *Team Planner* view after I dragged two tasks assigned to Nick Bock and reassigned them to Marilyn Ray. These two tasks were the tasks causing the resource overallocation for Nick Bock.

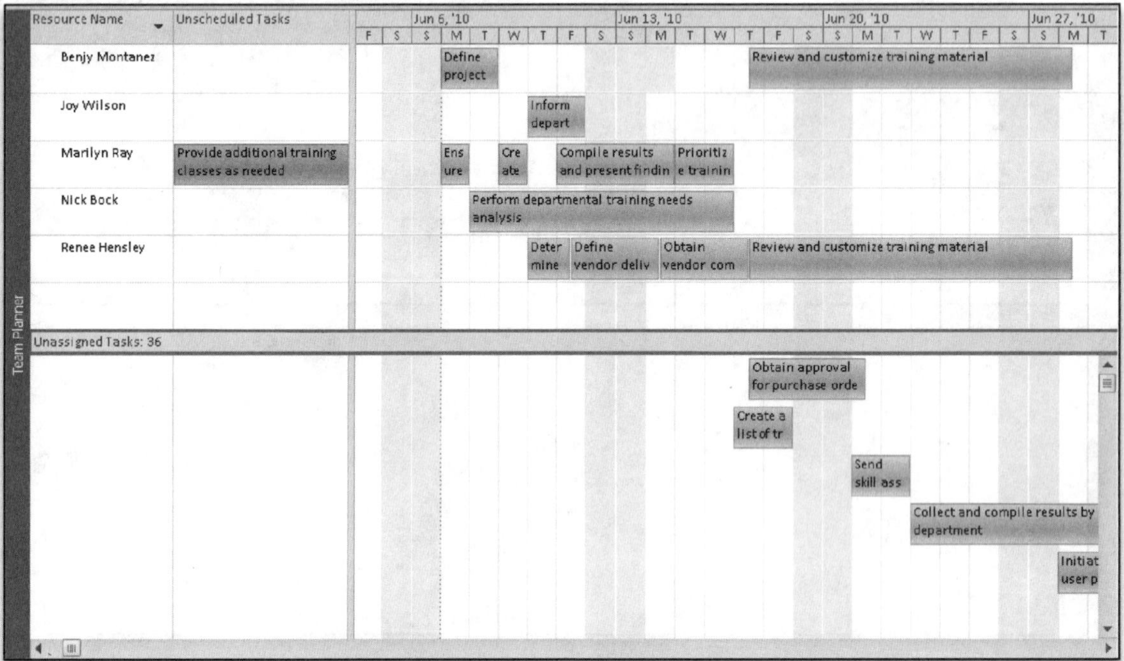

Figure 5 - 10: Resolve a resource overallocation by dragging tasks to another resource

You can also reassign a task to another resource by right-clicking on the Gantt bar for the task, choosing the *Reassign To* item on the shortcut menu, and then selecting the name of the new resource.

To assign an *Unassigned Task* to any resource using the *Team Planner* view, drag the task's Gantt bar from the bottom pane to the top pane and drop it in the time period during which you want to schedule the task. Keep in mind that when you assign a task to a resource using this method, Microsoft Project 2010 assigns the task to the resource at 100% Units automatically, indicating full-time work on the task.

To reassign or reschedule multiple tasks simultaneously, press and hold the Control key to select multiple tasks, and then drag and drop the block of selected tasks. Microsoft Project 2010 **does not** allow you to make multiple tasks assignments simultaneously in the *Team Planner* view.

Changing Schedule Information in the Team Planner View

As you analyze assignment information in the *Team Planner* view, at some point you may need to revise schedule information. Microsoft Project 2010 allows you to revise your project as follows in the *Team Planner* view:

- You can change the *Task Mode* option for a task by right-clicking on the Gantt bar for the task and choosing either the *Auto Schedule* or *Manually Schedule* item on the shortcut menu.
- You can set a task to *Inactive* status by right-clicking on the Gantt bar for the task and choosing the *Inactivate Task* item on the shortcut menu.
- You can change information for any task (such as setting a constraint or applying a task calendar) by double-clicking the Gantt bar for the task and entering the information in the *Task Information* dialog. You can also right-click on the Gantt bar for the task and choose the *Information* item on the shortcut menu.
- You can apply the *Task Details Form* in a split view arrangement with the *Team Planner* view by clicking the *Task* tab and then clicking the *Display Task Details* button in the *Properties* section of the *Task* ribbon. When you select the Gantt bar for any assigned task in the top pane, the *Task Details Form* in the bottom pane displays relevant information about the task and its assigned resources. Notice in Figure 5 - 11 that the *Task Details Form* displays information about the Perform Departmental Training Needs Analysis Task whose Gantt bar I selected in the top pane. To close the *Task Details Form*, click the *Display Task Details* button again in the *Task* ribbon.

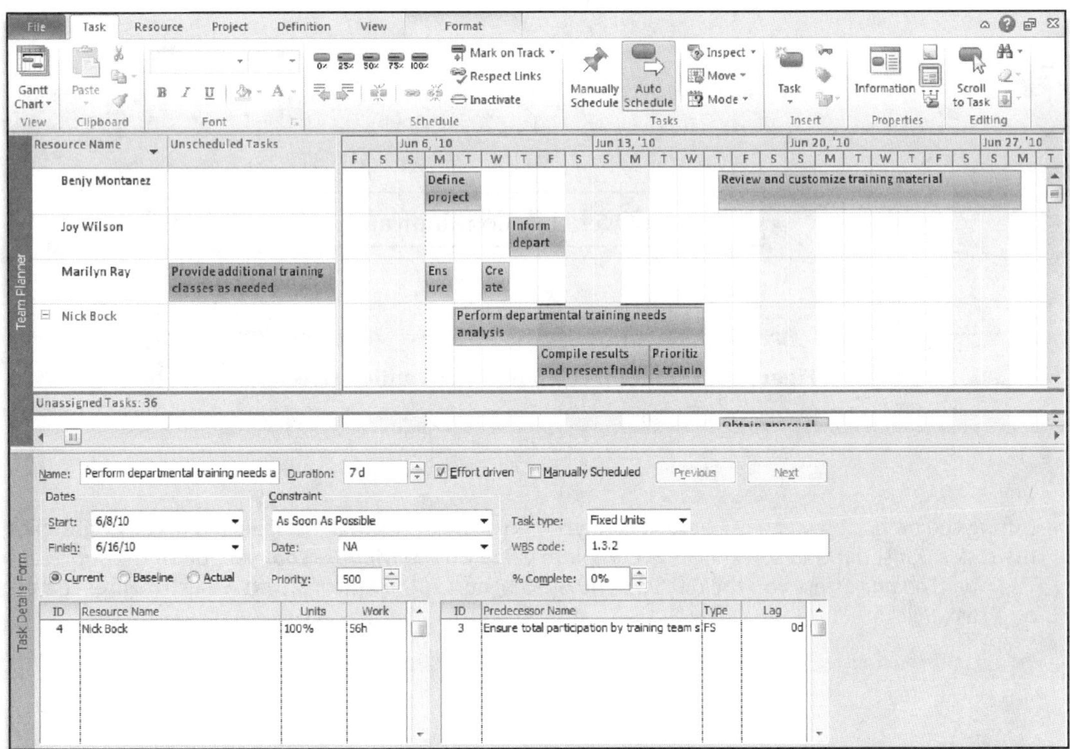

Figure 5 - 11: Task Details Form applied in a split-screen arrangement with the Team Planner view

- You can prevent resource overallocations in your project by clicking the *Format* tab and then clicking the *Prevent Overallocations* button in the *Format* ribbon. With this option selected, the software levels all existing overallocations in the project immediately, and levels any future resource overallocation when it occurs, such as when you drag a task or assign a task that causes a resource overallocation. Microsoft Project 2010 indicates in the *Team Planner* view that you selected this option by highlighting the *Prevent Overallocations* button and by displaying a *Prevent Overallocations: On* indicator at the left end of the Status bar at the bottom of the application window, as shown in Figure 5 - 12.

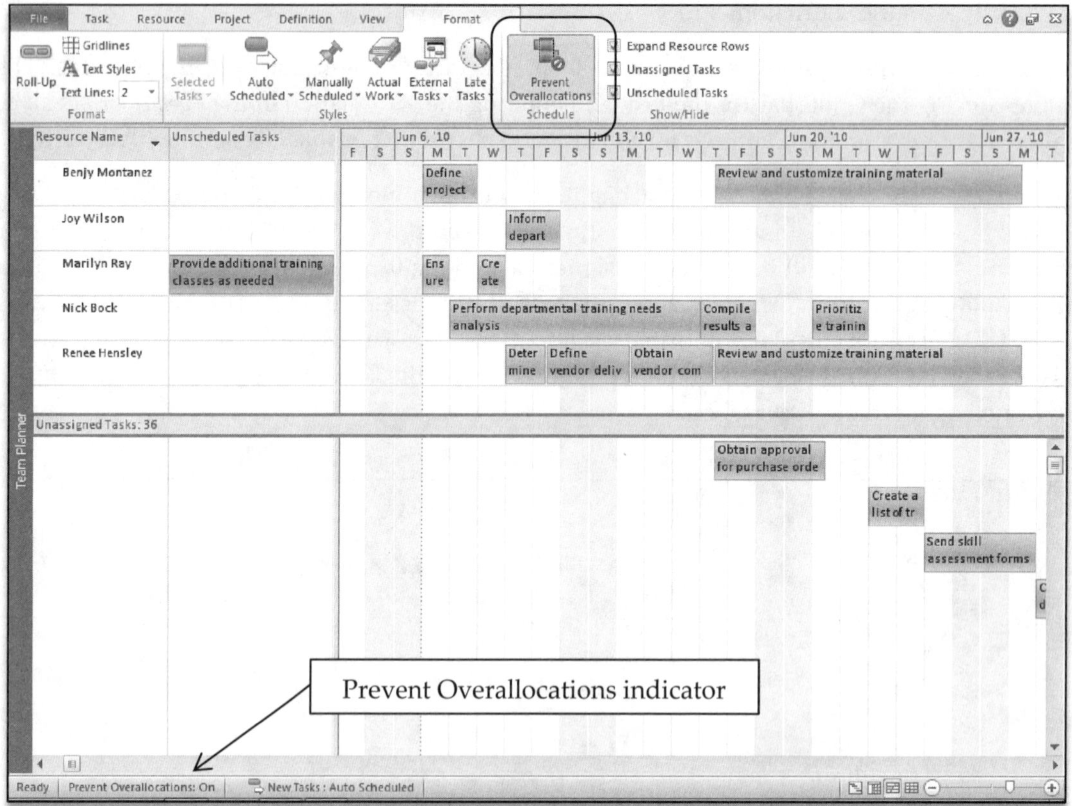

Figure 5 - 12: Prevent Overallocations option selected

During the execution stage of your project, you can also enter progress against a task by right-clicking on the task's Gantt bar and selecting a % Complete value on the *Mini Toolbar* section of the shortcut menu. The *Mini Toolbar* offers you the *0%, 25%, 50%, 75%,* and *100%* buttons with which to enter the progress on a task quickly.

Hands On Exercise

Exercise 5-4

Use the Team Planner view to analyze resource assignments and to level resource overallocations.

1. Navigate to your student folder and open the **Resource and Assignment Planning 2.mpp** sample file.
2. Click the *Resource* tab and then click the *Team Planner* button in the *Resource* ribbon.
3. Examine the tasks currently assigned to each resource. **Note:** Scroll to the right, as needed, to view task assignments for each resource.
4. In the *Resource* pane, scroll to the week of September 23, 2013 for Dan Morton and look for the week of nonworking time in the Gantt Chart (gray shaded cells).
5. Double-click in the gray shaded cells during the week of nonworking time for Dan Morton to display the *Change Working Time* dialog and reveal the reason for the nonworking time.
6. Click the *OK* button to close the *Change Working Time* dialog.
7. In the *Level* section of the *Resource* ribbon, click the *Leveling Options* button.
8. In the *Resource Leveling* dialog, click the *Leveling Order* pick list and select the *Priority, Standard* order.
9. Click the *OK* button to close the *Resource Leveling* dialog.
10. Select the overallocated resource, Dan Morton, and then click the *Level Resource* button in the *Resource* ribbon.

Notice that Microsoft Project 2010 delayed two of the tasks assigned to Dan Morton to resolve the overallocation.

11. Select the overallocated resource, Marilyn Ray, and then scroll to the right to locate her resource overallocation.
12. Drag the Gantt bar for the *Initiate End-User Placement Matrix* task from Marilyn Ray to Cassie Endicott. **Note:** Be sure to keep the same time schedule for the task when you drag the Gantt bar to Cassie Endicott.
13. Select the overallocated resource, Renee Hensley, and then click the *Level Resource* button in the *Resource* ribbon.

Notice that Microsoft Project 2010 delayed a task assigned to Renee Hensley to resolve the overallocation.

14. Save but do not close the **Resource and Assignment Planning 2.mpp** sample file.

Customizing the Team Planner View

Microsoft Project 2010 allows you to customize the *Team Planner* view. To customize this view, click the *Format* tab to display the *Format* ribbon, shown in Figure 5 - 13.

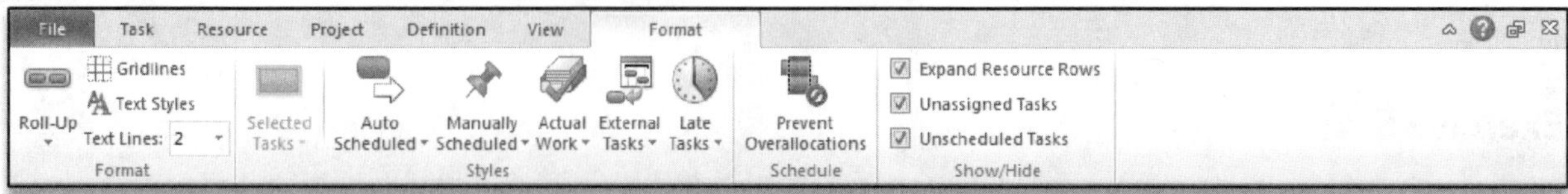

Figure 5 - 13: Format ribbon

Click the *Roll-Up* pick list button and select the level of WBS information to display for each Gantt bar shown in the *Team Planner* view. By default, the system selects the *All Subtasks* item on the *Roll-Up* pick list. When I created my project, I set it up so that summary tasks at *Outline Level 1* represent phases and summary tasks at *Outline Level 2* represent deliverables. Figure 5 - 14 shows the *Team Planner* view after selecting the *Outline Level 1* item on the *Roll-Up* pick list. Notice that Microsoft Project 2010 displays the name of each *Outline Level 1* summary task (the Phases) as Gantt bars in the *Team Planner* view. Notice also that the software displays the selected Outline Level for the *Team Planner* view with an indicator at the left end of the *Status bar* at the bottom of the application window.

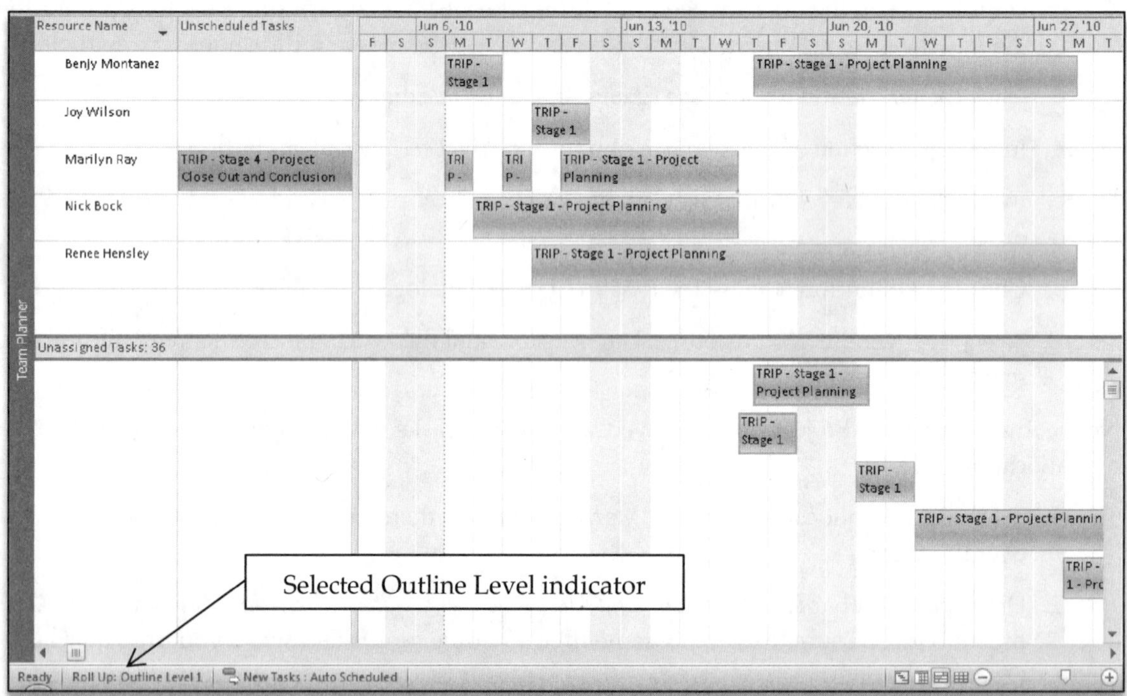

Figure 5 - 14: Team Planner view showing Outline Level 1 task information

Microsoft Project 2010 allows you to customize the display of gridlines and text in the *Team Planner* view. To change the gridline display, click the *Gridlines* button in the *Format* ribbon. The system displays the *Gridlines* dialog shown in Figure 5 - 15. In the *Gridlines* dialog, select an item in the *Line to Change* list and select the formatting on the *Type* and *Color* pick lists. When finished, click the *OK* button to apply the gridline formatting.

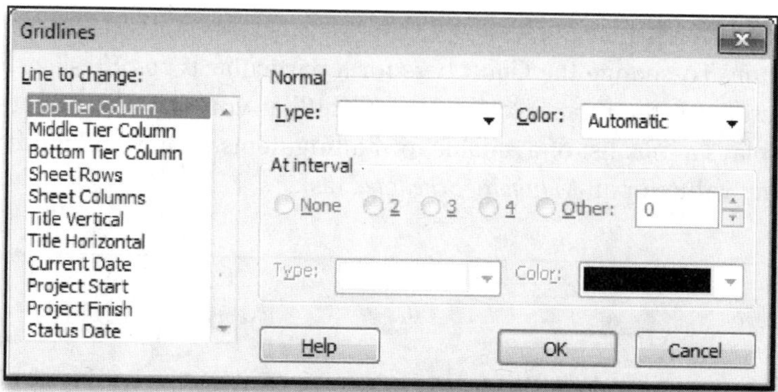

Figure 5 - 15: Gridlines dialog

To display the *Status Date* as a red dashed line in the *Team Planner* view, select the *Status Date* item in the *Line to Change* list, select the last item on the *Type* pick list, and choose the *Red* color on the *Color* pick list.

To customize how the software displays text in the *Team Planner* view, click the *Text Styles* button on the *Format* ribbon. The system displays the *Text Styles* dialog shown in Figure 5 - 16. In the *Text Styles* dialog, click the *Item to Change* pick list and choose a text style to format, and then select your desired formatting information for the selected text style in the other fields in the dialog. Click the *OK* button when finished.

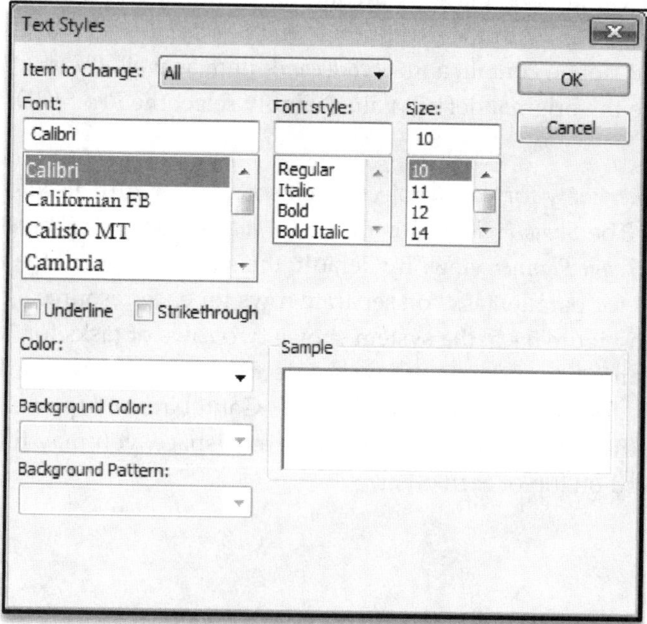

Figure 5 - 16: Text Styles dialog

Microsoft Project 2010 also allows you to format the colors of the Gantt bars shown in the *Team Planner* view. Notice in the *Format* ribbon shown previously in Figure 5 - 13 that the *Styles* section includes the *Selected Tasks, Auto Scheduled, Manually Scheduled, Actual Work, External Tasks,* and *Late Tasks* pick list buttons. To change the formatting of an individual Gantt bar or group of Gantt bars, select the Gantt bars you want to format and then click the

Selected Tasks pick list button. To change the Gantt bars for a particular type of tasks, such as *Manually Scheduled* tasks, click the pick list button for the type of task whose Gantt bar you want to format. When you click the pick list button, the system displays a pick list of available formatting items. Notice in Figure 5 - 17, for example, that I want to change the *Fill Color* value for all *Manually Scheduled* tasks.

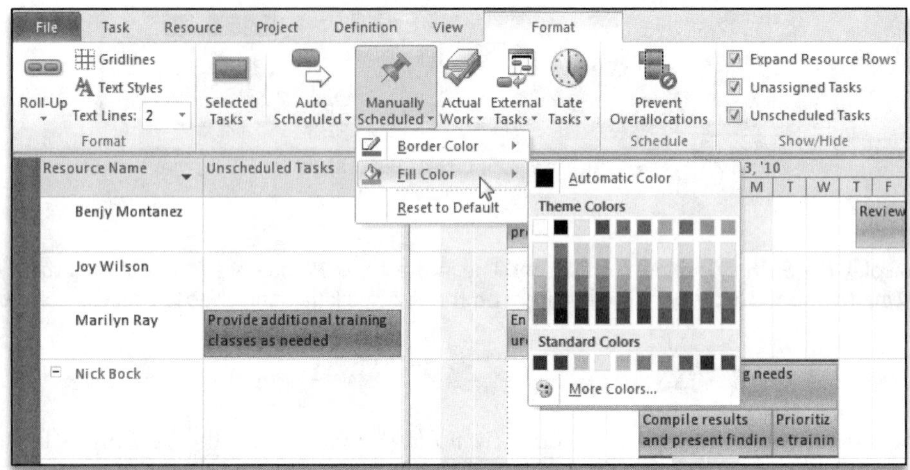

Figure 5 - 17: Format the Fill Color for Manually Scheduled tasks

To change the formatting for Gantt bars, the software allows you to specify both a *Border Color* value and a *Fill Color* value from a palette of values. With the exception of the *Selected Tasks* pick list, all of the other pick lists in the *Styles* section of the *Format* ribbon contain a *Reset to Default* item as well. If you change the color of any type of Gantt bar, and want to restore the original default value, simply select the *Reset to Default* item on the appropriate pick list.

As you format the *Team Planner* view for your project, Microsoft Project 2010 also allows you to determine which items to display in this view. The *Show/Hide* section of the *Format* ribbon offers three option checkboxes that control the items you see in the *Team Planner* view. By default, the software selects the *Expand Resource Rows* option so that you see the Gantt bars for parallel tasks on separate rows for each resource. For example, in the *Team Planner* view shown previously in Figure 5 - 5, the system shows two rows of tasks for Nick Bock, indicating parallel tasks occurring during the same time periods. If you deselect the *Expand Resource Rows* option, the system displays all tasks on a single row for each resource, and "stacks" Gantt bars on top of each other, as shown in Figure 5 - 18. Although deselecting this option may save vertical screen space, you may find it difficult to read the text contained in Gantt bars stacked on top of each other.

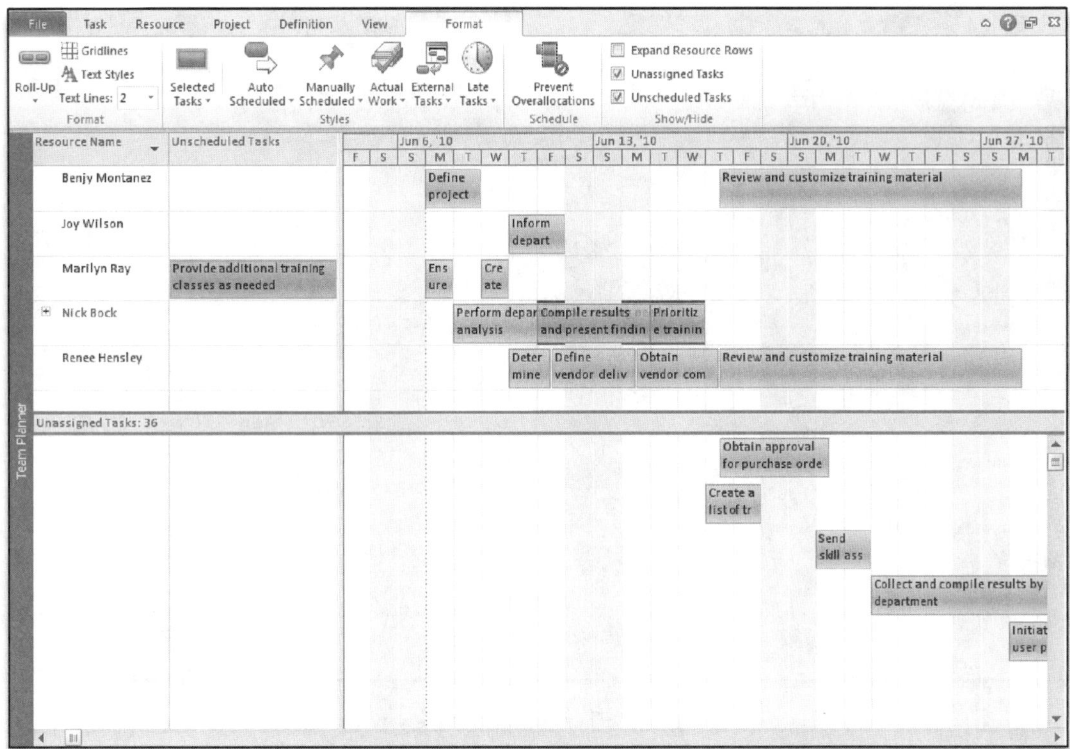

Figure 5 - 18: Expand Resource Names option deselected, Gantt bars stacked on a single row for each resource

You can also collapse parallel tasks onto one row for any resource by clicking the *Expand/Collapse* indicator to the left of the resource's name. For example, notice the *Expand/Collapse* indicator to the left of Nick Bock's name in Figure 5-18.

Microsoft Project 2010 also allows you to determine which type of tasks to display. By default, the software selects the *Unassigned Tasks* and *Unscheduled Tasks* options in the *Show/Hide* section of the *Format* ribbon. If you do not want to see the *Unassigned Tasks* pane in the bottom half of the *Team Planner* view, deselect the *Unassigned Tasks* option. If you do not want to see the *Unscheduled Tasks* column in the *Team Planner* view, deselect the *Unscheduled Tasks* option. Figure 5 - 19 shows the *Team Planner* view with the *Unassigned Tasks* and *Unscheduled Tasks* options deselected in the *Show/Hide* section of the *Format* ribbon.

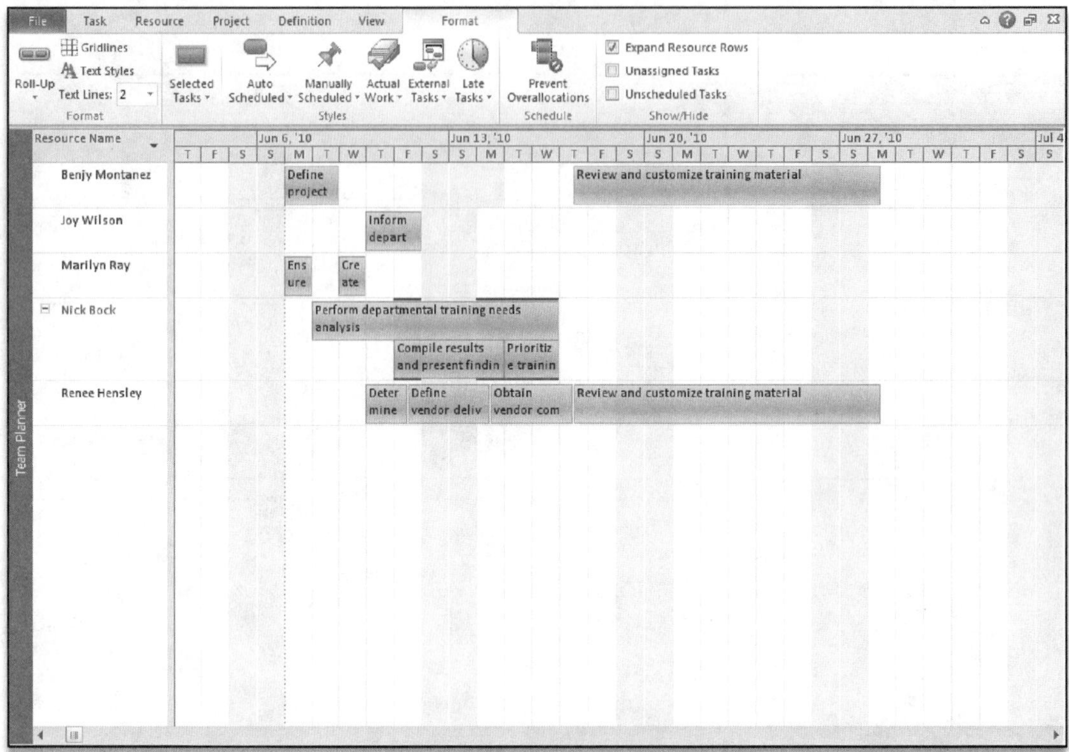

Figure 5 - 19: Team Planner view with Unassigned Tasks and Unscheduled Tasks hidden

A final formatting option in the *Team Planner* view is not obvious: zooming the Timescale in the Gantt Chart portion of the view. As I stated earlier in this section, Microsoft Project 2010 zooms the *Timescale* to the Weeks Over Days level of zoom. You can display any level of zoom you wish. If you added the *Zoom In* and *Zoom Out* buttons to your *Quick Access* menu (as specified previously in Hands On Exercise 1-4), you can use these buttons to zoom the Timescale in the *Team Planner* view. Otherwise, click the *View* tab and then click the *Zoom* pick list button in the *Zoom* section of the *View* ribbon to zoom in or zoom out as needed.

Printing the Team Planner View

You can print the *Team Planner* view by first formatting the *Team Planner* view to display according to your printing standards. Then click the *File* tab and click the *Print* tab in the *Backstage*. Microsoft Project 2010 displays the *Print* page of the *Backstage*, as shown in Figure 5 - 20. By default, the system sets the date in the *Dates* field to the Start date of the project, and sets the date in the *To* field to the Finish date of the project. Because of this, printing the *Team Planner* view can generate many pages in your printout. For example, notice in Figure 5 - 20 that the system needs 24 pages of paper to print my entire *Team Planner* view. If you do not need to print the entire date range of the project, change the dates in the *Dates* and *To* fields to reduce the page count. Otherwise, specify your settings on the *Print* page of the *Backstage* and then click the *Print* button to print the *Team Planner* view.

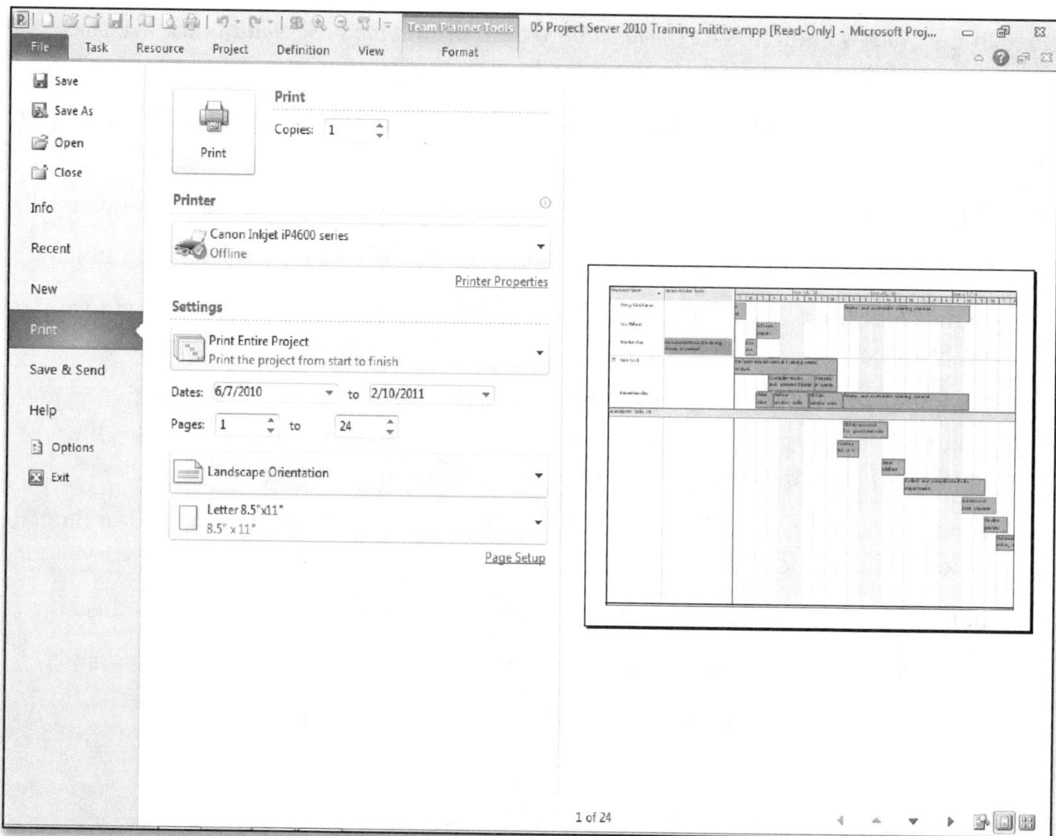

Figure 5 - 20: Print page of the Backstage, preparing to print the Team Planner view

Hands On Exercise

Exercise 5-5

Customize the Team Planner view.

1. Return to the **Resource and Assignment Planning 2.mpp** sample file.
2. While in the *Team Planner* view, click the *Format* tab to display the *Format* ribbon for the *Team Planner* view.
3. In the *Format* section of the *Format* ribbon, click the *Roll Up* pick list and select the *Outline Level 1* item on the list.

Notice how Microsoft Project 2010 displays the first-level summary tasks (Phases) for each resource in the *Team Planner* view.

4. Click the *Roll Up* pick list again and select the *All Subtasks* item on the list.

5. In the *Styles* section of the *Format* ribbon, click the *Manually Scheduled* pick list, select the *Fill Color* item, and then select a light green color on the color palette.

Notice how Microsoft Project 2010 changed the fill color for the *Manually Scheduled* task assigned to Marilyn Ray.

6. Click the *Manually Scheduled* pick list again and select the *Reset to Default* item on the list.
7. In the *Schedule* section of the *Format* ribbon, click the *Prevent Overallocations* button.
8. In the *Unassigned Tasks* pane, scroll to the right to locate tasks not yet assigned to any resource in this project.
9. Select the *Determine Course Dates, Start and End Times, and Locations* task, then drag and drop the Gantt bar to George Stewart. **Note:** Be sure to keep the same time schedule for the task and drop the Gantt bar on top of the Gantt bar of George Stewart's existing task.

With the *Prevent Overallocations* button selected, notice how Microsoft Project 2010 immediately leveled the new resource overallocation for George Stewart.

10. In the *Show/Hide* section of the *Format* ribbon, deselect the *Unscheduled Tasks* checkbox.

Notice that Microsoft Project 2010 hides the *Unscheduled Tasks* column in the *Resources* pane.

11. Save and close the **Resource and Assignment Planning 2.mpp** sample file.

Detecting and Resolving Resource Overallocations

Another powerful new feature in Microsoft Project 2010 helps you to detect and level resource overallocations on a task-by-task basis in any task view, such as the *Gantt Chart* view. Previous versions of the software, did not allow you to detect resource overallocations in a task view, displaying overallocation information and indicators only in a resource view, such as the *Resource Usage* view. In all previous versions of the software, the system allowed you to level resource overallocations in a task view, but it leveled the overallocations for all resources and all tasks simultaneously, which meant you lost control over the leveling process.

To detect a resource overallocation in a task view using Microsoft Project 2010, apply any task view, such as the *Gantt Chart* view. Look in the *Indicators* column for any task with a "burning man" indicator, as this indicator identifies the task as assigned to an overallocated resource. For example, Figure 5 - 21 shows the *Gantt Chart* view of my project. Notice the special indicator in the *Indicators* column for task IDs #6, #7, and #8, indicating that I have an overallocated resource assigned to these three tasks. In this situation, the overallocated resource is Nick Bock. The overallocation is a consequence of assigning Nick Bock at 100% Units on three tasks that run in parallel. Because he cannot work full-time on three tasks simultaneously, the system shows that Nick Bock is an overallocated resource on these three tasks.

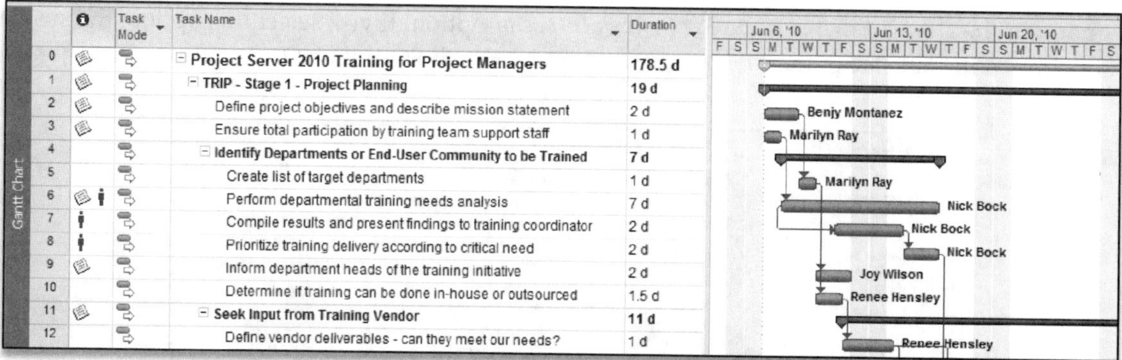

Figure 5 - 21: Three tasks with an overallocated resource assigned

As with previous versions of the software, Microsoft Project 2010 continues to allow you to level resource overallocations in the *Resource Usage* view for each resource individually. This method continues to offer you the most control over the leveling process. However, the 2010 version of the software does allow you to effectively level on a task-by-task basis in the *Gantt Chart* view, providing you with more control over the leveling process than in any other version. To level on a task-by-task basis, right-click in the *Indicators* column on any cell containing a "burning man" indicator. The system displays the shortcut menu shown in Figure 5 - 22, and offers three methods for dealing with the overallocation.

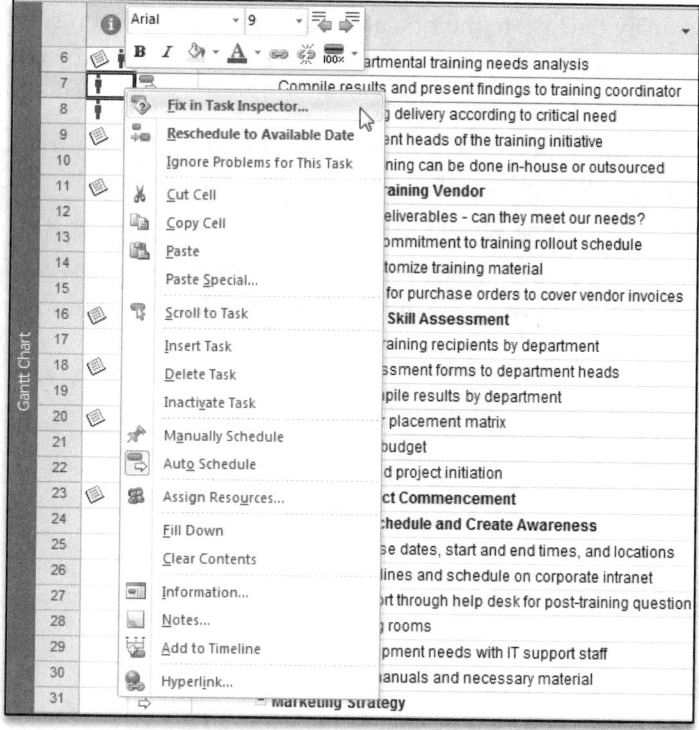

Figure 5 - 22: Shortcut menu for a task assigned to an overallocated resource

The first option in the shortcut menu is the *Fix in Task Inspector* option. If you select this option, the system opens the *Task Inspector* on the left side of the *Gantt Chart* view, as shown in Figure 5 - 23.

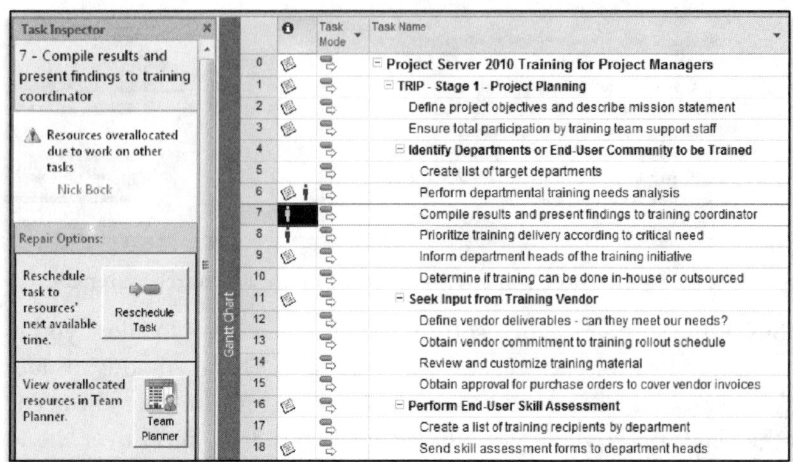

Figure 5 - 23: Task Inspector for a task assigned to an overallocated resource

The *Task Inspector* offers two options in the *Repair Options* section for resolving the resource overallocation. Click the *Reschedule Task* button to delay the task to the first available time period that resolves the overallocation. Click the *Team Planner* button to apply the *Team Planner* view, in which you can level the resource using any of the methods I discussed in the previous section of this module.

The second option in the shortcut menu is the *Reschedule to Available Date* option. If you select this option, Microsoft Project 2010 delays the task to the first available time period that resolves the overallocation. Selecting this option is the same as clicking the *Reschedule* button in the *Task Inspector*.

Lastly, you can use the third option on the shortcut menu, *Ignore Problems for This Task*. If you select this option, the system hides the "burning man" indicator for that task in the *Indicators* column, but does nothing to resolve the resource overallocation.

Hands On Exercise

Exercise 5-6

Locate and resolve resource overallocations in the Gantt Chart view.

1. Navigate to your student folder and open the **Resource and Assignment Planning 3.mpp** sample file.
2. Scroll down through the list of tasks and look for any task that shows the "burning man" indicator in the *Indicators* column, indicating the task has an overallocated resource assigned to it.

Note: You should see that task IDs #6, 7, 8, 13, 14, 15, 19, and 20 have an overallocated resource assigned to them.

3. Float your mouse pointer over the overallocation indicator for task ID #7, the *Compile Results and Present Findings to Training Coordinator* task, and read the text in the ScreenTip.
4. Right-click in the *Indicators* cell for task ID #7 and then select the *Fix in Task Inspector* item on the shortcut menu.
5. In the *Task Inspector*, read the available information about the resource overallocation on this task.
6. Click the *Reschedule Task* button in the *Task Inspector* to resolve the resource overallocation on this task.

Notice that this action resolved the resource overallocation on task IDs #6 and #8 as well.

7. Select task ID #14, the *Review and Customize Training Material* task, and then click the *Reschedule Task* button in the *Task Inspector*.
8. Select task ID #20, the *Initiate End-User Placement Matrix* task, and then click the *Reschedule Task* button in the *Task Inspector*.
9. Save and close the **Resource and Assignment Planning 3.mpp** sample file.

Module 06

What's New – Project Execution

Learning Objectives

After completing this module, you will be able to:

- Reschedule an unstarted project
- Move a task to a new Start date
- Cancel an unneeded task
- Understand the new Peak field
- Synchronize a project with a Tasks list in SharePoint

Inside Module 06

Rescheduling an Unstarted Project **153**

Rescheduling a Task **156**

Setting Tasks to Inactive **159**

Understanding the Peak Field **163**

Synchronizing with a SharePoint Tasks List **169**

Adding Fields to the Task Synchronization Process 175

Reporting Progress Using a SharePoint Tasks List 181

Rescheduling an Unstarted Project

Many project managers face the problem of rescheduling the start date of an unstarted project. Common reasons for rescheduling an unstarted project include budget shortfalls and lack of resources. For example, consider the unstarted project shown in Figure 6 - 1. When I planned the project originally, I did the following:

- I scheduled the project to start on April 16.
- I set a *Finish No Later Than* (FNLT) constraint of May 5 on the Phase I Complete milestone task.
- I set a *Start No Earlier Than* constraint (SNET) of June 18 on the Test Beta Classes task.
- I set a *Deadline* date of June 12 on the Phase II Complete milestone to signify the target finish date of Phase II.
- I set a *Deadline* date of July 20 on the Project Complete milestone to signify the target finish date of the entire project.

To make it easier for you to see the Deadline date symbols in the *Gantt Chart* shown in Figure 6 - 1, I removed the dates that Microsoft Project 2010 usually displays to the right of each Milestone symbol. This way you can easily see both the *Milestone* symbols and the *Deadline* date symbols on the Phase II Complete and Project Complete milestone tasks.

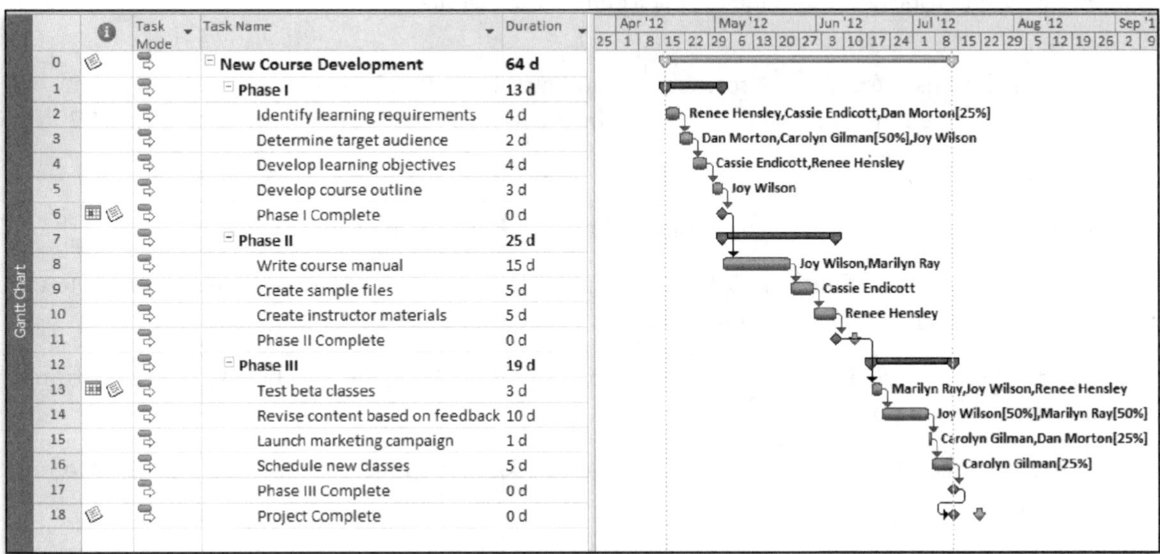

	Task Name	Duration
0	**New Course Development**	**64 d**
1	**Phase I**	**13 d**
2	Identify learning requirements	4 d
3	Determine target audience	2 d
4	Develop learning objectives	4 d
5	Develop course outline	3 d
6	Phase I Complete	0 d
7	**Phase II**	**25 d**
8	Write course manual	15 d
9	Create sample files	5 d
10	Create instructor materials	5 d
11	Phase II Complete	0 d
12	**Phase III**	**19 d**
13	Test beta classes	3 d
14	Revise content based on feedback	10 d
15	Launch marketing campaign	1 d
16	Schedule new classes	5 d
17	Phase III Complete	0 d
18	Project Complete	0 d

Figure 6 - 1: Unstarted project

Shortly before team members began work on this project, company management announced a 4-week delay to allow the project team members to work on a higher priority project. In previous versions of Microsoft Project, project managers can reschedule the project by clicking the *Adjust Dates* button on the *Analysis* toolbar. The limitation of the *Adjust Dates* dialog in previous versions of the software is that the tool does not reschedule *Deadline* dates, thus forcing the project manager to manually change *Deadline* dates after rescheduling the *Start* date of the project.

In Microsoft Project 2010, you can reschedule the *Start* date of an unstarted project by clicking the *Project* tab and then clicking the *Move Project* button in the *Schedule* section of the *Project* ribbon. When you click the *Move Project* button, the system displays the *Move Project* dialog shown in Figure 6 - 2

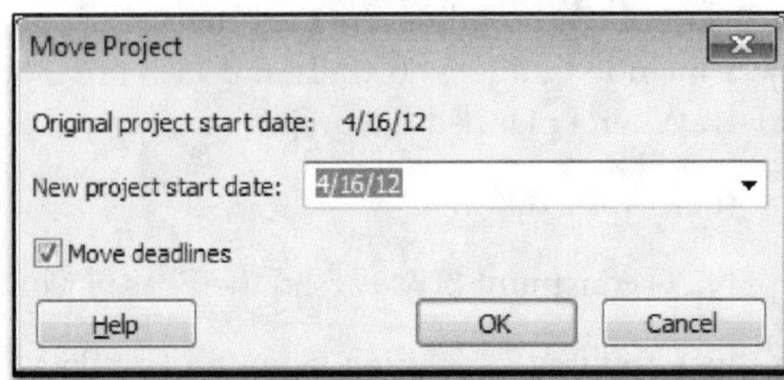

Figure 6 - 2: Move Project dialog

In the *Move Project* dialog, the system displays the current *Project Start* date in the *Original Project Start Date* field. To reschedule the project, enter or select a new *Project Start* date in the *New Project Start Date* field. If you want the system to reschedule *Deadline* dates, leave the *Move Deadlines* option selected. When you click the *OK* button, Microsoft Project 2010 reschedules your project using the following actions:

- The system enters your new *Project Start* date in the *Start Date* field of the *Project Information* dialog.
- The system reschedules the dates of constraints, based on the duration difference measured in working days between the original start date and the new start date of the project.
- The system reschedules *Deadline* dates, based on the duration difference measured in working days between the original start date and the new start date of the project.

Figure 6 - 3 shows the unstarted project rescheduled to start 4 weeks (20 working days) later than originally planned. After entering the new Start date of May 14 in the *Move Project* dialog, Microsoft Project 2010 did the following:

- The system entered May 14 in the *Start Date* field of the *Project Information* dialog.
- The system changed the *Finish No Later Than* (FNLT) constraint date on the Phase I Complete milestone task from May 5 to June 2 (20 working days).
- The system changed the *Start No Earlier Than* constraint (SNET) on the Test Beta Classes task from June 18 to July 16 (20 working days).
- The system changed the *Deadline* date on the Phase II Complete milestone task from June 12 to July 11 (20 working days).
- The system changed the *Deadline* date on the Project Complete milestone task from July 20 to August 18 (20 working days).

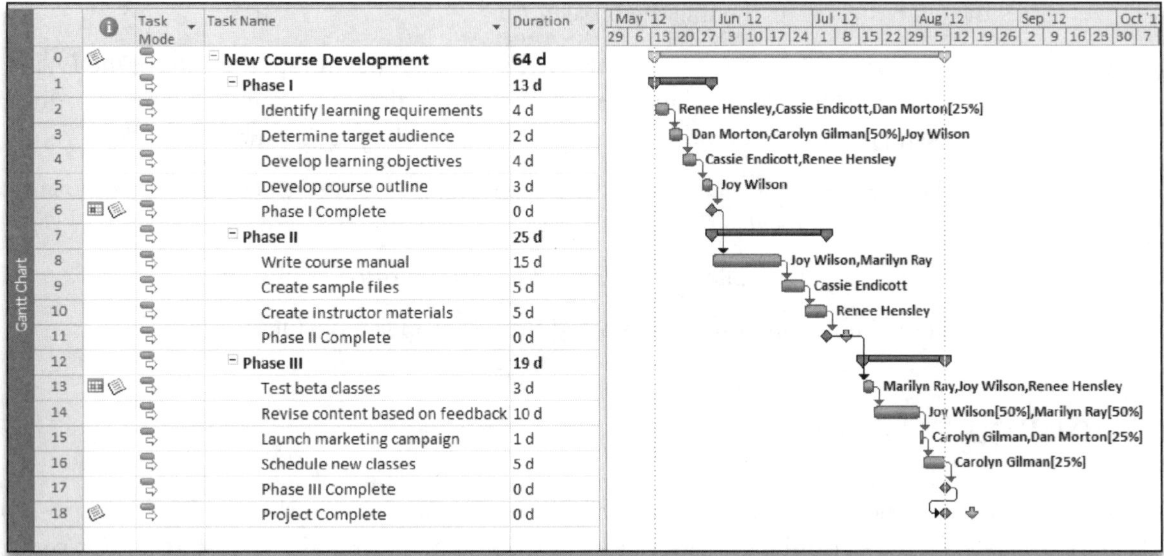

Figure 6 - 3: Unstarted project rescheduled 20 days later

Keep in mind that when you use the *Move Project* dialog to reschedule your project, Microsoft Project 2010 assumes that you want to move *Constraint* and *Deadline* dates exactly the same number of days that you moved the *Project Start* date. In reality, this may not be true, and you may need to change the *Constraint* dates and *Deadline* dates manually. In addition, if you set a *Baseline* for the unstarted project before rescheduling it, you may want to set a new *Baseline* for the project to capture the new schedule information.

Hands On Exercise

Exercise 6-1

Reschedule the *Project Start* date of an unstarted project to a date four months in the future due to a shortage of resources to work in the project.

1. Navigate to your student folder and open the **Reschedule an Unstarted Project.mpp** sample file.

Notice that three tasks in the project contain constraints and the *Project Complete* milestone tasks includes a deadline date.

2. Examine the constraint dates on the *Load and Configure Software* task, the *Testing Complete* milestone task, and the *Provide Training* task.
3. Examine the *Deadline* date on the *Project Complete* milestone task.
4. Click the *Project* tab and then click the *Move Project* button in the *Schedule* section.
5. In the *Move Project* dialog, enter the date **October 7, 2013** in the *New project start date* field.
6. In the *Move Project* dialog, leave the *Move deadlines* option selected.

7. Click the *OK* button to reschedule the project.

Notice that Microsoft Project 2010 displays *Change Highlighting* on the duration values of the *Project Summary Task* (Row 0) and on the *Training* summary task. This indicates a change in duration due to the Thanksgiving weekend company holidays after rescheduling the *Project Start* date.

8. Examine the **new** constraint dates on the *Load and Configure Software* task, the *Testing Complete* milestone task, and the *Provide Training* task.
9. Examine the **new** *Deadline* date on the *Project Complete* milestone task.
10. Save and close the **Reschedule an Unstarted Project.mpp** sample file.

Rescheduling a Task

Project managers occasionally need to reschedule one or more tasks in a project to show a delay in an in-progress project. Common reasons for rescheduling a task can include team members failing to start and/or complete a task in a previous reporting period or lack of resources to work on the task as currently scheduled. For example, consider the project shown in Figure 6 - 4. After team members completed all of the tasks in Phase I of the project, I learned that I must put the remainder of the project "on hold" for another month (4 weeks or 20 working days). Therefore, I must reschedule the tasks in the project beginning with the Write Course Manual task.

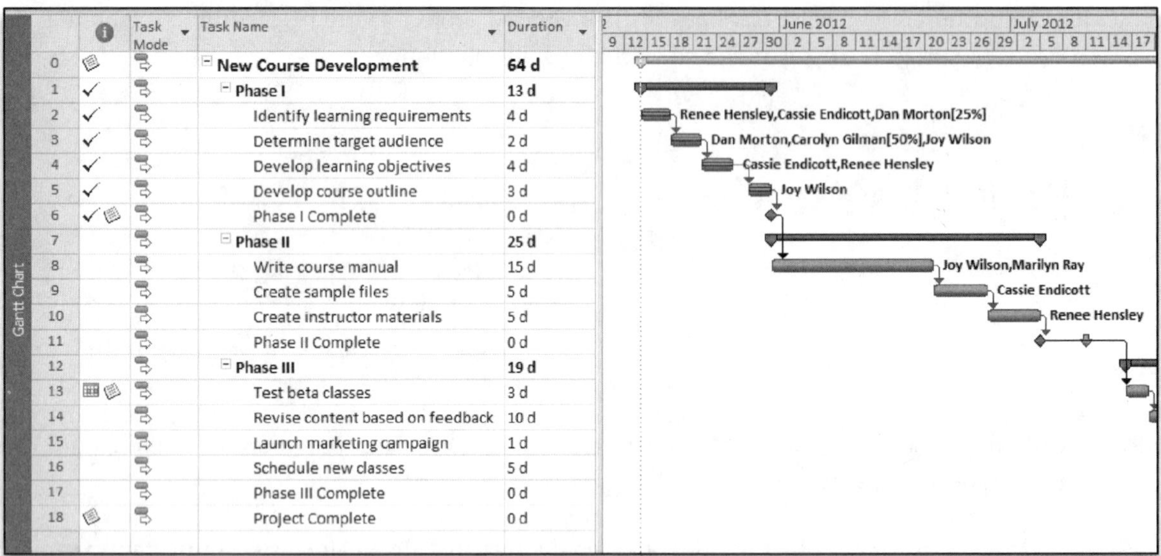

Figure 6 - 4: In-progress project

In previous versions of Microsoft Project, a project manager can reschedule tasks manually using one of two methods:

- On the *Advanced* tab of the *Task Information* dialog, set a *Start No Earlier Than* (SNET) constraint with the new Start date of the task as the Constraint Date.
- Use the *Reschedule Uncompleted Work* feature in the *Update Project* dialog (click Tools ➢ Tracking ➢ Update Project to access the dialog).

A new method for rescheduling one or more tasks in Microsoft Project 2010 allows you to select the tasks you want to reschedule and then click the *Move* pick list button in the *Tasks* section of the *Task* ribbon, as shown in Figure 6 - 5. The *Move* pick list includes three sections that allow you to reschedule the selected tasks.

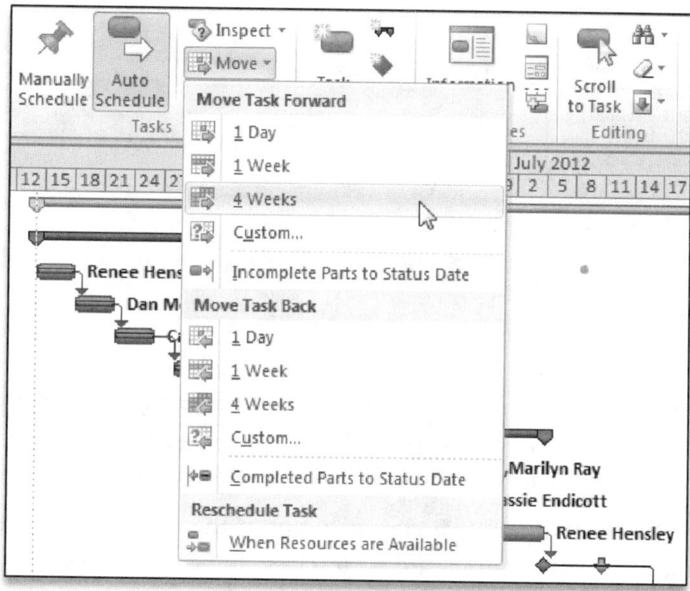

Figure 6 - 5: Move pick list

The *Move Task Forward* section offers options that allow you to reschedule the selected tasks into the future by 1 day, by 1 week, by 4 weeks, by a specific amount of time you specify, or by rescheduling uncompleted work forward past the *Status Date* of the project. The *Move Task Back* section offers you options that allow you reschedule the selected tasks into the past by 1 day, by 1 week, by 4 weeks, by a specific amount of time you specify, or by rescheduling completed work back to the *Status Date* of the project. The *Reschedule Task* section includes a single option that allows you to delay the task until the assigned resource is available. This final option allows you to manually level an overallocated resource assigned to the selected tasks.

To reschedule the tasks in the project shown previously in Figure 6 - 4, I selected the Write Course Manual task (the first task in Phase II), and then I selected the *4 Weeks* item on the *Move* pick list. Microsoft Project 2010 reschedules this task and all successor tasks 4 weeks into the future by setting a *Start No Earlier Than* (SNET) constraint on the task with a constraint date of June 28, as shown in Figure 6 - 6. June 28 is four weeks (20 working days) later than the original start date for the Write Course Manual task.

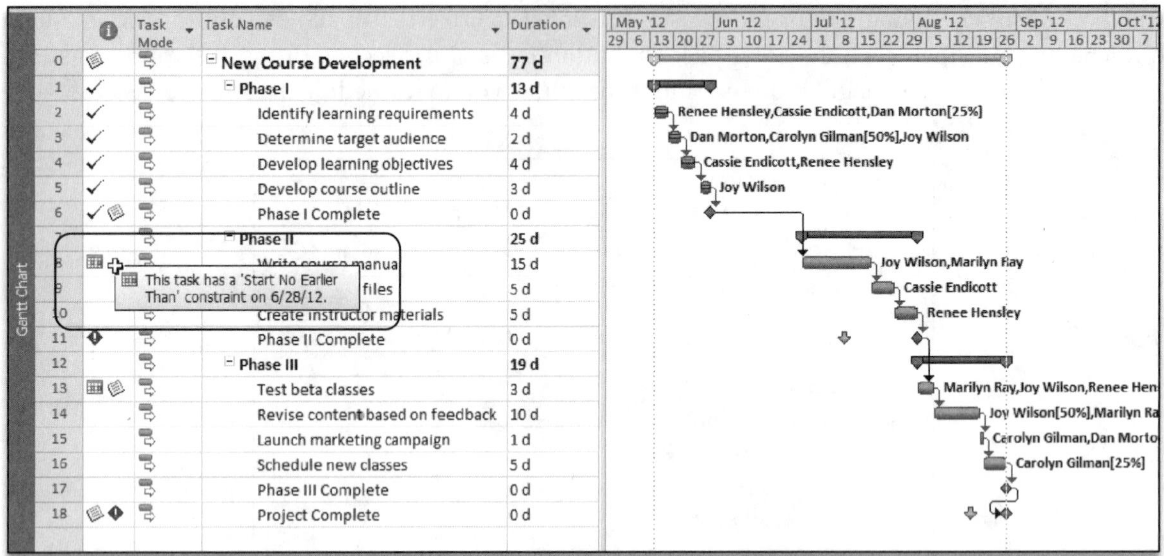

Figure 6 - 6: Start No Earlier Than constraint on the Write Course Manual task delays Phase II and Phase III by four weeks

Notice the special indicators displayed in the *Indicators* column for the Phase II Complete milestone task and the Project Complete milestone task, as shown in Figure 6 - 6. These indicators show that these two milestone tasks slipped past the *Deadline* dates I specified on these tasks. Because the project is slipping, this indicates that I will miss the original *Deadline* dates on these tasks, which is a natural consequence of a slipping project.

Hands On Exercise

Exercise 6-2

Due to a lack of resources, put a project "on hold" by rescheduling tasks in the project to a start date one week in the future.

1. Navigate to your student folder and open the **Reschedule Tasks.mpp** sample file.
2. Select the *Load and Configure Software* task, press and hold the **Control** key on your keyboard, and then select the *Create Training Module 01* task.
3. Release the **Control** key on your computer keyboard and then click the *Task* tab.
4. Click the *Move* pick list button in the *Tasks* section of the *Task* ribbon and then select the *1 Week* item on the pick list.

Notice how Microsoft Project 2010 splits the *Create Training Module 01* task and delays the entire *Load and Configure Software* task by setting a *Start No Earlier Than* (SNET) constraint on the task.

5. Save and close the **Reschedule Tasks.mpp** sample file.

Setting Tasks to Inactive

After you baseline a project and begin tracking progress, you may discover that you no longer need some tasks in the project. Although this is certainly not a bad situation, you should now cancel the unneeded tasks. Best practices with Microsoft Project dictate that you should never delete a task with a baseline, because in deleting the task you lose the baseline data on the task, therefore losing the ability to track variance on the deleted task. Instead, best practice dictates that you should **cancel** the unneeded task, rather than deleting it. To cancel an unneeded task using Microsoft Project 2007, for example, I recommend the following Best Practice approach:

1. Set the *Remaining Work* value to 0h on the task in the task *Work* table. When you complete this step, Microsoft Project 2007 changes the Gantt bar to the Milestone symbol (a black diamond).
2. Double-click the milestone symbol for the task and choose another symbol that you want to use to signify a cancelled task.
3. Change the *Cell Background Color* of the task to a color representing a cancelled task (I personally like the lime green color).
4. Add a note to the task to document the reason for cancelling it.

Warning: The Inactivate Task feature is available **only** in the Professional version of Microsoft Project 2010. You **cannot** use this feature if you have the Standard version of the software.

Cancelling an unneeded task in Microsoft Project 2010 is much simpler; to cancel a task you simply set the task to *Inactive* status. Consider the project shown in Figure 6 - 7. After the project team completed all tasks in Phase II and the first two tasks in Phase III, management cancelled the remainder of the project due to budgetary restrictions. Therefore, I can close out the project by setting the last four tasks in Phase III to *Inactive* status.

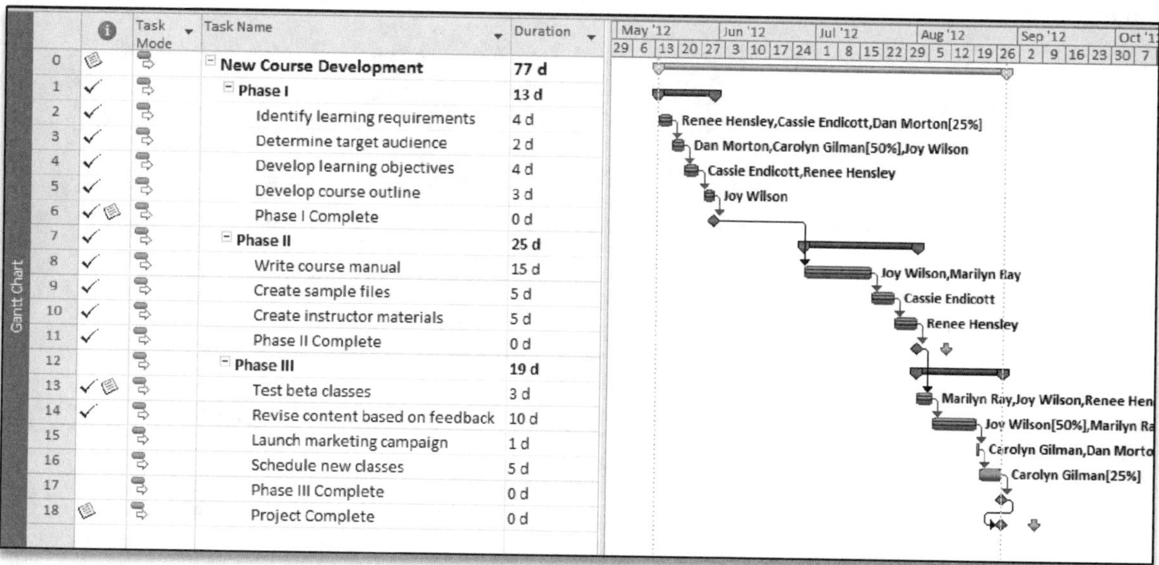

Figure 6 - 7: Project cancelled before completing Phase III

To set unneeded tasks to *Inactive* status in Microsoft Project 2010, select one or more tasks and then click the *Inactivate* button in the *Schedule* section of the *Task* ribbon. Figure 6 - 8 shows the *Inactivate* button on the *Task* ribbon, along with its floating Tooltip.

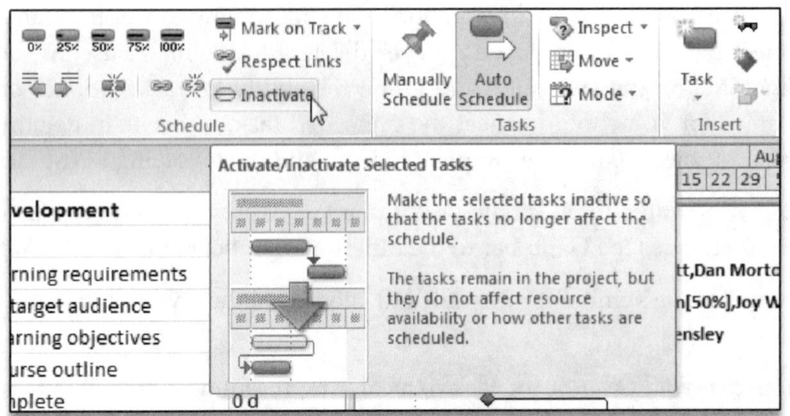

Figure 6 - 8: Inactivate button and Tooltip

Figure 6 - 9 shows the project after setting the last four tasks in Phase III to *Inactive* status. When you cancel a task using the *Inactivate* button, Microsoft Project 2010 does the following:

- The system formats the text of the *Inactive* task using the strikethrough font effect and the gray font color.
- The system formats the Gantt bar of the *Inactive* task using a hollow (unfilled) pattern.
- The system treats the *Inactive* task as if it has 0h of remaining work. This means the *Inactive* task no longer affects resource availability for resources assigned to it, as indicated in the Tooltip shown previously in Figure 6 - 8.
- Although the system continues to show link lines for the *Inactive* task, the system schedules successor tasks as if they are not linked to the *Inactive* task. This means that the duration of the *Inactive* task no longer affects the schedule of successor tasks, as indicated also in the Tooltip shown previously in Figure 6 - 8.

	Task Name	Duration
0	**New Course Development**	**71 d**
1	**Phase I**	**13 d**
2	Identify learning requirements	4 d
3	Determine target audience	2 d
4	Develop learning objectives	4 d
5	Develop course outline	3 d
6	Phase I Complete	0 d
7	**Phase II**	**25 d**
8	Write course manual	15 d
9	Create sample files	5 d
10	Create instructor materials	5 d
11	Phase II Complete	0 d
12	**Phase III**	**13 d**
13	Test beta classes	3 d
14	Revise content based on feedback	10 d
15	Launch marketing campaign	1 d
16	Schedule new classes	5 d
17	Phase III Complete	0 d
18	Project Complete	0 d

Gantt Chart
Aug 19, '12 | Aug 26, '12 | Sep 2, '12
enee Hensley
Joy Wilson[50%],Marilyn Ray[50%]
Carolyn Gilman,Dan Morton[25%]
Carolyn Gilman[25%]
8/28
8/28

Figure 6 - 9: Last four tasks cancelled in Phase III

Figure 6 - 10 shows the four Inactive tasks with the *Work* table applied in the *Gantt Chart* view. Notice that the system did not set the Remaining Work to 0h. Notice also that the system shows -20h of Work Variance (in the *Variance* column) on the Phase III summary task and on the *Project Summary Task,* caused by inactivating two tasks with 10h of work assigned to each task.

	Task Name	Work	Baseline	Variance	Actual	Remaining	% W. Comp.
0	**New Course Development**	**672 h**	**692 h**	**-20 h**	**672 h**	**0 h**	**100%**
1	**Phase I**	**200 h**	**200 h**	**0 h**	**200 h**	**0 h**	**100%**
2	Identify learning requirements	72 h	72 h	0 h	72 h	0 h	100%
3	Determine target audience	40 h	40 h	0 h	40 h	0 h	100%
4	Develop learning objectives	64 h	64 h	0 h	64 h	0 h	100%
5	Develop course outline	24 h	24 h	0 h	24 h	0 h	100%
6	Phase I Complete	0 h	0 h	0 h	0 h	0 h	100%
7	**Phase II**	**320 h**	**320 h**	**0 h**	**320 h**	**0 h**	**100%**
8	Write course manual	240 h	240 h	0 h	240 h	0 h	100%
9	Create sample files	40 h	40 h	0 h	40 h	0 h	100%
10	Create instructor materials	40 h	40 h	0 h	40 h	0 h	100%
11	Phase II Complete	0 h	0 h	0 h	0 h	0 h	100%
12	**Phase III**	**152 h**	**172 h**	**-20 h**	**152 h**	**0 h**	**100%**
13	Test beta classes	72 h	72 h	0 h	72 h	0 h	100%
14	Revise content based on feedback	80 h	80 h	0 h	80 h	0 h	100%
15	~~Launch marketing campaign~~	~~10 h~~	~~10 h~~	~~0 h~~	~~0 h~~	~~10 h~~	~~0%~~
16	~~Schedule new classes~~	~~10 h~~	~~10 h~~	~~0 h~~	~~0 h~~	~~10 h~~	~~0%~~
17	~~Phase III Complete~~	~~0 h~~	~~0 h~~	~~0 h~~	~~0 h~~	~~0 h~~	~~0%~~
18	~~Project Complete~~	~~0 h~~	~~0 h~~	~~0 h~~	~~0 h~~	~~0 h~~	~~0%~~

Figure 6 - 10: Work table shows cancelled tasks

Remember that when you set a task to *Inactive* status, Microsoft Project 2010 schedules successor tasks as if they are not linked to the *Inactive* task. For example, Figure 6 - 11 is the same schedule shown previously in Figure 6 - 9, except that I did not set the Phase III Complete and Project Complete milestone tasks to *Inactive* status. Notice that the system schedules these two Milestone tasks as if they are not linked to the two *Inactive* tasks by scheduling them on the Start date of the project. Because of this behavior, you should link successor tasks to the nearest *Active* predecessor task to reset the project schedule from that point forward.

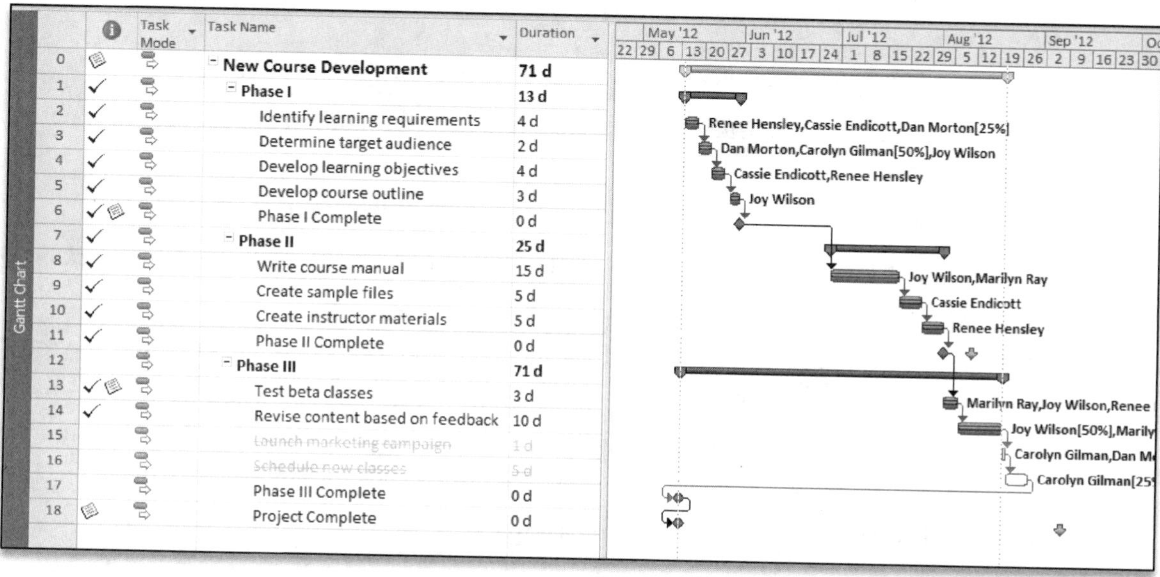

	Task Name	Duration
0	**New Course Development**	**71 d**
1	**Phase I**	**13 d**
2	Identify learning requirements	4 d
3	Determine target audience	2 d
4	Develop learning objectives	4 d
5	Develop course outline	3 d
6	Phase I Complete	0 d
7	**Phase II**	**25 d**
8	Write course manual	15 d
9	Create sample files	5 d
10	Create instructor materials	5 d
11	Phase II Complete	0 d
12	**Phase III**	**71 d**
13	Test beta classes	3 d
14	Revise content based on feedback	10 d
15	~~Launch marketing campaign~~	~~1 d~~
16	~~Schedule new classes~~	~~5 d~~
17	Phase III Complete	0 d
18	Project Complete	0 d

Figure 6 - 11: Inactive tasks do not control the schedule of successor tasks

Warning: Microsoft Project 2010 does not allow you to cancel a completed task or an in-progress task by setting it to *Inactive* status. To cancel the uncompleted work in an in-progress task, apply the task Work table and then set the *Remaining Work* value to 0h for the task.

If you set a task status to inactive using the *Inactivate* button, and later find you need the task after all, you can reset the task to *Active* status by selecting it and then clicking the *Inactivate* button again.

Hands On Exercise

Exercise 6-3

Cancel an unneeded task by setting its status to *Inactive*.

1. Navigate to your student folder and open the **Inactivate a Task.mpp** sample file.
2. Select the *Rewrite Training Module 03* task, which team members decided is no longer needed in the project.
3. Click the *Task* tab and then click the *Inactivate* button in the *Schedule* section.
4. Select the *Create Training Module 03* task, press and hold the **Control** key on your keyboard, and then select the *Training Materials Created* task.
5. Click the *Link Tasks* button in the *Schedule* section of the *Task* ribbon.
6. Double-click the *Rewrite Training Module 03* task and then click the *Notes* tab in the *Task Information* dialog.
7. Click to the right of the existing text in the *Notes* field and then press the **Enter** key on your keyboard to add a new blank line.
8. In the *Notes* field, add a Note to document the reason for setting the task to *Inactive* status (team members believe the task is no longer needed) and then click the *OK* button.
9. Save and close the **Inactivate a Task.mpp** sample file.

Understanding the Peak Field

The *Peak* field is another new feature of Microsoft Project 2010 that you can use during the execution stage of a project. Before I discuss this new feature, however, it helps to understand how the software works when you initially assign a resource to a task. Suppose that I assign Mickey Cobb to the Design task at 100% Units and 40 hour of Work, as shown in Figure 6 - 12. Notice that Microsoft Project 2010 calculates a 5-day *Duration* value for the task.

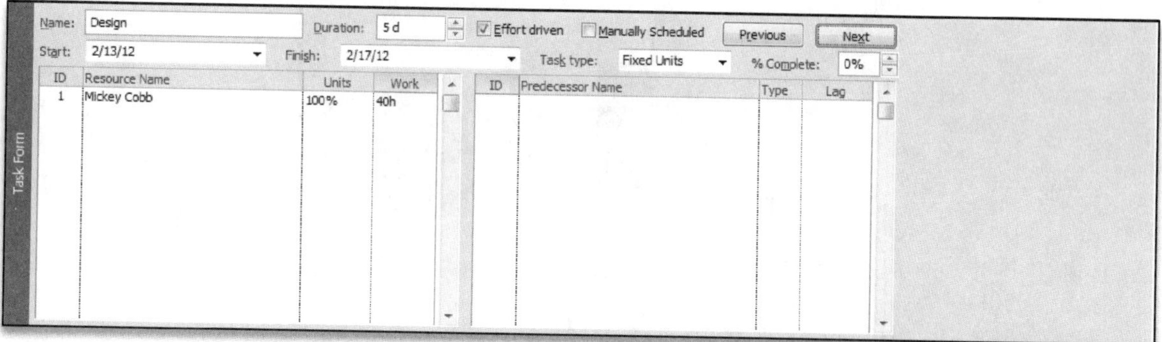

Figure 6 - 12: Resource assigned at 100% Units to the Design task

When I assign Mickey Cobb to the Design task at 100% Units, the system creates a resource assignment on the task and captures the original *Units* value of 100%. You can see the resource assignment information in either the *Task Usage* view or *Resource Usage* view of a project. Figure 6 - 13 shows the initial assignment information for Mickey Cobb's resource assignment on the Design task in the *Task Usage* view of my project. Notice that the system assigns the 40 hours of work using a flat pattern of 8 hours/day over the 5-day duration of the task.

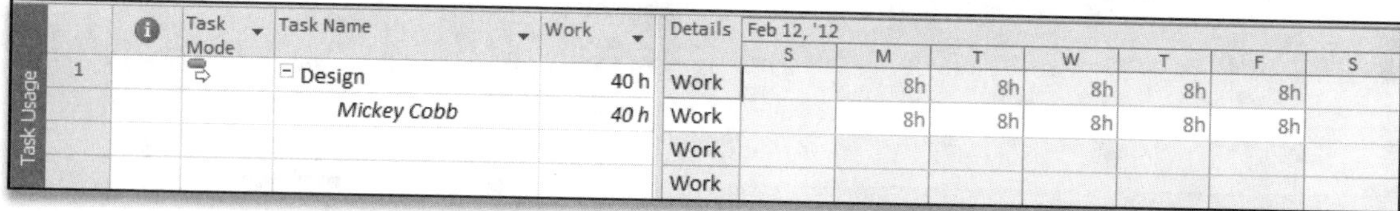

Figure 6 - 13: Task Usage view shows the resource assignment information

Although not displayed by default in either the *Task Usage* view or *Resource Usage* view, Microsoft Project 2010 offers several additional assignment fields you can use to understand how the software handles the original *Units* value on the resource assignment. These additional fields include:

- Assignment Units (an assignment field)
- Peak (an assignment field)
- Percent Allocation (a timephased assignment field)
- Peak Units (a timephased assignment field)

To add the *Assignment Units* field to the *Task Usage* view, right-click the *Work* column header. The system displays the shortcut menu shown in Figure 6 - 14

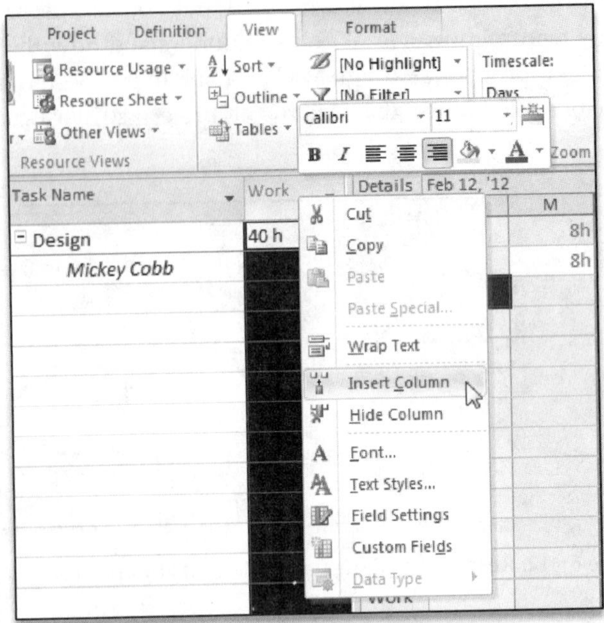

Figure 6 - 14: Shortcut menu to add a new field

Click the *Insert Column* item in the shortcut menu and then select the *Assignment Units* field from the lengthy pick list displayed by the system. Microsoft Project 2010 inserts the *Assignment Units* field to the left of the *Work* field, as shown in Figure 6 - 15.

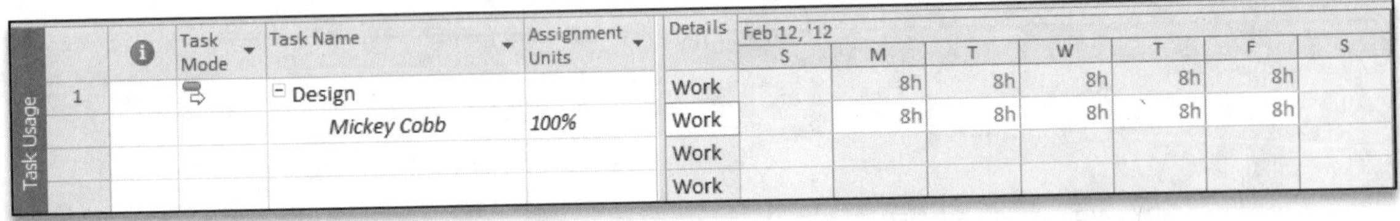

Figure 6 - 15: Assignment Units column added to the Task Usage view

After adding the *Assignment Units* field to the Task Usage view, you can also add the *Percent Allocation* time-phased assignment field to the timephased grid on the right side of the view. To add the *Percent Allocation* field, right-click anywhere in the timephased grid. On the shortcut menu, select the *Detail Styles* item at the top of the menu, as shown in Figure 6 - 16.

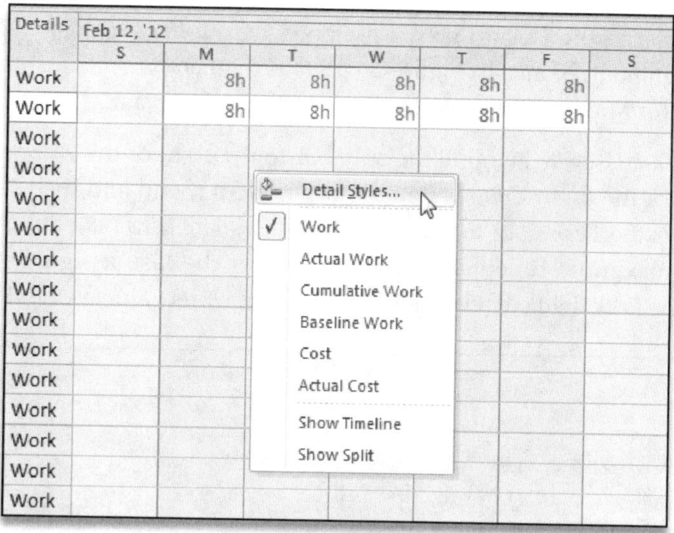

Figure 6 - 16: Shortcut menu to add a new timephased field to the timephased grid

The system displays the *Detail Styles* dialog shown in Figure 6 - 17. The *Detail Styles* dialog shows you the list of all available timephased fields in the *Available Fields* list on the left side of the dialog.

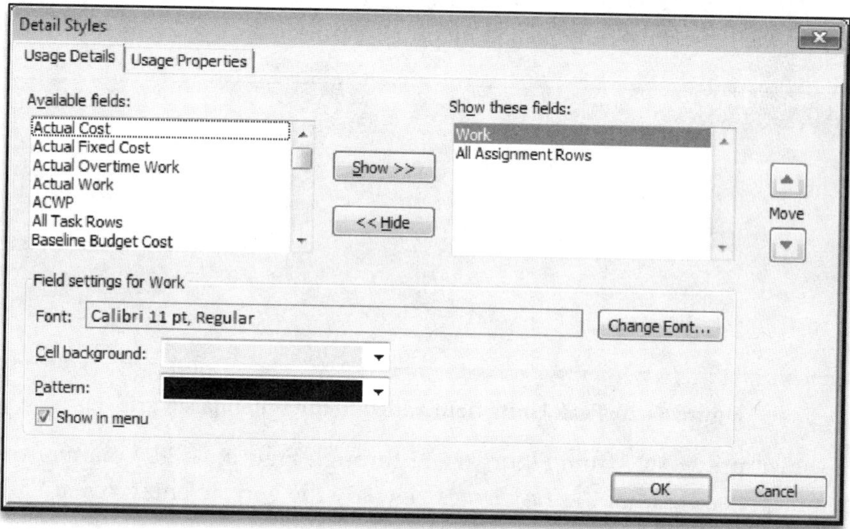

Figure 6 - 17: Detail Styles dialog

In the *Detail Styles* dialog, scroll to the bottom of the *Available Fields* list and select the *Percent Allocation* field. Click the *Show* button to add the *Percent Allocation* field to the *Show These Fields* list. Click the *OK* button to add the *Percent Allocation* timephased assignment field to the timephased grid, as shown in Figure 6 - 18.

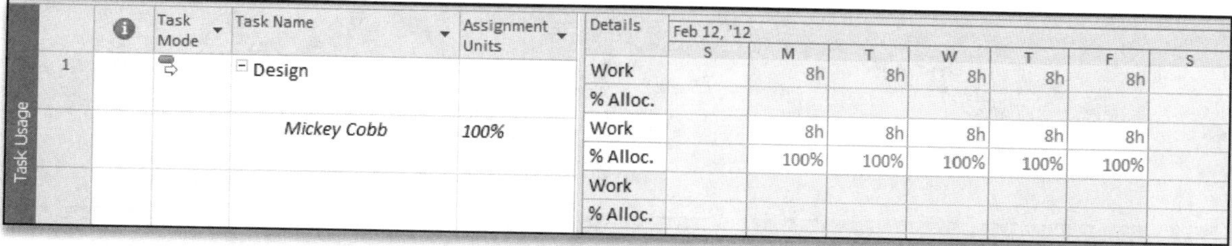

Figure 6 - 18: Percent Allocation field added to the timephased grid

When I assigned Mickey Cobb to the Design task, I assigned her at *100% Units,* which represents the original *Units* value for her task assignment. Notice in Figure 6 - 18 that the *Percent Allocation* timephased field shows the original *Units* value of 100% for Mickey Cobb's assignment on the Design task.

To add the *Peak* field to the *Task Usage* view, pull the split bar to the right of the *Work* column and then right-click the *Work* column header. Click the *Insert Column* item in the shortcut menu and then select the *Peak* field from the pick list. The system displays the *Peak* field to the right of the *Assignment Units* field, as shown in Figure 6 - 19. The *Peak* field displays the maximum timephased *Units* value for the task assignment during any time period. Notice in Figure 6 - 19 that the *Peak* field currently shows the same *Units* value as the *Assignment Units* field 100%.

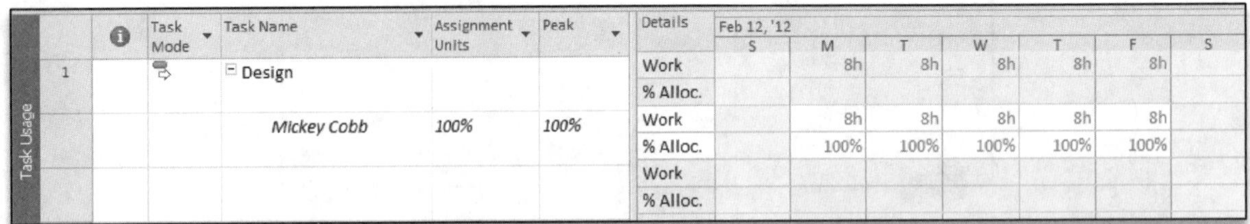

	Task Mode	Task Name	Assignment Units	Peak	Details	Feb 12, '12 S	M	T	W	T	F	S
1		Design			Work		8h	8h	8h	8h	8h	
					% Alloc.							
		Mickey Cobb	100%	100%	Work		8h	8h	8h	8h	8h	
					% Alloc.		100%	100%	100%	100%	100%	
					Work							
					% Alloc.							

Figure 6 - 19: Peak field added to the Task Usage view

To add the *Peak Units* timephased assignment field to the *Task Usage* view, right-click in the timephased grid and select the *Detail Styles* item at the top of the shortcut menu. In the *Detail Styles* dialog, select the *Peak Units* field from the *Available Fields* list. Click the *Show* button to add the *Peak Units* field to the *Show These Fields* list and then click the *OK* button to add the *Peak Units* timephased field to the timephased grid, as shown in Figure 6 - 20.

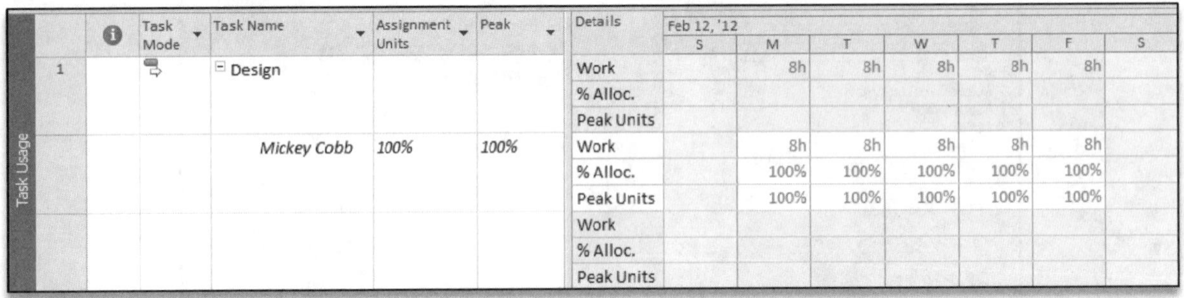

	Task Mode	Task Name	Assignment Units	Peak	Details	Feb 12, '12 S	M	T	W	T	F	S
1		Design			Work		8h	8h	8h	8h	8h	
					% Alloc.							
					Peak Units							
		Mickey Cobb	100%	100%	Work		8h	8h	8h	8h	8h	
					% Alloc.		100%	100%	100%	100%	100%	
					Peak Units		100%	100%	100%	100%	100%	
					Work							
					% Alloc.							
					Peak Units							

Figure 6 - 20: Peak Units field added to the timephased grid

In the sample project shown previously from Figure 6 - 12 through Figure 6 - 20, I manually entered *Actual Work* on a daily basis in the timephased grid of the *Task Usage* view. By the way, to enter *Actual Work* in the timephased grid, right-click anywhere in the timephased grid and select the *Actual Work* item on the shortcut menu. Figure 6 - 21 shows the sample project after I entered *Actual Work* for Mickey Cobb on the Design task.

		Task Mode	Task Name	Assignment Units	Peak	Details	Feb 12, '12 S	M	T	W	T	F	S
1	✓		Design			Work		8h	8h	8h	8h	12h	
						Act. Work		8h	8h	8h	8h	12h	
						% Alloc.							
						Peak Units							
			Mickey Cobb	100%	150%	Work		8h	8h	8h	8h	12h	
						Act. Work		8h	8h	8h	8h	12h	
						% Alloc.		100%	100%	100%	100%	150%	
						Peak Units		100%	100%	100%	100%	150%	
						Work							
						Act. Work							

Figure 6 - 21: Actual Work entered on a daily basis in the timephased grid

Notice the following facts in Figure 6 - 21 shown previously:

- On Monday through Thursday, I entered 8 hours of *Actual Work* each day.
- On Friday, I entered 12 hours of *Actual Work.*
- Based on the 12 hours of *Actual Work* entered on Friday, the system calculated the value in the *Peak* field at 150%.
- The system maintained the original 100% Units value for the task assignment in the *Assignment Units* field.

Microsoft Project 2010 calculates the value in the *Peak* field using the following formula:

Units = Work/Hours Per Day

Units = 12h/8h

Units = 150%

In Microsoft Project 2010, the default *Hours Per Day* value is 8h. You see the *Hours Per Day* value for your project in the *Schedule* page of the *Project Options* dialog.

In previous versions of Microsoft Project, such as Microsoft Project 2007, the software **does not** include a *Peak* field. Lacking a *Peak* field, previous versions of the software capture the *Peak* information in the *Assignment Units* field instead. This can cause assignment problems when you enter *Actual Work* greater than the original planned *Work* in the final time period to complete the task, and then later increase the *Remaining Work* value for the task. When Microsoft Project 2007 applies the new increased *Work* to the assignment, it assigns the additional *Work* at the **new** *Assignment Units* value instead of the **original** *Assignment Units* value. For example, Figure 6 - 22 shows the same sample project in Microsoft Project 2007. After entering *Actual Work* during the first week, I increased the *Remaining Work* by 24 hours. Although I assigned Mickey Cobb to the Design task at *100% Units* initially, notice that the system applied the 24 hours of additional Work using the new *Assignment Units* field value of 150% (12 hours/day instead of the original 8 hours/day).

		Task Name	Assignment Units	Details	Feb 12, '12 S	M	T	W	T	F	S	Feb 19, '12 S	M	T	W
1		− Design		Work		8h	8h	8h	8h	12h			12h	12h	
				Act. Work		8h	8h	8h	8h	12h					
				% Alloc.											
				Peak Units											
		Mickey Cobb	150%	Work		8h	8h	8h	8h	12h			12h	12h	
				Act. Work		8h	8h	8h	8h	12h					
				% Alloc.		100%	100%	100%	100%	150%			150%	150%	
				Peak Units		100%	100%	100%	100%	150%			150%	150%	
				Work											
				Act. Work											
				% Alloc.											
				Peak Units											

Figure 6 - 22: Microsoft Project 2007 - Additional Remaining Work assigned at 150% Units instead of the original 100% Units

By using the new *Peak* field, Microsoft Project 2010 eliminates this problem by **holding constant** the value in the *Assignment Units* field as you enter *Actual Work* on a task assignment. For example, Figure 6 - 23 shows the same sample project in Microsoft Project 2010. Notice how the system assigned the additional 24 hours of *Remaining Work* correctly, using the original 100% value in *Assignment Units* field.

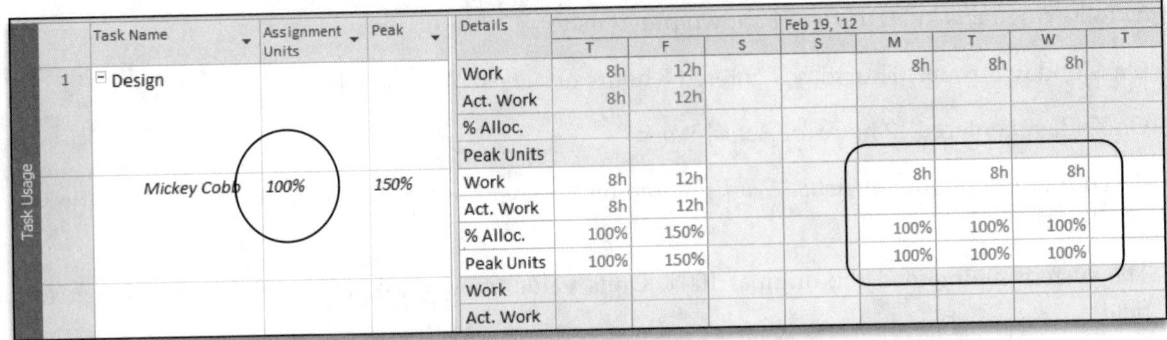

Figure 6 - 23: Microsoft Project 2010 – Additional Remaining Work assigned at the original 100% Units

Hands On Exercise

Exercise 6-4

Study the behavior of the new *Peak* field as you enter *Actual Work* and adjust the *Remaining Work* on a task.

1. Navigate to your student folder and open the **Using the Peak Field.mpp** sample file.
2. Click the *Task* tab to display the *Task* ribbon, if necessary.
3. Select the *Design P1* task and then click the *Scroll to Task* button in the *Editing* section of the *Task* ribbon to bring the timephased work into view.
4. Right-click on the *Work* column header, click the *Insert Column* item in the shortcut menu, and then select the *Assignment Units* field from the pick list.
5. Pull the split bar to the right of the *Work* column.
6. Right-click on the *Work* column header, click the *Insert Column* item in the shortcut menu, and then select the *Peak* field from the pick list.
7. Right-click anywhere in the timephased grid on the right side of the *Task Usage* view and select the *Detail Styles* item in the shortcut menu.
8. In the *Detail Styles* dialog, select the following fields individually in the *Available fields* list and then click the *Show* button to add them to the *Show these fields* list:
    - Actual Work
    - Peak Units
    - Percent Allocation
9. Click the *OK* button to close the *Detail Styles* dialog.

10. In the timephased grid, double-click the right edge of the *Details* column header to "best fit" the contents of the *Details* column.
11. In the timephased grid, select the *Actual Work* cell for George Stewart (white cell) for Monday, March 18, 2013.
12. Enter the following *Actual Work* values for George Stewart during the week of March 17, 2013:

Date	3/18/13	3/19/13	3/20/13	3/21/13	3/22/13
Actual Work	8	8	8	8	12

Notice how the value in the *Peak* field value changes from 100% to 150% due to entering 12 hours of *Actual Work* on Friday, March 22. Notice also how the *Assignment Units* field value remains constant at the 100% value.

13. Select the *Design P1* task again.
14. Click the *View* tab and then select the *Details* option in the *Split View* section of the *View* ribbon.
15. Right-click anywhere in the bottom pane and select the *Work* item on the shortcut menu to display the *Work* details in the *Task Form* view.
16. In the *Task Form*, change the *Remaining Work* field value to *24 hours* and then click the *OK* button.
17. Deselect the *Details* option in the *Split View* section of the *View* ribbon to close the *Task Form*.
18. Scroll the timephased grid to the week of March 24, 2013 to see the 24 hours of new *Work* scheduled during that week.

Notice how the system assigns the additional 24 hours of *Work* using the original 100% value in the *Assignment Units* field while maintaining the 150% value in the *Peak* field.

19. Save and close the **Using the Peak Field.mpp** sample file.

Synchronizing with a SharePoint Tasks List

If your organization uses Microsoft SharePoint Foundation 2010 or Microsoft SharePoint Server (MSS) 2010, but does not use the enterprise tool Microsoft Project Server 2010, you can leverage the power of SharePoint by publishing your project file to a SharePoint site as a Tasks list, and then synchronizing your project tasks with the SharePoint tasks list. This feature enables two-way communication between you and your project team members. It allows you to display the current task schedule to all team members, and allows your team members to submit task updates for their assigned tasks. Before you can use this feature, you must meet a number of requirements for both SharePoint and your Microsoft Project 2010 file. The requirements for SharePoint include:

- Your SharePoint administrator must create a SharePoint site for you.
- Your SharePoint administrator must create user accounts on the SharePoint site for all of the resources you intend to use in your projects.
- Your SharePoint administrator must supply you with the URL for the site.

Warning: The Synchronize with a SharePoint Tasks List feature is available **only** in the Professional version of Microsoft Project 2010. You **cannot** use this feature if you have the Standard version of the software.

Warning: Your organization **must** use either Microsoft SharePoint Foundation 2010 or Microsoft SharePoint Server 2010 before you can publish and synchronize your Microsoft Project 2010 tasks with a Tasks list in SharePoint. You **cannot** use any previous version of Windows SharePoint Services for this functionality.

The requirements for your Microsoft Project 2010 file include:

- You can save the project file in any location, including the SharePoint site, a network share, or even a folder on your workstation's hard drive.
- The name of each resource you enter in the Resource Sheet view of your project **must** exactly match the resource's User Name in the SharePoint site.
- You **must** use the *Manually Scheduled* task mode for **all tasks** in your project, including summary tasks.
- No two summary tasks at the same level of indenture can have the same name.
- You must use **only** Finish-to-Start (FS) dependencies to link tasks in your project. You **must not** use any other dependency relationship and you **must not** use Lag time or Lead time on the FS dependencies.
- You **must not** use any type of constraints in your project, other than the default *As Soon As Possible* (ASAP) constraint.
- You **cannot** assign generic resources to tasks in your project.
- You **must not** use any special characters in the names of summary tasks. Special characters include the following:

  ~ " # % : * & < > ? / { } |

Despite the many restrictions shown in the preceding list of bulleted items, you **can** use *Deadline* dates in your project!

Figure 6 - 24 shows a project that meets all of the requirements in the preceding list of bulleted items. Notice in particular that I set all tasks to Manually Scheduled, including summary tasks, and assigned only one resource per task.

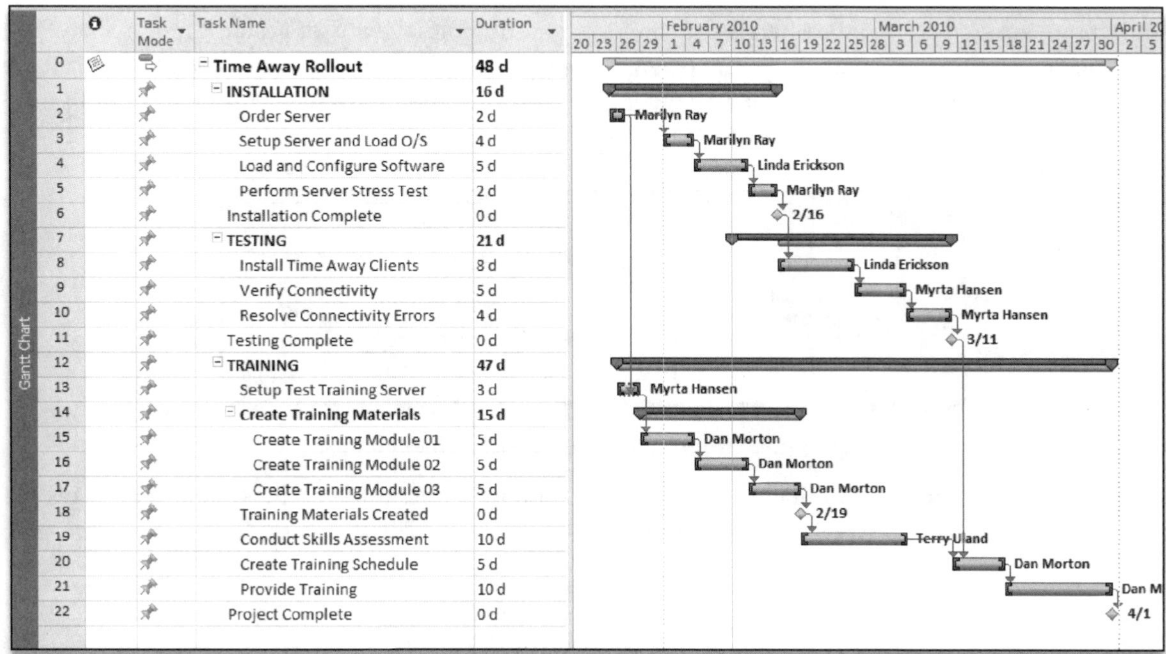

Figure 6 - 24: New project ready for synchronization with a Tasks list in SharePoint

To kick off the task synchronization with SharePoint feature in Microsoft Project 2010, you must publish your project to SharePoint by completing the following steps:

1. Click the *File* tab and then click the *Save & Send* tab in the Backstage.
2. On the *Save & Send* page, click the *Sync with Tasks List* tab.
3. In the *Sync with Tasks List* section on the *Save & Send* page, enter or paste the URL of the SharePoint site in the *Site URL* field, as shown in Figure 6 - 25.

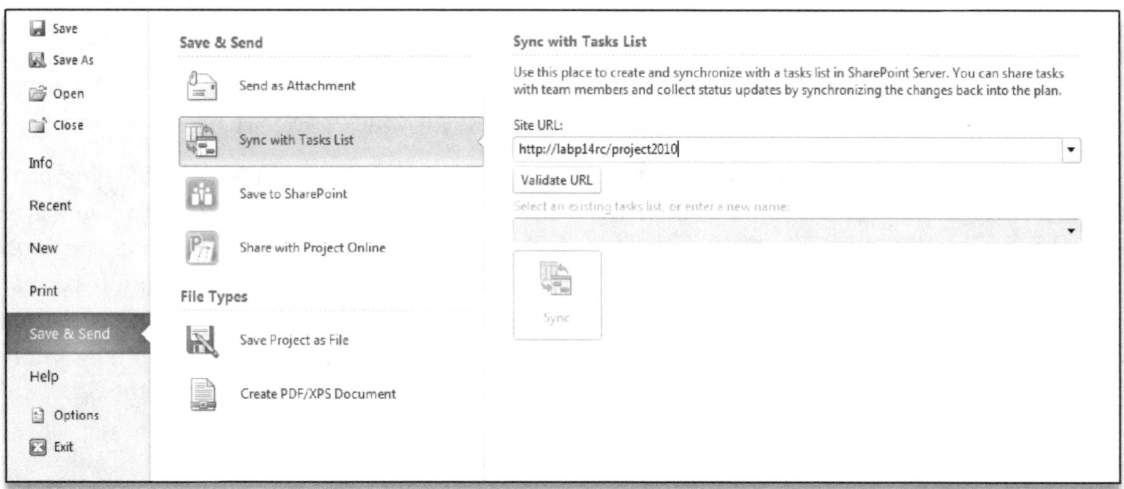

Figure 6 - 25: Enter Site URL in the Sync with Tasks List section

4. Click the *Validate URL* button to confirm the URL you entered.

If you enter an incorrect URL for the SharePoint site, or if you do not have a user account in the SharePoint site, the system displays the dialog shown in Figure 6 - 26. To resolve this problem, you may need to confirm the URL of the SharePoint site with your SharePoint administrator, and confirm you do have a user account in the SharePoint site.

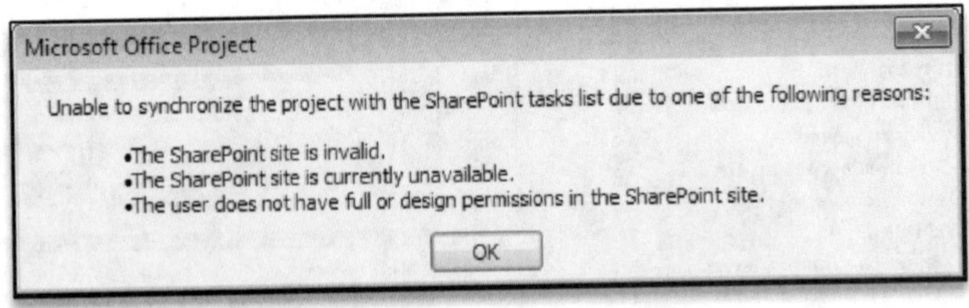

Figure 6 - 26: Error message in accessing SharePoint site

If you enter a valid URL and you do have a user account on the SharePoint site, the system redisplays the *Sync with Tasks List* section on the *Save & Send* page, and activates the *Select an existing tasks list or enter a new name* field and the *Sync* button, as shown in Figure 6 - 27.

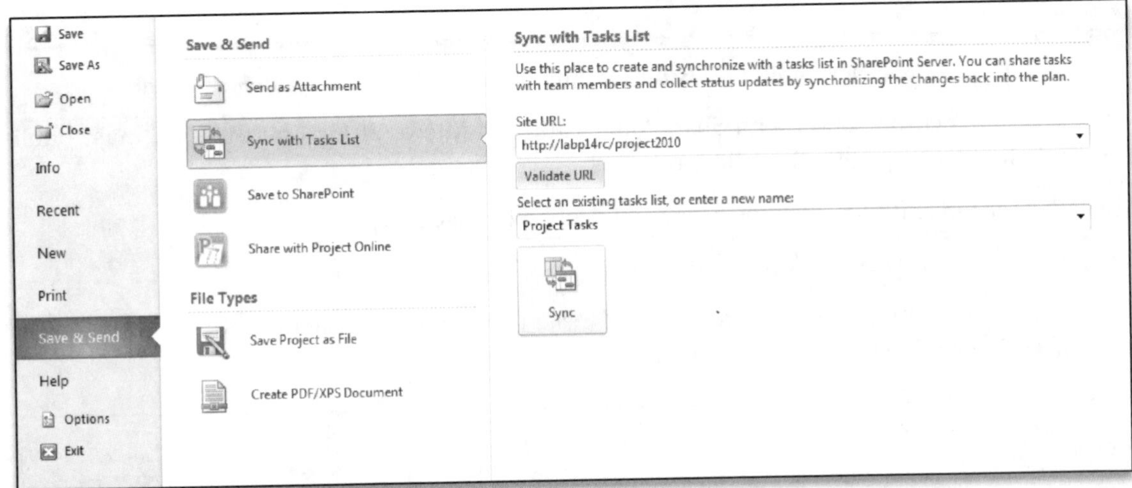

Figure 6 - 27: Save & Send page, ready to sync with a Tasks list

If a Tasks list already exists in the SharePoint site, for instance as a result of someone publishing a project to SharePoint, then you should see the name of that Tasks list in the *Select an existing tasks list or enter a new name* field. For example, notice in Figure 6 - 27 shown previously that the *Select an existing tasks list or enter a new name* field contains the name of the Project Tasks list. This is the tasks list shown previously in Module 03 that project managers use to create new projects in Microsoft Project 2010. If the SharePoint site does not contain an existing tasks list, then the *Select an existing tasks list or enter a new name* field is blank. When you initially publish your project to a SharePoint tasks list, you should manually enter the name of a new tasks list in the *Select an existing tasks list or enter a new name* field.

To minimize confusion in the minds of your team members about *Task* lists for multiple projects, MsProjectExperts recommends that you name your *Task* list using the same name of the project containing the tasks you want to sync with SharePoint.

After you enter the name of a new *Tasks* list in the *Select an existing tasks list or enter a new name* field, click the *Sync* button. As Microsoft Project 2010 publishes your project to the SharePoint tasks list, the system displays the SharePoint Synchronization dialog shown in Figure 6 - 28. This dialog shows the status of the synchronization process with the SharePoint tasks list and reports progress as it creates the *Tasks* list, reads the Properties of the *Tasks* list, downloads the *Tasks* list from SharePoint, compares the *Tasks* list in SharePoint with the tasks your Microsoft Project 2010 plan, and then writes *Tasks* list data to SharePoint and your project file.

Figure 6 - 28: SharePoint Synchronization dialog

During the publishing process, if the system encounters an error of any type, such as if you fail to meet the requirements specified for a project, then Microsoft Project 2010 displays an error dialog to document the error and suggest a solution. For example, the error dialog shown in Figure 6 - 29 warns you if you fail to set the *Task Mode* value to *Manually Scheduled* for each task in your project.

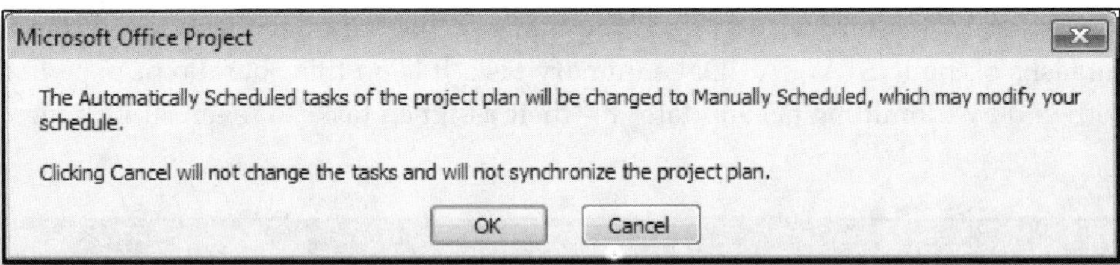

Figure 6 - 29: Error dialog about Automatically Scheduled tasks

After you publish your project successfully to a SharePoint tasks list, users can see the *Tasks* list in the SharePoint site. For example, Figure 6 - 30 shows a new *Tasks* list called Time Away Deployment in the SharePoint site. By default, the *Tasks* list shows only first-level tasks initially. This means I see only the Phase summary tasks (INSTALLATION, TESTING, and TRAINING) plus their corresponding milestone tasks.

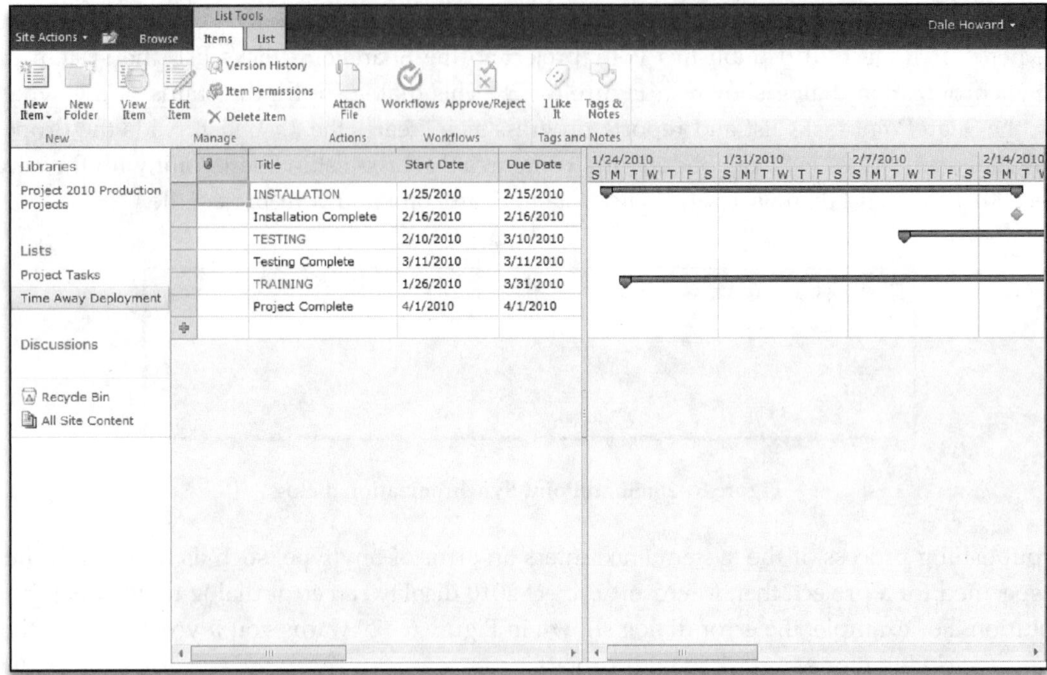

Figure 6 - 30: Tasks list for the Time Away Deployment project in a SharePoint site

To view the subtasks for any summary task, click the name of the summary task. For example, Figure 6 - 31 shows the four subtasks of the INSTALLATION summary task. It is on this SharePoint page that team members can collaborate with you by submitting task updates for their assigned tasks, or even submitting new tasks for the project.

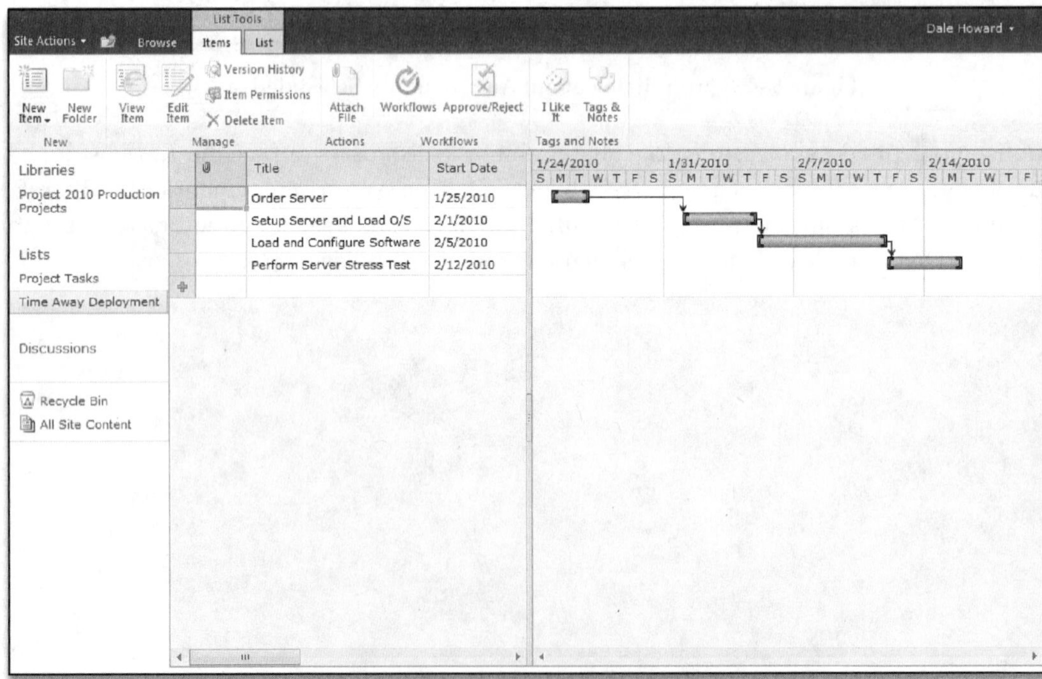

Figure 6 - 31: Subtasks of the INSTALLATION summary task

Adding Fields to the Task Synchronization Process

When you initially publish your project to a SharePoint *Tasks* list, Microsoft Project 2010 uses the information in the project to create a series of fields in the list. Most of the SharePoint fields map to a corresponding *Task* field in the project file, but several of the SharePoint fields do not map to any field in Microsoft Project 2010. Table 6 - 1 shows the list of SharePoint fields and the corresponding fields in Microsoft Project 2010.

SharePoint Tasks Field	Microsoft Project 2010 Field
Title	Name (Task Name)
Start Date	Start
Due Date	Finish
% Complete	% Complete
Assigned To	Resource Names
Predecessors	Predecessors
Priority	No corresponding field
Task Status	No corresponding field

Table 6 - 1: Corresponding fields in a SharePoint tasks list and the Microsoft Project 2010 file

In addition to the standard fields included in the task synchronization process, Microsoft Project 2010 allows you to add other fields, including both standard fields and custom fields, for reporting purposes or to give team members additional information about their task assignments. To add other fields to the task synchronization process, complete the following steps:

1. Click the *File* tab and then click the *Save & Send* tab in the Backstage.
2. On the *Save & Send* page, click the *Manage Fields* button in the *Manage Fields* section of the page.

After you publish your project tasks to SharePoint initially, you can also access the *Manage Fields* button and the *Synch* button on the *Info* page in the *Backstage,* however you cannot perform your initial publish from the *Info* page.

The system displays the *Manage Fields* dialog shown in Figure 6 - 32. Notice that the *Manage Fields* dialog confirms the field mapping I documented previously in Table 6 - 1.

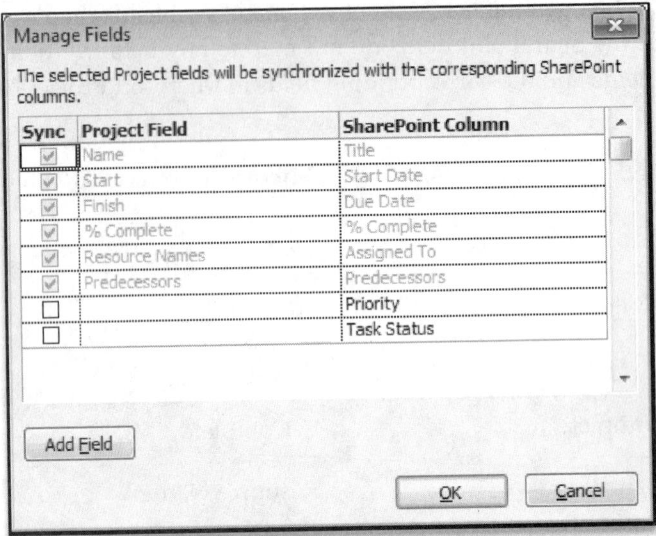

Figure 6 - 32: Manage Fields dialog

Microsoft Project 2010 does not allow you to select the *Sync* checkbox for the *Priority* and *Task Status* fields in SharePoint because there are no fields in Microsoft Project 2010 that correpond to these two SharePoint fields. You may not find them useful. If this is the case, you or your SharePoint administrator can remove these two fields from the Project Tasks view for your project in SharePoint. I discuss how to modify the Project Tasks view a little later in this section of the module.

3. In the *Manage Fields* dialog, click the *Add Field* button. The system displays the *Add Field* dialog shown in Figure 6 - 33.

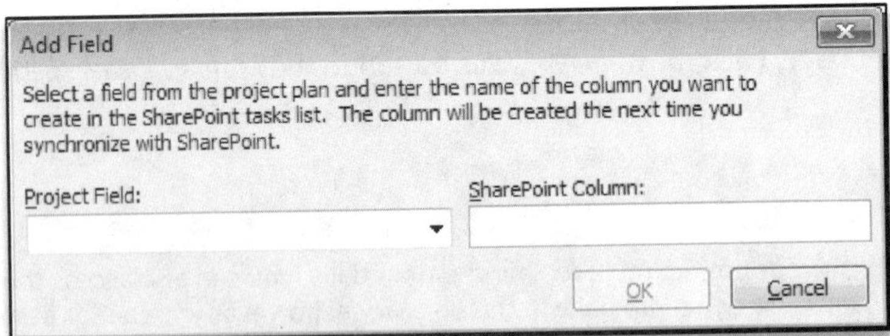

Figure 6 - 33: Add Field dialog

4. In the *Add Field* dialog, click the *Project Field* pick list and select a default or custom field in Microsoft Project 2010. The system enters the name of the field in the *SharePoint Column* field automatically.
5. In the *Add Field* dialog, optionally, enter an alternate name in the *SharePoint Column* field and then click the *OK* button.

The system displays the new field in the *Manage Fields* dialog, as shown in Figure 6 - 34. Notice in the *Manage Fields* dialog that I added the *Actual Start field* and the *Actual Finish* field. The next time I click the *Sync* button, Microsoft Project 2010 will create these two corresponding fields in the SharePoint tasks list.

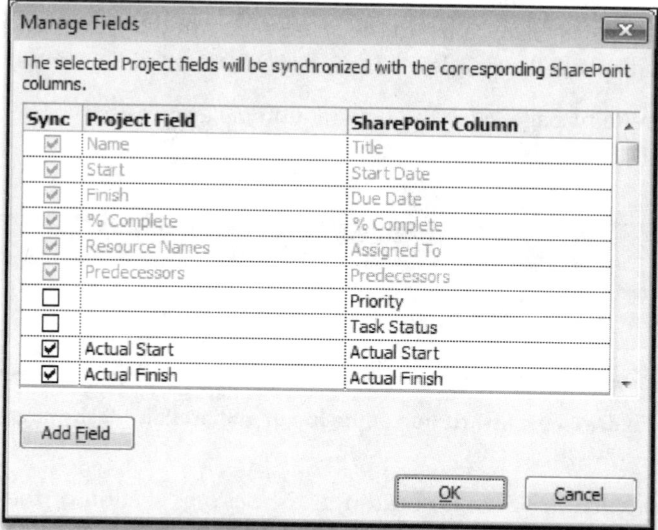

Figure 6 - 34: Manage Fields dialog shows two new fields added

6. Click the *OK* button to close the *Manage Fields* dialog.

The *Actual Start* and *Actual Finish* fields, shown in the Manage Fields dialog in the figure are two excellent examples of useful fields you can add to the SharePoint tasks list for your project. These two fields allow team members to report when when they **actually** started and finished a task, which allows you to see schedule variance if a team member starts or finishes a task on a different day than its baseline dates. Because of this, MSProjectExperts recommends as a best practice that you add the *Actual Start* and *Actual Finish* fields in the *Manage Fields* dialog for each project you publish to a SharePoint tasks list.

7. Click the *Sync* button to create the new field(s) in the SharePoint tasks list.

Modifying the Project Tasks View in SharePoint

After you sync your project tasks with the SharePoint tasks list, the system creates a new SharePoint field for each new Microsoft Project 2010 field you selected in the *Manage Fields* dialog. However, the system **does not** add the new fields to the default *Project Tasks* view for your project's SharePoint tasks list. This means that either you or your SharePoint administrator must add the new fields manually to the *Project Tasks* view in SharePoint. Before you can edit the *Project Tasks* view in SharePoint, your SharePoint administrator must make sure you are a member of the *Project 2010 Owners* group in SharePoint.

If you have the proper permissions in SharePoint, you can edit the default *Project Tasks* view for your project tasks list by completing the following steps:

1. Navigate to the SharePoint site where your organization stores projects and tasks lists.
2. Click the name of your project's tasks list in the *Lists* section of the Quick Launch Menu on the left side of the page. The system displays the first-level *Tasks for your project* view, shown previously in Figure 6 - 30.
3. At the top of the SharePoint page, click the *List* item on *the List Tools* tab. The system displays the *List* ribbon shown in Figure 6 - 35.

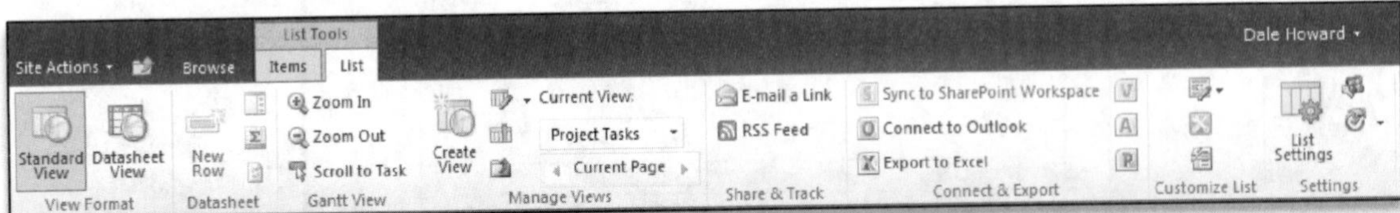

Figure 6 - 35: List ribbon at the top of a SharePoint tasks page

4. In the *List* ribbon, click the *List Settings* button in the *Settings* section of the ribbon. SharePoint displays the *List Settings* page shown in Figure 6 - 36 and Figure 6 - 37. Because of the length of the *List Settings* page, I need to break the screenshot into two separate figures.

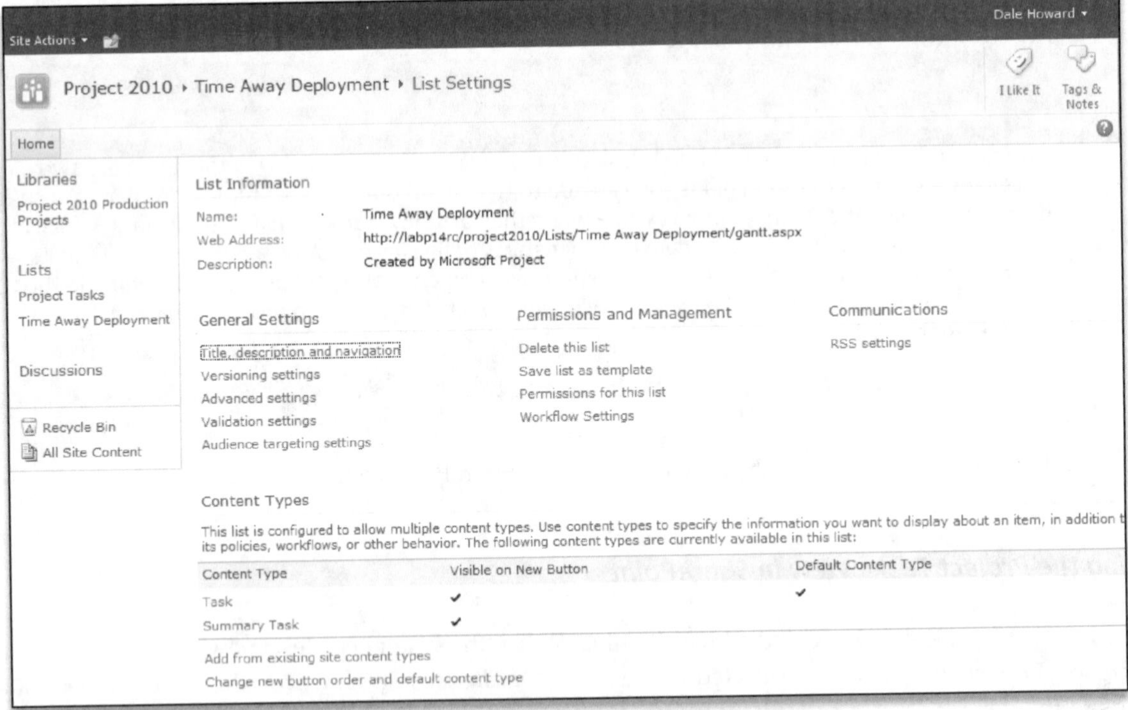

Figure 6 - 36: List Settings page, first three sections

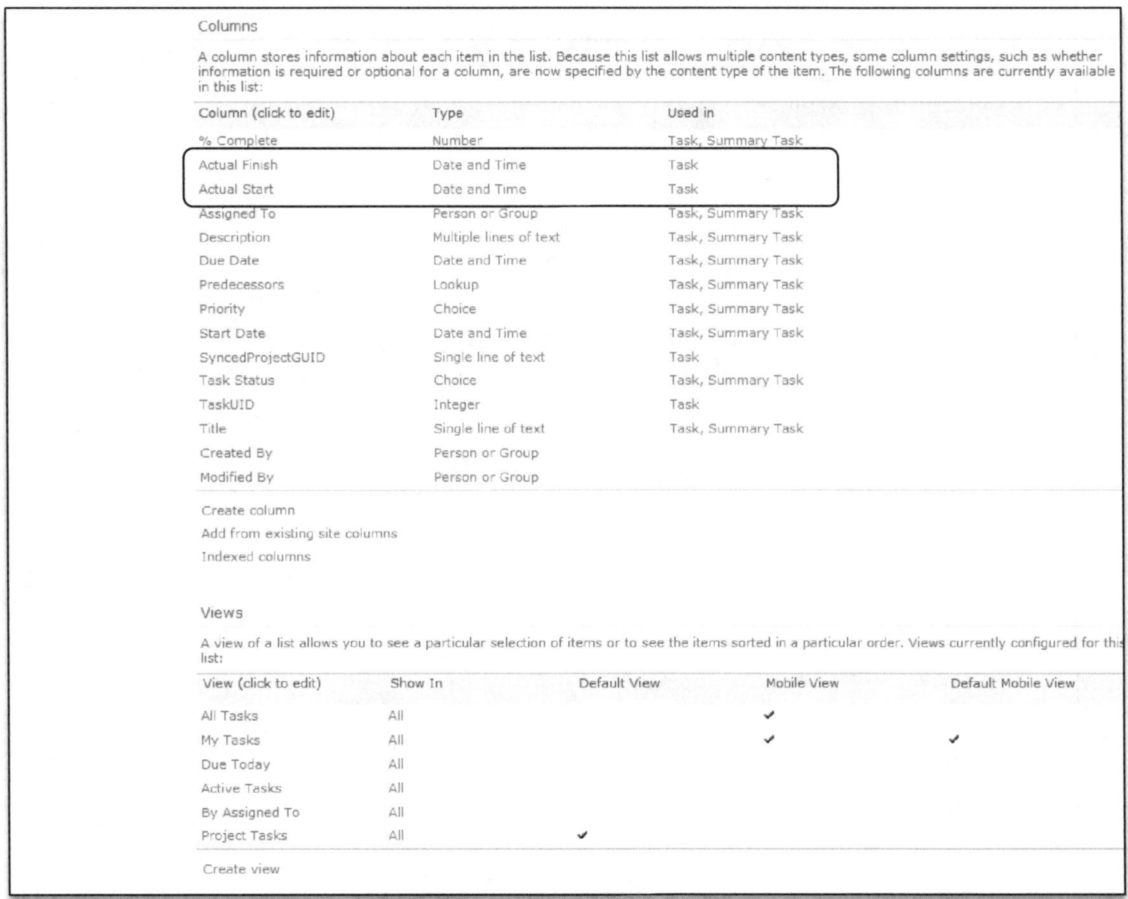

Figure 6 - 37: List Settings page, last two sections

Notice in the *Columns* section of the *List Settings* page shown previously in Figure 6 - 36 that the system created the *Actual Start* and *Actual Finish* fields in SharePoint tasks list, as expected.

5. In the *Views* section of the *List Settings* page, click the name of the *Project Tasks* view to open this View for editing. The system displays the *Edit View* page shown in Figure 6 - 38.

When you navigate to the *Edit View* page, the system expands the *Gantt Columns*, *Sort*, and *Filter* sections by default. For the sake of brevity, however, I collapsed these three sections, as shown in Figure 6 - 38. You do not need to change any settings in these three sections to modify the *Project Tasks* view to include the *Actual Start* and *Actual Finish* fields.

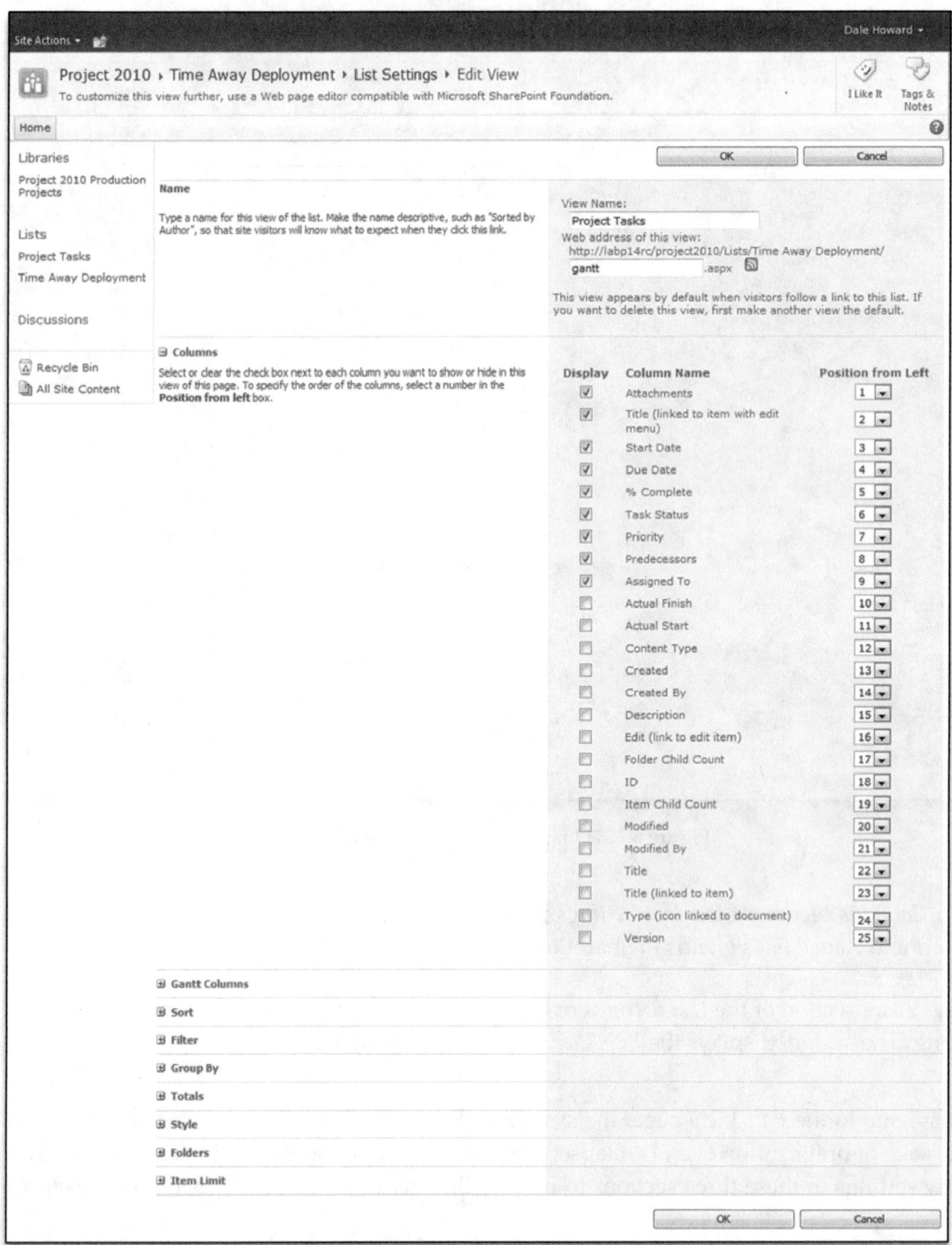

Figure 6 - 38: Edit View page

6. In the *Columns* section of the *Edit View* page, select the checkbox for the *Actual Start* field and the *Actual Finish* field.

7. In the *Columns* section of the *Edit View* page, select a value in the *Position from Left* pick list for the *Actual Start* field and the *Actual Finish* field to control the order of the columns displayed in the View.

8. Click the *OK* button to save the changes to the Project Tasks view.

Figure 6 - 39 shows the edited Project Tasks view applied to the tasks in the INSTALLATION phase of the project.

Title	Actual Start	% Complete	Actual Finish	Start Date	Due Date
Order Server		0 %		1/25/2010	1/26/2010
Setup Server and Load O/S		0 %		2/1/2010	2/4/2010
Load and Configure Software		0 %		2/5/2010	2/11/2010
Perform Server Stress Test		0 %		2/12/2010	2/15/2010

Figure 6 - 39: Project Tasks view shows new display order of columns

Keep in mind that the *Project Tasks* view is the default view for the SharePoint page that displays first-level summary tasks **and** for the SharePoint page that shows subtasks for these summary tasks. Therefore, if you modify the default *Project Tasks* view, you see the same columns in the same order on **both pages**.

Notice in Figure 6 - 39 that the display order of columns in my edited Project Tasks view is as follows: Title, Actual Start, % Complete, Actual Finish, Start Date, and Due Date. To take maximum advantage of using the Sync to SharePoint Tasks List functionality, I recommend you use these columns in the order I specified for my project.

Reporting Progress Using a SharePoint Tasks List

In the Tasks list for your project, SharePoint allows your project team members to collaborate with you using each of the following features:

- Enter task progress.
- Adjust the planned Start date or Finish date of a task.
- Create a new task.

If you use the column order shown previously in Figure 6 - 39, I recommend you teach your team members to report task progress on their SharePoint tasks using the following methodology:

1. When you start work on a new task, enter the date you began work on the task in the *Actual Start* field.
2. Enter your estimate of the percentage of work completed to date on the task in the *% Complete* field.
3. When you complete work on a task, enter the date you finished work on the task in the *Actual Finish* field.
4. Attach a document to the task, if needed, to provide supporting information.
5. Use the date in the *Start Date* field to determine when you **should** begin work on a task.
6. Use the date in the *Due Date* field to determine when you **should** finish work on a task.

MsProjectExperts recommends as a best practice that you use the display order of columns shown in Figure 6 - 39 and that you use the progress reporting methodology documented above. Doing so allows you to truly "harness the power" of the Syc with SharePoint Tasks List functionality!

Warning: If you use the *Actual Start* and *Actual Finish* fields in the synchronization process, keep in mind that SharePoint assumes **12:00 AM** as the time for any date entered by a team member in both of these fields. To make the best use of these two fields in SharePoint, team members should enter both the **date and time** they started or finished a task. For example, the team member might enter "1/25/2010 8:00 AM" in the *Actual Start* field or enter "1/26/2010 5:00 PM" in the *Actual Finish* field. If you lack team member cooperation for this process, you may wish to omit using the *Actual Start* and *Actual Finish* fields and use only the *% Complete* field for SharePoint synchronization.

To enter progress on a task, at a minimum the team member needs to enter a value in the *% Complete* field for the task. If you follow the methodology I recommend above, the team member should also enter or select a date in the *Actual Start* field and/or *Actual Finish* date field as per best practice. When finished, the team member should also press the **Enter** key on the keyboard to save the data in the SharePoint database. For example, notice in Figure 6 - 40 that Mickey Cobb entered data in the *Actual Start, % Complete,* and *Actual Finish* fields to indicate that she started and finished work on the task during the same week. Notice the icon to the left of the task indicates that she has not yet pressed the **Enter** key to save the data.

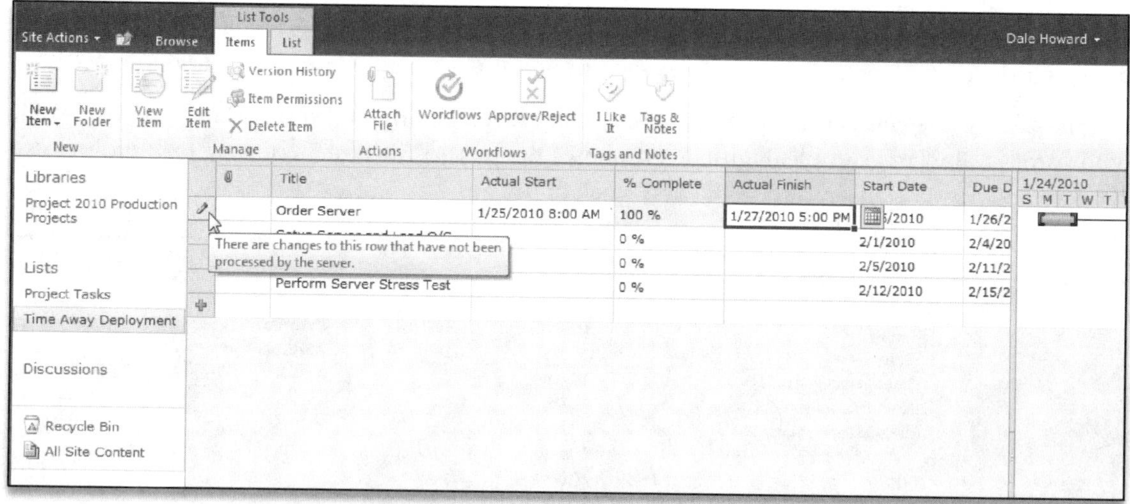

Figure 6 - 40: Progress entered on the Order Server task but not yet saved to the SharePoint database

Notice in Figure 6 - 40 that the team member entered both a date and a time in the *Actual Start* and *Actual Finish* fields for the Order Server task. Remember that if a team member does not enter a time value with the date value, SharePoint sets the time value to 12:00 AM (midnight) for the date entered.

After the team member presses the **Enter** key to save the data to the SharePoint database, the system briefly displays another indicator for the progress of the save, and then removes the indicator. To update the progress entered by your team members, open the project and then click the *Sync* button on the *Save & Send* page in the *Backstage*. After Microsoft Project 2010 synchronizes the task progress data from the SharePoint tasks list, you may see a *Conflict Resolution* dialog such as the one shown in Figure 6 - 41.

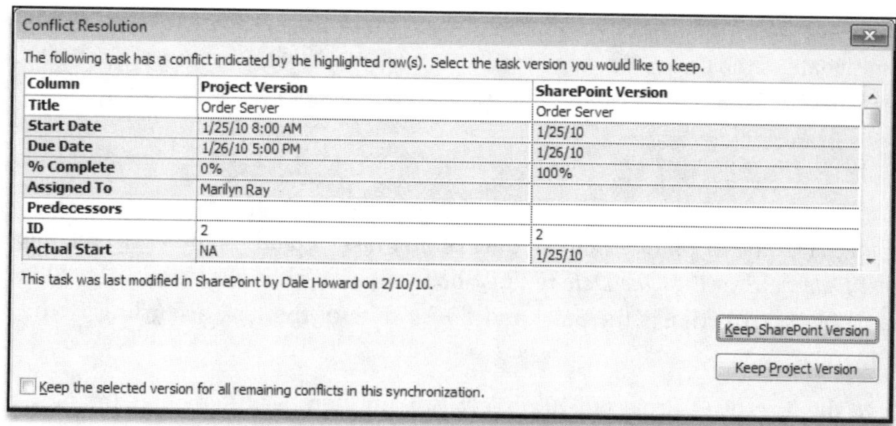

Column	Project Version	SharePoint Version
Title	Order Server	Order Server
Start Date	1/25/10 8:00 AM	1/25/10
Due Date	1/26/10 5:00 PM	1/26/10
% Complete	0%	100%
Assigned To	Marilyn Ray	
Predecessors		
ID	2	2
Actual Start	NA	1/25/10

Figure 6 - 41: Conflict Resolution dialog

The *Conflict Resolution* dialog shows you the differences between the tasks in SharePoint and the tasks in your Microsoft Project 2010 project file. To accept the task updates from your team members, click the *Keep SharePoint Version* button. To reject the task updates from your team members, and reset the SharePoint tasks to the schedule in the Microsoft Project 2010 file, click the *Keep Project Version* button. If you have multiple pending task updates from your team members, you can also select the *Keep the selected version for all remaining conflicts in this synchronization* option before you click either button to auto-accept or auto-reject all pending task updates.

If you click the *Keep SharePoint Version* button in the *Conflict Resolution* dialog, you see the progress applied to the tasks in your project file. For example, Figure 6 - 42 shows the project file after accepting task progress submitted by Marilyn Ray and Myrta Hansen during the first week of the project.

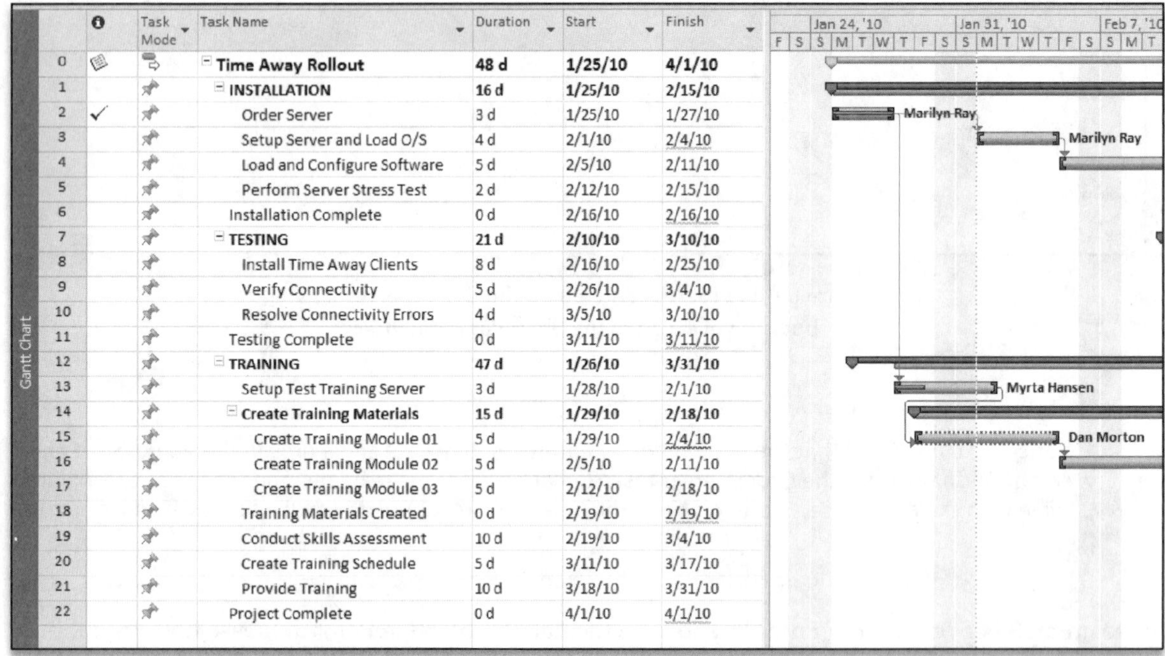

		Task Mode	Task Name	Duration	Start	Finish
0			Time Away Rollout	48 d	1/25/10	4/1/10
1			INSTALLATION	16 d	1/25/10	2/15/10
2	✓		Order Server	3 d	1/25/10	1/27/10
3			Setup Server and Load O/S	4 d	2/1/10	2/4/10
4			Load and Configure Software	5 d	2/5/10	2/11/10
5			Perform Server Stress Test	2 d	2/12/10	2/15/10
6			Installation Complete	0 d	2/16/10	2/16/10
7			TESTING	21 d	2/10/10	3/10/10
8			Install Time Away Clients	8 d	2/16/10	2/25/10
9			Verify Connectivity	5 d	2/26/10	3/4/10
10			Resolve Connectivity Errors	4 d	3/5/10	3/10/10
11			Testing Complete	0 d	3/11/10	3/11/10
12			TRAINING	47 d	1/26/10	3/31/10
13			Setup Test Training Server	3 d	1/28/10	2/1/10
14			Create Training Materials	15 d	1/29/10	2/18/10
15			Create Training Module 01	5 d	1/29/10	2/4/10
16			Create Training Module 02	5 d	2/5/10	2/11/10
17			Create Training Module 03	5 d	2/12/10	2/18/10
18			Training Materials Created	0 d	2/19/10	2/19/10
19			Conduct Skills Assessment	10 d	2/19/10	3/4/10
20			Create Training Schedule	5 d	3/11/10	3/17/10
21			Provide Training	10 d	3/18/10	3/31/10
22			Project Complete	0 d	4/1/10	4/1/10

Figure 6 - 42: Microsoft Project 2010 file after synchronizing task progress on two tasks

Notice in the project shown in Figure 6 - 42 that Microsoft Project 2010 displays a schedule *Warning* on the Finish date of the Create Training Module 01 task. To maintain an accurate project schedule, I need to respond to all schedule *Warnings* and then synchronize this project again.

To adjust the planned Start date or planned Finish date of any task, a team member needs only to enter or select a new date in the *Start Date* field or the *Due Date* field. When you synchronize your project file with the SharePoint tasks list, Microsoft Project 2010 adjusts the *Start* and *Finish* date of the task according to the new schedule estimated by the team member.

To add a new task to the Microsoft Project 2010 project, a team member must enter the new task information in the last line of the SharePoint task list, indicated by green plus sign (+) indicator at the left end of the row. At a minimum, the team member should enter a task name in the *Title* field, but can optionally enter a planned Start date or Finish date in the *Start Date* and *Due Date* fields, can select a predecessor for the new task in the *Predecessors* field, and can even select an assigned resource in the *Assigned To* field. For example, Figure 6 - 43 shows a team member entering a new task named Tune Server.

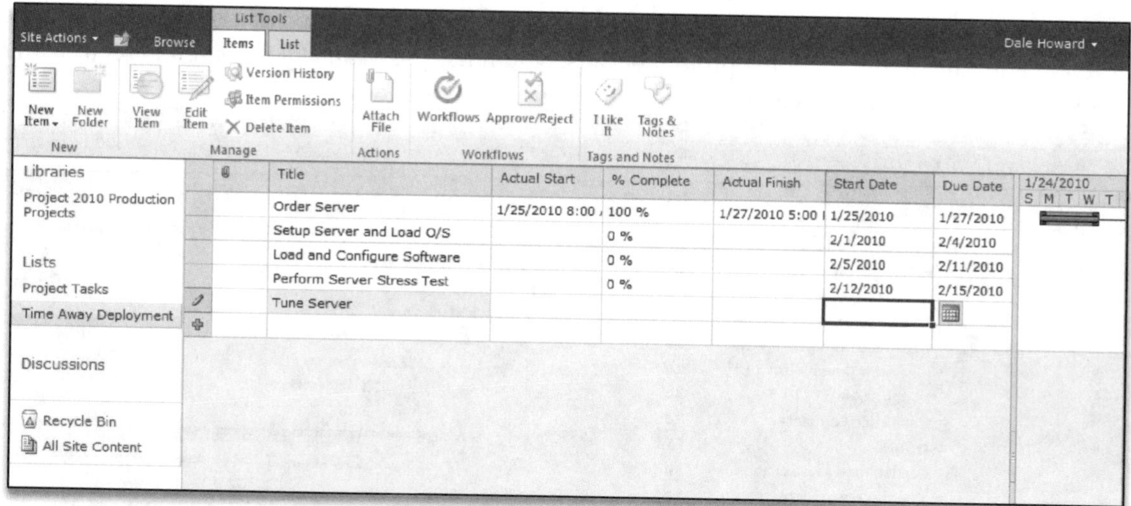

Figure 6 - 43: New task submitted from SharePoint

When you accept a new task update from SharePoint, Microsoft Project 2010 adds the new task at the beginning of the summary section in which the team member created it. If the team member specified information in the *Start Date, Due Date, Predecessors,* or *Assigned To* fields, Microsoft Project 2010 accepts this information and schedules the task accordingly. Keep in mind that when the system adds the new task to the Microsoft Project 2010 project file, this can result in schedule *Warnings* and resource overallocations, such as those shown in the project in Figure 6 - 44. After accepting the new task, you must move the task manually into its correct position in the project file and then synchronize with SharePoint again.

	Task Name	Duration
0	Time Away Rollout	48 d
1	INSTALLATION	16 d
2	Tune Server	3 d
3	Order Server	3 d
4	Setup Server and Load O/S	4 d
5	Load and Configure Software	5 d
6	Perform Server Stress Test	2 d
7	Installation Complete	0 d
8	TESTING	21 d
9	Install Time Away Clients	8 d
10	Verify Connectivity	5 d
11	Resolve Connectivity Errors	4 d
12	Testing Complete	0 d
13	TRAINING	47 d
14	Setup Test Training Server	3.64 d
15	Create Training Materials	17 d
16	Create Training Module 01	5 d
17	Create Training Module 02	5 d
18	Create Training Module 03	5 d
19	Training Materials Created	0 d
20	Conduct Skills Assessment	10 d
21	Create Training Schedule	5 d
22	Provide Training	10 d
23	Project Complete	0 d

Figure 6 - 44: New task accepted from SharePoint into the Microsoft Project 2010 project file

Figure 6 - 45 shows the Microsoft Project 2010 project file after accepting two progress updates and a new task from SharePoint after the first week of the project. Because you must use *Manually Scheduled* tasks in your project, you must continuously deal with schedule *Warnings* and resource overallocations.

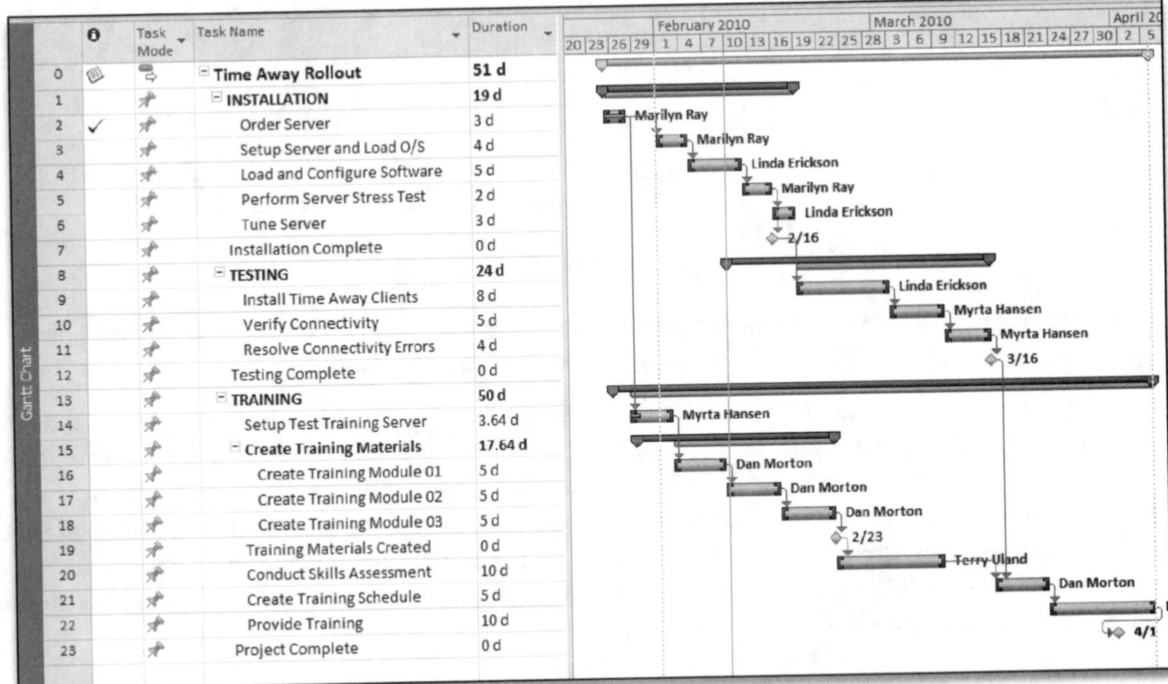

Figure 6 - 45: Microsoft Project 2010 file is current after task updates during the first week of the project

Warning: If you set a task to *Inactive* status at any point in the life of the project, the system sets the task to *Inactive* status in your Microsoft Project 2010 plan, but SharePoint continues to show the task as an *Active* task. Because of this, you may want to cancel the task by setting its Remaining Work value to 0h instead of setting it to *Inactive* status.

Module 07

What's New – Reporting

Learning Objectives

After completing this module, you will be able to:

- Use enhanced Copy and Paste features with the Microsoft Office applications
- Understand the new standard fields in Microsoft Project 2010
- Format the Gantt Chart view
- Use and customize the Timeline
- Create a new custom View and Table
- Use enhancements with Visual Reports
- Use new features in the Compare Project Versions tool

Inside Module 07

Using Enhanced Copy and Paste **189**

Understanding New Fields **193**

Using the Active Field........ 194

Using the Task Mode Field........ 194

Using the Scheduled Fields........ 195

Using the Warning Field........ 196

Using the Baseline Estimated Fields 197

Formatting the Gantt Chart **202**

Using the Format Tools........ 202

Using the Columns Tools 205

Using the Bar Styles Tools........ 207

Using the Gantt Chart Style Tools........ 212

Using the Show/Hide Tools 212

Using the Drawing Tools........ 214

Formatting Other Views **217**

Using the Timeline with the Gantt Chart View **218**

Adding a Task to the Timeline.......220
Formatting the Timeline View.......221
Adding Tasks Using the Contextual Format Ribbon.......225
Exporting the Timeline View.......229
Creating a New View.......231
Creating a New Table.......232
Creating a New Filter.......234
Creating a New Group.......234
Creating the New View.......237
Using the Add New Column Feature.......242
Creating a New View by Customizing an Existing View.......248
Resetting a Default View after Customization.......250
Using Visual Reports Improvements.......252
Using New Features in the Compare Project Versions Tool.......256

Using Enhanced Copy and Paste

During the reporting process in the execution stage of a project, you may need to copy and paste project data to another application. When you copy data from Microsoft Project 2010 and paste the data into another application in the Microsoft Office family, the paste operation works as follows:

- The Microsoft Office application pastes the Microsoft Project 2010 data in a table format that you can modify as needed.
- The Microsoft Office application indents tasks to reflect their hierarchy in the project.
- The Microsoft Office application retains field names as column headers for each column of data.
- The Microsoft Office application maintains complete text and cell background color formatting. The text formatting includes the fonts, font sizes, font styles, and font colors, as well as other formatting such as bold, italic, underline, strikethrough, etc.

For example, Figure 7 - 1 shows a task list for the project shown previously in Module 06. Notice the work breakdown structure in my project, along with the tasks highlighted using cell background formatting. I select the task information from the *Task Name* column through the *Finish* column, and from the *Project Summary Task* (Row 0) to the *Project Complete* milestone task, and then copy the information to the clipboard.

	Task Mode	Task Name	Duration	Start	Finish
0		**Time Away Rollout**	**50 d**	**1/25/10**	**4/2/10**
1		**INSTALLATION**	**18 d**	**1/25/10**	**2/17/10**
2		Order Server	2 d	1/25/10	1/26/10
3		Setup Server and Load O/S	4 d	2/3/10	2/8/10
4		Load and Configure Software	5 d	2/9/10	2/15/10
5		Perform Server Stress Test	2 d	2/16/10	2/17/10
6		Installation Complete	0 d	2/17/10	2/17/10
7		**TESTING**	**17 d**	**2/18/10**	**3/12/10**
8		Install Time Away Clients	8 d	2/18/10	3/1/10
9		Verify Connectivity	5 d	3/2/10	3/8/10
10		Resolve Connectivity Errors	4 d	3/9/10	3/12/10
11		Testing Complete	0 d	3/12/10	3/12/10
12		**TRAINING**	**48 d**	**1/27/10**	**4/2/10**
13		Setup Test Training Server	3 d	1/27/10	1/29/10
14		**Create Training Materials**	**18 d**	**2/1/10**	**2/24/10**
15		Create Training Module 01	5 d	2/1/10	2/5/10
16		Create Training Module 02	5 d	2/8/10	2/12/10
17		Create Training Module 03	5 d	2/15/10	2/19/10
18		Rewrite Training Module 03	3 d	2/22/10	2/24/10
19		Training Materials Created	0 d	2/24/10	2/24/10
20		Conduct Skills Assessment	10 d	2/25/10	3/10/10
21		Create Training Schedule	5 d	3/15/10	3/19/10
22		Provide Training	10 d	3/22/10	4/2/10
23		Project Complete	0 d	4/2/10	4/2/10

Figure 7 - 1: Task list in Microsoft Project 2007

After opening a new blank document in Microsoft Word 2007, I paste the contents of the clipboard directly into the document, shown in Figure 7 - 2. Notice how Microsoft Word 2007 pastes the project data into a table with the correct column headers at the top of each column. Notice also how Microsoft Word 2007 maintains the level of indenture for each task, along with the cell background formatting.

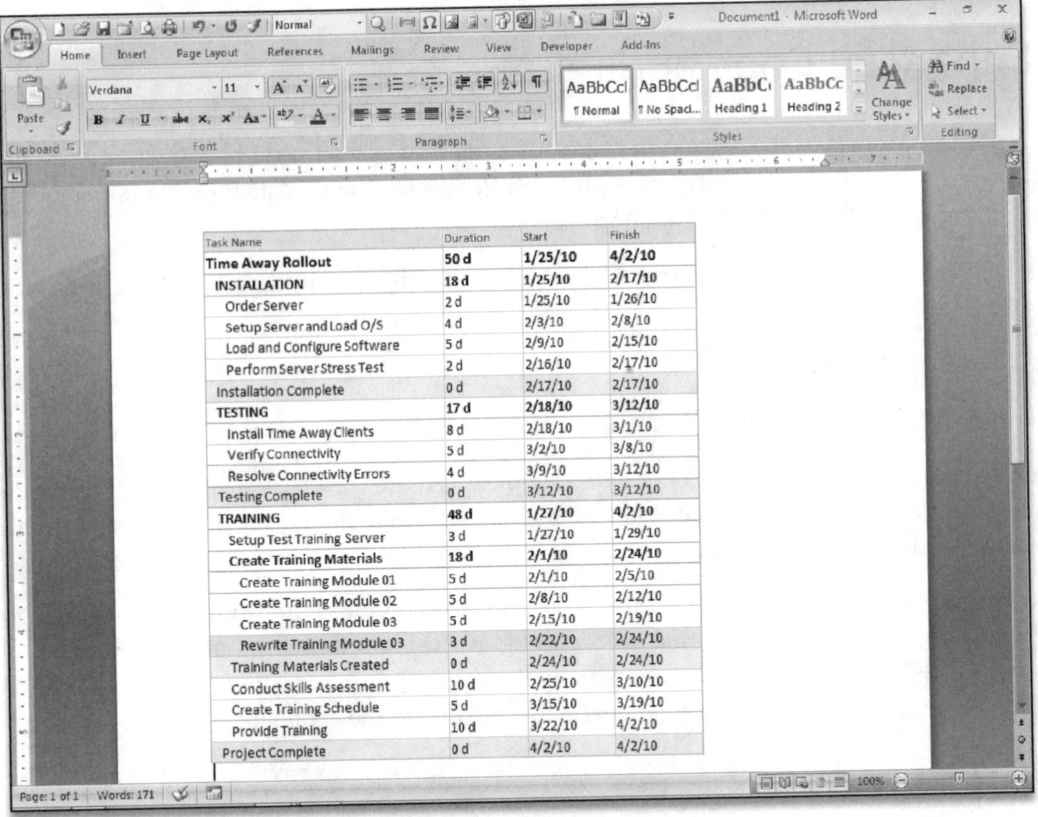

Task Name	Duration	Start	Finish
Time Away Rollout	**50 d**	**1/25/10**	**4/2/10**
INSTALLATION	**18 d**	**1/25/10**	**2/17/10**
Order Server	2 d	1/25/10	1/26/10
Setup Server and Load O/S	4 d	2/3/10	2/8/10
Load and Configure Software	5 d	2/9/10	2/15/10
Perform Server Stress Test	2 d	2/16/10	2/17/10
Installation Complete	0 d	2/17/10	2/17/10
TESTING	**17 d**	**2/18/10**	**3/12/10**
Install Time Away Clients	8 d	2/18/10	3/1/10
Verify Connectivity	5 d	3/2/10	3/8/10
Resolve Connectivity Errors	4 d	3/9/10	3/12/10
Testing Complete	0 d	3/12/10	3/12/10
TRAINING	**48 d**	**1/27/10**	**4/2/10**
Setup Test Training Server	3 d	1/27/10	1/29/10
Create Training Materials	**18 d**	**2/1/10**	**2/24/10**
Create Training Module 01	5 d	2/1/10	2/5/10
Create Training Module 02	5 d	2/8/10	2/12/10
Create Training Module 03	5 d	2/15/10	2/19/10
Rewrite Training Module 03	3 d	2/22/10	2/24/10
Training Materials Created	0 d	2/24/10	2/24/10
Conduct Skills Assessment	10 d	2/25/10	3/10/10
Create Training Schedule	5 d	3/15/10	3/19/10
Provide Training	10 d	3/22/10	4/2/10
Project Complete	0 d	4/2/10	4/2/10

Figure 7 - 2: Microsoft Project 2010 task data pasted into a Microsoft Word 2007 document

When you copy data in an application in the Microsoft Office family, and paste the data into Microsoft Project 2010, the paste operation retains custom text and cell background color formatting. Depending on the Office application, the paste operation may also retain other information. For example, if you paste a bulleted list from Microsoft Word into the *Task Name* field in Microsoft Project 2010, the paste operation converts the bulleted tasks into subtasks of the first task, making it a summary task.

Warning: Be very wary about pasting data from Microsoft PowerPoint into your Microsoft Project 2010 project files. Keep in mind that the paste operation retains **complete** text formatting information, including bullets and the very large font sizes used in PowerPoint.

Figure 7 - 3 shows a project task list created in Microsoft Word 2007. Notice that I used several levels of bulleted text to indicate phase and deliverable summary tasks, and used the highlight feature in the application to highlight the Deliverable 1 Complete and Deliverable 2 Complete tasks. I selected and copied the entire task list to the Clipboard.

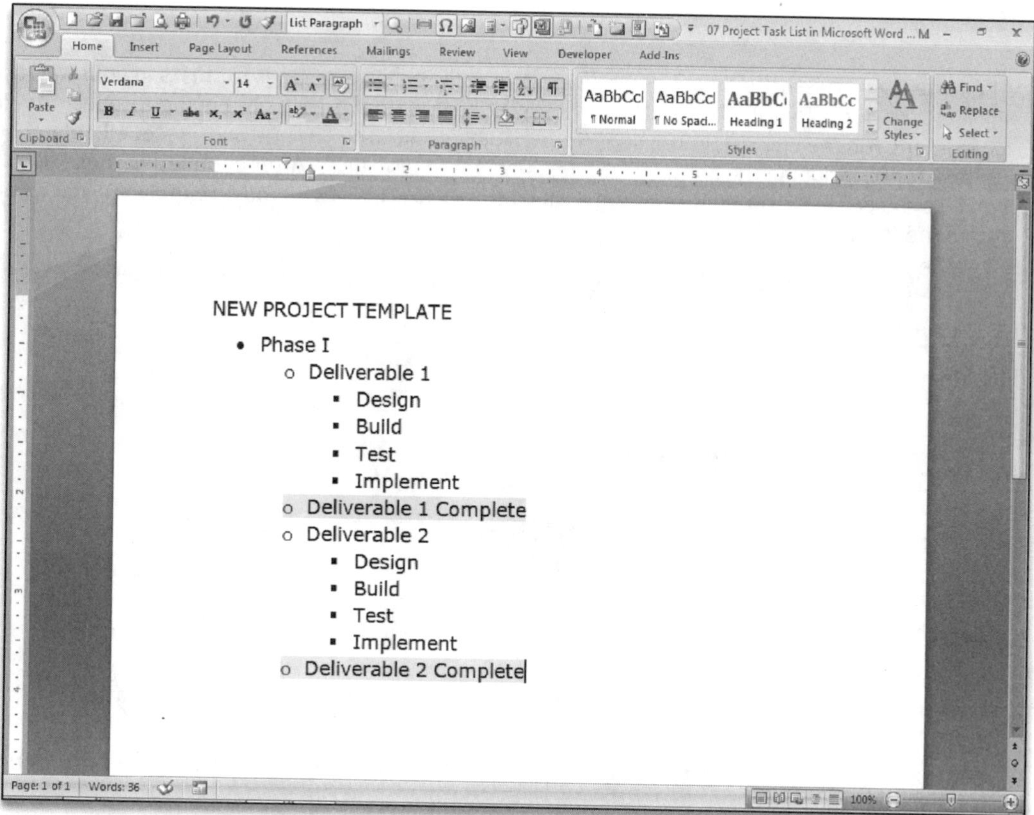

Figure 7 - 3: Task list created in Microsoft Word 2007

After opening a new blank project in Microsoft Project 2010, I pasted the contents of the clipboard directly into the first blank line of the project, as shown in Figure 7 - 4. Notice how Microsoft Project 2010 uses the various levels of the bulleted text to create summary tasks and subtasks, and that the software applies Cell Background Formatting to the Deliverable 1 Complete and Deliverable 2 Complete tasks. Notice also that Microsoft Project 2010 uses the font and font size settings from Microsoft Word. After pasting text from another Office application, you may need to change the font and font size settings on the tasks in your Microsoft Project 2010 plan.

	Task Mode	Task Name	Duration
1		NEW PROJECT TEMPLATE	1 d
2		Phase I	1 d
3		Deliverable 1	1 d
4		Design	1 d
5		Build	1 d
6		Test	1 d
7		Implement	1 d
8		Deliverable 1 Complete	1 d
9		Deliverable 2	1 d
10		Design	1 d
11		Build	1 d
12		Test	1 d
13		Implement	1 d
14		Deliverable 2 Complete	1 d

Figure 7 - 4: Task list from Microsoft Word 2007 pasted into a blank Microsoft Project 2010 project

The fastest way to set the default *Font*, *Font Style*, and *Font Size* settings for tasks in your Microsoft Project 2010 file is to click the *Gantt Chart* pick list button on the *Task* ribbon and to select the *Reset to Default* item on the pick list. In the confirmation dialog, click the *Yes* button to reset all default settings for task fonts, including the *Font*, *Font Style*, and *Font Size* settings. After completing these two steps, you lose the cell background formatting applied to any tasks, and you must reapply it if you want to retain the formatting.

Hands On Exercise

Exercise 7-1

Copy and paste data from Microsoft Project 2010 to another Microsoft Office application.

1. Navigate to your student folder and open the **Project Navigation 2010.mpp** sample file.
2. Click the *Task* tab to display the *Task* ribbon.
3. Pull the split bar to the right to display the *Start* and *Finish* columns.
4. Select the information in the *Task Name, Duration, Start,* and *Finish* columns for all of the tasks in the Pre-Renovation section of the project (task IDs #1-17).
5. Click the *Copy* button in the *Clipboard* section of the *Task* ribbon.
6. Launch Microsoft Word.
7. In a new blank Word document, click the *Paste* button.

Notice how Microsoft Word pastes the Microsoft Project 2010 data into a table, and maintains the levels of indenture for every task.

8. Close the Microsoft Word document without saving it.
9. In Microsoft Project 2010, close but **do not** save the **Project Navigation 2010.mpp** sample file.

Exercise 7-2

Copy and paste data from a Microsoft Office application to Microsoft Project 2010.

1. Return to your Microsoft Word application window.
2. Navigate to your student folder and open the **Task List for Phases I and II.doc** sample document.
3. Select all of the tasks shown in the sample document and then click the *Copy* button.

4. Return to your Microsoft Project 2010 application window.
5. Click the *File* tab and then click the *New* menu item in the *Backstage*.
6. In the *Available Templates* page, double-click the *Blank Project* template to create a new blank project.
7. Click the cell in the *Task Name* column for the first blank row.
8. Click the *Paste* button in the *Clipboard* section of the *Task* ribbon.

Notice how Microsoft Project 2010 pastes the Word data into the project, creating summary tasks and subtasks, while maintaining the font formatting for each task.

9. Click the *Gantt Chart* pick list button in the *View* section of the *Task* ribbon, and then *Reset to Default* item at the bottom of the menu.
10. When prompted in a warning dialog, click the *Yes* button to reset the task list to the default settings for the *Gantt Chart* view.
11. Close the new project without saving it.
12. Return to your Microsoft Word application window.
13. Close the **Task List for Phases I and II.doc** sample document without saving it and then exit Microsoft Word.

Understanding New Fields

Microsoft Project 2010 offers a number of new fields, most of which you use primarily with the new *Manually Scheduled* tasks feature. All of these new fields contain task data, and you can use them in any task view, such as the *Gantt Chart* view. These new fields include:

- Active
- Task Mode
- Scheduled Start
- Scheduled Finish
- Scheduled Duration
- Warning
- Ignore Warnings
- Baseline Estimated Start 0-10
- Baseline Estimated Finish 0-10
- Baseline Estimated Duration 0-10

Using the Active Field

The *Active* field is the only new field not used primarily with *Manually Scheduled* tasks. The *Active* field is a *Flag* field and contains a *Yes* or *No* value for every task in your project. When you select a task and click the *Inactivate* button on the *Task* ribbon, Microsoft Project 2010 sets a *No* value in the *Active* field for the selected task, as shown in Figure 7 - 5. By default, the system sets the *Active* field value to *Yes* for every task.

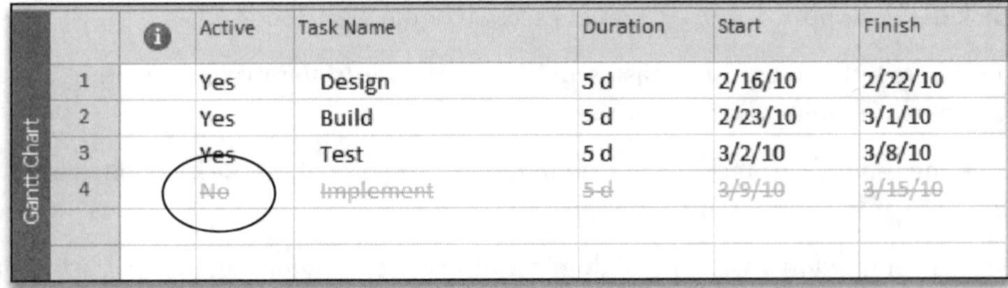

	Active	Task Name	Duration	Start	Finish
1	Yes	Design	5 d	2/16/10	2/22/10
2	Yes	Build	5 d	2/23/10	3/1/10
3	Yes	Test	5 d	3/2/10	3/8/10
4	~~No~~	~~Implement~~	~~5 d~~	~~3/9/10~~	~~3/15/10~~

Figure 7 - 5: Inactive field inserted in the Gantt Chart view

An alternate way to set a task to *Inactive* status is to temporarily insert the *Active* field in any task view, such as the Gantt Chart view, and then set the value to *No* in the *Active* field for each task you want to inactivate.

Using the Task Mode Field

Microsoft Project 2010 displays the *Task Mode* field automatically in the task *Entry* table of the *Gantt Chart* view. In spite of the fact that the system displays the *Manually Scheduled* and *Auto Scheduled* text values in the field, the *Task Mode* field is **actually** a *Flag* field and contains a *Yes* or *No* value for every task in your project. When you select the *Manually Scheduled* option in the *Task Mode* field for a task, the system selects the *Yes* value in the field, indicating the task **is** a *Manually Scheduled* task. When you select the *Auto Scheduled* option in the *Task Mode* field for a task, the system selects the *No* value in the field, indicating the task **is not** a *Manually Scheduled* task.

To confirm the behavior of the *Task Mode* field, examine the project shown in Figure 7 - 6. In this sample project, notice the custom field I created called *Value in the Task Mode Field*. This custom field is a *Flag* field and contains the simple formula *[Task Mode]* that extracts the literal value in the *Task Mode* field. Notice the custom field reveals that the *Task Mode* field contains a literal *No* value for the first two tasks, which are *Auto Scheduled* tasks. Notice also that the custom field reveals that the *Task Mode* field contains a literal *Yes* value for the last two tasks, which are *Manually Scheduled* tasks.

	Task Mode	Value in the Task Mode Field	Task Name	Duration
1		No	Design	1 d
2		No	Build	1 d
3		Yes	Test	
4		Yes	Implement	

Figure 7 - 6: Literal values for the Task Mode field

Using the Scheduled Fields

The *Scheduled Start* field is a *Date* field and contains date information. When you enter a new *Manually Scheduled* task, Microsoft Project 2010 leaves the *Start* field blank and enters a suggested start date in the *Scheduled Start* field. You cannot edit the date in the *Scheduled Start* field as this data is read only. When you enter a new *Auto Scheduled* task, or convert a *Manually Scheduled* task to an *Auto Scheduled* task, Microsoft Project 2010 calculates the start date of the task and enters this information in both the *Start* field and the *Scheduled Start* field. In other words, for *Auto Scheduled* tasks, the dates are the same in both the *Start* and *Scheduled Start* fields.

The *Scheduled Finish* field is a *Date* field and contains date information. When you enter a new *Manually Scheduled* task, Microsoft Project 2010 leaves the *Finish* field blank and enters a suggested finish date in the *Scheduled Finish* field. You cannot edit the date in the *Scheduled Finish* field as this data is read only. When you enter a new *Auto Scheduled* task, or convert a *Manually Scheduled* task to an *Auto Scheduled* task, Microsoft Project 2010 calculates the finish date of the task and enters this information in both the *Finish* field and the *Scheduled Finish* field. In other words, for *Auto Scheduled* tasks, the dates are the same in both the *Finish* and *Scheduled Finish* fields.

The *Scheduled Duration* field is a *Duration* field and contains duration information. When you enter a new *Manually Scheduled* task, Microsoft Project 2010 leaves the *Duration* field blank and enters a suggested duration in the *Scheduled Duration* field. You cannot edit the number in the *Scheduled Duration* field as this data is read only. If you enter a duration value in the *Duration* field, such as *5d*, the system updates the value in the *Scheduled Duration* field automatically to the new value in the *Duration* field. When you enter a new *Auto Scheduled* task, or convert a *Manually Scheduled* task to an *Auto Scheduled* task, Microsoft Project 2010 enters the default *1d* duration value in both the *Duration* field and the *Scheduled Duration* field. In other words, for *Auto Scheduled* tasks, the duration values are the same in both the *Duration* and *Scheduled Duration* fields.

In the project shown in Figure 7 - 7, you see the initial values in the *Scheduled Duration, Scheduled Start,* and *Scheduled Finish* fields for the five tasks in the project. Notice that the system enters no value in the *Duration, Start,* and *Finish* fields because each task is a *Manually Scheduled* task. Notice that the system enters a *1d* value in the *Scheduled Duration* field for each task, and enters *3/19/12* as the suggested date in the *Scheduled Start* and *Scheduled Finish* fields for each task as well.

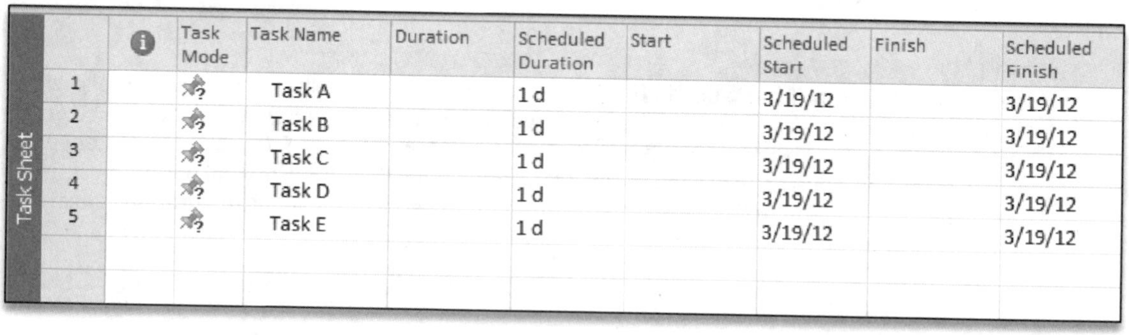

		Task Mode	Task Name	Duration	Scheduled Duration	Start	Scheduled Start	Finish	Scheduled Finish
1			Task A		1 d		3/19/12		3/19/12
2			Task B		1 d		3/19/12		3/19/12
3			Task C		1 d		3/19/12		3/19/12
4			Task D		1 d		3/19/12		3/19/12
5			Task E		1 d		3/19/12		3/19/12

Figure 7 - 7: Initial values for the Scheduled Duration, Scheduled Start, and Scheduled Finish fields for Manually Scheduled tasks

When you enter values in the *Duration, Start,* and *Finish* fields for *Manually Scheduled* tasks, you may see unexpected behavior in the *Scheduled Start* and *Scheduled Finish* fields. Consider the following scenarios:

- If you enter a value in the *Duration* field, Microsoft Project 2010 recalculates the date in the *Scheduled Finish* field by adding the value in the *Duration* field to the date in the *Scheduled Start* field. You see this behavior on Task B shown in Figure 7 - 8. Notice the date in the *Scheduled Finish* field is now *03/23/12*, calculated by adding the *Duration* value of *5d* to the date in the *Scheduled Start* field.

- If you enter a date value in the *Start* field for a *Manually Scheduled* task, Microsoft Project 2010 **does not** change the date in the *Scheduled Start* field. Instead, the system maintains the original suggested start date in this field. You see this behavior in Task C shown in Figure 7 - 8.
- If you enter dates in both the *Start* and *Finish* fields for a *Manually Scheduled* task, Microsoft Project 2010 calculates the value in the *Duration* field automatically, based on the difference in working days between the dates in the *Start* and *Finish* fields. The system then calculates a new date in the *Scheduled Finish* date by adding the value in the *Duration* field to the date in the *Scheduled Start* field. You see this behavior in Task D shown in Figure 7 - 8. For Task D, I entered *3/26/12* in the *Start* field and *4/6/12* in the *Finish* field. The system automatically calculated *10d* in the *Duration* field and then recalculated a new date of *3/30/12* in the *Scheduled Finish* field by adding 10 working days to the date in the *Scheduled Start* field.
- If you enter a value in the *Duration* field and enter a date in the *Start* field, Microsoft Project 2010 calculates the date in the *Finish* field, and then recalculates the date in the *Scheduled Finish* field by adding the value in the *Duration* field to the date in the *Scheduled Start* field. You see this behavior in Task E shown in Figure 7 - 8. For Task E, I entered *15d* in the *Duration* field and entered *4/9/12* in the *Start* field. The system recalculated a new date of *4/6/12* in the *Scheduled Finish* field by adding 15 working days to the date in the *Scheduled Start* field.

		Task Mode	Task Name	Duration	Scheduled Duration	Start	Scheduled Start	Finish	Scheduled Finish
1			Task A		1 d		3/19/12		3/19/12
2			Task B	5 d	5 d		3/19/12		3/23/12
3			Task C		1 d	3/26/12	3/19/12		3/19/12
4			Task D	10 d	10 d	3/26/12	3/19/12	4/6/12	3/30/12
5			Task E	15 d	15 d	4/9/12	3/19/12	4/27/12	4/6/12

Figure 7 - 8: Behavior of the Scheduled Duration, Scheduled Start, and Scheduled Finish fields when entering Duration, Start, or Finish values

When you enter textual information in the *Duration*, *Start*, or *Finish* fields for a *Manually Scheduled* task, Microsoft Project 2010 **does not** change the values in the *Scheduled Duration*, *Scheduled Start*, or *Scheduled Finish* fields. For example, after creating a new *Manually Scheduled* task, the system enters a suggested duration value of *1d* in the *Scheduled Duration* field. If I enter a textual duration value of *About 5 days* in the *Duration* field, the system continues to show the original *1d* duration value in the *Scheduled Duration* field.

Using the Warning Field

The *Warning* field is a *Flag* field and contains a *Yes* or *No* value for every task in your project. The default value is *No* in the *Warning* field, and you cannot edit the value in the *Warning* field as this data is read only. When you create a potential scheduling conflict for a *Manually Scheduled* task, Microsoft Project 2010 calculates a *Yes* value in the *Warning* field and applies a red wavy underline to the date in the *Finish* field, such as for the scheduling conflict on Task B shown in Figure 7 - 9.

	Task Mode	Warning	Task Name	Duration	Start	Finish
1		No	Task A	5 d	2/17/10	2/23/10
2		Yes	Task B	1 d	2/18/10	2/18/10
3		No	Task C	1 d	2/19/10	2/19/10
4		No	Task D	1 d	2/22/10	2/22/10

Figure 7 - 9: Scheduling conflict causes a Yes value in the Warning field

The *Ignore Warnings* field is a *Flag* field and contains a *Yes* or *No* value for every task in your project. The default value is *No* in the *Ignore Warnings* field. When you create a scheduling conflict such as the one shown previously in Figure 7 - 9, you can choose to hide the conflict warning (red wavy underline) by right-clicking anywhere on the task and selecting the *Ignore Problems for this Task* item on the shortcut menu. When you choose to ignore a scheduling conflict and hide the warning, Microsoft Project 2010 sets a *Yes* value in the *Ignore Warnings* field, as shown in Figure 7 - 10. Beyond the automatic behavior of the *Ignore Warnings* field, you also have the option to select a *Yes* value manually in this field.

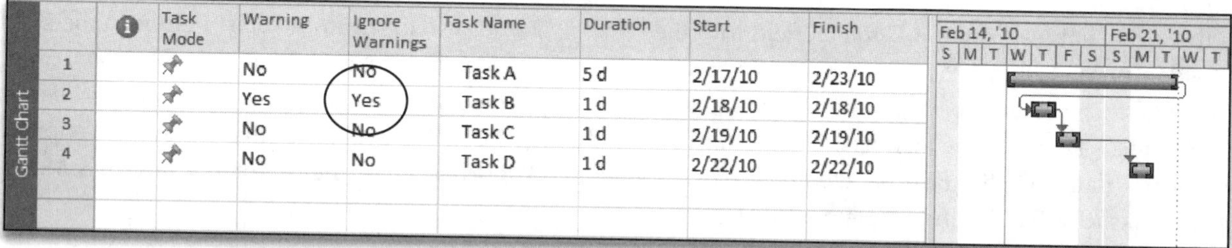

	Task Mode	Warning	Ignore Warnings	Task Name	Duration	Start	Finish
1		No	No	Task A	5 d	2/17/10	2/23/10
2		Yes	Yes	Task B	1 d	2/18/10	2/18/10
3		No	No	Task C	1 d	2/19/10	2/19/10
4		No	No	Task D	1 d	2/22/10	2/22/10

Figure 7 - 10: Ignore Warnings field value set to Yes

You can also hide the warning about a schedule conflict by displaying the Task Inspector sidepane and then **deselecting** the *Show Warning and Suggestion Indicators for this Task* option at the bottom of the sidepane.

Using the Baseline Estimated Fields

Microsoft Project 2010 maintains two sets of fields for tracking the Baseline values in a project. As with previous versions of the software, the system uses the *Baseline Duration, Baseline Start, Baseline Finish, Baseline Work,* and *Baseline Cost* fields. New for 2010 are the *Baseline Estimated Duration, Baseline Estimated Start,* and *Baseline Estimated Finish* fields. As with previous versions, you can use ten additional sets of Baseline fields, named *Baseline 1-10,* which include the *Baseline Duration 1-10, Baseline Start 1-10, Baseline Finish 1-10, Baseline Work 1-10,* and *Baseline Cost 1-10* fields. New for 2010 are the *Baseline Estimated Duration 1-10, Baseline Estimated Start 1-10,* and *Baseline Estimated Finish 1-10* fields.

Figure 7 - 11 shows a new project consisting of two phases, ready to set a baseline. Notice that all of the tasks in the Phase I section are *Auto Scheduled* tasks, while all of the tasks in the Phase II section are *Manually Scheduled* tasks (including the Phase II summary task). Notice further that I entered textual data in the *Duration, Start,* and *Finish* fields for the Test P2 task, and in the *Duration* field only for the Implement P2 task.

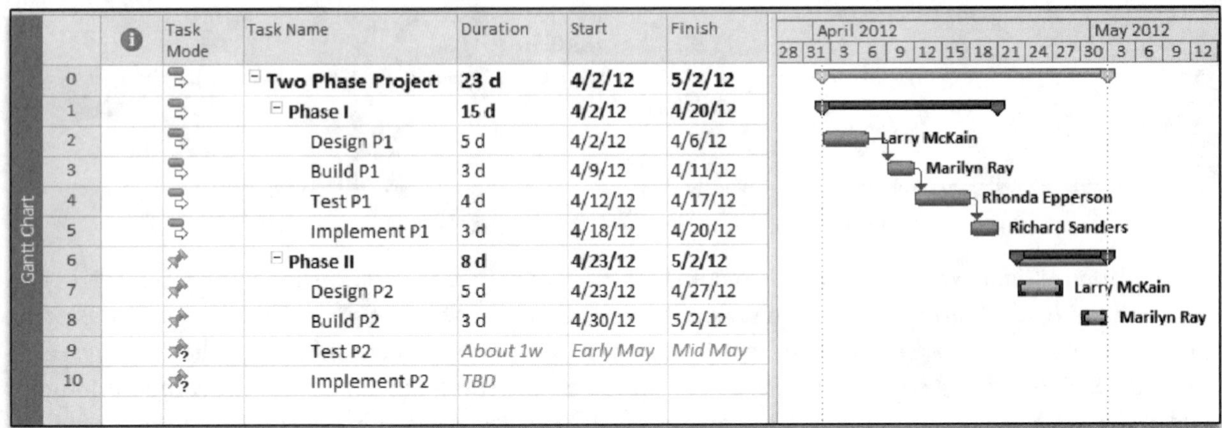

	Task Mode	Task Name	Duration	Start	Finish
0		Two Phase Project	23 d	4/2/12	5/2/12
1		Phase I	15 d	4/2/12	4/20/12
2		Design P1	5 d	4/2/12	4/6/12
3		Build P1	3 d	4/9/12	4/11/12
4		Test P1	4 d	4/12/12	4/17/12
5		Implement P1	3 d	4/18/12	4/20/12
6		Phase II	8 d	4/23/12	5/2/12
7		Design P2	5 d	4/23/12	4/27/12
8		Build P2	3 d	4/30/12	5/2/12
9		Test P2	About 1w	Early May	Mid May
10		Implement P2	TBD		

Figure 7 - 11: New project ready to be Baselined

When you save a baseline for your project, Microsoft Project 2010 saves the current values for every task in the *Baseline Duration, Baseline Start, Baseline Finish, Baseline Work,* and *Baseline Cost* fields. This means that the software saves the literal values from the *Duration* field into the *Baseline Duration* field, from the *Start* field into the *Baseline Start* field, etc. For *Manually Scheduled* tasks, this means that when you enter textual data in the *Duration, Start,* or *Finish* fields, the system copies the literal textual data in the *Baseline Duration, Baseline Start,* and *Baseline Finish* fields. Figure 7 - 12 shows the task *Baseline* table applied in the *Gantt Chart* view. Notice that the system copied the literal textual data into the *Baseline Duration, Baseline Start,* and *Baseline Finish* fields for the last two *Manually Scheduled* tasks (the Test P2 and Implement P2 tasks).

	Task Name	Baseline Duration	Baseline Start	Baseline Finish	Baseline Work	Baseline Cost
0	Two Phase Project	23 d	4/2/12	5/2/12	184 h	$9,200.00
1	Phase I	15 d	4/2/12	4/20/12	120 h	$6,000.00
2	Design P1	5 d	4/2/12	4/6/12	40 h	$2,000.00
3	Build P1	3 d	4/9/12	4/11/12	24 h	$1,200.00
4	Test P1	4 d	4/12/12	4/17/12	32 h	$1,600.00
5	Implement P1	3 d	4/18/12	4/20/12	24 h	$1,200.00
6	Phase II	8 d	4/23/12	5/2/12	64 h	$3,200.00
7	Design P2	5 d	4/23/12	4/27/12	40 h	$2,000.00
8	Build P2	3 d	4/30/12	5/2/12	24 h	$1,200.00
9	Test P2	About 1w	Early May	Mid May	0 h	$0.00
10	Implement P2	TBD			0 h	$0.00

Figure 7 - 12: Baseline table applied in the Gantt Chart view

When you save a baseline for your project, Microsoft Project 2010 also saves baseline data in the *Baseline Estimated Duration* field. For each task, if the *Duration* field contains numeric data, the system saves the current numeric value in the *Baseline Estimated Duration* field. If the *Duration* field contains textual data for a *Manually Scheduled* task, such as the Test P2 and Implement P2 tasks shown previously in Figure 7 - 11 and Figure 7 - 12, the system saves the default value of *1 day* in the *Baseline Estimated Duration* field for that task.

When you save a baseline for your project, Microsoft Project 2010 also saves baseline data in the *Baseline Estimated Start* and *Baseline Estimated Finish* fields. For each task, if the *Start* or *Finish* field contains date data, the system saves the current date value from the *Start* field into the *Baseline Estimated Start* and from the *Finish* field into the *Baseline Estimated Finish* field. If the *Start* field or *Finish* field contains textual data for a *Manually Scheduled* task, the system saves the date from the *Scheduled Start* field into the *Baseline Estimated Start* and from the *Scheduled Finish* field into the *Baseline Estimated Finish* field. Figure 7 - 13 shows a custom task table I created to show all of the corresponding *Baseline* fields and *Baseline Estimated* fields discussed in this topical section. Notice how Microsoft Project 2010 captured different baseline information between the *Baseline Duration* and *Baseline Estimated Duration* fields, between the *Baseline Start* and *Baseline Estimated Start* fields, and between the *Baseline Finish* and *Baseline Estimated Finish* fields for the last two *Manually Scheduled* tasks.

	Task Name	Baseline Duration	Baseline Estimated Duration	Baseline Start	Baseline Estimated Start	Baseline Finish	Baseline Estimated Finish
0	**Two Phase Project**	**23 d**	**23 d**	**4/2/12**	**4/2/12**	**5/2/12**	**5/2/12**
1	**Phase I**	**15 d**	**15 d**	**4/2/12**	**4/2/12**	**4/20/12**	**4/20/12**
2	Design P1	5 d	5 d	4/2/12	4/2/12	4/6/12	4/6/12
3	Build P1	3 d	3 d	4/9/12	4/9/12	4/11/12	4/11/12
4	Test P1	4 d	4 d	4/12/12	4/12/12	4/17/12	4/17/12
5	Implement P1	3 d	3 d	4/18/12	4/18/12	4/20/12	4/20/12
6	**Phase II**	**8 d**	**8 d**	**4/23/12**	**4/23/12**	**5/2/12**	**5/2/12**
7	Design P2	5 d	5 d	4/23/12	4/23/12	4/27/12	4/27/12
8	Build P2	3 d	3 d	4/30/12	4/30/12	5/2/12	5/2/12
9	Test P2	About 1w	1 d	Early May	4/23/12	Mid May	4/23/12
10	Implement P2	TBD	1 d		4/23/12		4/23/12

Figure 7 - 13: Custom task table shows all Baseline fields

Remember that Microsoft Project 2010 includes the ten additional sets of *Baseline* fields, named *Baseline 1-10*. When you capture baseline information in one of these ten additional sets of fields, the system captures additional information in the corresponding *Baseline Estimated* set of fields. For example, if you baseline your project using the *Baseline 1* set of fields, the system also captures baseline information in the *Baseline Estimated Duration 1* field, *Baseline Estimated Start 1* field, and the *Baseline Estimated Finish 1* field using the process I described previously.

For *Auto Scheduled* tasks, the baseline set of fields always contain the exact same data as the baseline estimated set of fields. This means the data is identical in the *Baseline Duration* and *Baseline Estimated Duration* fields, the *Baseline Start* and *Baseline Estimated Start* fields, as well as the *Baseline Finish* and *Baseline Estimated Finish* fields. Because of this, you may find the *Baseline Estimated* fields of little value unless you use *Manually Scheduled* tasks in your projects.

Hands On Exercise

Exercise 7-3

Explore the new *Active, Task Mode, Warning,* and *Ignore Warnings* fields available in Microsoft Project 2010.

1. Navigate to your student folder and open the **Using New Fields.mpp** sample file.
2. Select task ID #22, *Re-test modified code.*
3. Click the *Task* tab and then click the *Inactivate* button on the *Task* ribbon.

Notice how Microsoft Project 2010 sets a *No* value in the *Active* field for the *Inactive* task.

4. Select task ID #18, *Review modular code.*
5. On the *Task* ribbon, click the *Auto Schedule* button.

Notice how the system changes the indicator shown in the *Task Mode* field for the task you set to *Auto Scheduled* mode.

6. Click the *View* tab to apply the *View* ribbon.
7. In the *Data* section of the *View* ribbon, click the *Tables* pick list button and select the *_Warning Fields* custom table.
8. Drag your split bar to the right edge of the *Finish* column.
9. Change the value in the *Duration* field to *8 days* for task ID #18, *Review modular code.*

Notice how the system indicates a schedule conflict by setting a *Yes* value in the *Warning* field for task ID #19, *Test component modules to product specifications,* and by applying a red wavy underline to the date in the *Finish* field.

10. Select task ID #19, *Test component modules to product specifications.*
11. Click the *Task* tab and then click the *Inspect* button in the *Tasks* section of the *Task* ribbon.
12. In the *Task Inspector* sidepane, click the *Respect Links* button.

Notice how the system shows a new schedule conflict for task ID #20, *Identify anomalies to product specifications.*

13. Select task ID #20, *Identify anomalies to product specifications.*
14. Scroll to the bottom of the *Task Inspector* sidepane and **deselect** the *Show warning and suggestion indicators for this task* option.

Notice how the system sets a *Yes* value in the *Ignore Warnings* field for task ID #20, *Identify anomalies to product specifications,* and removes the red wavy underline in the *Finish* field as well.

15. Close the *Task Inspector* sidepane and then save the **Using New Fields.mpp** sample file.

Exercise 7-4

Explore the six new date fields available in Microsoft Project 2010.

1. Return to the **Using New Fields.mpp** sample file, if necessary.
2. Right-click on the *Select All* button (blank gray button above the row 0 ID number) and select the *_Scheduled Date Fields* custom table.
3. Drag your split bar to the right edge of the *Scheduled Finish* column.
4. Scroll to the bottom of the project and examine the information for the last five tasks (the *Manually Scheduled* tasks) in the each of the columns in the *_Scheduled Date Fields* custom table.

Notice that the system shows information in the *Scheduled Duration, Scheduled Start,* and *Scheduled Finish* fields for the last three *Manually Scheduled* tasks, even though there are no numbers in the *Duration* field and no dates in the *Start* and *Finish* fields for these tasks.

5. Right-click on the *Select All* button again and select the *_Estimated Baseline Fields* custom table.
6. Drag your split bar to the right edge of the *Baseline Estimated Finish* column.

Notice that the all of the columns are empty in this custom table. This is because you have not yet saved a baseline for this project.

7. Click the *Project* tab to display the *Project* ribbon.
8. In the *Schedule* section of the *Project* ribbon, click the *Set Baseline* pick list button and select the *Set Baseline* item on the list.
9. In the *Set Baseline* dialog, leave all default options selected and then click the *OK* button.
10. Scroll to the bottom of the project and examine the information shown for the last five tasks (the *Manually Scheduled* tasks) in the each of the columns in the *_Baseline Estimated Fields* custom table.

For the last three *Manually Scheduled* tasks, notice the differences in the data between the *Baseline Duration* and *Baseline Estimated Duration* fields, between the *Baseline Start* and *Baseline Estimated Start* fields, and between the *Baseline Finish* and *Baseline Estimated Finish* fields.

11. Save and close the **Using New Fields.mpp** sample file.

Formatting the Gantt Chart

As part of your organization's project reporting process, you may need to format the *Gantt Chart* view for printing or display purposes. In all previous versions of Microsoft Project, you needed to use the *Gantt Chart Wizard* tool to format the Gantt Chart to your reporting specifications. In Microsoft Project 2010, you no longer need to use the *Gantt Chart Wizard* tool because the system provides you with many simple ways to format the Gantt Chart manually.

To format the Gantt Chart, apply the *Gantt Chart* view and then click the *Format* tab. The system displays the contextual *Format* ribbon with the *Gantt Chart Tools* applied, as indicated by the purple area above the *Format* tab, as shown in Figure 7 - 14.

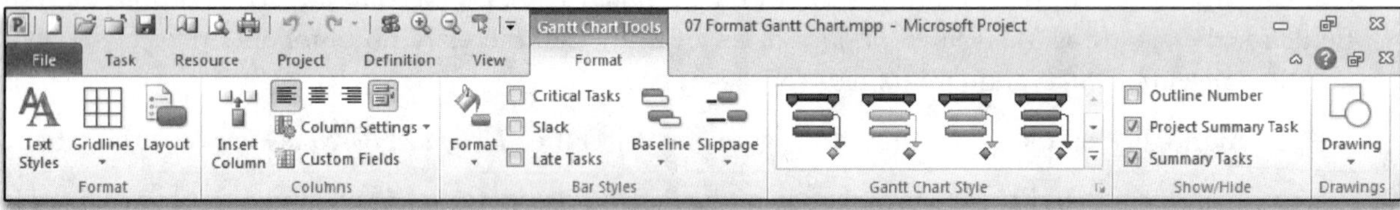

Figure 7 - 14: Format ribbon with the Gantt Chart Tools applied

Using the Format Tools

The *Format* section of the contextual *Format* ribbon contains buttons that display dialogs found in previous versions of Microsoft Project. When you click the *Text Styles* button, the system displays the *Text Styles* dialog. Although this dialog is not itself a new feature, it does contain several new capabilities. When you click the *Item to Change* pick list, you see the first new feature, the *Inactive Tasks* item shown in Figure 7 - 15.

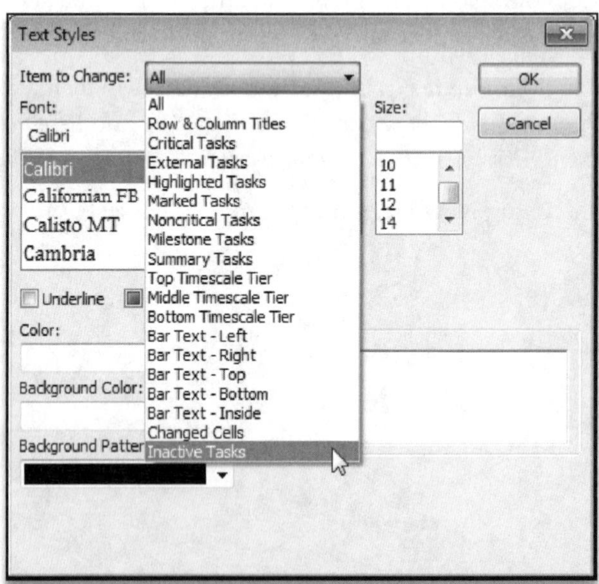

Figure 7 - 15: Text Styles dialog
Item to Change pick list

If you select the *Inactive Tasks* item on the *Item to Change* pick list, you see the second new feature in the *Text Styles* dialog, the a new *Strikethrough* checkbox. Microsoft Project 2010 uses the *Strikethrough* font formatting by default on *Inactive* tasks, as shown in Figure 7 - 16. Notice in the *Text Styles* dialog that the system disables the *Background Color* and *Background Pattern* pick lists, as the system does not allow any kind of cell background formatting on *Inactive* tasks.

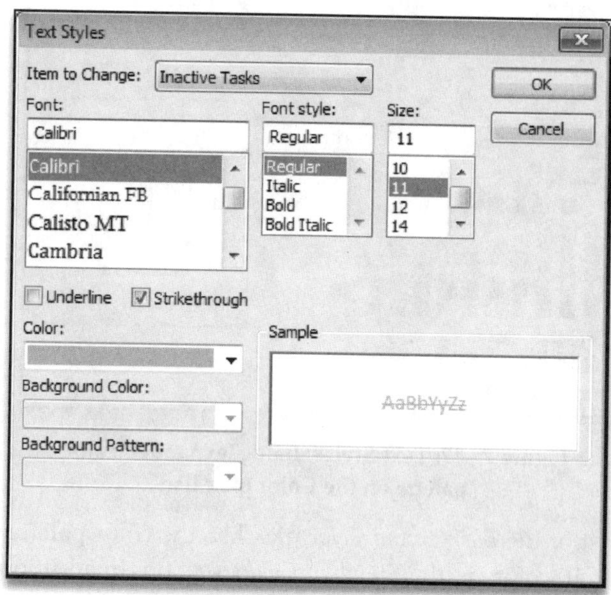

Figure 7 - 16: Text Styles dialog Strikethrough font formatting option

If you want to change the values in either the *Color* pick list or *Background Color* pick list, you see the third new feature, the expanded color palette. In all previous versions of the software, the system offered a small color palette with only sixteen standard colors. Microsoft Project 2010 now offers an expanded color palette with thousands of colors, available for font colors, cell background colors, Gantt bar colors, hyperlink colors, and grouping colors. You see the expanded color palette in the *Text Styles* dialog if you click either the *Color* pick list or the *Background Color* pick list. For example, Figure 7 - 17 shows the expanded color palette in the *Color* pick list with the *Critical Tasks* item selected on the *Item to Change* pick list.

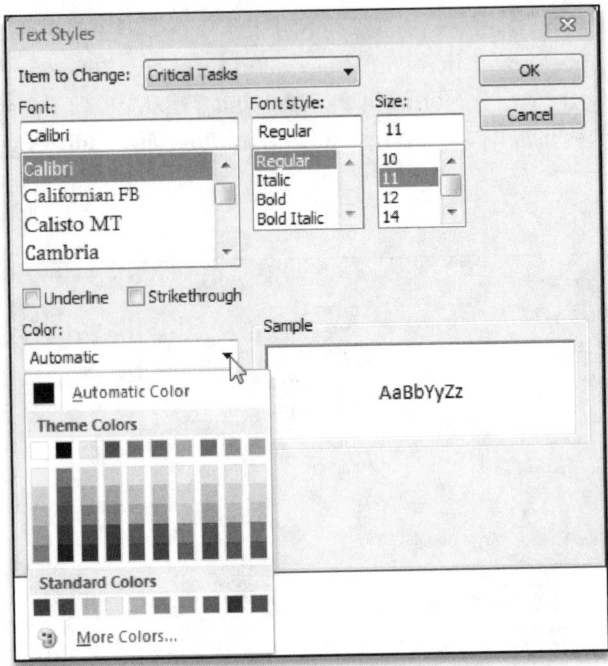

Figure 7 - 17: Text Styles dialog, expanded color palette on the Color pick list

When you click the *Color* pick list or the *Background Color* pick list, the color palette offers a set of 60 colors in the *Theme Colors* section and a set of 10 colors in the *Standard Colors* section. In addition, if you select the *More Colors* item in the pick list, the system displays the *Colors* dialog shown in Figure 7 - 18. This dialog allows you to select a color from among the thousands of colors on either the *Standard* or *Custom* tab.

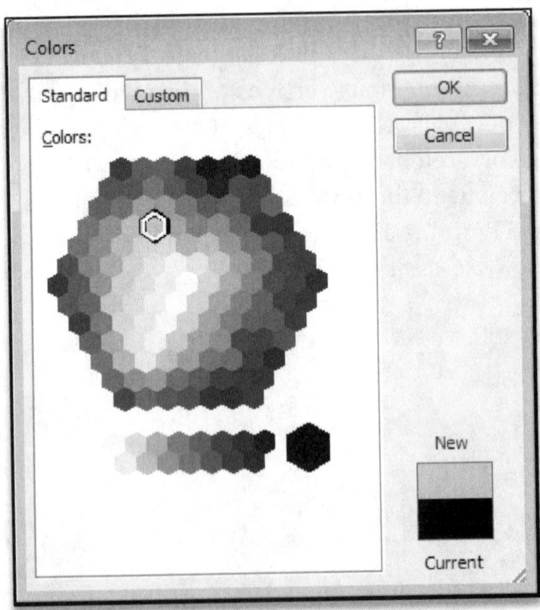

Figure 7 - 18: Color dialog

When you click the *Gridlines* pick list button, the system displays two options on the list: the *Gridlines* item and the *Progress Lines* item. If you click the *Gridlines* item, Microsoft Project 2010 displays the *Gridlines* dialog shown in Figure 7 - 19. Although this dialog is not new, the system does use different default formatting for several types of gridlines in the *Line to Change* list. Gridlines with new formatting include the *Current Date, Project Start,* and *Project Finish* gridlines. Figure 7 - 19 shows the formatting for the *Current Date* gridline in the *Gridlines* dialog, for example.

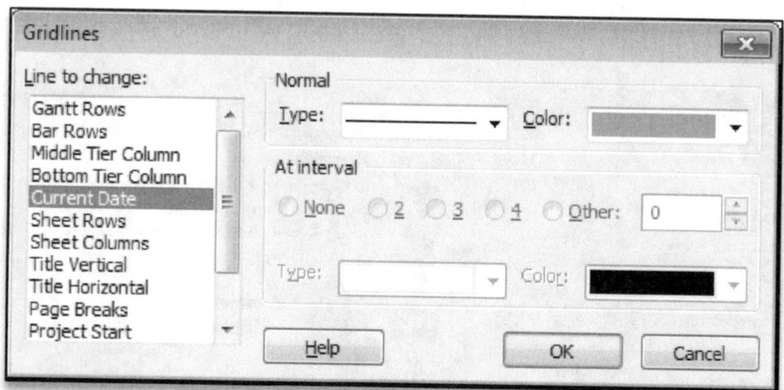

Figure 7 - 19: Gridlines dialog, Current Date formatting

When you click the *Gridlines* pick list button and then click the *Progress Lines* item, the system displays the *Progress Lines* dialog. This dialog contains no new features in Microsoft Project 2010; therefore, I do not show or discuss this dialog.

When you click the *Layout* button, the system displays the *Layout* dialog. This dialog contains no new features in Microsoft Project 2010; therefore, I do not show or discuss this dialog.

Using the Columns Tools

The *Columns* section of the contextual *Format* ribbon contains buttons that allow you to insert and format columns in the *Gantt Chart* view. To insert a new column in the *Gantt Chart* view, select the column where you want to insert the new column, and then click the *Insert Column* button. Microsoft Project 2010 inserts a new column to the left of the selected column and displays the list of available task fields, as shown in Figure 7 - 20. To complete the insertion process, scroll the list and select the column you want to insert.

Alternately, you can also type the name of the column you want to insert. When you type the name of a column, the system creates a new custom *Text* field using the name you enter. I discuss how to create new custom fields later in this module.

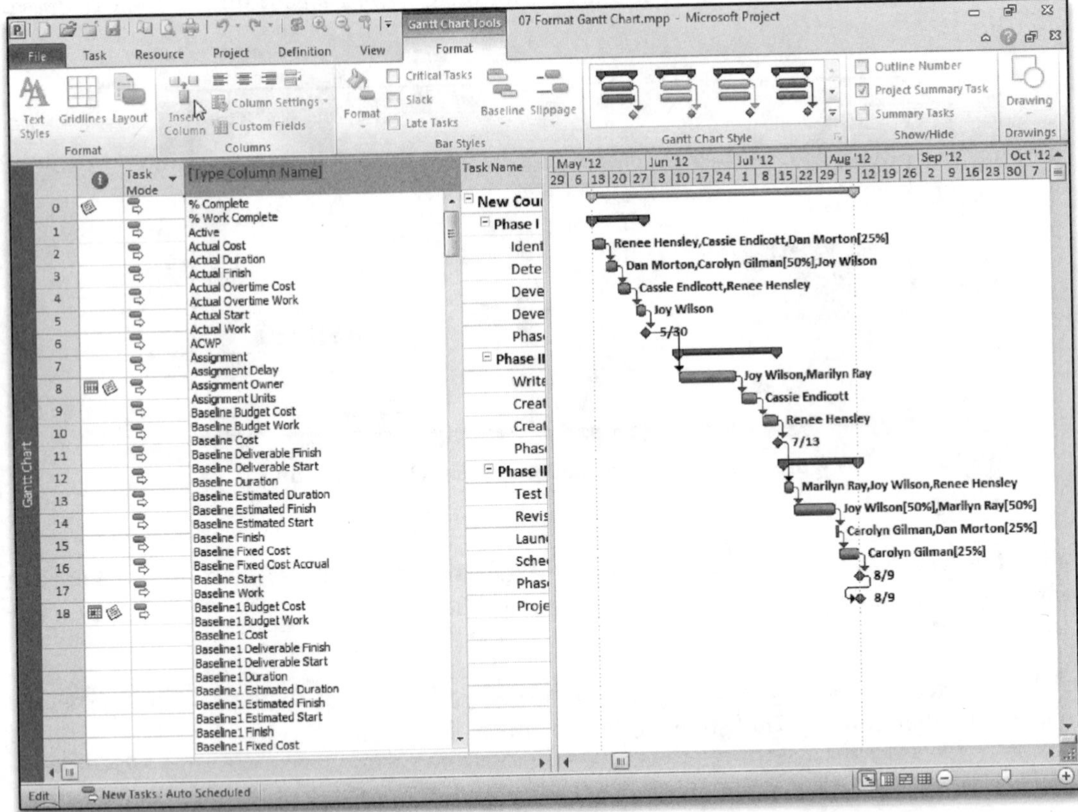

Figure 7 - 20: Insert a new column to the left of the Task Name column

To align the data in any column, select anywhere in a column and then click the *Align Text Left*, *Center*, or *Align Text Right* button. The system changes the alignment of the data in the column, but does not change the alignment of the text in the column header.

To control text wrapping for any column, select anywhere in the column you want to change and then select or deselect the *Wrap Text* button. By default, Microsoft Project 2010 enables the *Wrap Text* feature for only the *Task Names* column in task views and the *Resource Names* column in resource views. With the *Text Wrapping* feature enabled, the system increases the row height of tasks automatically for task names that are longer than the new width of the *Task Name* column.

Before you attempt to use the *Column Settings* pick list button, be certain to select a column in your Microsoft Project 2010 project file. When you click the *Column Settings* pick list button, the system displays the pick list menu shown in Figure 7 - 21.

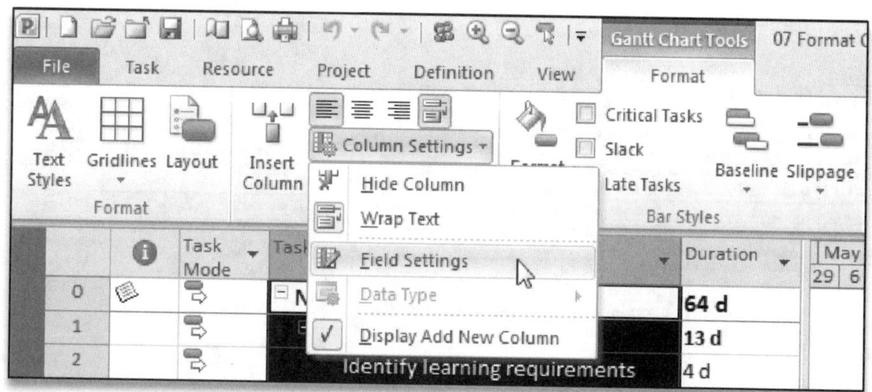

Figure 7 - 21: Column Settings pick list menu

On the *Column Settings* pick list menu, click the *Hide Column* item to hide the selected column. Select or deselect the *Wrap Text* item to enable or disable automatic text wrapping in the selected column. Click the *Field Settings* item to display the *Field Settings* dialog shown in Figure 7 - 22. The *Field Settings* dialog is identical to the *Column Definition* dialog found in previous versions of Microsoft Project; therefore, I do not discuss this feature.

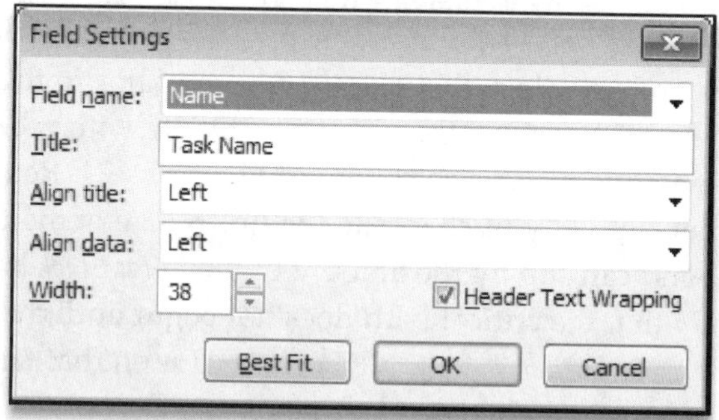

Figure 7 - 22: Field Settings dialog

In the *Column Settings* pick list menu, deselect the *Display Add New Column* item if you do not want to display the *Add New Column* virtual column on the far right side of the current table. You can display or hide the *Add New Column* virtual column for each table individually; however, the system displays the *Add New Column* virtual column in every default table included in Microsoft Project 2010.

Using the Bar Styles Tools

The *Bar Styles* section of the contextual *Format* ribbon contains a number of powerful tools that allow you to customize the Gantt Chart to show exactly the type of information you want to see. When you click the *Format* pick list button, the system displays two options on the pick list menu: the *Bar* item and the *Bar Styles* item. If you click the *Bar* item, Microsoft Project 2010 displays the *Format Bar* dialog. This dialog contains no new features in Microsoft Project 2010; therefore, I do not show or discuss this dialog.

If you click the *Bar Styles* item on the *Format* pick list, the system displays the *Bar Styles* dialog shown in Figure 7 - 23. Although this dialog is not new in Microsoft Project 2010, this dialog does contain many new Gantt bar objects, such as the *Manual Task* item I selected in Figure 7 - 23. Remember that the information shown in the *Bar Styles* dialog controls how Microsoft Project 2010 draws each of the objects shown in the *Gantt Chart* view. You can change the appearance of an object by selecting its definition row in the *Bar Styles* dialog and then editing the information in the *Start, Middle,* and *End* sections of the *Bars* tab at the bottom of the dialog.

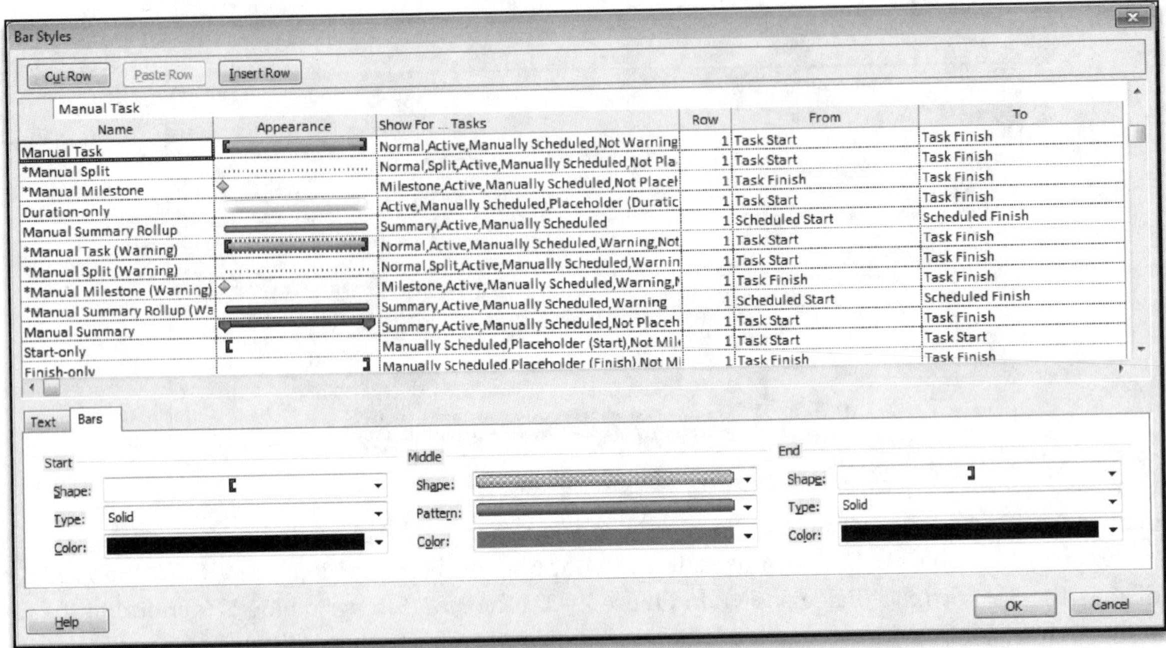

Figure 7 - 23: Bar Styles dialog with Manual Task item selected

To display the Critical Path in your project, select the *Critical Tasks* checkbox in the *Bar Styles* section of the contextual *Format* ribbon. Microsoft Project 2010 formats the *Gantt Chart* view with red bars representing critical tasks, and with blue bars representing non-critical tasks, as shown in Figure 7 - 24. Remember that critical tasks have a *Total Slack* value of *0 days* and cannot slip without changing the finish date of the project. Non-critical tasks have a *Total Slack* value *greater than 0 days* and can slip by the amount of the *Total Slack* before they impact the finish date of the project. Notice in Figure 7 - 24 that the critical path does not begin until the first task in the Phase II section of the plan. This is because of a *Start No Earlier Than* (SNET) constraint on that task, which creates *Total Slack* value greater than 0 days for the tasks in the Phase I section of the plan.

	Task Name	Duration
0	**New Course Development**	**64 d**
1	**Phase I**	**13 d**
2	Identify learning requirements	4 d
3	Determine target audience	2 d
4	Develop learning objectives	4 d
5	Develop course outline	3 d
6	Phase I Complete	0 d
7	**Phase II**	**25 d**
8	Write course manual	15 d
9	Create sample files	5 d
10	Create instructor materials	5 d
11	Phase II Complete	0 d
12	**Phase III**	**19 d**
13	Test beta classes	3 d
14	Revise content based on feedback	10 d
15	Launch marketing campaign	1 d
16	Schedule new classes	5 d
17	Phase III Complete	0 d
18	Project Complete	0 d

Gantt Chart
May '12 | Jun '12 | Jul '12 | Aug '12
29 6 13 20 27 3 10 17 24 1 8 15 22 29 5 12 19
Renee Hensley,Cassie Endicott,Dan Morton[25%]
Dan Morton,Carolyn Gilman[50%],Joy Wilson
Cassie Endicott,Renee Hensley
Joy Wilson
5/30
7/13
8/9
8/9

Figure 7 - 24: Critical Path displayed in the Gantt Chart view

Warning: Because of an unfixed bug in the release version of Microsoft Project 2010, when you select the *Critical Tasks* checkbox on the *Format* ribbon, the system removes the names of assigned resources displayed to the right of Gantt bars for critical tasks. To display the names of your assigned resources, double-click anywhere in the white part of the Gantt Chart to display the *Bar Styles* dialog. Scroll to the bottom of the list, select the *Critcal* item, and then select the *Text* tab. On the Text tab, click the Right pick list and select the *Resource Names* field. Click the OK button when finished.

To display the *Total Slack* in your project, select the *Slack* checkbox in the *Bar Styles* section of the contextual *Format* ribbon. Microsoft Project 2010 displays a dark blue underscore stripe to the right of the Gantt bar of every task with a *Total Slack* value greater than 0 days. Notice in Figure 7 - 25 that both the Phase I summary task and the Phase I Complete milestone task have a *Total Slack* value greater than 0 days, indicated by the dark blue underscore stripe to the right of their Gantt bars.

	Task Mode	Task Name	Duration
0		**New Course Development**	**64 d**
1		**Phase I**	**13 d**
2		Identify learning requirements	4 d
3		Determine target audience	2 d
4		Develop learning objectives	4 d
5		Develop course outline	3 d
6		Phase I Complete	0 d
7		**Phase II**	**25 d**
8		Write course manual	15 d
9		Create sample files	5 d
10		Create instructor materials	5 d
11		Phase II Complete	0 d
12		**Phase III**	**19 d**
13		Test beta classes	3 d
14		Revise content based on feedback	10 d
15		Launch marketing campaign	1 d
16		Schedule new classes	5 d
17		Phase III Complete	0 d
18		Project Complete	0 d

Figure 7 - 25: Total Slack displayed in the Gantt Chart view

In Microsoft Project 2010, a late task is any task whose cumulative *Percent Complete* value is less than the *Status Date* value specified for the project. For example, Figure 7 - 26 shows the project after entering progress for the first week of the project. Notice that the assigned resources did not complete work on the Identify Learning Requirements task as expected. Because the task is not complete by the *Status Date,* indicated by the red dashed line on May 18, the system considers this task as a late task.

	Task Mode	Task Name	Duration
0		**New Course Development**	**64 d**
1		**Phase I**	**14 d**
2		Identify learning requirements	5 d
3		Determine target audience	2 d
4		Develop learning objectives	4 d
5		Develop course outline	3 d
6		Phase I Complete	0 d

Figure 7 - 26: Progress entered for the first week

To display the Late tasks in your project, select the *Late Tasks* checkbox in the *Bar Styles* section of the contextual *Format* ribbon. Microsoft Project 2010 displays late tasks with black Gantt bars, as shown in Figure 7 - 27.

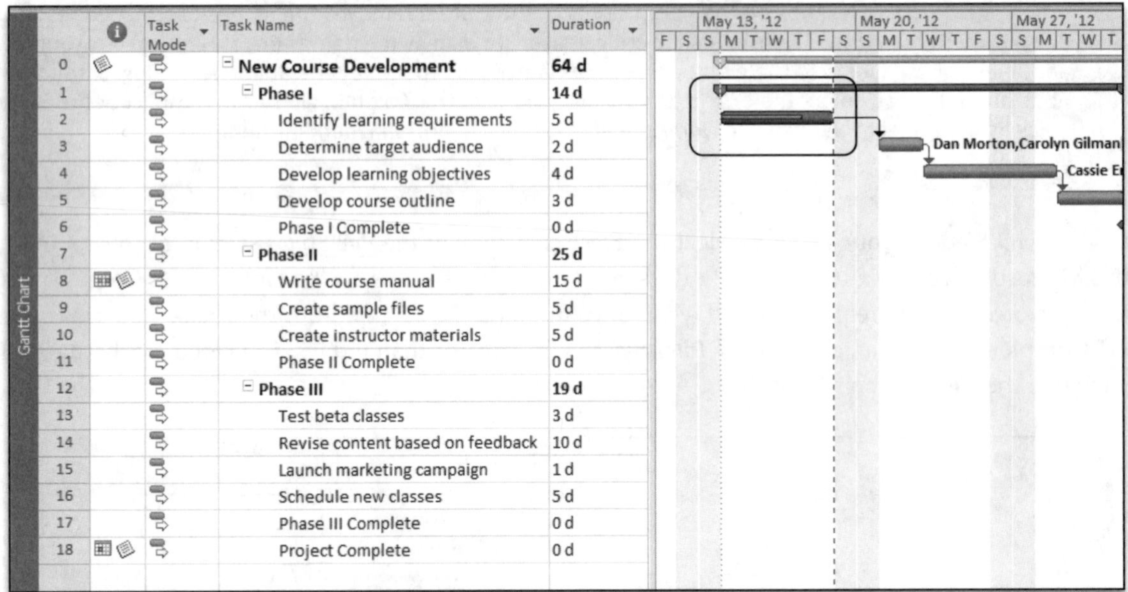

Figure 7 - 27: Late tasks displayed in the Gantt Chart view

To display your operating baseline in the *Gantt Chart* view, click the *Baseline* pick list button in the *Bar Styles* section of the contextual *Format* ribbon. The *Baseline* pick list displays a list of eleven available sets of *Baseline* fields, and indicates the save date for each set of *Baseline* fields, as shown in Figure 7 - 28.

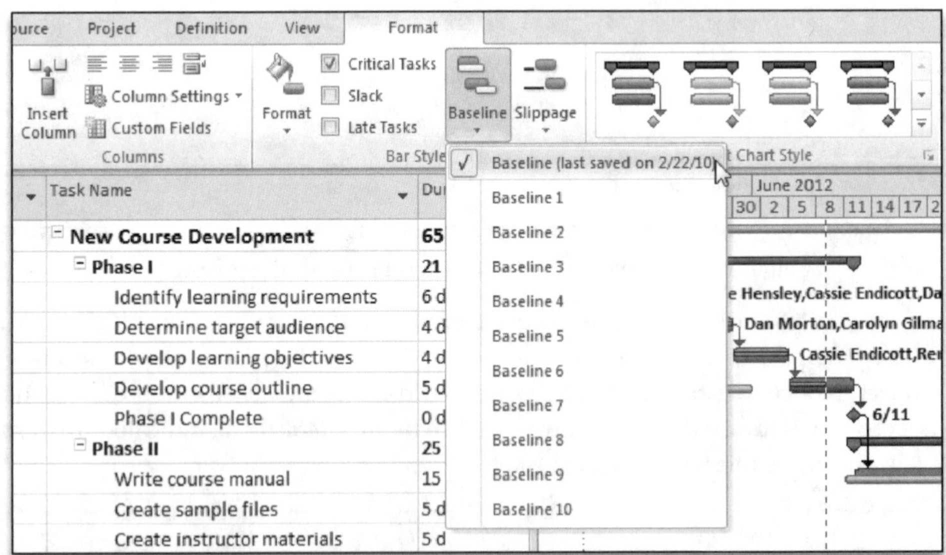

Figure 7 - 28: List of available Baselines on the Baseline pick list

On the *Baseline* pick list, select the baseline you want to show in the *Gantt Chart* view. Microsoft Project 2010 displays the selected baseline information using a gray bar for each task to represent the original baseline schedule for the task, as shown in Figure 7 - 29. After you apply the baseline information to your *Gantt Chart* view, compare the current schedule of each task with its baseline schedule. If the current schedule for any task is to the right of its accompanying gray Gantt bar, then the task is slipping. Notice in Figure 7 - 29 that my project is slipping after entering task progress for the first four weeks of the project.

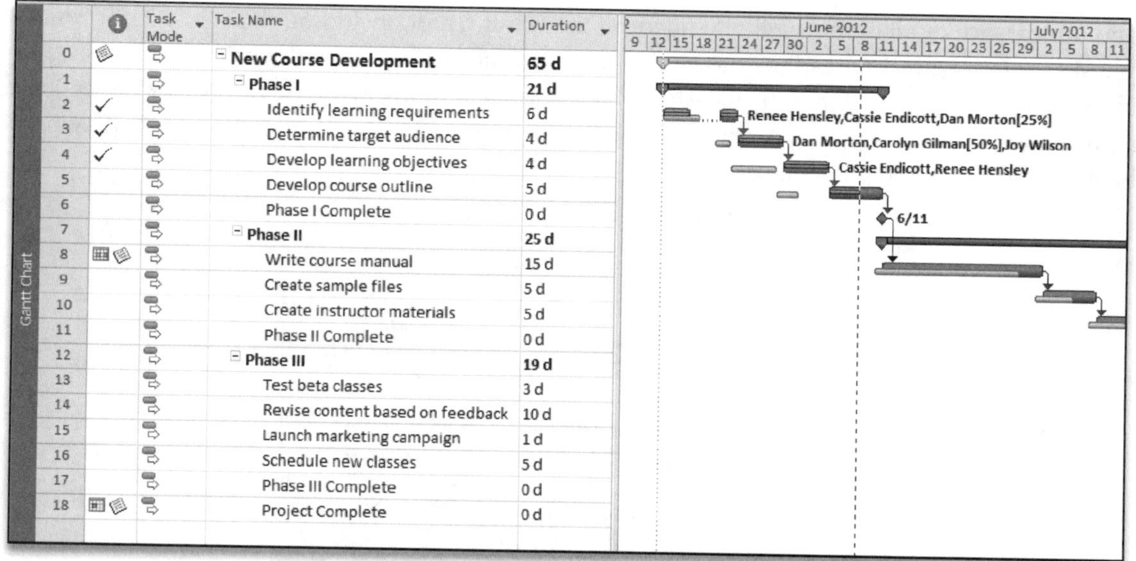

Figure 7 - 29: Baseline schedule applied to the Gantt Chart

To view the current amount of schedule slippage in your *Gantt Chart* view, click the *Slippage* pick list button in the *Bar Styles* section of the contextual *Format* ribbon. The *Slippage* pick list includes the same list of *Baseline* fields as on the *Baseline* pick list shown previously in Figure 7 - 28. Select one of the available sets of *Baseline* fields on the *Slippage* pick list. Microsoft Project 2010 displays a gray underscore stripe to the left of the Gantt bar for every slipping task, as shown in Figure 7 - 30. The length of the *Slippage* indicator represents the amount of slippage for each task.

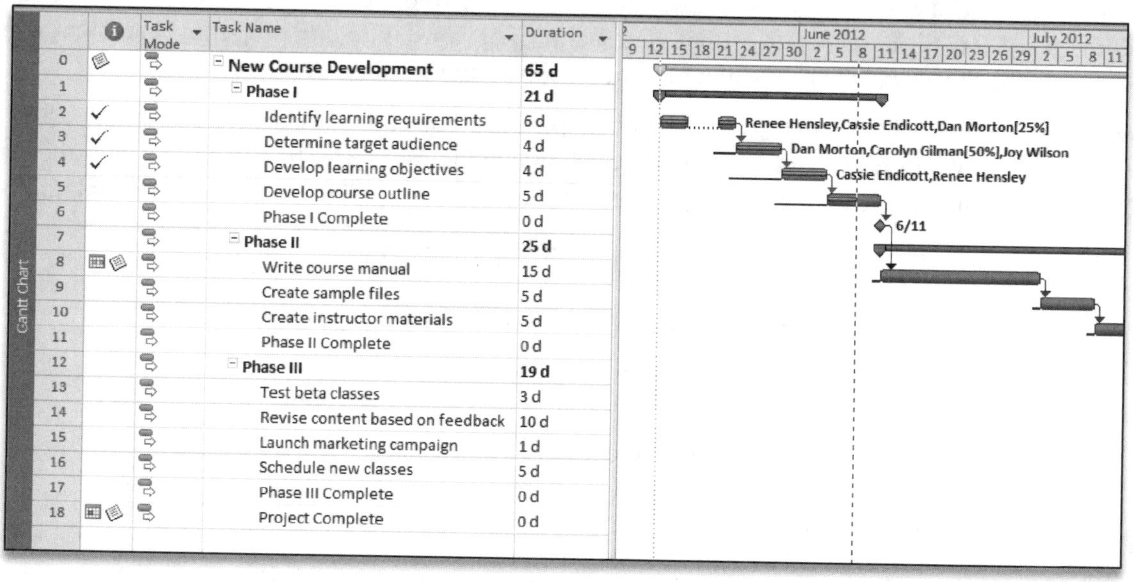

Figure 7 - 30: Slipping task information applied to the Gantt Chart

Using the Gantt Chart Style Tools

The single option in the *Gantt Chart Style* section of the contextual *Format* ribbon allows you to customize the color scheme and appearance of all of the symbols shown in the Gantt Chart, including the symbols for regular tasks, summary tasks, milestone tasks, deadline date indicators, and more. To change the color scheme used for every symbol in the Gantt Chart, click either the *up-arrow* or *down-arrow* buttons in the *Gantt Chart Style* section to view the list of available color scheme, and then select a color scheme. Click the *More* button to display a list of all available color schemes, as shown in Figure 7 - 31.

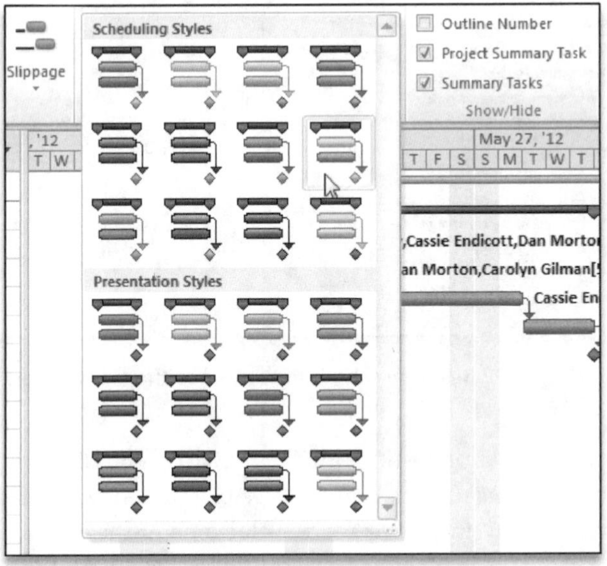

Figure 7 - 31: Available color styles in the Gantt Chart Styles pick list

Notice that the *Gantt Chart Styles* pick list organizes the available color schemes into two sections. Use a color scheme in the *Scheduling Styles* section to format your Gantt Chart for day-to-day project management work. Use a color scheme in the *Presentation Styles* section to format your Gantt Chart for a presentation.

After you select a color scheme on the *Gantt Chart Styles* pick list, you can also click the *Format Bar Styles* dialog launcher icon in the lower right corner of the section, as shown in Figure 7 - 32. The system launches the *Bar Styles* dialog shown previously in Figure 7 - 23, with the selected color scheme applied to objects in the dialog.

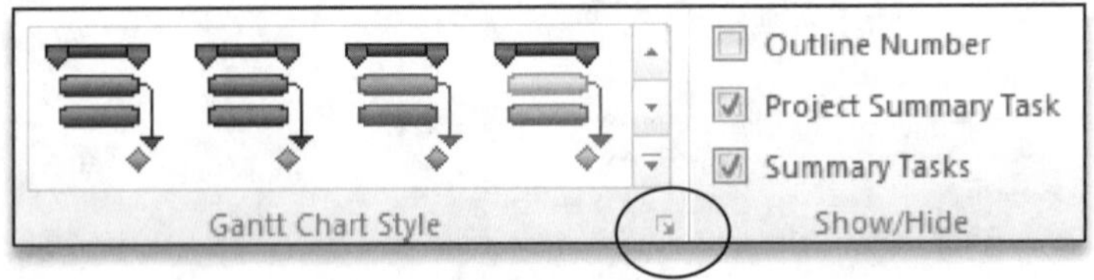

Figure 7 - 32: Format Bar Styles dialog launcher icon

Using the Show/Hide Tools

The *Show/Hide* section of the contextual *Format* ribbon contains three option checkboxes that allow you to show extra detail in the *Task Sheet* part of your *Gantt Chart* view. Unless you specify otherwise in the *Project Options* dialog, the system selects only the *Summary Tasks* option by default in each new project you create. Deselect the

Summary Tasks option to hide summary tasks in your project temporarily, and to show only regular tasks and milestone tasks in your project, as shown in Figure 7 - 33.

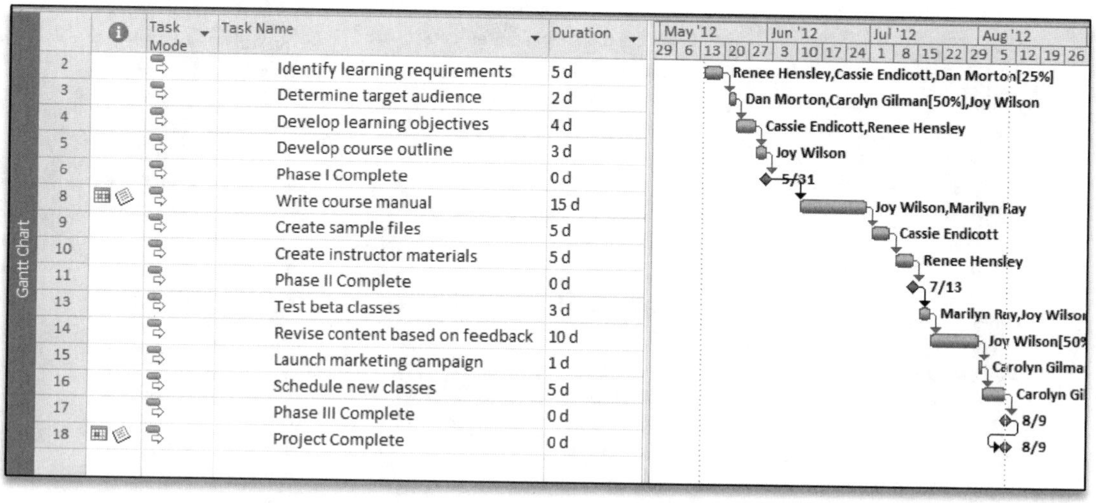

Figure 7 - 33: Summary Tasks option deselected in the Show/Hide section

With the *Summary Tasks* option selected, you can also select the *Project Summary Task* option to display the Project Summary Task (Row 0 or Task 0) in your project. Remember that the Project Summary Task is the highest level summary task in your project, and summarizes all of the information in the project. It shows you the current Start date and current calculated finish date of the project, the current duration of the project, the current amount of work and cost for the project, and shows you all variance for the project as well. Because of this, I strongly recommend you include the Project Summary Task in the *Gantt Chart* view of every project you manage! Figure 7 - 34 shows the Project Summary Task in a project.

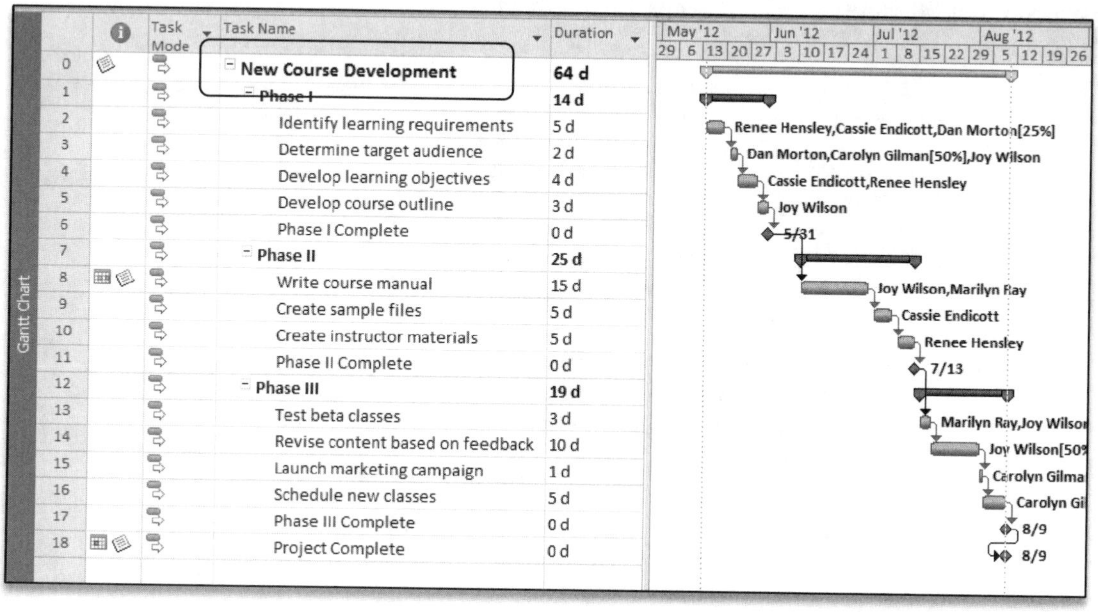

Figure 7 - 34: Project Summary Task option selected in the Show/Hide section

The final option you can select in the *Show/Hide* section of the contextual *Format* ribbon is the *Outline Number* option. When you select this option, Microsoft Project 2010 displays an outline number to the left of each task in the *Task Sheet* part of the *Gantt Chart* view, as shown in Figure 7 - 35.

	Indicators	Task Mode	Task Name	Duration	Start	Finish
0			**New Course Development**	**64 d**	**5/14/12**	**8/9/12**
1			**1 Phase I**	**14 d**	**5/14/12**	**5/31/12**
2			1.1 Identify learning requirements	5 d	5/14/12	5/18/12
3			1.2 Determine target audience	2 d	5/21/12	5/22/12
4			1.3 Develop learning objectives	4 d	5/23/12	5/28/12
5			1.4 Develop course outline	3 d	5/29/12	5/31/12
6			1.5 Phase I Complete	0 d	5/31/12	5/31/12
7			**2 Phase II**	**25 d**	**6/11/12**	**7/13/12**
8			2.1 Write course manual	15 d	6/11/12	6/29/12
9			2.2 Create sample files	5 d	7/2/12	7/6/12
10			2.3 Create instructor materials	5 d	7/9/12	7/13/12
11			2.4 Phase II Complete	0 d	7/13/12	7/13/12
12			**3 Phase III**	**19 d**	**7/16/12**	**8/9/12**
13			3.1 Test beta classes	3 d	7/16/12	7/18/12
14			3.2 Revise content based on feedba	10 d	7/19/12	8/1/12
15			3.3 Launch marketing campaign	1 d	8/2/12	8/2/12
16			3.4 Schedule new classes	5 d	8/3/12	8/9/12
17			3.5 Phase III Complete	0 d	8/9/12	8/9/12
18			3.6 Project Complete	0 d	8/9/12	8/9/12

Figure 7 - 35: Outline Number option selected in the Show/Hide section

Using the Drawing Tools

The *Drawing* section of the contextual *Format* ribbon contains a single option. When you click the *Drawing* pick list button, the system displays the pick list shown in Figure 7 - 36. Use the items on this pick list to draw objects in your *Gantt Chart* view. Because the *Drawing* pick list contains all of the same items found on the *Drawing* toolbar in previous versions of Microsoft Project, I do not discuss this feature.

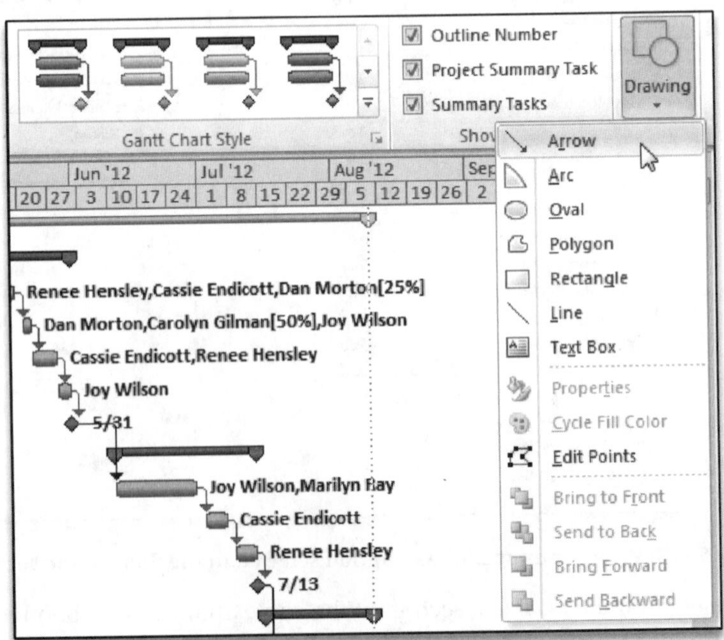

Figure 7 - 36: Drawing pick list

Hands On Exercise

Exercise 7-5

Format Text Styles and Gridlines in the Gantt Chart view of a project.

1. Navigate to your student folder and open the **Format Views.mpp** sample file.
2. Click the *Format* tab to display the contextual *Format* ribbon with the *Gantt Chart Tools* applied.
3. Click the *Text Styles* button in the *Format* section of the *Format* ribbon.
4. In the *Text Styles* dialog, click the *Item to Change* pick list and select the *Milestone Tasks* item.
5. Click the *Background Color* pick list and select the *Orange, Lighter 80%* color (lightest orange color) in the *Theme Colors* section of the dialog.
6. Click the *OK* button.

Notice how Microsoft Project 2010 formats the cell background color of every milestone task with the light orange color.

7. Click the *Gridlines* pick list button and then click the *Gridlines* item on the list.
8. In the *Gridlines* dialog, select the *Status Date* item at the bottom of the *Line to Change* list.
9. Click the *Type* pick list and select the last item on the list (the -- - -- - -- - item).
10. Click the *Color* pick list and select the *Red* color in the *Standard Colors* section of the dialog.
11. Click the *OK* button.

Notice how Microsoft Project 2010 displays the Status Date of the project using a red dashed vertical line in the Gantt Chart.

12. Save but do not close the **Format Views.mpp** sample file.

Exercise 7-6

Format the columns in the Gantt Chart view of a project.

1. Click the *Task Mode* column header to select the entire column.
2. Click the *Insert Column* button in the *Columns* section of the *Format* ribbon, and then select the *% Complete* field from the list of available fields.
3. Double-click on the right edge of the *% Complete* column header to "best fit" the column automatically.
4. Click the *% Complete* column, if necessary to select the entire *% Complete* column again.
5. Click the *Center* button to center the data in the *% Complete* column.

6. With the *% Complete* column still selected, click the *Column Settings* pick list button and then click the *Field Settings* item.
7. In the *Field Settings* dialog, click the *Align Title* pick list and select the *Center* item.
8. Click the *OK* button.
9. Click the *Task Mode* column header to select the entire column.
10. Click the *Column Settings* pick list button and select the *Hide Column* item on the pick list.
11. In the *Show/Hide* section of the *Format* ribbon, select the *Outline Number* option.

Notice how Microsoft Project 2010 displays the *Outline Number* value to the left of each task in the *Task Name* field.

12. Save but do not close the **Format Views.mpp** sample file.

Exercise 7-7

Format the items displayed in the Gantt Chart view of a project.

1. In the *Bar Styles* section of the *Format* ribbon, select the *Critical Tasks* option.
2. Scroll through the *Gantt Chart* and look for critical tasks (tasks with red Gantt bars).
3. Leave the *Critical Tasks* option selected and then select the *Slack* option.
4. Scroll through the *Gantt Chart* and look for tasks with slack (tasks with a dark blue underscore stripe to the right of the Gantt bar).
5. **Deselect** both the *Critical Tasks* and *Slack* options.
6. Click the *Baseline* pick list button and select the *Baseline* item (the first Baseline listed).
7. Scroll through the *Gantt Chart* and look for the Baseline schedule of each task (gray Gantt bars).
8. Click the *Baseline* pick list button again and **deselect** the *Baseline* item.
9. Click the *Slippage* pick list button and select the *Baseline* item (the first Baseline listed).
10. Scroll through the *Gantt Chart* and look for slipping tasks (tasks with a dark blue underscore stripe to the left of the Gantt bar).
11. Click the *Slippage* pick list button again and **deselect** the *Baseline* item.
12. In the *Gantt Chart Style* section of the *Format* ribbon, click the *More* button to see the complete list of styles available.
13. In the *Presentation Styles* section of the menu, select the second style in the first row (light blue Gantt bars).
14. In the *Gantt Chart Style* section of the *Format* ribbon, click the *Format Bar Styles* dialog launcher icon to open the *Bar Styles* dialog.
15. In the *Bar Styles* dialog, examine the formatting of each object in the *Gantt Chart* view.
16. Click the *Cancel* button to close the *Bar Styles* dialog when finished.
17. Save but do not close the **Format Views.mpp** sample file.

Formatting Other Views

As I noted in Module 01, Microsoft Project 2010 offers a contextual *Format* ribbon for every view in the system. When you select any view and click the contextual *Format* ribbon, the ribbon contains a set of options unique to the selected view. For example, if you select the *Task Usage* view, the system displays the contextual *Format* ribbon with the *Task Usage Tools* applied, as shown in Figure 7 - 37. With the *Task Usage* view displayed, the contextual *Format* ribbon contains several of the same sections shown for the *Gantt Chart* view, and contains two additional sections as well.

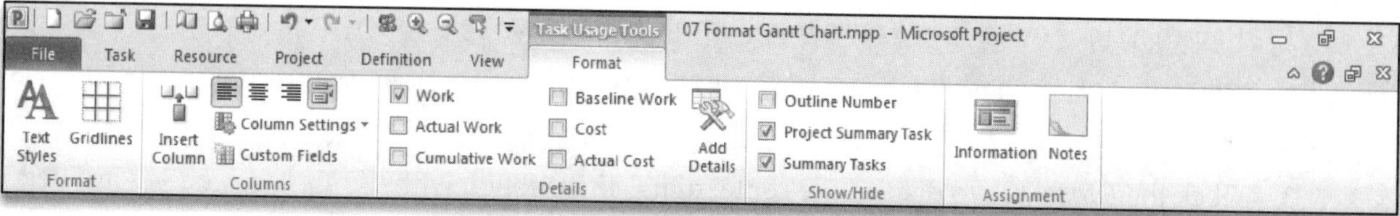

Figure 7 - 37: Format ribbon with the Task Usage Tools applied

The *Details* section contains six option checkboxes that control the details (rows) displayed in the timephased grid on the right side of the view (gray and white timesheet-like grid). By default, Microsoft Project 2010 selects only the *Work* option, which displays only the *Work* details in the timephased grid. Select additional checkboxes in the *Details* section as you require. To choose from a complete list of details available for the timephased grid, click the *Add Details* button in the *Details* section. The system displays the *Detail Styles* dialog, in which you can select from a complete list of rows for the timephased grid. Because the *Detail Styles* dialog is the same dialog found in previous versions of Microsoft Project, I do not discuss this feature.

When you select a resource assignment (italicized resource name below a task) in the *Task Usage* view, the system activates the two buttons in the *Assignment* section of the contextual *Format* tab. Click the *Information* button to display the *Assignment Information* dialog for the selected resource assignment. To add a note to a resource assignment, click the *Notes* button to display the *Assignment Information* dialog with the *Notes* tab selected. Because these dialogs are the same as in previous versions of Microsoft Project, I do not discuss these two features.

The contextual *Format* ribbon for the *Resource* view is identical to the ribbon shown for the *Task Usage* view. This is because both of these views are assignment views that display assignment information, along with a timephased grid on the right side of the view.

I do not discuss the contextual *Format* ribbon for every view in Microsoft Project 2010. However, the information in the Formatting the Gantt Chart section and the Formatting Other Views section of this module can serve as an effective guide for you to explore the contextual *Format* ribbon for any view in the software.

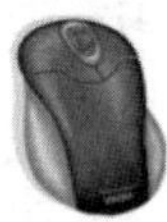

Hands On Exercise

Exercise 7-8

Format the Task Usage view of a project.

1. Return to the **Formatting Views.mpp** sample file, if necessary.
2. Click the *View* tab and then click the *Task Usage* button in the *Task Views* section of the *View* ribbon.
3. Click the *Format* tab to display the contextual *Format* ribbon with the *Task Usage Tools* applied.
4. In the *Details* section of the *Format* ribbon, select the *Actual Work* and *Baseline Work* details.

Notice how Microsoft Project 2010 displays these two additional detail rows in the timephased grid on the right side of the *Task Usage* view.

5. Double-click on the right edge of the *Details* column header in the timephased grid to "best fit" the column automatically.
6. Click the *Add Details* button in the *Details* section of the *Format* ribbon.
7. In the *Detail Styles* dialog, select the *Actual Work* item in the *Show these fields* list and then click the *Hide* button.
8. In the *Available fields* list, select the *Cost* field, click the *Show* button, and then click the *OK* button.
9. In the *Available fields* list, select the *Baseline Cost* field and then click the *Show* button again.
10. Save and close the **Formatting Views.mpp** sample file.

Using the Timeline with the Gantt Chart View

Microsoft Project 2010 includes the new *Timeline* view that displays the current project schedule using a timeline presentation similar to what you see in Microsoft Visio or in any other timeline software application. You can modify the default *Timeline* view to show your current project schedule according to your reporting requirements. You can also export the *Timeline* view to other Microsoft Office applications, such as Microsoft PowerPoint.

The *Gantt with Timeline* view is the default view for every new project you create in Microsoft Project 2010. In fact, you see this view every time you launch the software, because the system always creates a new blank project on application launch. The *Gantt with Timeline* view is a split view that shows the *Timeline* view in the top pane and the *Gantt Chart* view in the bottom pane. Figure 7 - 38 shows the *Gantt with Timeline* view applied to an in-progress project.

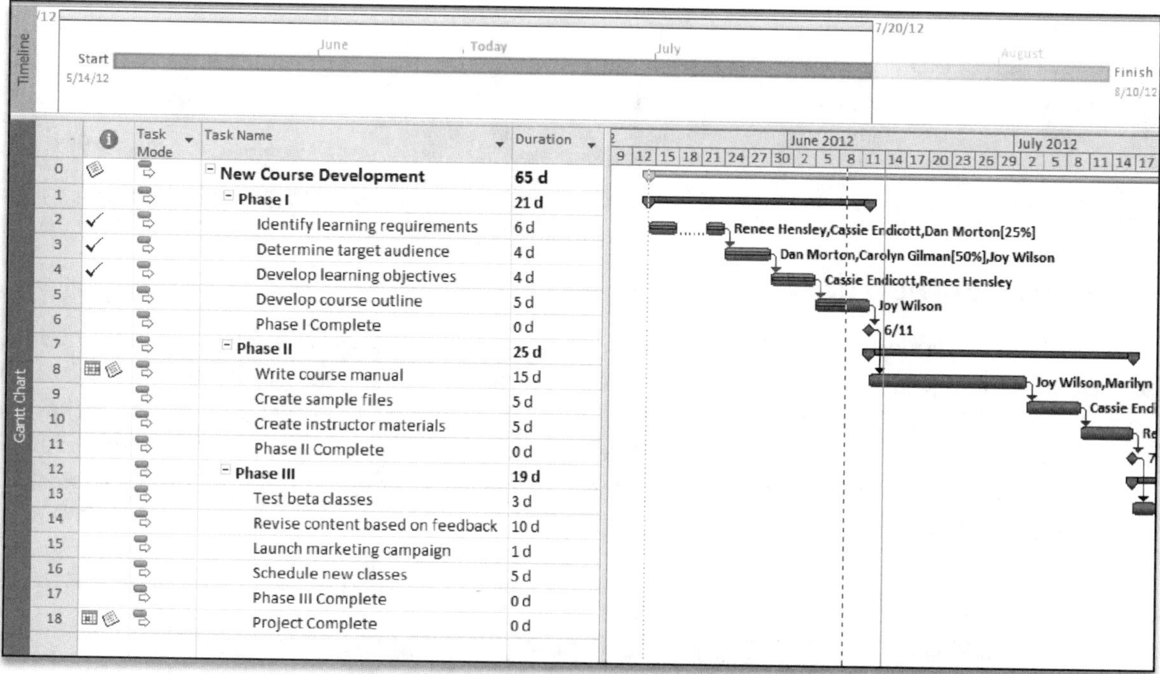

Figure 7 - 38: Gantt with Timeline view for an in-progress project

If you do not see the *Gantt with Timeline* view when you open a project, apply the *Gantt Chart* view and then click the *View* tab. In the *Split View* section of the *View* ribbon, select the *Timeline* option.

Depending on your level of zoom applied in your project, the *Timeline* view shows the following information by default:

- The gray *Timeline* bar represents the time span of the entire project, with the project *Start* date on the left end of the bar and the project *Finish* date on the right end of the bar. Notice in Figure 7 - 38 that the project runs from 5/14/12 to 8/10/12, indicated by the dates to the left and right of the gray *Timeline* bar.
- The system divides the *Timeline* bar into one-month segments using light blue tick marks, and displays the name of the month above each segment. Figure 7 - 38 shows that the project spans a partial month of May (not shown as a month name), plus the months of June, July, and August.
- The system indicates the current date with the word *Today* formatted with orange text above the *Timeline* bar and with an orange dashed line in the *Timeline* bar.
- The light blue *Pan and Zoom* bar above the *Timeline* bar represents the time span of the project currently visible in the *Gantt Chart* view. At the ends of the *Pan and Zoom* bar, the system displays the beginning and ending dates of the time span currently visible in the *Gantt Chart* view. Notice in Figure 7 - 38 that the gray *Timeline* bar extends only to 7/20/12, indicated by the date on the right end of the *Pan and Zoom* bar.
- The system uses light gray shading for the portion of the *Timeline* bar not visible in the *Gantt Chart* view. Figure 7 - 38 shows that project information is not visible past 7/20/12 in the *Gantt Chart* view, indicated by the light gray shading in the gray *Timeline* bar after that date.

As you scroll right or left in the *Gantt Chart* view, the *Pan and Zoom* bar scrolls with you to indicate the portion of the timeline currently visible in the Gantt Chart.

Adding a Task to the Timeline

To add any task to the *Timeline* view, right-click on the name of the task in the *Task Sheet* part of the *Gantt Chart* view and then click the *Add to Timeline* item on the shortcut menu. To add multiple tasks to the *Timeline* view, select a block of tasks, right-click anywhere in the selected block of tasks, and then click the *Add to Timeline* item on the shortcut menu. Microsoft Project 2010 adds the selected tasks to the *Timeline* view as shown in Figure 7 - 39. Notice that I added the Phase I and Phase II tasks to the *Timeline* view, along with the first three subtasks in the Phase II section of the project.

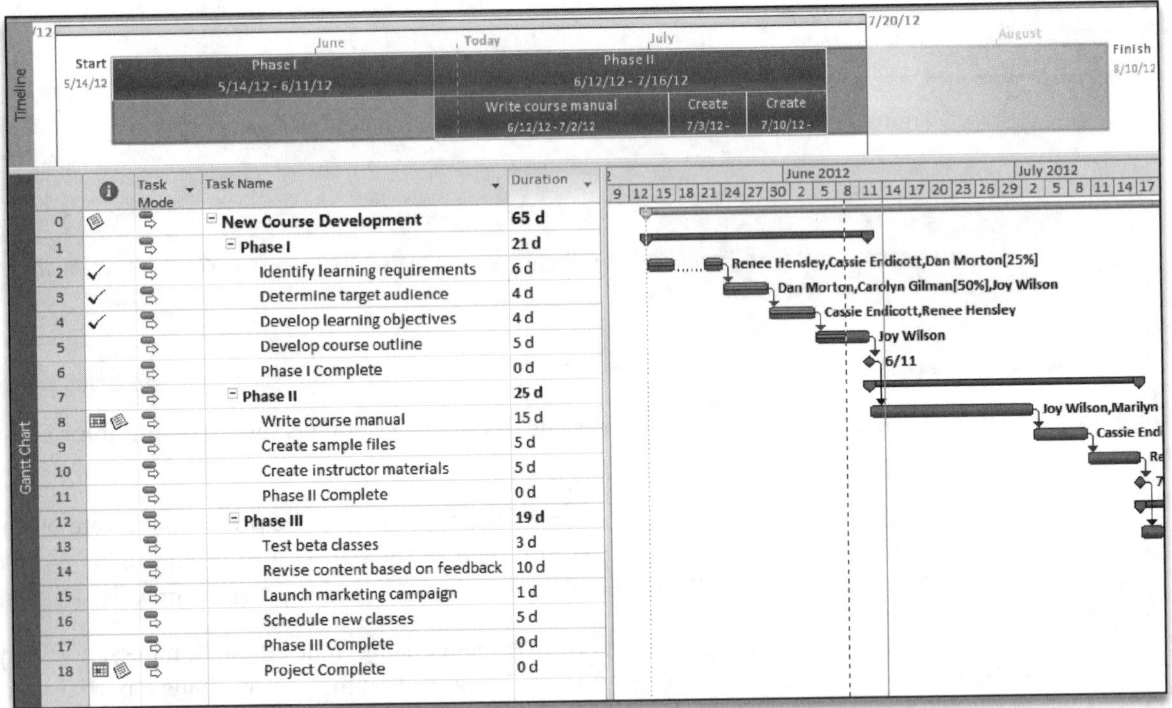

Figure 7 - 39: Tasks added to the Timeline view

You can also add a task in the *Timeline* view by double-clicking the task and then selecting the *Display on Timeline* option in the *General* page of the *Task Information* dialog. If you select multiple tasks, you can add a task in the *Timeline* view by selecting the *Task* ribbon and then clicking the *Information* button in the *Properties* section of the *Task* Ribbon. In the *Multiple Task Information* dialog, select the the *Display on Timeline* option in the *General* page.

After you add tasks to the *Timeline* view, you can rearrange the tasks on the *Timeline* bar using any of the following techniques:

- Drag a task to a new row above or below its current position in the *Timeline* bar.
- Drag a task above or below the *Timeline* bar to display the task as a callout.
- Drag a block of tasks by selecting them while pressing and holding the *Control* key on your keyboard, and then dragging the block of the selected tasks to a new position.
- Right-click on any task in the *Timeline* bar and select the *Display as Callout* item on the shortcut menu.
- Drag a new callout from the top of the *Timeline* bar to a position below the *Timeline* bar.
- Convert a callout to a task bar by right-clicking on the callout and then clicking the *Display as Bar* item on the shortcut menu.

When you drag tasks into a new position in the *Timeline* bar, or create callouts above or below the *Timeline* bar, Microsoft Project 2010 adjusts the height of the *Timeline* view automatically to accommodate the new information. For example, Figure 7 - 40 shows my *Timeline* view after I created two callouts and dragged the Phase II task and its subtask to a new row in the *Timeline* bar.

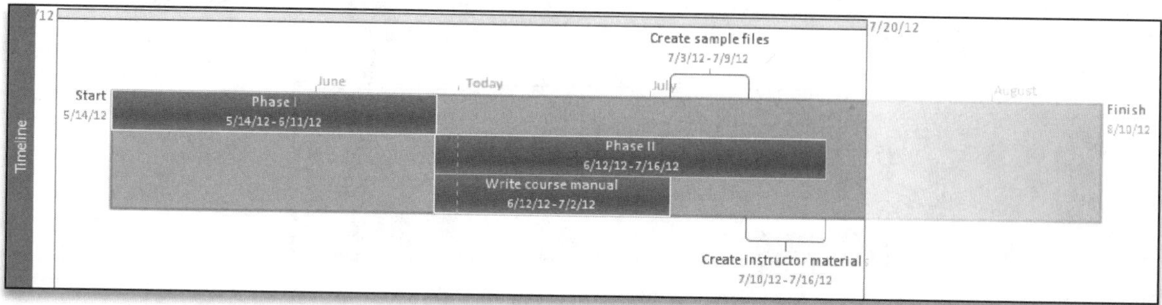

Figure 7 - 40: Rearranged tasks in the Timeline view

To remove a task or a callout from the *Timeline* view, right-click the task or the callout and then click the *Remove from Timeline* item on the shortcut menu.

Formatting the Timeline View

To format the *Timeline* view, click anywhere in the *Timeline* view to select it and then click the *Format* tab. The system displays the contextual *Format* ribbon with the *Timeline Tools* applied, shown in Figure 7 - 41. The process for formatting the *Timeline* view is similar to the process of formatting the *Gantt Chart* view that you learned earlier in this module.

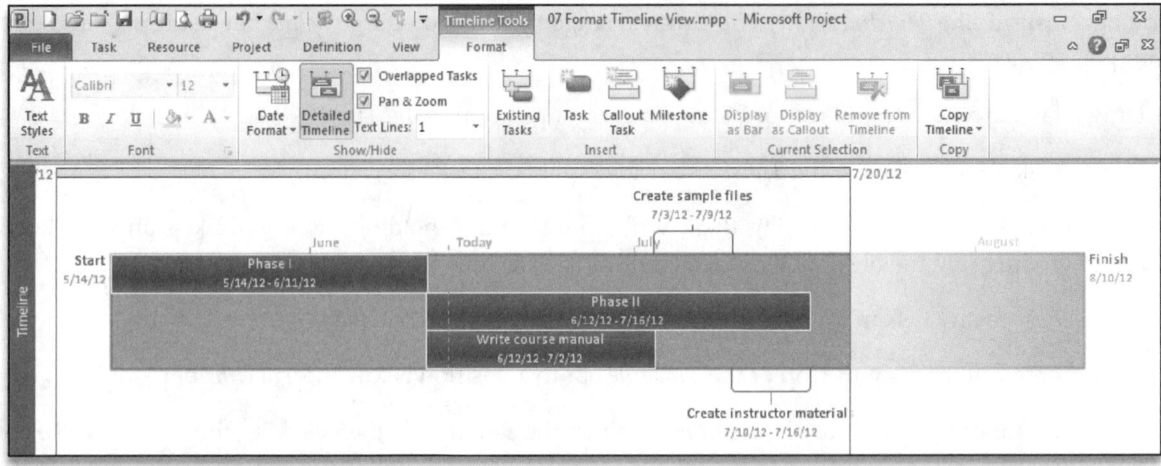

Figure 7 - 41: Format ribbon with the Timeline Tools applied

Using the Text Tools

To format the text for any set of objects shown in the *Timeline* view, click the *Text Styles* button in the *Text* section of the contextual *Format* ribbon. Microsoft Project 2010 displays the *Text Styles* dialog. Although this *Text Styles* dialog is similar to the same-named dialog shown previously in Figure 7 - 15, the *Item to Change* pick list includes a completely different list of items available for formatting, as shown in Figure 7 - 42.

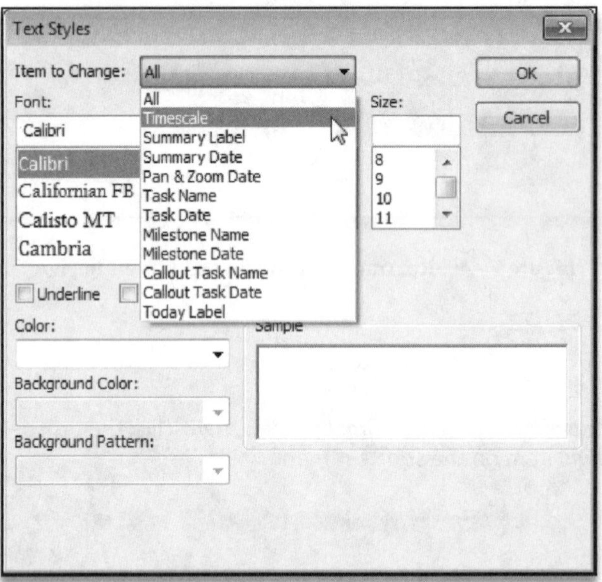

Figure 7 - 42: Text Styles dialog Item to Change pick list

Notice in Figure 7 - 42 that Microsoft Project 2010 does not allow you to change the *Background Color* or *Background Pattern* options in the *Text Styles* dialog for the *Timeline* view. The system limits you to changing only text formatting options such as the *Font* and *Color* items, for example.

You can also display the *Text Styles* dialog by right-clicking anywhere in the white part of the *Timeline* view and then clicking the *Text Styles* item on the shortcut menu.

Using Font Tools

To change the font or the cell background color of an individual object in the *Timeline* view, select the object and then change the formatting options in the *Font* section of the contextual *Format* ribbon. To display the *Font* dialog, click the *Font* dialog launcher icon in the lower right corner of the *Font* section of the ribbon. To change the background color of a task, for example, select the task and choose a new color on the *Background Color* pick list.

Using Show/Hide Tools

To change the date format of the dates shown in the *Timeline* view, click the *Date Format* pick list button in the *Show/Hide* section and select a new date format. By default, the *Timeline* view uses the date format specified in the *Date Format* field on the *General* page of the *Project Options* dialog. On the *Date Format* pick list, Microsoft Project 2010 also allows you to hide some of the dates shown by default on the *Timeline* view. To hide the dates shown for each task, click the *Date Format* pick list and deselect the *Task Dates* option. To hide the current date, deselect the *Current Date* option on the *Date Format* pick list. To hide the dates shown above the *Timeline* bar, deselect the *Timescale* option on the *Date Format* pick list.

To remove the details from the *Timeline* view, such as the names of tasks and task dates, deselect the *Detailed Timeline* option in the *Show/Hide* section of the contextual *Format* ribbon. The system completely removes all details from the *Timeline* view. As you can see in Figure 7 - 43, without the details, the *Timeline* view is probably not very useful to you.

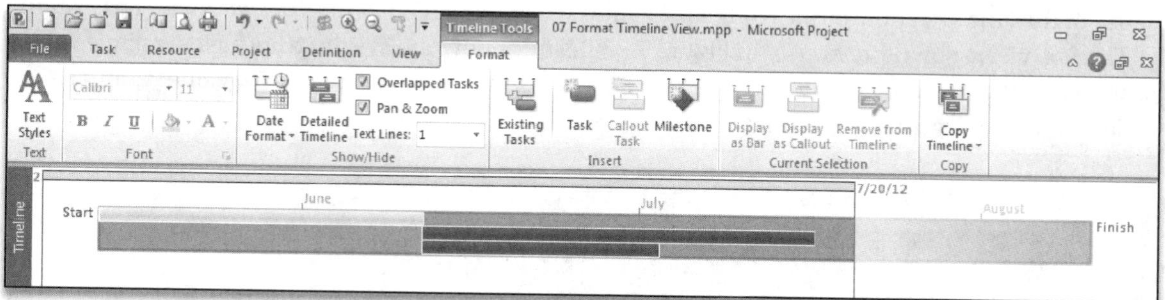

Figure 7 - 43: Timeline view with details removed

If your project contains parallel task sections, and you display overlapping tasks from these parallel sections in the *Timeline* view, the *Overlapped Tasks* option in the *Show/Hide* section works to your advantage. When selected, the *Overlapped Tasks* option displays each overlapping task on its own row in the *Timeline* view. For example, Figure 7 - 44 shows a different project with multiple parallel task sections and with each summary task section displayed on the *Timeline* view. Notice how Microsoft Project 2010 displays each overlapping section on its own task row in the *Timeline* view.

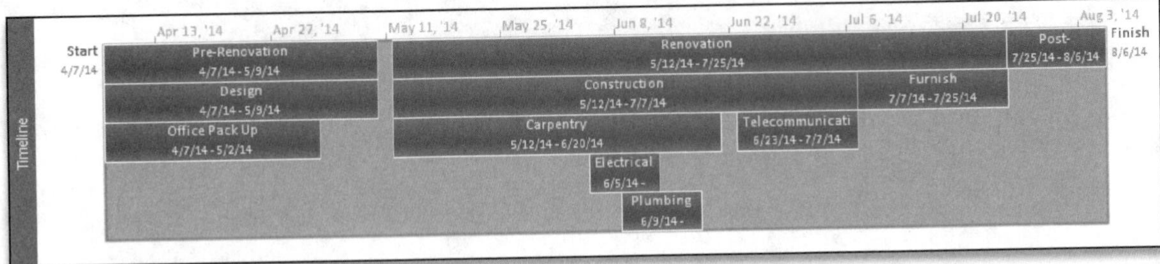

Figure 7 - 44: Timeline with Overlapped Tasks option selected

Figure 7 - 45 shows the same *Timeline* view with the *Overlapped Tasks* option deselected. Notice how the system displays all tasks on a single task row in the *Timeline* view, rendering the information all but impossible to read. For this reason, I recommend you leave the *Overlapped Tasks* option selected for the *Timeline* view when you build a timeline presentation containing numerous overlapping tasks.

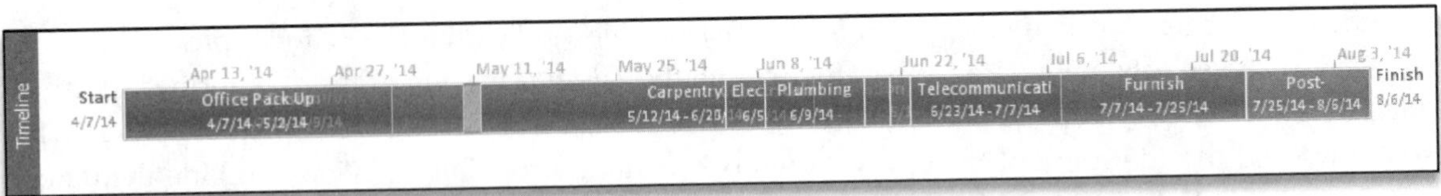

Figure 7 - 45: Timeline with Overlapped Tasks option deselected

In the *Show/Hide* section of the contextual *Format* ribbon, the *Pan & Zoom* option allows you to display or hide the light blue *Pan and Zoom* bar shown at the top of the *Timeline* view. If you select the *Pan & Zoom* option, the system displays the *Pan and Zoom* bar; if you deselect this option, the system hides the *Pan and Zoom* bar.

The final option in the *Show/Hide* section is the *Text Lines* option, which allows you to determine how many lines of text to display for every task shown in the *Timeline* view. By default, the system sets the *Text Lines* value to *1 line*. Because of this, the system truncates long task names when displayed in the *Timeline* view. For example, consider the *Timeline* view shown previously in Figure 7 - 39. Notice how the system truncates the names of the three subtasks shown in the Phase II section with the *Text Lines* value set to the default *1 line* value. Compare the same *Timeline* view shown in Figure 7 - 46 with the *Text Lines* value set to *3 lines*.

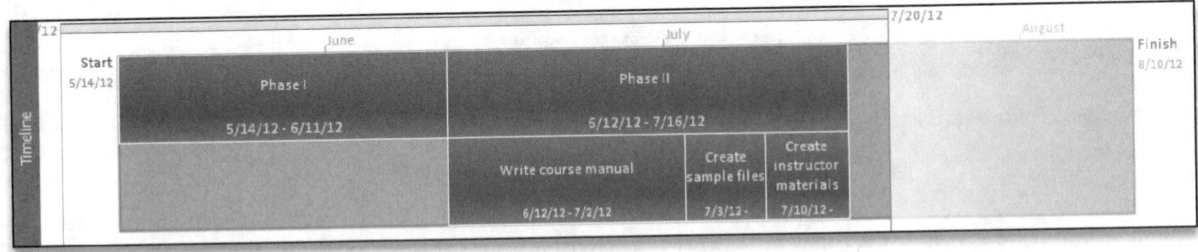

Figure 7 - 46: Timeline view with the Text Lines option set to 3 lines

Figure 7 - 47 shows the completed *Timeline* view after I formatted it using methods I documented in this section of the module. To format the *Timeline* view, I did the following:

- I added the Phase III task to the *Timeline* view.
- I changed the Create Instructor Materials task to a callout.

- I dragged the new callout to a position below the *Timeline* bar.
- I changed the *Date Format* option to the *Jan 28* format.
- I changed the *Background Color* setting for each task individually.
- Using the *Text Styles* dialog, I changed the *Font Color* setting to *Red* for the names of all callout items.

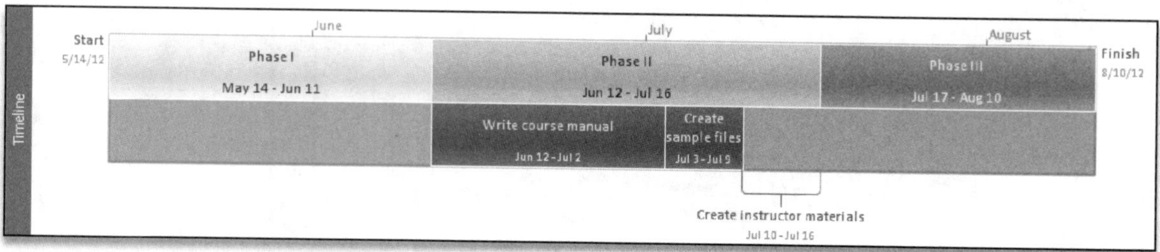

Figure 7 - 47: Timeline view after applying custom formatting

Notice in Figure 7 - 47 that the *Timeline* view no longer includes the light blue *Pan and Zoom* bar at the top of the view. This is because I zoomed the *Gantt Chart* view to show the complete time span of the project. When you zoom the Gantt Chart view to show the Gantt bars for all tasks in the project, Microsoft Project 2010 removes the Pan and Zoom bar from the Timeline view automatically.

To change the type of object displayed in the *Timeline* view, or to remove an object from the *Timeline* view, use the buttons in the *Current Selection* section of the contextual *Format* ribbon. For example, to change a callout to a task bar, select the callout and then click the *Display as Bar* button. To change a task bar to a callout, select the task bar and then click the *Display as Callout* button. To remove a task or a callout from the *Timeline* view, select the task or callout and then click the *Remote from Timeline* button.

Adding Tasks Using the Contextual Format Ribbon

In addition to the formatting options available on the contextual *Format* ribbon for the *Timeline* view, this ribbon also offers options for adding or removing tasks in the *Timeline* view. In the *Insert* section, Microsoft Project 2010 includes four buttons that allow you to add new tasks to the *Timeline* view. To add a new existing task to the *Timeline* view, click the *Existing Tasks* button. The system displays the *Add Tasks to Timeline* dialog shown in Figure 7 - 48. Select the checkbox to the left of the task name and then click the *OK* button.

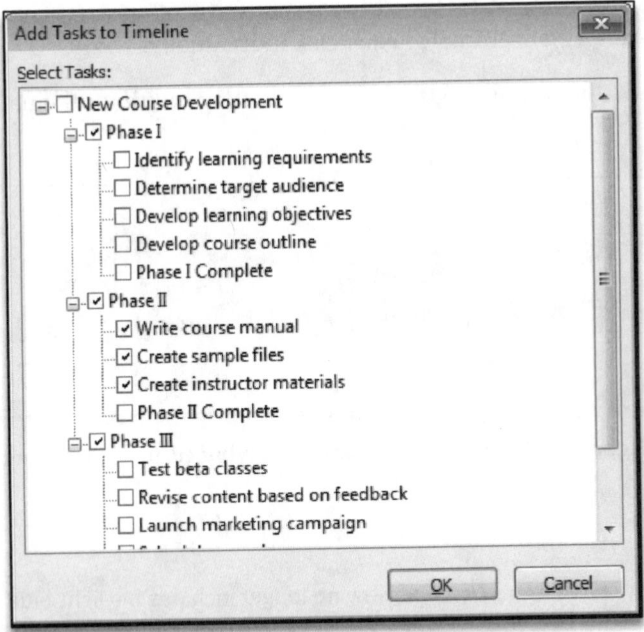

Figure 7 - 48: Add Tasks to Timeline dialog

The system adds the selected task(s) to the *Timeline* view. For example, notice in Figure 7 - 49 that I added the Project Complete milestone task to the *Timeline* view.

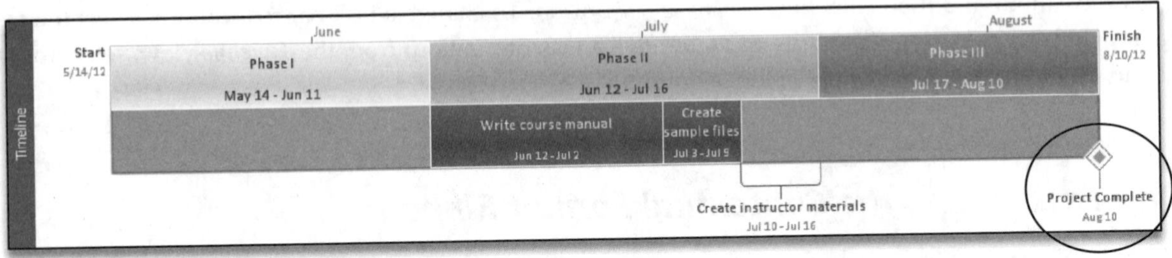

Figure 7 - 49: Milestone task added to the Timeline view

To add a completely new task to your project and add the new task to the *Timeline* view, click the *Task* button, the *Callout Task* button, or the *Milestone* button in the *Insert* section of the contextual *Format* ribbon. When you click any of these three buttons, Microsoft Project 2010 displays the *Task Information* dialog shown in Figure 7 - 50.

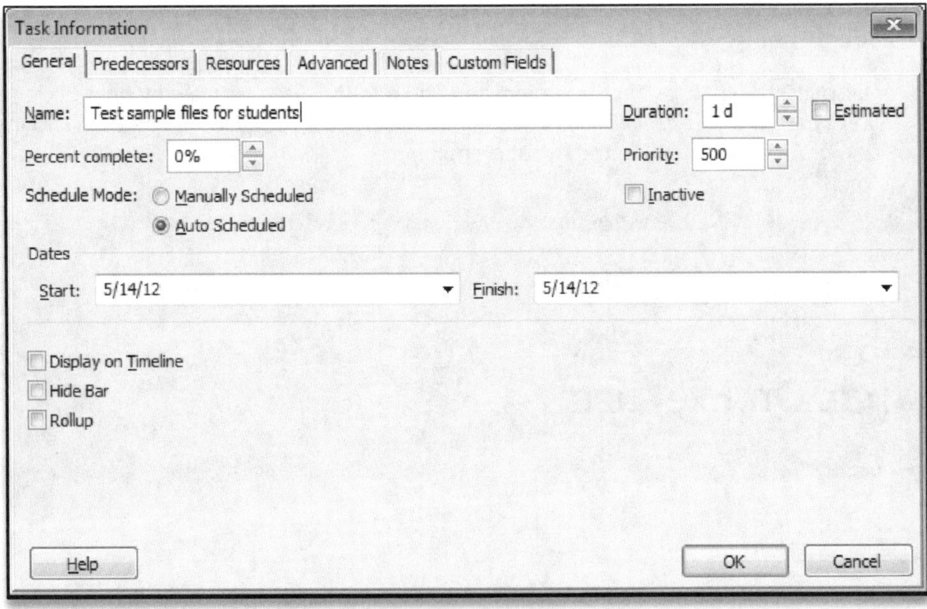

Figure 7 - 50: Task Information dialog

In the *Task Information* dialog, enter complete information about the new task, including information in the *Name* and *Duration* fields, and select the desired *Schedule Mode* option. Assuming you want to display the new task in the *Timeline* view, be sure to select the *Display on Timeline* option. If necessary, select predecessor tasks on the *Predecessors* page and assign resources to the new task on the *Resources* page. Click the *OK* button to finish. Microsoft Project 2010 creates the new task as the last task in the task list, and adds the new task to the *Timeline* view. Figure 7 - 51 shows a new task I added, Test Student Sample Files. After creating the new task, you must drag the task to the correct place in the project and set additional dependencies.

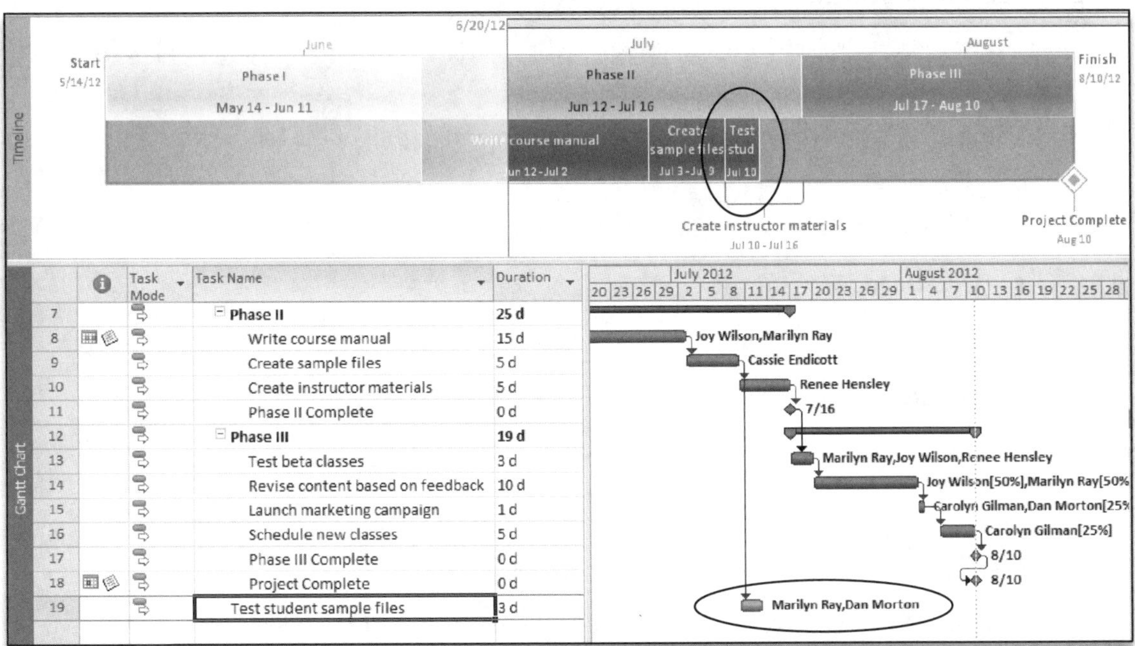

Figure 7 - 51: New task added to the project and to the Timeline view

You can also insert a new task in the project and add it to the *Timeline* view by right-clicking anywhere in the white part of the *Timeline* view, selecting the *Insert Task* menu item, and then clicking the *Callout Task*, *Task*, or *Milestone* item on the flyout menu.

Hands On Exercise

Exercise 7-9

Add tasks to the Timeline view.

1. Navigate to your student folder and open the **Format the Timeline View.mpp** sample file.
2. Click the *View* tab and then select the *Timeline* option in the *Split View* section of the *View* ribbon.
3. Grab the split bar along the bottom edge of the *Timeline* view and drag it down to approximately **triple** the height of the *Timeline* view.
4. Right-click on the name of the *Pre-Renovation* summary task and then click the *Add to Timeline* item on the shortcut menu.

Notice how Microsoft Project 2010 adds a bar to the *Timeline* view representing the Pre-Renovation summary task.

5. Using the *Control* key on your keyboard, select and highlight the following summary tasks as a group:
   - Renovation
   - Construction
   - Furnish
   - Post Renovation
6. Release the *Control* key, then right-click anywhere in one of the selected tasks and click the *Add to Timeline* item on the shortcut menu.
7. Press the *Control* key on your keyboard and highlight as a group the three tasks highlighted with *Lime* as their cell background color (task IDs #22, 24, and 25).
8. Release the *Control* key, then right-click anywhere in one of the selected tasks and then click the *Add to Timeline* item on the shortcut menu.
9. In the *Timeline* view, right-click on the *Obtain asbestos removal permit* task bar and click the *Display as Callout* item on the shortcut menu.

10. In the *Timeline* view, right-click on the task bar for the *Asbestos removal inspection* task bar and click the *Display as Callout* item on the shortcut menu.
11. Grab the split bar along the bottom edge of the *Timeline* view and drag it down to add approximately one inch to the height of the *Timeline* view.
12. In the *Timeline* view, drag the *Remote asbestos in ceiling* task bar **below** the *Timeline* bar to display this task as a Callout below the Timeline.
13. Press the *Control* key on your keyboard and select the task bars as a block for the *Renovation, Construction,* and *Furnish* tasks in the *Timeline* view.
14. Release the *Control* key, and then drag the block of three selected task bars **one row below** their current position in the *Timeline* view.
15. Save but do not close the **Format the Timeline View.mpp** sample file.

Exercise 7-10

Customize the Timeline view.

1. Click anywhere in the *Timeline* view to select the view.
2. Click the *Format* tab to display the contextual *Format* ribbon with the *Timeline Tools* applied.
3. Click the *Text Styles* button in the *Text* section of the *Format* ribbon.
4. In the *Text Styles* dialog, click the *Item to Change* pick list and select the *Callout Task Name* item.
5. Click the *Color* pick list and select the *Red* color in the *Standard Colors* section of the dialog.
6. Click the *OK* button.
7. In the *Timeline* view, click the task bar for the Construction task.
8. In the *Font* section of the *Format* ribbon, click the *Background Color* pick list button and select the *Red* color in the first row of the *Theme Colors* section.
9. In the *Font* section of the *Format* ribbon, click the *Color* pick list button and select the *Yellow* color in the *Standard Colors* section.
10. In the *Show/Hide* section of the *Format* ribbon, click the *Date Format* pick list button and then **deselect** the *Timescale* item at the bottom of the pick list.
11. In the *Show/Hide* section of the *Format* ribbon, **deselect** the *Pan & Zoom* option.
12. Click the *Existing Tasks* button in the *Insert* section of the *Format* ribbon.
13. In the *Add Tasks to Timeline* dialog, select the checkbox for the Project Complete milestone task and then click the *OK* button.
14. Save but do not close the **Format the Timeline View.mpp** sample file.

Exporting the Timeline View

One additional feature of the new *Timeline* view allows you to export the entire *Timeline* view to any Microsoft Office application, such as Microsoft PowerPoint or Microsoft Visio, for example. To copy the *Timeline* view, click the *Copy Timeline* pick list button in the *Copy* section of the contextual *Format* ribbon. The *Copy Timeline* pick list contains three choices, including *For E-Mail, For Presentation,* and *Full Size.*

If you select the *Full Size* item on the *Copy Timeline* pick list, Microsoft Project 2010 copies the full-size image of the *Timeline* view to your Windows clipboard. If you select the *For Presentation* item, the system optimizes the image for use in Microsoft PowerPoint by reducing the image size to approximately 90% of full size. If you select the *For E-Mail* item, the system optimizes the image for use in Microsoft Outlook by reducing the image size to approximately 60% of full size.

After copying the *Timeline* view to your clipboard, paste the image in one of the Microsoft Office applications. If you use an application that has image editing capabilities, such as Microsoft Word or Microsoft PowerPoint, you can continue to refine your *Timeline* view presentation. For example, Figure 7 - 52 shows the *Timeline* view after I pasted the image into a Microsoft PowerPoint presentation and applied additional formatting. Notice that I used the *Bevel* feature to give the tasks a 3-D appearance, and I used the *Glow* feature to alter the appearance of the Project Complete milestone task.

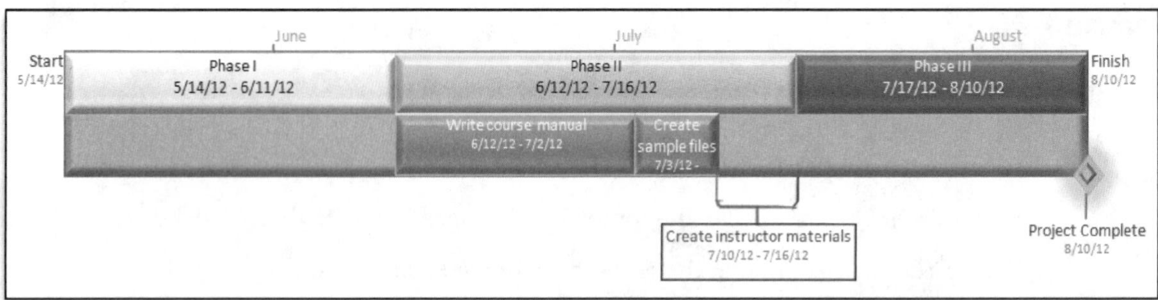

Figure 7 - 52: Timeline view formatted in Microsoft PowerPoint

You can also copy the *Timeline* view by right-clicking anywhere in the white part of the *Timeline* view, selecting the *Copy Timeline* item from the shortcut menu, and then clicking the *For E-Mail, For Presentation*, or *Full Size* item on the flyout menu.

Exercise 7-11

Export the Timeline view to another Microsoft Office application.

1. Return to the **Format the Timeline View.mpp** sample file, if necessary, and then click anywhere in the *Timeline* view to select it.
2. Click the *Copy Timeline* pick list button in the *Copy* section of the *Format* ribbon and then select the *For E-Mail* item on the pick list.
3. Launch Microsoft PowerPoint and create a new blank slide with no placeholder information.
4. Click the *Paste* button in Microsoft PowerPoint.

Notice the size of the Timeline image for an e-mail message.

5. Return to your Microsoft Project 2010 application window.

6. Click the *Copy Timeline* pick list button and then select the *For Presentation* item on the pick list.
7. Return to your Microsoft PowerPoint application and click the *Paste* button again.
8. Drag the pasted Timeline image to the middle of the PowerPoint slide.

Notice the difference in size between the timeline images for a presentation and for an e-mail message.

9. Select the timeline image for an e-mail message and then delete it.
10. Zoom your PowerPoint slide to the *100%* level of zoom.
11. Double-click one of the task bars in the timeline image to launch the *Drawing Tools* feature in Microsoft PowerPoint.
12. Using the *Control* key on your computer keyboard, select each of the task bars in the Timeline image, and then release the *Control* key.
13. Use any of the object formatting features in Microsoft PowerPoint to format the selected task bars in the timeline image. For example, if you have Microsoft PowerPoint 2007, format the task bars using one of the *Bevel* items in the *Shape Effects* pick list.
14. Exit your Microsoft PowerPoint application and save the presentation, if you wish.
15. Return to your Microsoft Project 2010 application window, and then save and close the **Format the Timeline View.mpp** sample file.

Creating a New View

When working with Microsoft Project 2010 files, most of us think of a view as a "way of looking at our data." However, the system formally defines a view as follows:

View = Table + Filter + Group + Screen

The system uses each part of the view as follows:

- The table displays columns of data you want to see.
- The filter displays the rows of data you want to see.
- The group organizes the rows the way you want to see them.
- The screen determines what appears on the right side of the view. For example, you may see a Gantt Chart screen, a timephased screen, or no screen at all (such as in the *Task Sheet* view).

Microsoft Project 2010 allows you to create your own custom views, which may include a custom table, a custom filter, and a custom group. To create a custom view, MSProjectExperts recommends as a best practice that you use the following four-step process:

1. Select an existing table or create a new table.
2. Select an existing filter or create a new filter.
3. Select an existing group or create a new group
4. Create your custom view using the table, filter, group, and screen you need for the view.

Although this process is not new with Microsoft Project 2010, there are several new features you use during these four steps.

Creating a New Table

A quick way to create a new table is to copy an existing table and then modify the copy. To create a new table using this method, complete the following steps:

1. Click the *View* tab to display the *View* ribbon.
2. Click the *Tables* pick list in the *Data* section of the ribbon and then click the *More Tables* item. Microsoft Project 2010 displays the *More Tables* dialog shown in Figure 7 - 53.

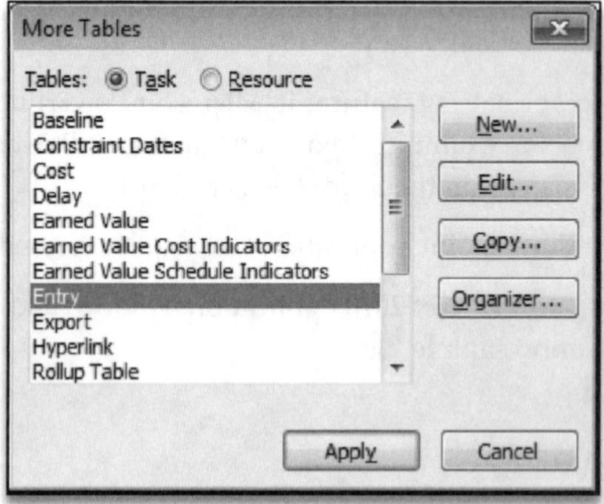

Figure 7 - 53: More Tables dialog

3. From the list of tables shown in the *More Tables* dialog, select a table and then click the *Copy* button. Microsoft Office Project 2010 displays the *Table Definition* dialog shown Figure 7 - 54.

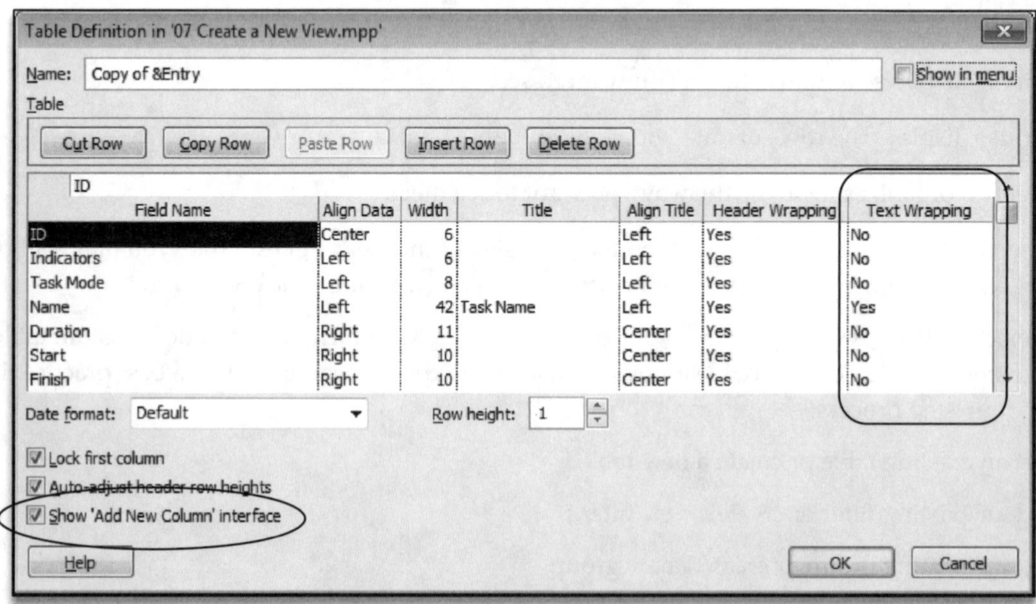

Figure 7 - 54: Table Definition dialog

4. Enter a new name for the table in the *Name* field.

5. Select the *Show in Menu* option if you wish to see the table displayed on *Tables* pick list menu.
6. In the *Field Name* column, add the fields you wish to see in the new table and delete the fields you do not want to appear in your new table.

The preceding is the same process you used in previous versions of Microsoft Project, but the *Table Definition* dialog contains several new features that you should be aware of. The dialog contains a new *Text Wrapping* column that allows you to specify whether the system wraps text in the field automatically when the length of the text string exceeds the width of the field. Notice in Figure 7 - 54 that Microsoft Project 2010 wraps text in the *Name* field (*Task Name* column) by default. When you add new fields to the table, the system sets the *Text Wrapping* value to *No* for each new field, but you can change the value to *Yes* as needed.

The dialog also contains the new *Show 'Add New Column' Interface* option in the lower left corner of the dialog. The system enables this option by default. When selected, this option displays the *Add New Column* virtual column as the last column on the right side of the table. If you do not want to see the *Add New Column* virtual column in your new table, deselect this option.

7. Click the *OK* button to close the *Table Definition* dialog and then click the *Apply* button to display your new table.

After you create and apply your new table, Microsoft Project 2010 uses another new feature to make your new table available in every current and future project. The system copies your new table to the Global.mpt file on your hard drive. Remember that the Global.mp file is your "library" of default and custom objects in Microsoft Project 2010, including views, tables, filters, groups, reports, etc. To see your new table in the Global.mpt file, click the *File* tab and then click the *Organizer* button on the *Info* tab of the *Backstage*. In the *Organizer* dialog, click the *Tables* tab, as shown in Figure 7 - 55. Notice that the *Organizer* dialog shows my new *_Duration and Work Comparison* table in the list on the left (in the Global.mpt file) and in the list on the right (in the active project).

If you do not want to include your new table in the Global.mpt file, click the name of the new table in the *Global.MPT* list on the left side of the dialog and click the *Delete* button. When the system prompts you in a warning dialog, click the *OK* button to confirm the deletion.

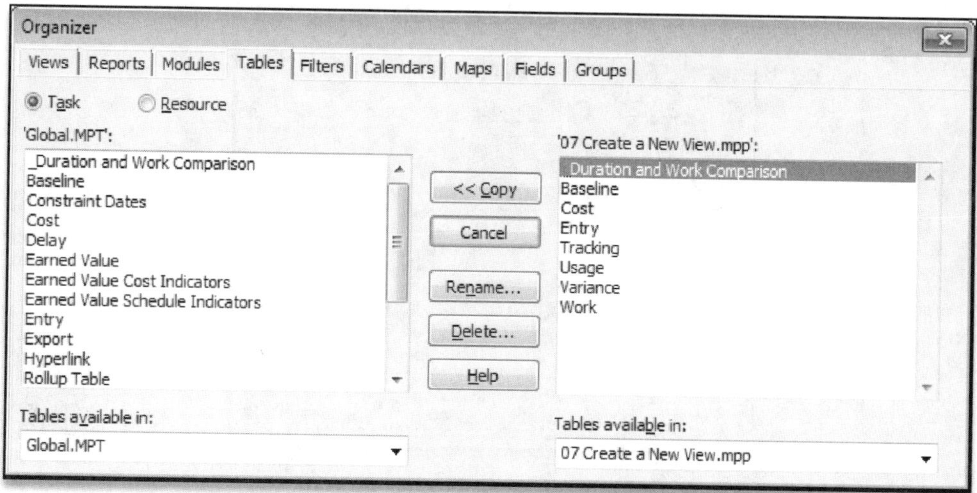

Figure 7 - 55: Organizer dialog shows the new table

If you want to create custom tables on a project-by-project basis, and do not want to include the new tables in the Global.mpt file, you can disable this automatic functionality. Click the *File* tab and then click the *Options* tab in the Backstage. In the *Project Options* dialog, select the *Advanced* tab. In the *Display* section of the *Advanced* page, deselect the the *Automatically Add New Views, Tables, Filters, and Groups to the Global* option and then click the *OK* button.

Creating a New Filter

To create a new filter, click the *View* tab to display the *View* ribbon. In the *Data* section of the ribbon, click the *Filter* pick list and select the *More Filters* item on the list. The system displays the *More Filters* dialog. This dialog is identical to the *More Filters* dialog used in previous versions of Microsoft Project. In the *More Filters* dialog, click the *New* button. The system displays the *Filter Definition* dialog. This dialog is identical to the *Filter Definition* dialog in previous versions of Microsoft Project. Because of this, I do not discuss how to create a new filter. When you create a new filter, Microsoft Project 2010 copies the new filter to the Global.mpt file automatically so that you can use the new filter in all current and future projects.

Creating a New Group

To create a new group, complete the following steps:

1. Click the *View* tab to display the *View* ribbon. In the *Data* section of the ribbon, click the *Group By* pick list and select the *More Groups* item on the list. Microsoft Project 2010 displays the *More Groups* dialog shown in Figure 7 - 56.

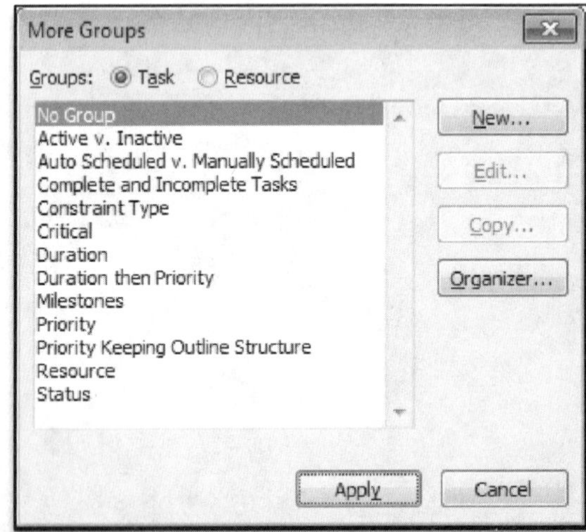

Figure 7 - 56: More Groups dialog

2. In the *More Groups* dialog, click the *New* button. Microsoft Project 2010 displays the *Group Definition* dialog shown in Figure 7 - 57.

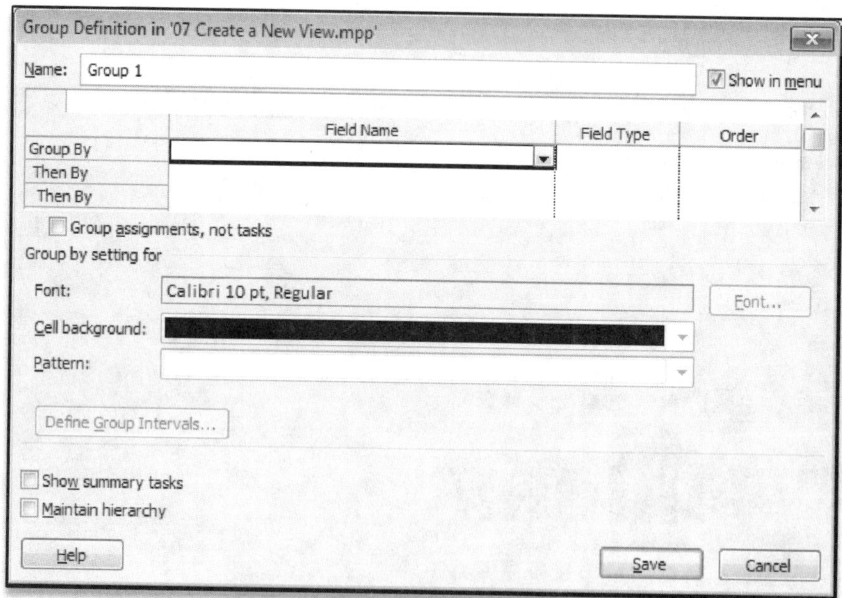

Figure 7 - 57: Group Definition dialog

You can bypass the *More Groups* dialog and access the *Group Definition* dialog directly by clicking the *New Group By* item on the *Group By* pick list in the *Data* section of the *View* ribbon.

3. Enter a name for the new group in the *Name* field and then select the *Show in menu* option if you want the new group to display in the *Group by* menu.
4. In the data grid, enter the desired grouping information on the *Group By* line in the *Field Name, Field Type,* and *Order* columns.

At this point in the group creation process, Microsoft Project 2010 offers two new features in the *Group Definition* dialog. When you click the *Cell Background* pick list, you see the expanded color palette of thousands of colors, as shown in Figure 7 - 58.

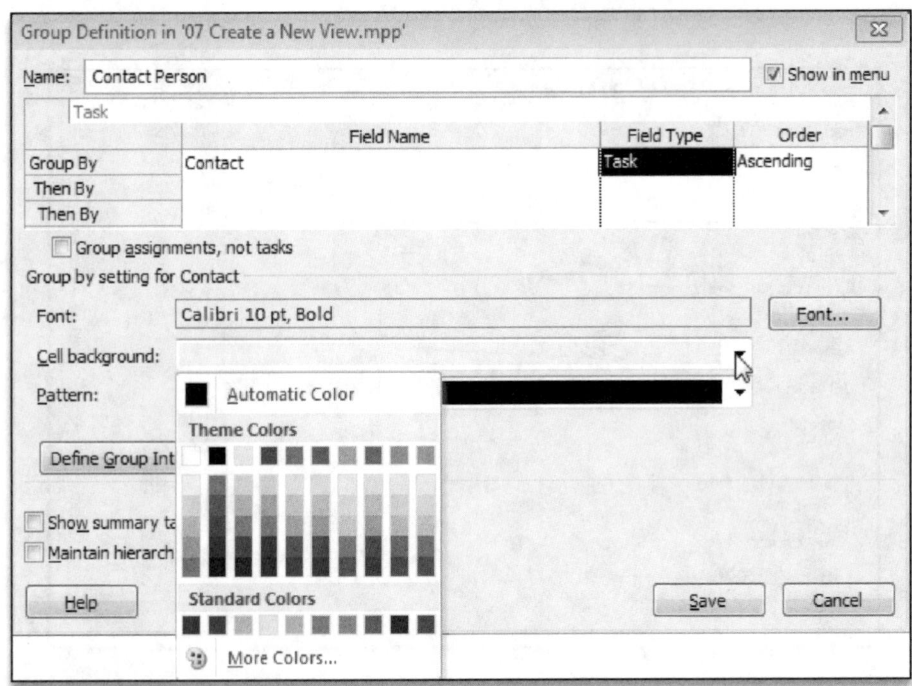

Figure 7 - 58: Expanded color palette on the Cell Background pick list

The other new feature is the *Maintain hierarchy* option in the lower left of the dialog. If you want to display the WBS for the tasks in a new task group, select the *Maintain hierarchy* option when you create your custom group.

Remember that the *Maintain hierachy* option is available only for task groups. You cannot display the hierarchy information for resource groups because resources do not have any Work Breakdown Structure information. This means that the software disables the the *Maintain hierarchy in Current Group* item on the *Group By* pick list in any resource view, and disables the *Maintain hierarchy in Current Group* option in the *Group Definition* dialog when creating a resource group.

Click the *Save* button and then click the *Apply* button in the *More Groups* dialog to apply the new group in the current view. Figure 7 - 59 shows a new custom group I created named *Contact Person,* applied in the *Task Sheet* view of my project. Notice that I selected the *Maintain hierarchy* option in the *Group Definition* dialog to display the WBS for each task. You see the WBS information as the second-level grouping below the name of each person listed in my custom group.

	Task Mode	Task Name	Duration	Start	Finish	Predecessors	Resource Names
		⊟ Contact: George Stewart	**0d**	**8/12/13**	**8/12/13**		
		⊟ 5 Projct Complete	**0d**	**8/12/13**	**8/12/13**		
23		Projct Complete	0 days	8/12/13	8/12/13	22	
		⊟ Contact: Linda Erickson	**5d**	**7/19/13**	**8/12/13**		
		⊟ 4 Testing	**5d**	**7/19/13**	**8/12/13**		
17		Review modular code	5 days	7/19/13	7/25/13	15	Bob Jared
18		Test component modules to product specifications	2 days	7/26/13	7/29/13	17	Software Tester
19		Identify anomalies to product specifications	3 days	7/30/13	8/1/13	18	Software Tester
20		Modify code	5 days	8/2/13	8/8/13	19	Jeff Holly[50%]
21		Re-test modified code	2 days	8/9/13	8/12/13	20	Bob Jared
22		Testing Complete	0 days	8/12/13	8/12/13	21,20	
		⊟ Contact: Richard Sanders	**20d**	**5/23/13**	**7/18/13**		
		⊟ 2 Design	**6d**	**5/23/13**	**6/7/13**		
8		Develop functional specifications	5 days	5/23/13	5/30/13	6	Jeff Holly
9		Develop prototype based on functional specifications	6 days	5/31/13	6/7/13	8	Jeff Holly
10		Design complete	0 days	6/7/13	6/7/13	9	
		⊟ 3 Development	**20d**	**6/10/13**	**7/18/13**		
12		Identify design parameters	5 days	6/10/13	6/14/13	10	Jeff Holly[50%]
13		Develop code	20 days	6/17/13	7/15/13	12	Jeff Holly
14		Developer testing (primary debugging)	20 days	6/20/13	7/18/13	13SS+1 day	Software Tester
15		Development complete	0 days	7/18/13	7/18/13	14	

Figure 7 - 59: Contact Person group applied in the Task Sheet view

Creating the New View

After completing the first three steps in the four-step process, you are ready to create the new view using the table, filter, group, and screen you want in the view. To create the new view, complete the following steps:

1. Click the *View* tab to display the *View* ribbon.
2. Click **any** pick list button in the *Task Views* section or *Resource Views* section of the *View* ribbon and then select the *More Views* item on the list. For example, you can click the *Gantt Chart* pick list button in the *Task Views* section or the *Team Planner* pick list button in the *Resource Views* section of the *View* ribbon. Microsoft Project 2010 displays the *More Views* dialog shown in Figure 7 - 60.

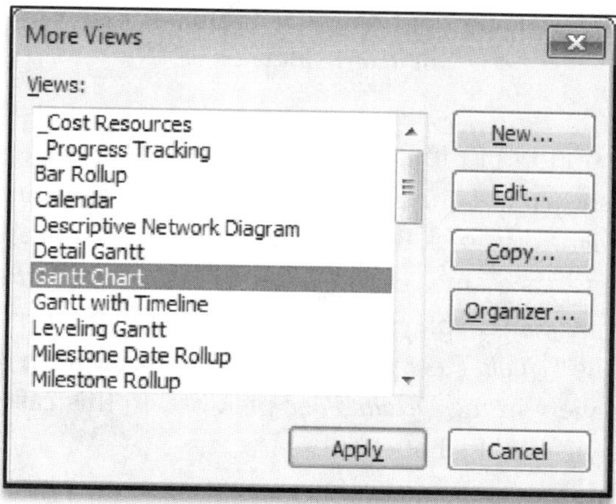

Figure 7 - 60: More Views dialog

3. In the *More Views* dialog, click the *New* button. The system displays the *Define New View* dialog shown in Figure 7 - 61.

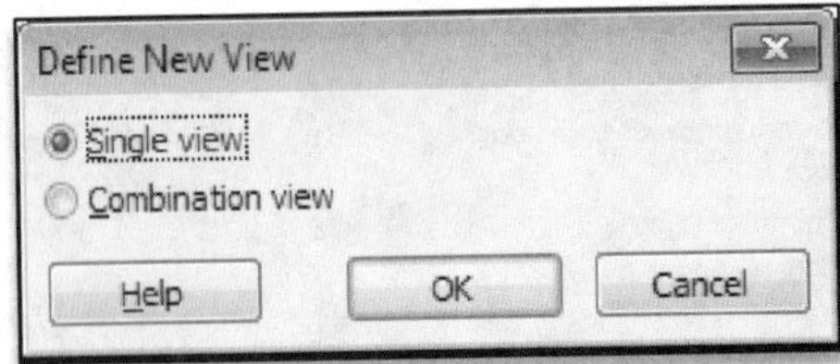

Figure 7 - 61: Define New View dialog

In the *Define New View* dialog, Microsoft Project 2010 allows you to create two types of views. A **single view** is a view that fills the entire Microsoft Project 2010 application window. The *Gantt Chart* view and the *Resource Sheet* view are two common examples of a single view. A **combination view** is a split view consisting of two different views, each displayed in its own viewing pane. The *Task Entry* view and the *Gantt with Timeline* view are two common examples of a combination view.

If you select the default *Single View* option in the *Define New View* dialog and then click the *OK* button, the system displays the *View Definition* dialog for a new single view, as shown in Figure 7 - 62. This dialog is identical to the *View Definition* dialog for a single view used in previous versions of Microsoft Project; therefore, I do not discuss this feature any further.

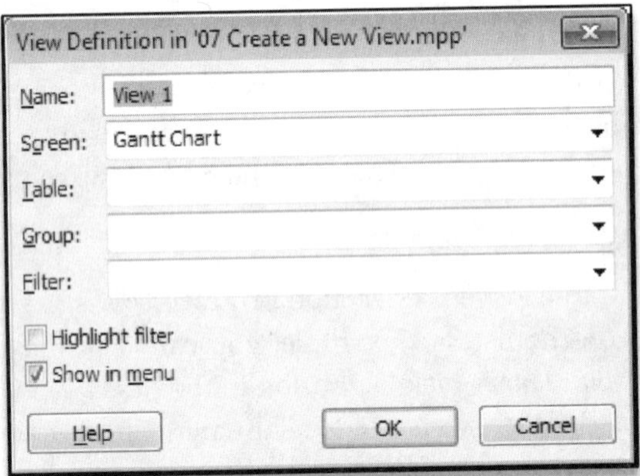

Figure 7 - 62: View Definition dialog for a new single view

If you select the *Combination View* option in the *Define New View* dialog, the system displays the *View Definition* dialog for a combination view, as shown in Figure 7 - 63. To create the new combination view in the *View Definition* dialog, select a view in the *Primary View* pick list and then select a different view in the *Details Pane* pick list as well. Although this dialog is not new, the names of the *Primary View* and *Details Pane* pick lists **are** new in Microsoft Project 2010. In most cases, the system displays the view selected in the *Primary View* pick list in the **top pane**, and displays the view selected in the *Details Pane* pick list in the **bottom pane**. The exception to this rule, however, is when you select the *Timeline* view in the *Details Pane* pick list. In this case, the system displays the *Timeline* view in the top pane and the other view in the bottom pane.

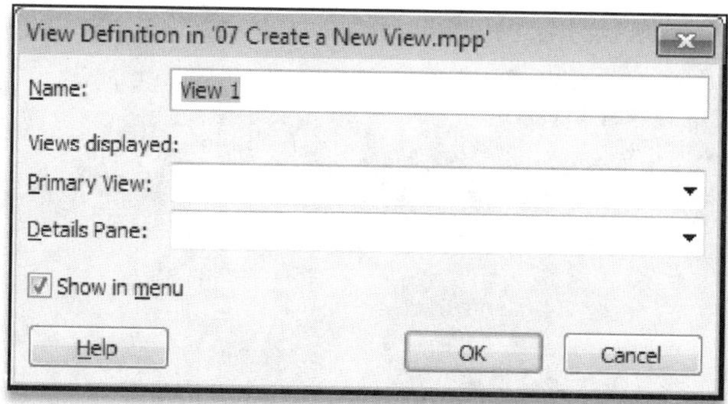

Figure 7 - 63: View Definition dialog for a new combination view

To finish creating your new view, click the *OK* button and then click the *Apply* button in the *More Views* dialog. As with tables, filters, and groups, Microsoft Project 2010 adds the new view to the Global.mpt file for use with all current and future projects. Figure 7 - 64 shows a new combination view with the *Timeline* view in the top pane and the *Tracking Gantt* view in the bottom pane.

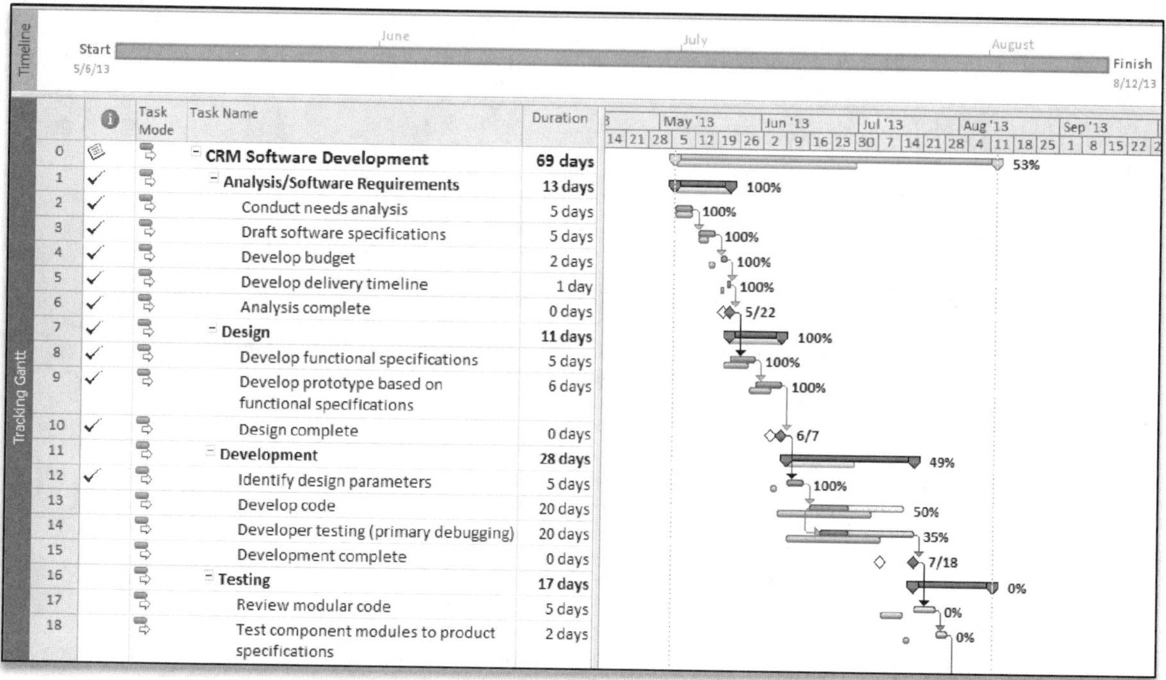

Figure 7 - 64: Combination view with Timeline view in the top pane and the Tracking Gantt view in the bottom pane

Hands On Exercise

Exercise 7-12

Create a new custom table that includes columns that show Duration variance information.

1. Navigate to your student folder and open the **Create a View.mpp** sample file.
2. Click the *View* tab to display the *View* ribbon.
3. Click the *Tables* pick list in the *Data* section of the ribbon and then click the *More Tables* item.
4. In the *More Tables* dialog, select the *Entry* table and then click the *Copy* button.
5. Enter the name *_Duration* in the *Name* field.
6. Select the *Show in Menu* option.
7. Select the following fields individually and then click the *Delete Row* button to delete them:
   - Duration
   - Start
   - Finish
   - Predecessors
   - Resource Names
8. Below the *Name* field, add the following fields to the *Table Definition* dialog:
   - Duration Variance
   - Duration
   - Baseline Duration
   - Actual Duration
   - Remaining Duration
   - % Complete
9. Change the *Width* value to *12* for each of the fields added in the preceding step.
10. Deselect the *Show 'Add New Column' interface* option.
11. Click the *OK* button to close the *Table Definition* dialog.
12. Select the new table and then click the *Apply* button in the *More Tables* dialog.
13. Pull the split bar to the right to view the new table in the *Gantt Chart* view.
14. Save but do not close the **Create a View.mpp** sample file.

Exercise 7-13

Create a new custom filter to locate tasks with Duration Variance greater than 0 days.

1. In the *Data* section of the *View* ribbon, click the *Filter* pick list and select the *More Filters* item on the list.
2. Click the *New* button in the *More Filters* dialog.
3. In the *Filter Definition* dialog, enter the following filter criteria:

Name	_Duration Variance > 0d		
Show in menu	Selected		
And/Or	**Field Name**	**Test**	**Value(s)**
	Duration Variance	is greater than	0
Show related summary rows	Selected		

4. Click the *Save* button to close the *Filter Definition* dialog.
5. In the *More Filters* dialog, select the new filter and then click the *Apply* button to apply and test the new filter.

Notice that Microsoft Project 2010 displays all tasks with a Duration Variance value greater than 0 days, as specified in the filter criteria.

6. In the *Data* section of the *View* ribbon, click the *Filter* pick list and select either the *[No Filter]* or *Clear Filter* item on the list.
7. In the *Data* section of the *View* ribbon, click the *Tables* pick list and select the *Entry* table.
8. Pull the split bar to the right edge of the *Duration* column.
9. Save but do not close the **Create a View.mpp** sample file.

Exercise 7-14

Create a new custom view to show all tasks with a Duration Variance value greater than 0 days. Apply the filter as a highlighter filter in the custom view.

1. In the *Task Views* section of the *View* ribbon, click the *Gantt Chart* pick list button and then select the *More Views* item on the list.
2. In the *More Views* dialog, select the *Tracking Gantt* view and then click the *Copy* button.
3. In the *View Definition* dialog, enter or select the following information:

Field Name	Value
Name	_Duration Variance
Table	_Duration
Group	No Group
Filter	_Duration Variance > 0d
Highlight filter	Selected
Show in menu	Selected

4. Click the *OK* button to close the *View Definition* dialog.
5. In the *More Views* dialog, select the new view and then click the *Apply* button to apply and test the new custom view.

Notice in the new custom view that Microsoft Project 2010 uses yellow cell background formatting to highlight tasks with a duration variance value greater than 0 days. Notice that the new custom view also includes a *Tracking Gantt* screen on the right side of the view.

6. Save but do not close the **Create a View.mpp** sample file.

Using the Add New Column Feature

As I noted previously in this module, every default table in Microsoft Project 2010 includes the new *Add New Column* virtual column on the far right side of the table. You can use this feature to supplement the list of columns in a default table, and you can use this feature as an alternate method of adding columns in a new custom table. The system offers you several ways to insert a new column using the *Add New Column* virtual column:

- Click the column header at the top of the *Add New Column* virtual column and select a field from the list of available fields. This functionality behaves the same as the *Insert Column* button on the contextual *Format* ribbon, shown previously in this module in Figure 7 - 20.
- Click the column header at the top of the *Add New Column* virtual column and then enter the name of a new custom field in the blank column header.
- Type data in any cell in the *Add New Column* virtual column.

When you type the name of a new custom field in the *Add New Column* virtual column header, the system creates a new custom *Text* field automatically, using the next available unused *Text* field. The system then redisplays the *Add New Column* virtual column to the right of the new custom column. For example, Figure 7 - 65 shows the new *Schedule Risk* column I added to a custom table using the *Add New Column* virtual column.

	Indicators	Task Mode	Task Name	Duration	Schedule Risk	Add New Column
0			CRM Software Development	69 d		
1	✓		Analysis/Software Requirements	13 d		
2	✓		Conduct needs analysis	5 d		
3	✓		Draft software specifications	5 d		
4	✓		Develop budget	2 d		
5	✓		Develop delivery timeline	1 d		
6	✓		Analysis complete	0 d		
7	✓		Design	11 d		
8	✓		Develop functional specifications	5 d		
9	✓		Develop prototype based on functional specifications	6 d		
10	✓		Design complete	0 d		
11			Development	28 d		
12	✓		Identify design parameters	5 d		
13			Develop code	20 d		
14			Developer testing (primary debugging)	20 d		
15			Development complete	0 d		
16			Testing	17 d		
17			Review modular code	5 d		
18			Test component modules to product specifications	2 d		
19			Identify anomalies to product specifications	3 d		
20			Modify code	5 d		

Figure 7 - 65: New custom Schedule Risk column added

When you create a new custom column using this method, keep in mind that Microsoft Project 2010 offers only 30 custom *Text* fields. If you attempt to exceed this number by creating the thirty-first custom column, the system displays the *Delete Custom Fields* dialog shown in Figure 7 - 66. Because of the limit of 30 custom *Text* fields, you must delete an existing custom *Text* field by selecting the option checkbox for one or more fields and then clicking the *Delete Custom Fields* button in the dialog. When prompted in a confirmation dialog, click the *Yes* button to delete the selected fields.

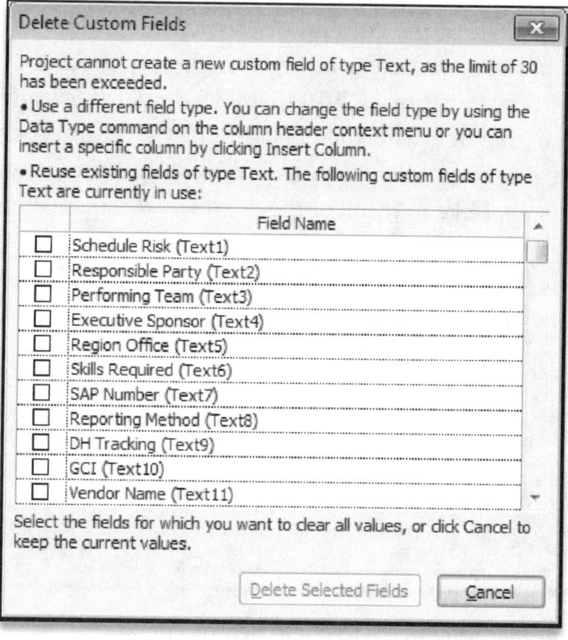

Figure 7 - 66: Delete Custom Fields dialog

When you type data in the *Add New Column* virtual column, Microsoft Project 2010 automatically selects the next available custom field using the data type you entered. For example, if you type *$500* in the *Add New Column* field, the software selects and inserts the next unused custom *Cost* field. If you enter *5d* in the *Add New Column* field, the software selects and inserts the next unused custom *Duration* field. For example, Figure 7 - 67 shows the new *Number1* column that the system added automatically after I typed a number in the *Add New Column* virtual column.

		Task Mode	Task Name	Duration	Schedule Risk	Number1	Add New Column
0			**CRM Software Development**	**69 d**		**0**	
1	✓		**Analysis/Software Requirements**	**13 d**		**0**	
2	✓		Conduct needs analysis	5 d		12357	
3	✓		Draft software specifications	5 d		0	
4	✓		Develop budget	2 d		0	
5	✓		Develop delivery timeline	1 d		0	
6	✓		Analysis complete	0 d		0	
7	✓		**Design**	**11 d**		**0**	
8	✓		Develop functional specifications	5 d		0	
9	✓		Develop prototype based on functional specifications	6 d		0	
10	✓		Design complete	0 d		0	
11			**Development**	**28 d**		**0**	
12	✓		Identify design parameters	5 d		0	
13			Develop code	20 d		0	
14			Developer testing (primary debugging)	20 d		0	
15			Development complete	0 d		0	
16			**Testing**	**17 d**		**0**	
17			Review modular code	5 d		0	
18			Test component modules to product specifications	2 d		0	
19			Identify anomalies to product specifications	3 d		0	
20			Modify code	5 d		0	

Figure 7 - 67: New custom Number column

After you create a new custom column by typing a value in the *Add New Column* virtual column, I strongly recommend that you either change the *Title* of the column or rename the field to display relevant information that identifies the column. To change the *Title* of a column, right-click on the column header and select the *Field Settings* item on the shortcut menu. Microsoft Project 2010 displays the *Field Settings* dialog shown in Figure 7 - 68. Enter a name for the column in the *Title* field and then click the *OK* button. When you enter a *Title* for a column, the column continues to retain its original name, such as *Number1*, but the column header displays the *Title* information instead of the column name. I like to think of the column *Title* as the "nickname" of the column.

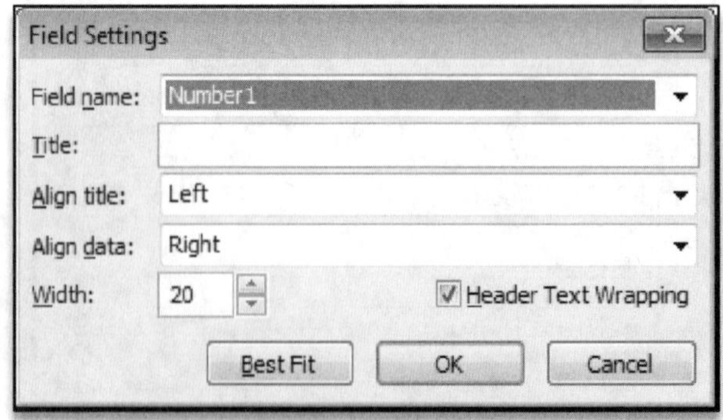

Figure 7 - 68: Field Settings dialog

To rename a column to give it a new name, right-click on its column header and select the *Custom Fields* item on the shortcut menu. The system displays the *Custom Fields* dialog shown in Figure 7 - 69. Click the *Rename* button, enter a new name for the field, and then click the *OK* button. Because the *Custom Fields* dialog does not contain any new features in Microsoft Project 2010, I do not discuss this dialog any further.

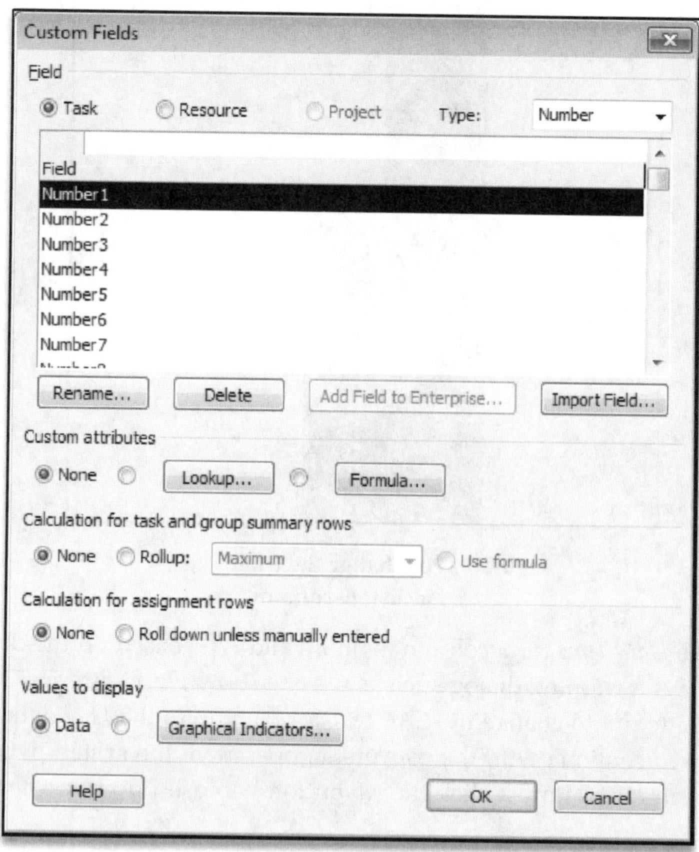

Figure 7 - 69: Custom Fields dialog

After creating a new custom column using either of the two previous methods, Microsoft Project 2010 also allows you to change the *Data Type* used for the column. For example, after I typed a number in the *Add New Column* virtual column, the system added the *Number1* field automatically. However, if for example I need to enter alphanumeric data in this column, I would need to convert the *Data Type* from *Number* to *Text* instead. To change the *Data Type* for any custom column, right-click on the column header, select the *Data Type* item on the shortcut menu, and then select the desired *Data Type* item on the fly out menu as shown in Figure 7 - 70. Notice that I renamed the custom *Number1* column to *SAP Number* instead. Notice also that the fly out menu shows the original *Data Type* value for this column, the *Number* type.

When you change the *Data Type* for a custom column, Microsoft Project 2010 selects the next available unused column with that *Data Type*. In my project, after converting the *SAP Number* column from a *Number* field to a *Text* field, the system selected the *Text2* field, applied the *SAP Number* name to the *Text2* field, and then removed the *SAP Number* name from the *Number1* field.

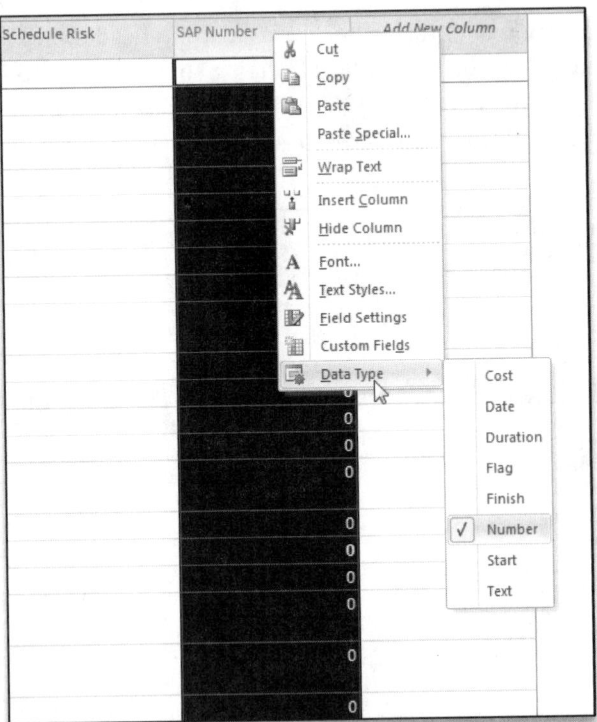

Figure 7 - 70: Change the Data Type for a custom column

If you attempt to convert the *Data Type* for a column to an invalid type based on the data already in the column, Microsoft Project 2010 displays a warning dialog such as the one shown in Figure 7 - 71. For example, the system displays this dialog when I attempt to change the *SAP Number* column to the *Flag* data type. Notice in the dialog that if I click the *Yes* button to continue with the conversion operation, the system will delete all of the existing data in this column. In my situation, I must click the *No* button because I do not want to delete the data in this column.

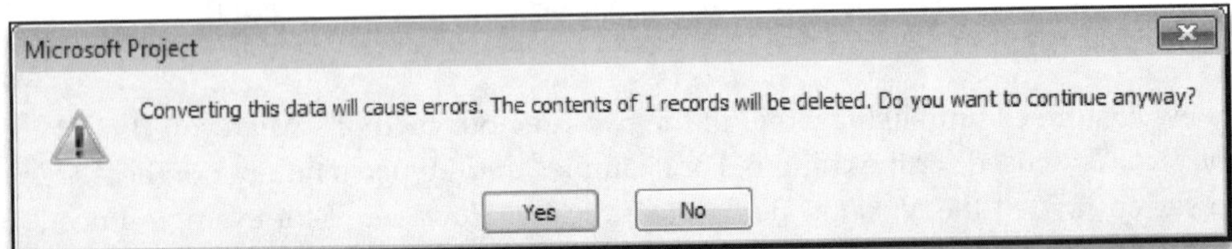

Figure 7 - 71: Warning dialog after changing to an invalid Data Type

Warning: When you add columns to any default table, remember that this action changes the definition of the table from this point forward. Because a number of views share common tables between them, adding columns to the table in one view causes the columns to appear in other views. For example, if you add columns to the *Entry* table in the *Gantt Chart* view, you see these additional columns in the *Tracking Gantt* view and the *Task Sheet* view because all three views use the Entry table by default.

Hands On Exercise

Exercise 7-15

Create several new custom columns using the *Add New Column* virtual column.

1. Return to the **Create a View.mpp** sample file, if necessary.
2. In the *Task Views* section of the *View* ribbon, click the *Gantt Chart* pick list button and then select the *Gantt Chart* item on the list.
3. In the *Data* section of the *View* ribbon, click the *Tables* pick list and select the *Entry* table, if not already selected.
4. Pull the split bar to the far right side of the *Gantt Chart* view to expose all of the columns in the *Entry* table.
5. Click and drag across the column headers of the *Duration, Start, Finish, Predecessors,* and *Resource Names* columns to select these five columns.
6. Right-click anywhere in the column headers of the five selected columns, then click the *Hide Column* item on the shortcut menu to hide the five selected columns.
7. Click the column header of the *Add New Column* virtual column and select the *Responsible Person (Text1)* column.

Notice how Microsoft Project 2010 adds the new *Responsible Person* column to the left of the *Add New Column* virtual column.

8. Click the column header of the *Add New Column* virtual column and select the *Cost Center ID (Text2)* column.
9. In the *Add New Column* virtual column, select the cell for task ID #17, the Pre-Renovation Complete milestone task.
10. Type a *Yes* value in the selected cell in the *Add New Column* virtual column.

Notice how Microsoft Project 2010 adds the new *Flag1* column to the left of the *Add New Column* virtual column.

11. In the *Flag1* column, enter a *Yes* value for the following tasks:
    - Task ID #69, the Renovation Complete milestone task
    - Task ID #76, the Post-Renovation Complete milestone task
    - Task ID #77, the PROJECT COMPLETE milestone task
12. Right-click in the *Flag1* column header and click the *Custom Fields* item on the shortcut menu.
13. In the *Custom Fields* dialog, select the *Flag1* field and then click the *Rename* button.

14. In the *Rename Field* dialog, enter the name *Major Milestone* in the *New name for Flag1* field and then click the *OK* button.
15. Click the *OK* button to close the *Custom Fields* dialog.
16. Right-click in the *Major Milestone* column header and click the *Field Settings* item on the shortcut menu.
17. In the *Field Settings* dialog, select the *Center* value in the *Align Title* and *Align Data* fields.
18. Set the *Width* field value to *14* and then click the *OK* button.
19. Save but do not close the **Create a View.mpp** sample file.

Creating a New View by Customizing an Existing View

Earlier in this module, I presented detailed information on how to format the *Gantt Chart* view to customize it to meet your project management and reporting needs. In the previous topical section, I documented how to add new custom columns to any view. After you customize any default view, including adding custom columns, Microsoft Project 2010 allows you to save the customized view as an entirely new custom view. For example, Figure 7 - 72 shows a customized *Gantt Chart* view.

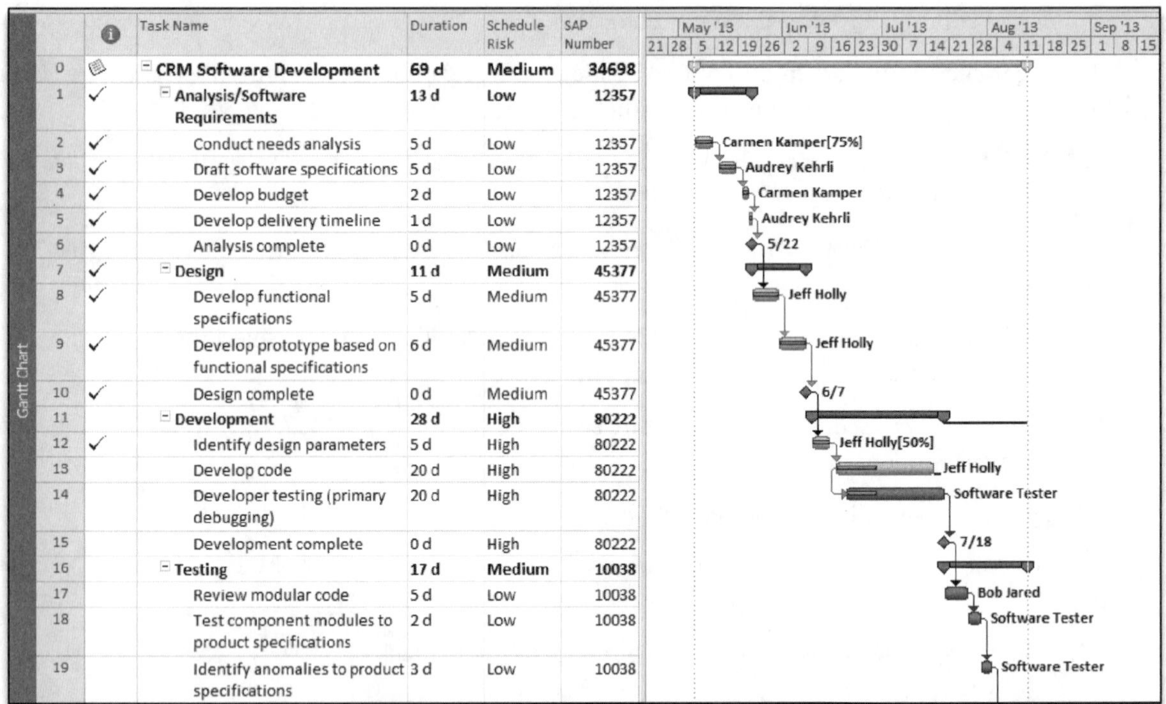

Figure 7 - 72: Customized Gantt Chart view

To customize the default *Gantt Chart* view shown in Figure 7 - 72, I completed the following steps:

- I removed the *Task Mode* column.
- I created two new columns called *Schedule Risk* and *SAP Number*, and then populated a value in each of these fields for every task in the project.

- I formatted the *Gantt Chart* by selecting the *Critical Path* and *Slack* options in the *Bar Styles* section of the *Format* ribbon.
- I changed the color scheme of the *Gantt Chart* view using one of the color schemes in the *Gantt Chart Style* section of the *Format* ribbon.

After customizing the default *Gantt Chart* view with all of the above changes, I am ready to save this customized view as a new custom view for use with all current and future project. To save a customized default view as a new custom view, complete the following steps:

1. Display the customized view, including the table to which you added the custom columns.
2. Click the *Task* tab to display the *Task* ribbon.
3. In the *View* section of the *Task* ribbon, click the *Gantt Chart* pick list button and then click the *Save View* item on the pick list menu. Microsoft Project 2010 displays the *Save View* dialog shown in Figure 7 - 73.

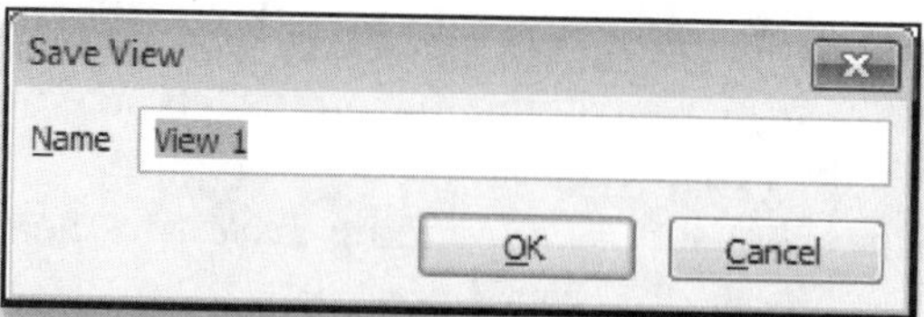

Figure 7 - 73: Save View dialog

4. In the *Save View* dialog, enter an original name for the custom view in the *Name* field and then click the *OK* button.

You can also add a customized default view as a new view using several other ribbons. For example, on the *Resource* ribbon, click the *Team Planner* pick list button and then select the *Save View* item on the menu. On the *View* ribbon, click **any** pick list button in either the *Task Views* or *Resource Views* section of the ribbon and then click the *Save View* item on the menu.

After completing the previous set of steps, Microsoft Project 2010 adds your new view and table to your current project and to your Global.mpt file. By adding the view and table to the Global.mpt file, the system makes your new view available in all current and future projects. To see your new view and table, click the *File* tab and then click the *Organizer* button in the *Info* tab of the *Backstage*. The system displays the *Views* page of the *Organizer* dialog shown in Figure 7 - 74. Notice that the system added the new custom view named *_Company Tracking* to the list on the left side of the dialog (in the Global.mpt file) and to the list on the right side of the dialog (in the active project).

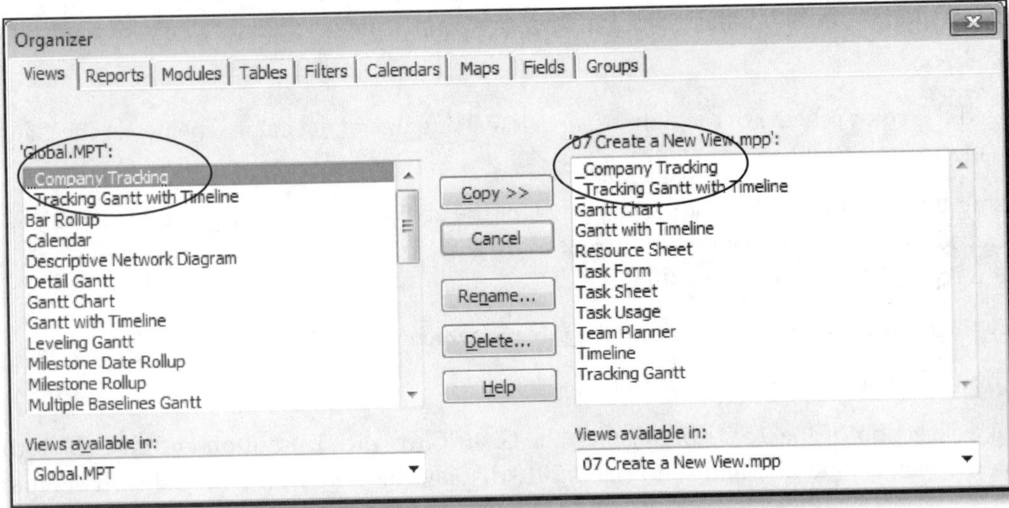

Figure 7 - 74: Organizer dialog, Views tab

If you click the *Tables* tab, you can see your new custom table on the left side of the dialog (in the Global.mpt file) and in the right side of the dialog (in the active project). Notice in Figure 7 - 75 that the system named my new custom table by using the name of the view and by appending *Table 1* to the name of the table. In this case, the system named my new custom table *_Company Tracking Table 1*.

At this point, you have the option to edit the name of the table, if necessary. To edit the table name, select the table on the left side of the dialog and then click the *Rename* button. In the *Rename* dialog, enter a new name for the table (such as removing the *Table 1* text from the table name, for example) and then click the *OK* button. Repeat this process for the name of the table on the right side of the dialog. Click the *Close* button to close the *Organizer* dialog and then click the *File* tab to exit the *Backstage*.

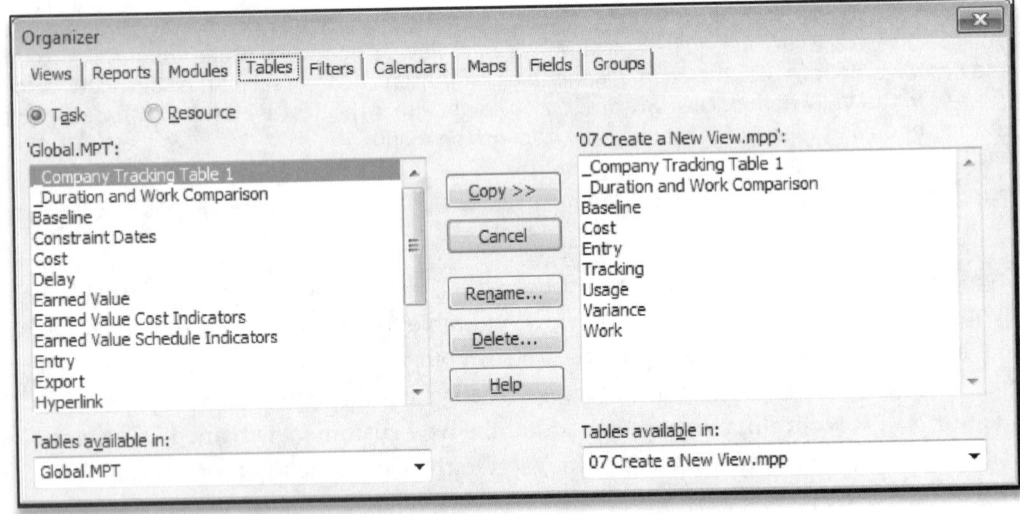

Figure 7 - 75: Organizer dialog, Tables tab

Resetting a Default View after Customization

After you create a new custom view and table from a customized default view, I strongly recommend that you reset the customized default view and table to their original default condition before customization. To do this, complete the following steps:

1. Display the default view and table you customized previously.
2. Click the *Task* tab to display the *Task* ribbon.
3. In the *View* section of the *Task* ribbon, click the *Gantt Chart* pick list button and then click the *Reset to Default* item on the pick list menu. Microsoft Project 2010 displays the confirmation dialog shown in Figure 7 - 76.

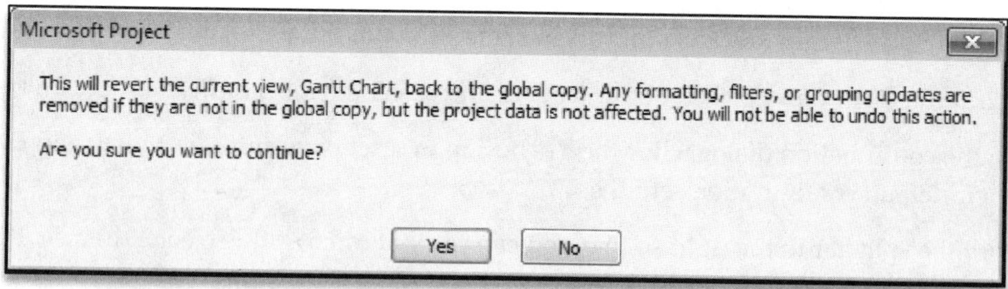

Figure 7 - 76: Confirmation dialog to reset a view to its default settings

4. In the confirmation dialog, click the *Yes* button.

As noted in the previous topical section, you can reset a view to its default settings by clicking any view pick list button on either the *Resource* ribbon or the *View* ribbon.

The system resets both the view and table to their original default settings prior to customization. This means if you removed columns from the table or added columns to the table, the system resets the table to the original default list of columns and resets the column width for every column. It has never been this easy to reset a customized view and table to their default settings in any previous version of Microsoft Project!

Hands On Exercise

Exercise 7-16

Create and a new custom view by saving a customized default view.

1. Return to the **Create a View.mpp** sample file, if necessary.
2. Double-click the right edge of the *Cost Center ID* column header to "best fit" the width of this column.
3. Pull the split bar to the right edge of the *Responsible Person* column.
4. Click the *Format* tab to display the contextual *Format* ribbon with the *Gantt Chart Tools* applied.
5. In the *Bar Styles* section of the *Format* ribbon, select the *Critical Tasks* option and the *Slack* option.

6. Select any color scheme in the *Gantt Chart Style* section of the *Format* ribbon.
7. Click the *Task* tab to display the *Task* ribbon.
8. Click the *Gantt Chart* pick list button and then click the *Save View* item on the list.
9. In the *Save View* dialog, enter the name *_Corporate Information* in the *Name* field and then click the *OK* button.
10. Click the *Gantt Chart* pick list button and select the *Gantt Chart* view.
11. Click the *Gantt Chart* pick list button again and select the *Reset to Default* item on the list.
12. In the confirmation dialog, click the *Yes* button to reset the *Gantt Chart* view and *Entry* table to their default configuration settings.
13. Pull the split bar to the right so that you can see that Microsoft Project 2010 reset the *Entry* table to its default list of columns.
14. Click the *File* tab and then click the *Organizer* button in the *Info* tab of the *Backstage*.

Notice the new *_Corporate Information* view in the *Global.MPT* section of the *Organizer* dialog.

15. Click the *Tables* tab.

Notice the new *_Corporate Information Table 1* table in the *Global.MPT* section of the *Organizer* dialog.

16. Click the *Cancel* button to close the *Organizer* dialog.
17. Click the *File* tab again to exit the *Backstage*.
18. Save and close the **Create a View.mpp** sample file.

Using Visual Reports Improvements

To use the Excel visual reports feature in Microsoft Project 2010, you must have Excel 2003, 2007, or 2010 installed on your PC. To use the Visio visual reports feature, you must have Visio **Professional** 2007 or 2010 installed on your PC.

Microsoft added visual reports as a new feature in Microsoft Project 2007, and improved visual reports functionality in Microsoft Project 2010. These improvements are minor, and include the following:

- You can add custom fields to the OLAP cubes used for the *Assignment Usage* and *Assignment Summary* visual reports.
- Visual reports now support custom field names of up to 100 characters, increased from 25 characters in Microsoft Project 2007.

You can view the first improvement by completing the following steps:

1. Open a project to create a visual report for either Microsoft Excel or Microsoft Visio.
2. Click the *Project* tab and then click the *Visual Reports* button in the *Reports* section of the *Project* ribbon. The system displays the *Visual Reports – Create Report* dialog shown in Figure 7 - 77.

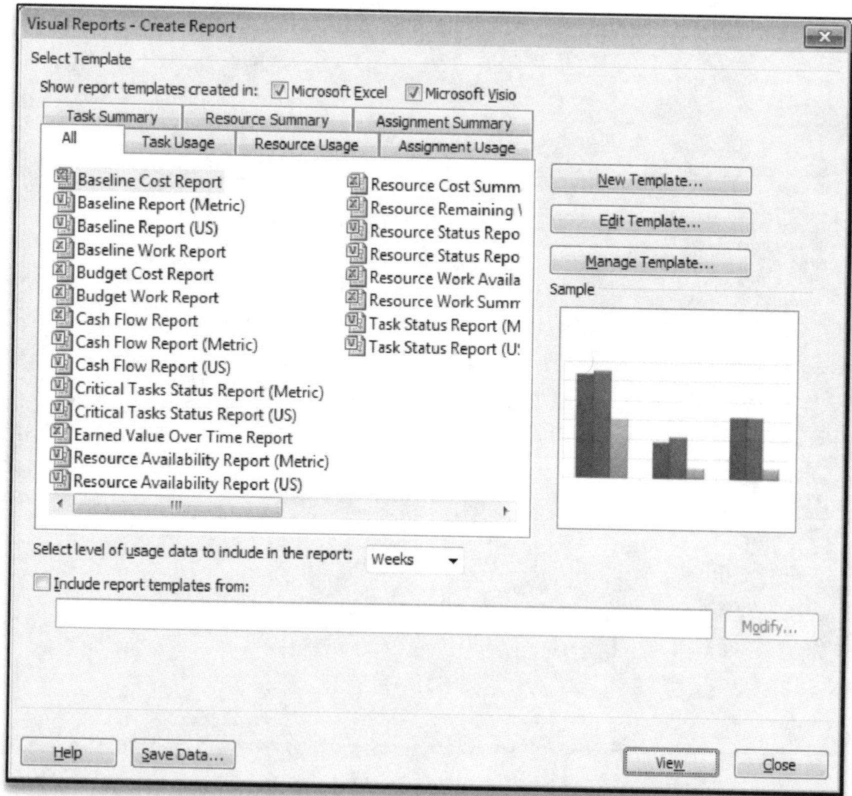

Figure 7 - 77: Visual Reports – Create Report dialog

3. Select the *Assignment Usage* tab to view the available *Assignment Usage* reports.
4. Select a visual report for either Microsoft Excel or Microsoft Visio, such as the *Budget Cost Report*, for example.
5. Click the *Edit Template* button. The system displays the *Visual Reports – Field Picker* dialog shown in Figure 7 - 78.
6. Select a custom field in the *Available Custom Fields* list on the left side of the dialog and then click the *Add* button to add the field to the *Selected Custom Fields* list on the right side of the dialog.

Notice in the *Visual Reports – Field Picker* dialog shown in Figure 7 - 78 that the *Available Custom Fields* list includes the *SAP Number* and *Schedule Risk* custom fields I created and used in the previous topical sections of this module. Notice that the dialog refers to each custom field by appending the *Task (dimension)* text string at the end of the field name.

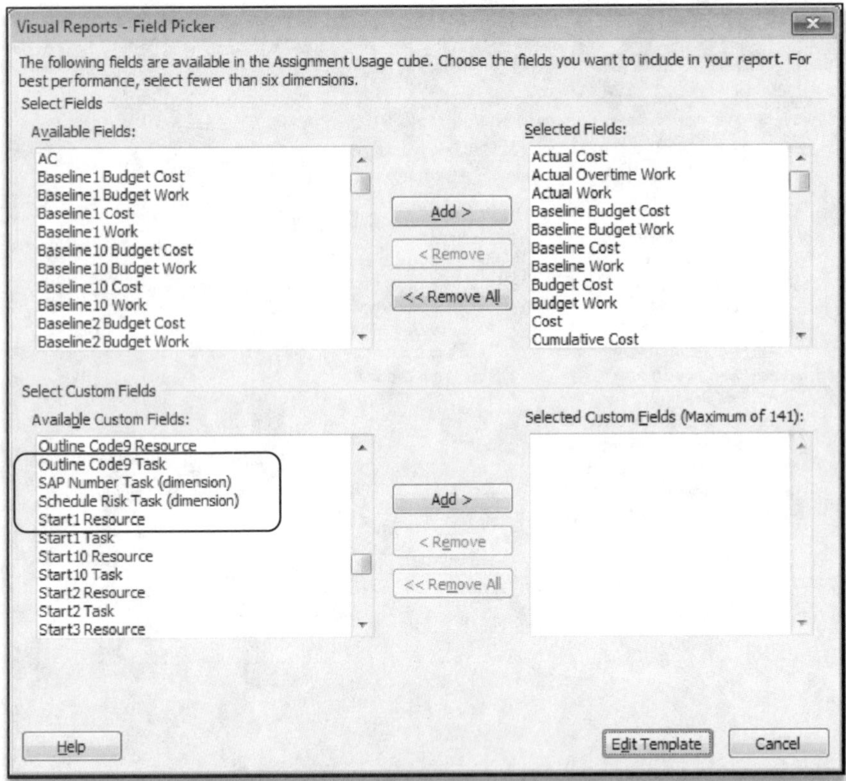

Figure 7 - 78: Visual Reports – Field Picker dialog

7. After adding custom fields to the *Selected Custom Fields* list, click the *Edit Template* button.

The system totals all of the assignment data for work and cost in the project, builds the local OLAP cube using this data, and then launches Microsoft Excel and creates the visual report. Figure 7 - 79 shows the *Assignment Usage* worksheet of the resulting *Budget Cost* visual report. You see your selected custom fields in the *Choose Fields to Add to Report* list at the top of the *PivotTable Field List* pane on the right side of the worksheet. Notice that the *PivotTable Field List* pane includes the *SAP Number* and *Schedule Risk* custom fields shown previously in the *Visual Reports – Field Picker* dialog in Figure 7 - 78.

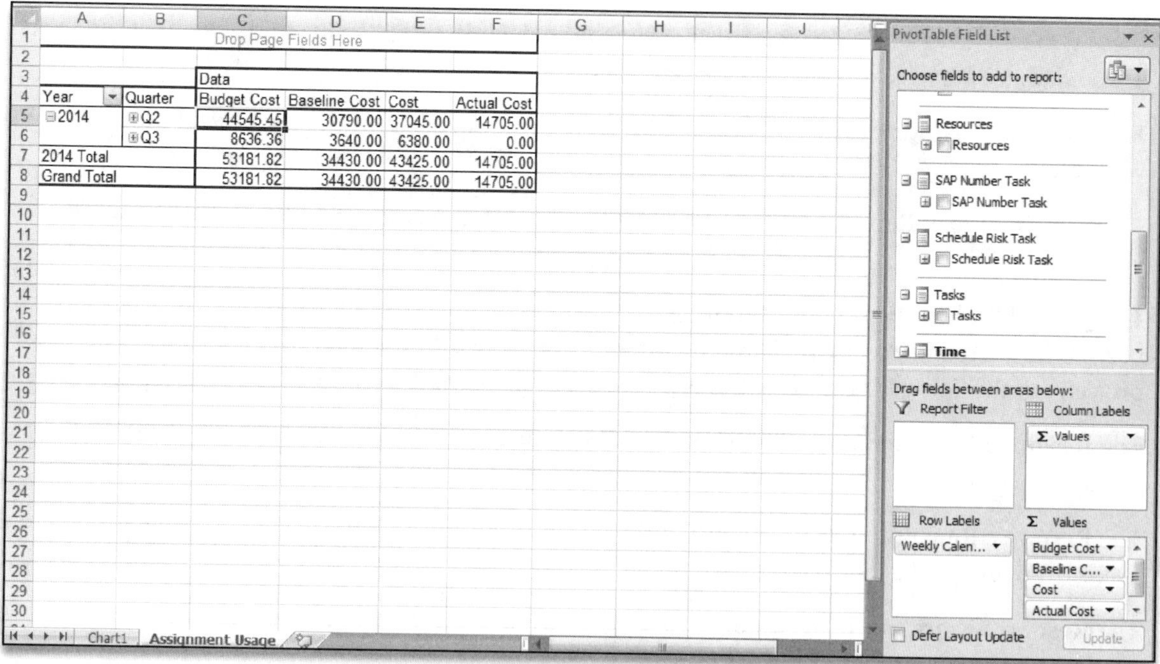

Figure 7 - 79: Budget Cost Visual Report in Microsoft Excel

At this point, you can customize the visual report to meet your reporting requirements, including adding any of the custom fields you added previously in the *Visual Reports – Field Picker* dialog. Figure 7 - 80 shows the resulting PivotChart after adding the *Schedule Risk* field to the PivotTable for the *Budget Cost* visual report.

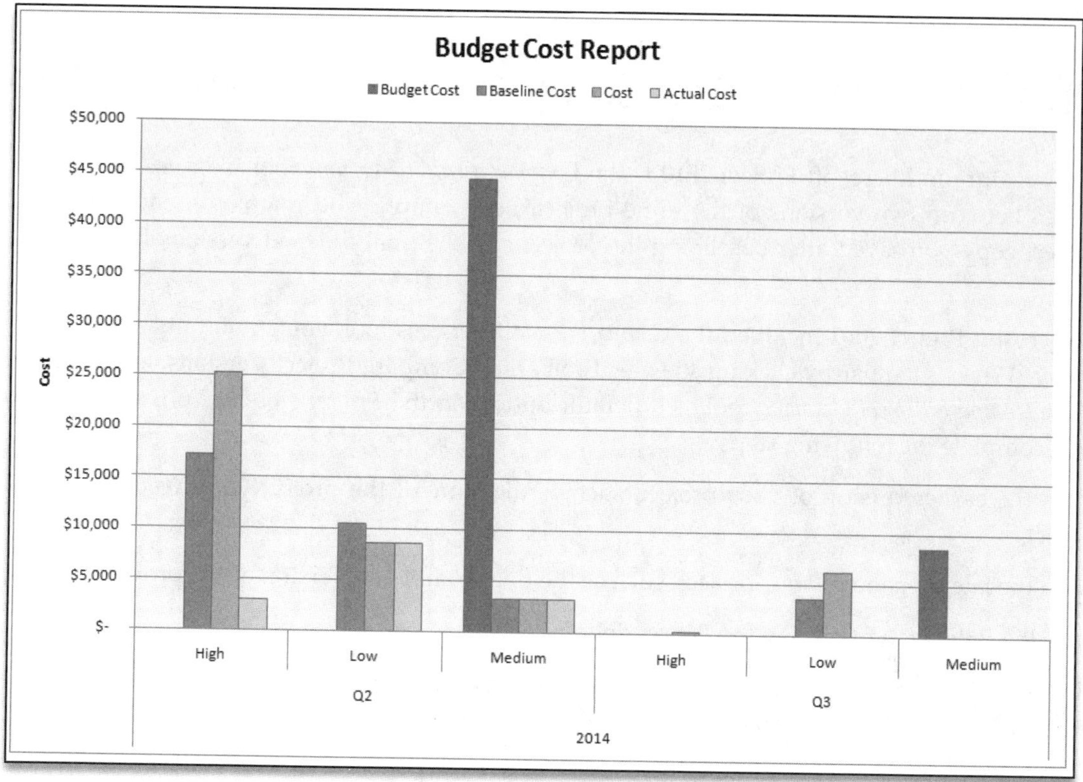

Figure 7 - 80: PivotChart shows the Schedule Risk field data added to the Visual Report

Beyond these two improvements, Microsoft also changed the default data displayed in several of the Excel visual reports. These changes are as follows:

- The **Baseline Cost Report** no longer includes the *Tasks* dimension in the *Row Labels* drop area of the PivotTable.
- The **Baseline Work Report** no longer includes the *Tasks* dimension in the *Row Labels* drop area of the PivotTable.
- The **Earned Value Over Time Report** shows Earned Value data only through the Status Date of the project. In Microsoft Project 2007, the report showed Earned Value data over the entire time span of the project, but the Earned Value dropped to 0 for every time period after the Status Date of the project.
- The **Resource Cost Summary Report** no longer includes the *Type* dimension in the *Row Labels* drop area of the PivotTable.
- The **Resource Remaining Work Report** no longer includes the *Type* and *Resources* dimensions in the *Row Labels* drop area of the PivotTable.
- The **Resource Work Summary Report** no longer includes the *Type* and *Resources* dimensions in the *Row Labels* drop area of the PivotTable.

For the Visio visual reports, Microsoft made only one minor change to the default data shown in the **Resource Status Report,** which displays information for a new default resource named *Task's Fixed Cost*. This new resource displays any extra task costs you add to the *Fixed Cost* column.

Using New Features in the Compare Project Versions Tool

The final new feature in Microsoft Project 2010 is the *Compare Project Versions* tool. You use this tool to compare the differences between two versions of the same project. For example, you might compare the differences between a project copy you saved after baselining the project and the final finished version after you closed out in the project.

Although Microsoft Project 2007 included the *Compare Project Versions* tool, you could only access the tool on the *Compare Project Versions* toolbar by clicking View ➤ Toolbars ➤ Compare Project Versions. Microsoft Project 2010 integrates the *Compare Project Versions* tool as a default button on the *Project* ribbon. To use the *Compare Project Versions* tool, complete the following steps:

1. Open the earlier version of your project, such as the copy of the project you saved after baselining the project.
2. Open the later version of your project, such as the final completed version of the project.
3. Click the *Project* tab to display the *Project* ribbon.
4. Click the *Compare Projects* button in the *Reports* section of the *Project* ribbon. Microsoft Project 2010 displays the *Compare Project Versions* dialog shown in Figure 7 - 81.

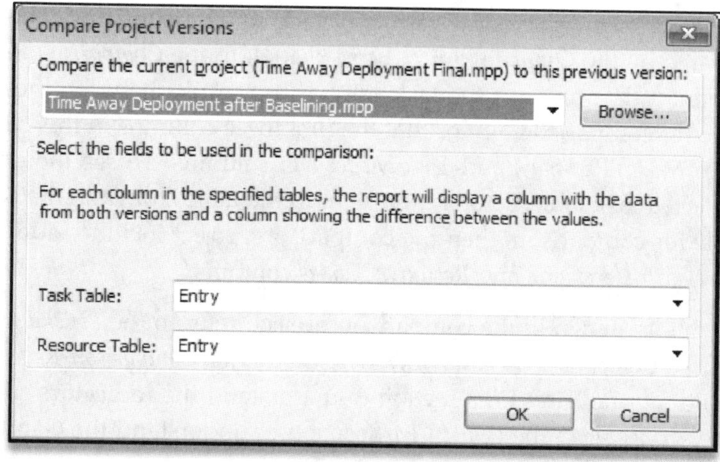

Figure 7 - 81: Compare Project Versions dialog

5. Click the pick list at the top of the dialog and select the earlier version, if necessary.
6. Click the *Task Table* pick list and select the table containing the task data you want to compare.
7. Click the *Resource Table* pick list and select the table containing the resource data you want to compare.
8. Click the *OK* button.

The system finds the differences between the two selected projects, and then displays the *Comparison Report* view shown in Figure 7 - 82. Notice that the *Comparison Report* view consists of a combination of three project windows, a *Legend* window, and the *Compare Projects* ribbon.

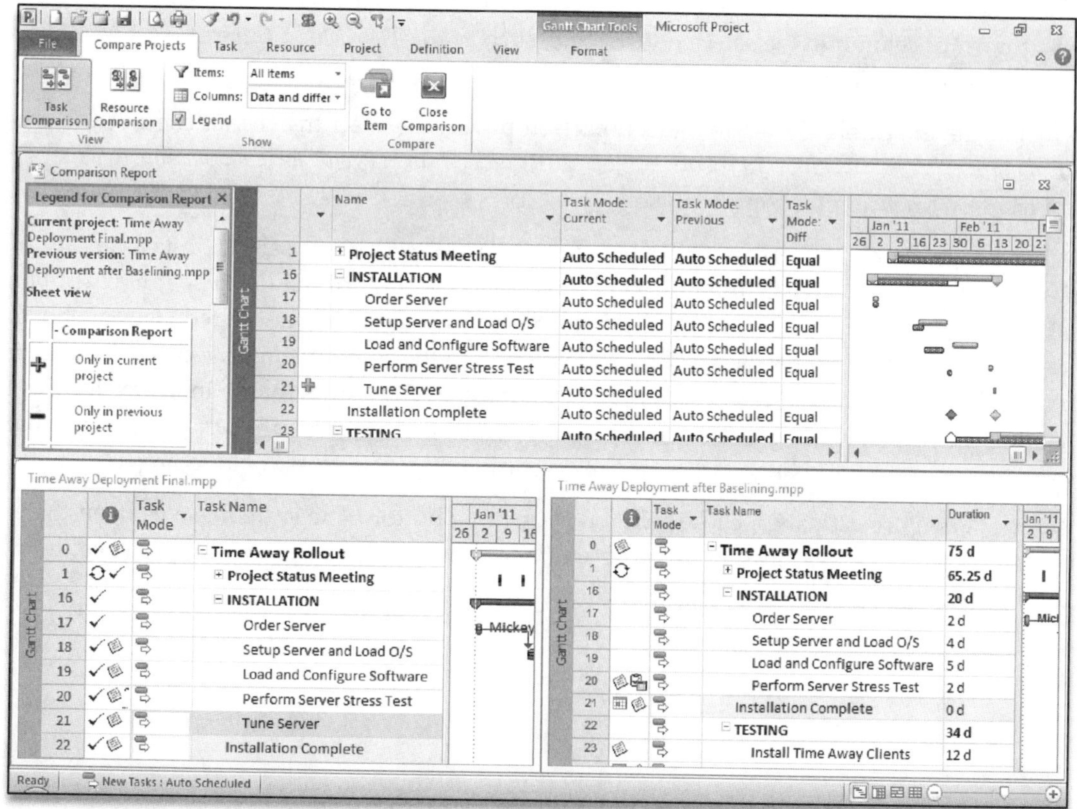

Figure 7 - 82: Comparison Report for two projects

By default, the *Comparison Report* view shows the results of task comparisons first. The bottom two panes show you the two projects compared by the *Compare Project Versions* tool. In the *Comparison Report* pane at the top, you see a special comparison project that contains the task comparison results between these two projects. Because I selected the task *Entry* table for comparison, notice that the first three columns in this comparison project include the *Task Mode: Current, Task Mode: Previous,* and *Task Mode: Diff* columns. To see the comparison between other columns of data in your selected task table, scroll to the right in the table shown in the comparison project. If you selected the task *Entry* table for comparison, then the comparison project includes additional columns that compare the *Duration, Start, Finish, Predecessors,* and *Resource Names* columns.

To understand all of the symbols shown in the comparison project, refer to the *Legend for Comparison Report* pane in the upper left corner of the *Comparison Report* view. The *Legend for Comparison Report* pane contains two sections. Refer to the information in the *Sheet View* section to understand the indicators shown in the *Indicators* column of the comparison project. Refer to the *Gantt Chart* section to understand the Gantt bars shown in the *Gantt Chart* portion of the comparison project.

To compare the resource information between the two projects, click the *Resource Comparison* button in the *View* section of the *Compare Projects* ribbon. The system displays a similar *Comparison Report* view, except with the *Resource Sheet* view in all three project windows. Again, the *Legend for Comparison Report* pane helps you to understand the indicators shown in the *Indicators* column in the comparison project. Click the *Task Comparison* button to return to the *Comparison Report* view for tasks.

Click the *Items* pick list in the *Show* section of the *Compare Projects* ribbon to choose the exact type of comparison data you want to see in the *Comparison Report* view. For example, to see only the tasks with differences between the two projects, select the *All Differences* item on the *Items* pick list. Click the *Columns* pick list in the *Show* section of the *Compare Projects* ribbon to choose the sets of columns you want to see in the *Comparison Report* view. By default, the system selects the *Dates and Differences* item on the *Columns* pick list. This means that you see a set of three columns for every column in the selected task table, such as the *Task Mode: Current, Task Mode: Previous,* and *Task Mode: Diff* columns shown previously in Figure 7 - 82.

If you understand the indicators shown in the comparison project, deselect the *Legend* checkbox in the *Show* section of the *Compare Projects* ribbon. Microsoft Project 2010 closes the *Legend for Comparison Report* pane and expands the comparison project in the top pane.

To focus your analysis on an individual task in the *Comparison Report* view, select the task in any of the three project panes and then click the *Go to Item* button in the *Compare* section of the *Compare Projects* ribbon. The system selects the task in all three project panes and scrolls to the Gantt bars for the selected tasks as shown in Figure 7 - 83. Notice that I selected the Verify Server Connectivity task in the comparison project pane and clicked the *Go to Item* button to view this task in all three project panes. Notice the "question mark" indicator for this task in the *Indicators* column of the comparison project. Finally, in the *Legend for Comparison Report* pane notice that the question mark indicator means that I changed the name of this task in the later version of the project.

To close the bottom two project panes, click the *Close Comparison* button. The system leaves open the comparison project pane and the *Legend for Comparison Report* pane for further analysis. If you want to save the comparison project for additional analysis, you may do so as well.

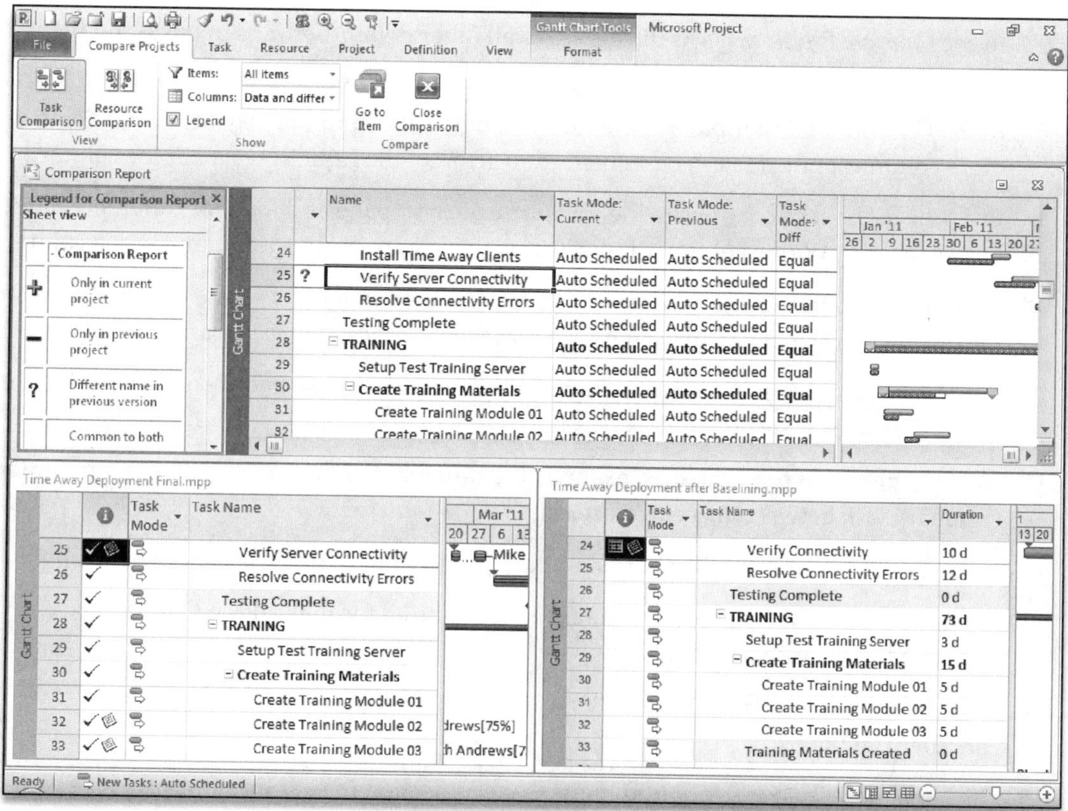

Figure 7 - 83: Go to Item for selected task

Hands On Exercise

Exercise 7-17

Use the Compare Project Versions tool to compare two different versions of the same project.

1. Navigate to your student folder and open the **Project Buddy 2010 Macro Development - Original.mpp** sample file.
2. Open the **Project Buddy 2010 Macro Development - Completed.mpp** sample file as well.

These two sample files are two different versions of the same project. One represents the project immediately after the project manager set the original baseline for the plan. The other represents the final finished version of the project.

3. Click the *Project* tab to display the *Project* ribbon.
4. Click the *Compare Projects* button in the *Reports* section of the *Project* ribbon.
5. In the *Compare Project Versions* dialog, make sure the pick list at the top displays the *Project Buddy 2010 Macro Development - Original.mpp* sample file.

6. In the *Compare Project versions* dialog, leave all other default settings in place and then click the *OK* button.
7. In the *Comparison Report* pane at the top, pull the split bar all the way to the right side to view more columns in the table. You may need to scroll to the right to see all of the columns.
8. Examine each set of columns in the *Comparison Report* pane and look for differences for the tasks in each project. Widen columns, if necessary, to examine the information in each column.
9. Examine the indicators shown in the *Indicators* column in the *Comparison Report* pane. Determine the meaning of the indicators using the *Legend for Comparison Report* pane.
10. In the *Comparison Report* pane, select the Design summary task and then click the *Go to Item* button in the *Compare* section of the *Compare Projects* ribbon.
11. In the bottom two project panes, examine the differences in the *Task Mode* column for the *Design* summary task between these two projects.
12. Click the *Resource Comparison* button in the *View* section of the *Compare Projects* ribbon.
13. Examine the indicators shown in the *Indicators* column for the DaleCo Contractor Tester resource and for Myrta Hansen.
14. In the *Show* section of the *Compare Projects* ribbon, click the *Items* pick list and select the *All Differences* item on the list.
15. Click the *Close Comparison* button in the *Compare* section of the *Compare Projects* ribbon.
16. Close the Comparison Report project file without saving it.
17. Save and close the **Project Buddy 2010 Macro Development - Completed.mpp** sample file.
18. Save and close the **Project Buddy 2010 Macro Development - Original.mpp** sample file.

Index

A

Add New Column feature **207, 242–46**
- deselecting 207
- using 242–46

Assign Resources dialog **127–28**

Assign resources to tasks **126–28**
- using the Assign Resources dialog 127–28
- using the Task Entry view 126–27

B

Backstage **11–23**

Bar Styles dialog **207–8**

Baseline, displaying in the Gantt Chart **210–11**

C

Compare Project Versions tool **256–59**

Copy and paste **189–92**

Critical Path, displaying in the Gantt Chart **208–9**

F

Field Settings dialog **207**

Fields **193–99**

File tab **11–23**

Filters **52–54, 234**
- applying and removing a highlight filter 53–54
- applying and removing a standard filter 52–53
- creating a new filter 234
- new filters described 52

G

Gantt Chart view, formatting **201–14**

Gridlines dialog **204–5**

Groups **55–59, 234–37**
- applying and removing a group 56–59
- creating a new group 234–37
- Maintain Hierarchy in Current Group new feature 57–59
- new groups described 55–56

I

Inactive tasks **159–62**

K

Keyboard shortcuts and KeyTips **26**

L

Late tasks, displaying in the Gantt Chart ... **209–10**
Legacy Formats page – Project Options dialog ... **89–90**
Leveling resource overallocations in the Gantt Chart view ... **146–49**

M

Macro Settings page – Project Options dialog ... **87–88**
Manually Scheduled tasks ... **69–70, 76, 112–20, 193–99**
- creating and using ... 112–14
- linking ... 114–16
- new fields used with Manually Scheduled tasks ... 193–99
- setting the Task Mode option for all new projects ... 76
- setting the Task Mode option for the current project ... 69–70
- using Manually Scheduled summary tasks ... 120
- using the Respect Links feature ... 118
- using the Task Inspector ... 118–20
- Warnings and Suggestions ... 117–18

Microsoft Project 2007 ... **5–9, 70–90**
- corresponding commands on the ribbon ... 5–9
- corresponding project options settings ... 70–90

Milestone task, inserting ... **111**
Mini Toolbar ... **24–25**

O

Organizer dialog ... **16**

P

PDF, saving a project as a PDF or XPS document ... **94–96**
Peak field ... **163–68**
Project ... **11–23, 63–67, 68–69, 69–90, 92–105, 98, 100–105, 105–6, 153–58, 169–86, 225–28**
- adding tasks to the project using the Timeline view ... 225–28
- closing a project ... 14
- creating a new project ... 18–19, 63–67
  - from a SharePoint task list ... 63–66
- defining a new project ... 68–69
- Help page ... 21–22
- opening a project ... 14, 16–18, 98
- pinning a project in the Recent Project page in the Backstage ... 17–18
- printing a project ... 19–20
- rescheduling projects and tasks ... 153–58
- saving a project ... 13–14, 92–105, 100–105
  - as a PDF or XPS document ... 94–96
  - as an alternate file type ... 92–105
  - to a SharePoint site ... 100–105
- setting project options ... 22–23, 69–90
- setting project Properties ... 14–16

sharing a project with others....20–21, 105–6

synchronizing with a SharePoint task list....169–86

using the Organizer dialog....16

Project Options dialog....22–23, 30, 70–90

Project Properties dialog....16

Project Server Accounts dialog....15

Project Summary Task, displaying in the Gantt Chart....212–14

Q

Quick Access Toolbar....35–43

customizing and resetting the Quick Access Toolbar....35–43

importing/exporting a Quick Access Toolbar customization file....41–43

showing the Quick Access Toolbar below the ribbon....36

R

Rescheduling a project....153–55

Rescheduling tasks....156–58

Resource Leveling dialog....133–35

Ribbon....4–11, 29–34, 41–43

collapsing....10–11

customizing and resetting the ribbon....29–34

importing/exporting a ribbon customization file....41–43

using the ribbon....4–11

S

SharePoint....63–66, 100–105, 169–86

creating a new project from a SharePoint task list....63–66

saving a project to a SharePoint site....100–105

synchronizing a project with a SharePoint task list....169–86

Shortcut menus....24–25

Slippage, displaying in the Gantt Chart....211

Summary tasks, inserting for "top down" planning....109–11

T

Tables....50–51, 232–34

creating a new table....232–34

using....50–51

Task Entry view....126–27

Task Inspector....118–20

Task Usage view, formatting....217

Team Planner view....48–49, 131–45

described....48–49

dragging tasks....135–36

formatting....140–44

leveling resource overallocations....133–35

printing....144–45

revising the schedule....137–38

understanding and using ... 131–45
Templates ... **18–19, 66–67**
Text Styles dialog ... **202–4**
Timeline view ... **48, 218–30**
described ... 48
exporting and formatting in another Office application ... 229–30
formatting ... 221–25
using with the Gantt Chart ... 218–30
Total Slack, displaying in the Gantt Chart ... **209**
Trust Center options ... **86–90**

U

User interface ... **3**

V

Views ... **47–49, 140–44, 201–14, 217, 221–25, 231–39, 248–51**
creating a new view ... 231–39
formatting ... 140–44, 201–14, 217, 221–25
formatting the Gantt Chart view ... 201–14
formatting the Task Usage view ... 217
formatting the Team Planner view ... 140–44
formatting the Timeline view ... 221–25
resetting a custom view to its default settings ... 250–51
saving a custom view as a new view ... 248–51
using ... 47–49
Visual Reports ... **252–56**

Z

Zooming the Timescale ... **26–28**
using the View ribbon buttons ... 26–28
using the Zoom Slider ... 28